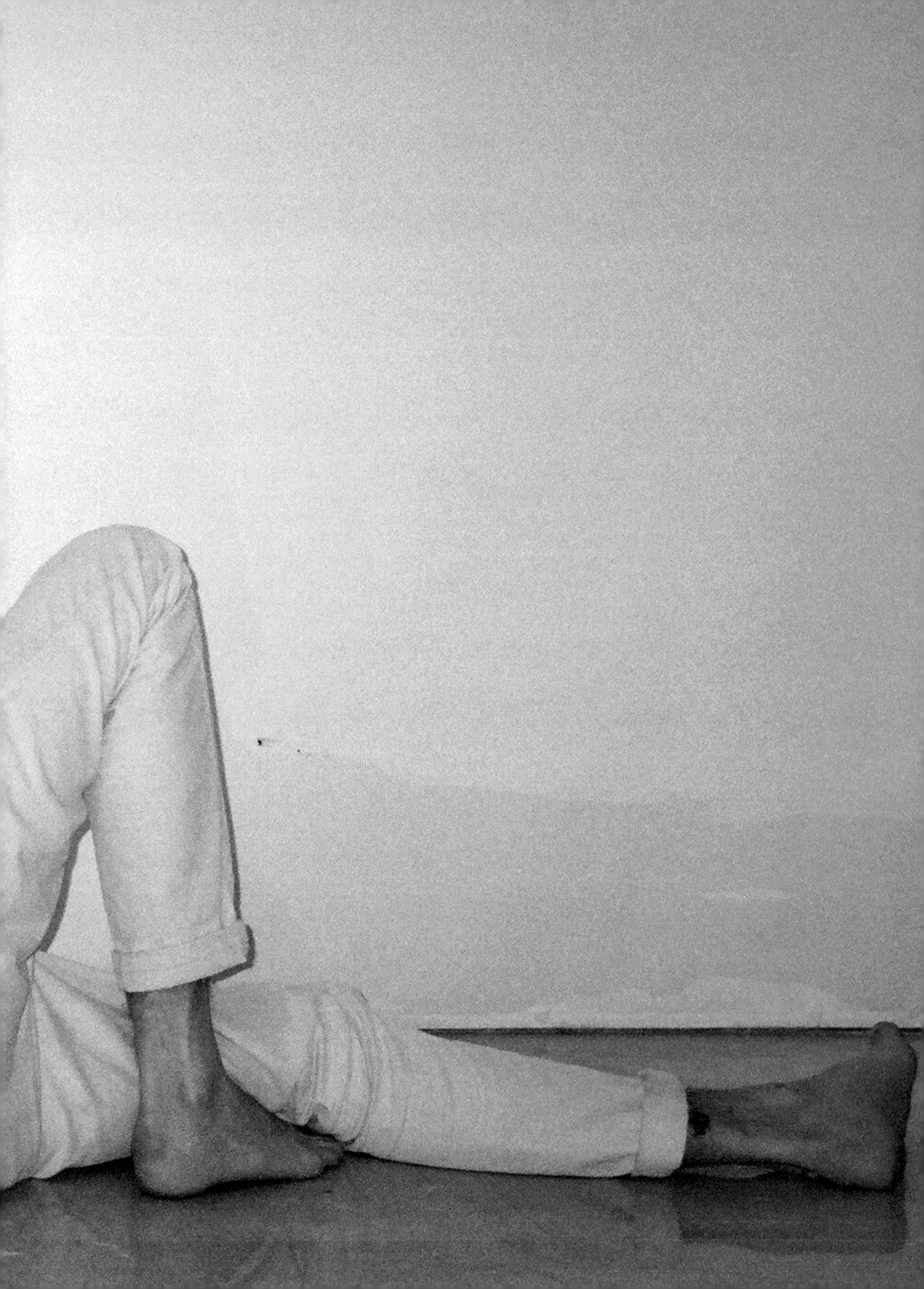

I LEFT MY NOODLE ON RAMEN STREET

DEVENDRA BANHART

PRESTEL MUNICH · LONDON · NEW YORK

Prestel Verlag, Munich
A member of Verlagsgruppe Random House GmbH

Prestel Verlag
Neumarkter Strasse 28
81673 Munich
Tel. +49 (89) 4136-0

Prestel Publishing Ltd.
14-17 Wells Street
London W1T 3PD
Tel. +44 (20) 7323-5004

Prestel Publishing
900 Broadway, Suite 603
New York, NY 10003
Tel. +1 (212) 995-2720

www.prestel.com

Library of Congress Control Number: 2014958073
British Library Cataloguing-in-Publication Data: a catalogue record for this book is available from the British Library; Deutsche Nationalbibliothek holds a record of this publication in the Deutsche Nationalbibliografie; detailed bibliographical data can be found under: http://www.dnb.de.

Prestel books are available worldwide. Please contact your nearest bookseller or one of the above addresses for information concerning your local distributor.

Design and layout:
Devendra Banhart with Carl Williamson / Familiar, New York

Editorial direction: Curt Holtz
Copyediting: Jonathan Fox, Barcelona
Cover photo / art direction: Osk Studio
Production: Friederike Schirge
Origination: Reproline Mediateam, Munich
Printing and binding: TBB, a.s., Banská Bystrica

FSC www.fsc.org MIX From responsible sources FSC® C022120

Verlagsgruppe Random House FSC® N001967
The FSC®-certified paper Arctic Volume has been supplied by Berberich, Germany

ISBN 978-3-7913-4908-4

WITH TEXTS BY

ANTONY

DIEGO CORTEZ

BECK HANSEN

JEFFREY DEITCH

ADAM GREEN

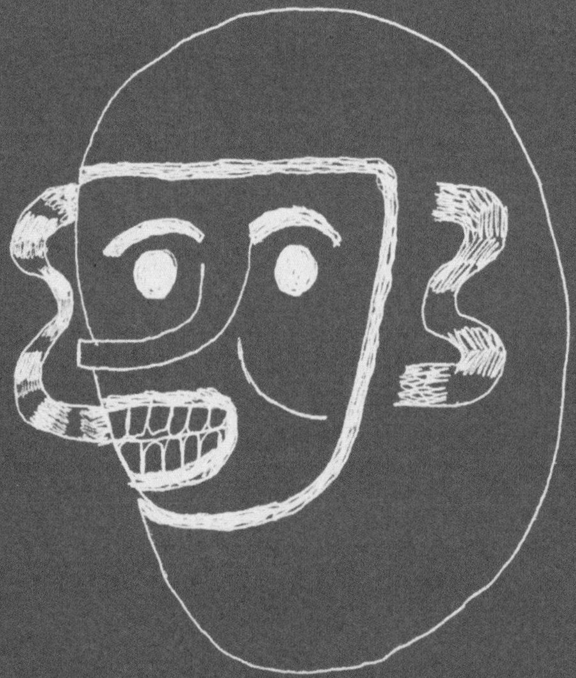

HONG KONG CHARLIE

Turnip greens yarrow ricebean rutabaga endive cauliflower sea lettuce kohlrabi amaranth water spinach avocado daikon napa cabbage asparagus winter purslane kale. Celery potato scallion desert raisin horseradish spinach carrot. Lotus root water spinach fennel kombu maize bamboo shoot green bean swiss chard seakale pumpkin onion chickpea gram corn pea. Brussels sprout coriander water chestnut gourd swiss chard wakame kohlrabi beetroot carrot watercress. Corn amaranth salsify bunya nuts nori azuki bean chickweed potato bell pepper artichoke.

SO TRUE

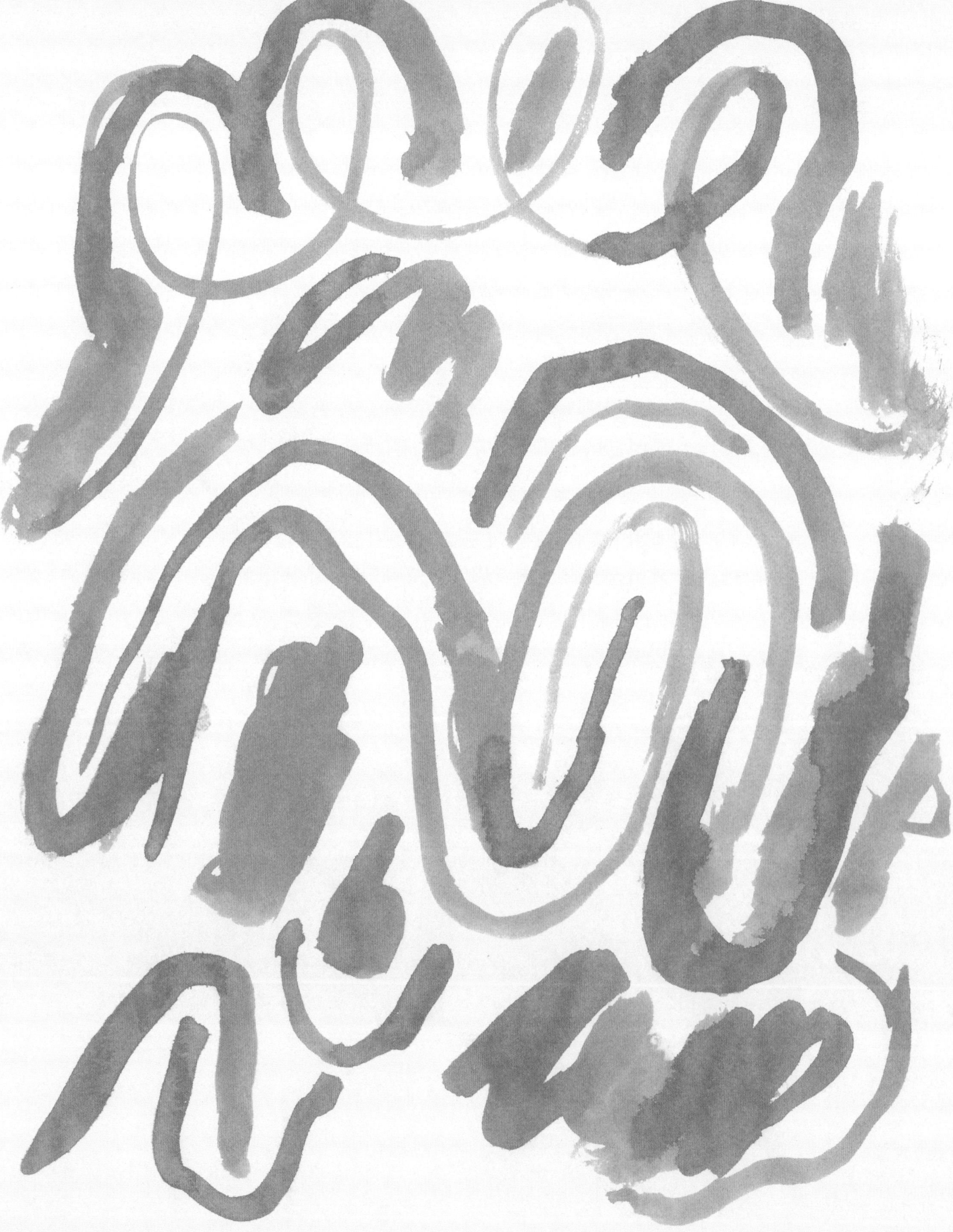

a holey ghost pours from my hands
it gapes in thirsty cups!
all my eyes wide open
wanna whistle free the heart

I saw Devendra's drawings for the first time on his early cds, and then for an exhibition at Canada Art Gallery around 2003. They were all these little masterpieces, tiny delicate lines, feeling like lost Indonesian or Native American scriptures, depicting a pantheon of surreal characters and forms in shuddering or billowing states, animals and clouds, insects, praying circles of hands and lines, scrawled on worn papers, book leaves, and imbued with a sense of magic. I remember seeing on the cover of *Rejoicing in the Hands* that he had drawn a tiny little black hole. I surrendered to that mystic artwork. It was stressful watching those drawings sell for 500 dollars each, each to a different Tom, Dick or Harriet. I wanted to buy them all, just to keep them together for him. He was so young and he was not proprietary about his work; he gave it away like handfuls of olives.

I watched the way his lines curled, in words and licks of hair, each gesture a sailboat plump with laughter, tenderness and generosity. It was a crying and intimate time... a golden time. In 2004 I wrote a song about the way Devendra's work and presence changed me, called "Everything is New." I saw him perform at Other Music standing on a table, and I felt like I could see shapeshifting spirits pour through his body as he sang, a wolf and a craggy old man wrestling for control of his frame. Devendra was having an ecstatic awakening as a performer, and it was coinciding with his rising fame. His kindness and gentleness, and his willingness to organize community, placed him in the center of a burgeoning scene that he would spend the next several years seeking to quietly extricate himself from.

Three years ago Devendra started showing me his recent drawings and paintings. He had returned to his inspiration, implementing even more structure in the ways that he applied himself, as in the case with the series of sphinxes. I felt such joy to see these works, so breathing, dancing, gold and new.

Antony, NYC, 2014

Devendra asked me Dearest James, to write dreamy Diego, "something Homeric, Miltonian, *out there*, monumental, barbaric (qué te parece?)" about mi amor! his works I write to on paper. you from Soon, he began to ask me every few days if I my first had begun my text. day at I insisted there was the LA no hurry. painting When he moved the deadline studio, up from December 1 to October 15, 2014, I asked him to send me a list of 20 points or ideas which he would like you'll have me to cover. to brave the He sent alley and a long rambling visit soon... letter which As for bullet was too good not points, more to incorporate will come, here into my but upon essay which I am finally sitting sitting down down and to write. going through some key influencers/possible Devendra helpful fodder for your text, asked this is what I came up with... me to none need to be included, "keep it light, they are all merely keep signposts it funny." and inspirations It and is influencers with this in mind through the that I years... construct a As a child in mishap mash-up. Caracas, the When viewing Devendra's drawings, we see first work I saw that very little really of what resonated he himself with says are his major me was influences. a Rufino I begin to Tamayo, just the realize then that poster for a show, artists reference things of course, held but it beguiled dear, me, drew me but by the time they express into themselves its worn they have already and mystic transformed blue such information and influences hues... into newer I always got entities a good which stand as art, laugh apart from from Botero's the original inspirational sculptures data. too... Later, Artists around 12, rebel against I moved themselves and their affinities to create something to Encinal alien Canyon in to their California, own interests. where my neighbor They happened to be transcend Lita themselves to become Albuquerque. someone or something else. I'm still Artists fashion new very identities, close into universal selves, with her and even and in Devendra's case, closer it is something hyper- or micro-organic. with He is a true organic her two creature—visible through his previous long, daughters, flowing hair, Jasmine or his more recent (an cropped hair—these are Devendra's amazing dancer and visual artist visible organic opposites. who happens to His drawings be married to Rodrigo Amarante) also resemble patches of hair or patches of and Isabelle weeds—wild bits of (Hecuba... animal and planted nature. Germ Records, Osk If Devendra's visuals are organic, Studio...), his performances are is one of my hyper-expressionistic and dearest gender-liberative—they closest stretch the boundaries of friends/heroes. what musically can be done. Lita Banhart's art straddles the cusp basically of fine put versus folk books by art. His drawings are the labor-intensive following artists and detailed, in my pre-teen not myopic. The color hands, palette destroying is reduced, basic, the world I but not thin. There are figures, thought I selves, but knew: Beuys, more the particulars of Eva Hesse, molecular life—striations, Agnes Martin, marks, stains, growths, Twombly, doodled lines which Sol Lewitt, fill spaces— Basquiat, Lygia Clark, fields of patterns, De Kooning, interspersed with fragments Lee Lozano, of elaborate handwritten Hannah poetry. Wilke, Ana Mendieta, They function as Jay DeFeo, markers, indicators, Robert signs, titles, Smithson, Walter De stars, asterisks— Maria reminders. and of Devendra's poetic course texts are not as her surrealist as own his images, rather absurdist— work... playfully (it's misleading. amazing, "Never sing alone!" check he cries. it out!). He often sings Later alone, especially at the San in his art-making. "Lay low" Francisco implies Art Institute (where invisibility, Bill Berkson was the only faculty transparency, member to lightness express of being— interest in my work), alluding a little to the crew consisting of space between things. Sarah A spiritual art is Cain, born. But "spiritual" is not a reality, Matteah only a genre. Baim, "Sphinx Interiors" and Colter portray a Jacobsen Europeanization was born. or Mediterranization of Banhart's work— Our first Egypt being shows the locale were at for this recent the Luggage series. The details of his organicism Store (love Darryl Smith and Laurie Lazer) are now neatly where we stored or contained in got cookie-cutter to meet Sphinx our structures, heroes wrought in in (Italian?) person, design. Alessandro Mendini, the Ettore Sottsass, and so-called Mission Aldo Rossi, come to mind. School of The operative word Barry McGee, in the title *Sphinx Interiors* Margaret Kilgallen, is "Interiors," Alicia not "Sphinx." McCarthy, The word "Interiors" Jo implies a spiritual Jackson, center, Chris which fills Johanson, and all variant containers, Christopher shapes, contexts. Garrett, The *South* among *American* others... *Creeps* series My is a further other heroes collapsing of forms at the into time were a crude *graffito* (Italian for "a little scratch"), Motherwell and Bas Jan a crude cartoon. It is counter-spiritual Ader... in Throughout, of that it is course, there's music non-pedagogical, and Cage in opposition to a "preaching" might be the of spirit. biggest guide The *Vessels* series for me is an outsider, throughout... asymmetric, the polyrhythmic, great dweller on that offbeat design—actually something threshold between more painterly (Giorgio Morandi) aural/ than design (Mendini). John Cage visual... is Devendra's true forebearer— I another music creator took who turned a Duchampian sound philosophical base inside-out. classes This is found at the at source of both Banhart's the Art musical Institute and entangled visual work. and One soon had all must throw his books Lucio Fontana into of the drawings, writings, "Vessels" mix, except etc.... the usual cuts, I was named lacerations, scars, Devendra tats, by Maharaji become more emblematic Prem and Rawat. whole than the younger You work. Devendra have been an always-by-my-side is less supporter of my work and thanks a collagist to you I met Mazzoli than a scatter and had the artist. It is in the ASIF and supercolliders Roth of the world that exhibitions, a possible we find physical truth by Japan one in shaking it. Devendra shakes, in voice and hand, a and moves (again having moved to few LA). months... When countless other his hand shakes amazing it is gifts/opportunities... a precious, There's non-pedestrian Keegan McHargue, movement, Louise unlike Despont, Julia Leonard, Luckey Remington, contemporary Antony, dance, Nathaniel Russell, which Dylan Marcus, collapsed Chris Fallon, Kori Girard, Ross Simonini, Chris Vassell, ballet Mel Shimkovitz, into Cliff Hengst, modern Ana Kraš, Scott dance, Hewicker, Ry Fyan, finally Will Lemon, to mere Adam "movement." Tullie, That's Adam Green, and awesome Angeline Rivas who for a are great thinker and friends that recovered make opiater— amazing work... normally To palate still, cleanse engaged in life I turn somewhat to Japan, from a distance. always enamored These are with the "disappointed," the philosophy disappointed by and the the conformism of our society— general what we fail aesthetic... to see and understand. Perhaps we appear to still hoping them as in you'll a sweeping, introduce me to Hosono-san and panoramic Sakamoto-san film shot someday... of a distended Lately cocktail party. loving the work In their of Sarah critical stillness abides Charlesworth, an intense meditation on Forrest Bess, truth, Bodys Isek Kingelez, accuracy, Karl Wirsum, reality, Nathalie Du Pasquier, Kenojuak Ashevak, Marcel Storr and wisdom, perspective, Carroll Dunham... relevance, And I love you heartfelt feeling, and lemme and love. know if this helps!!!!
Diego Cortez

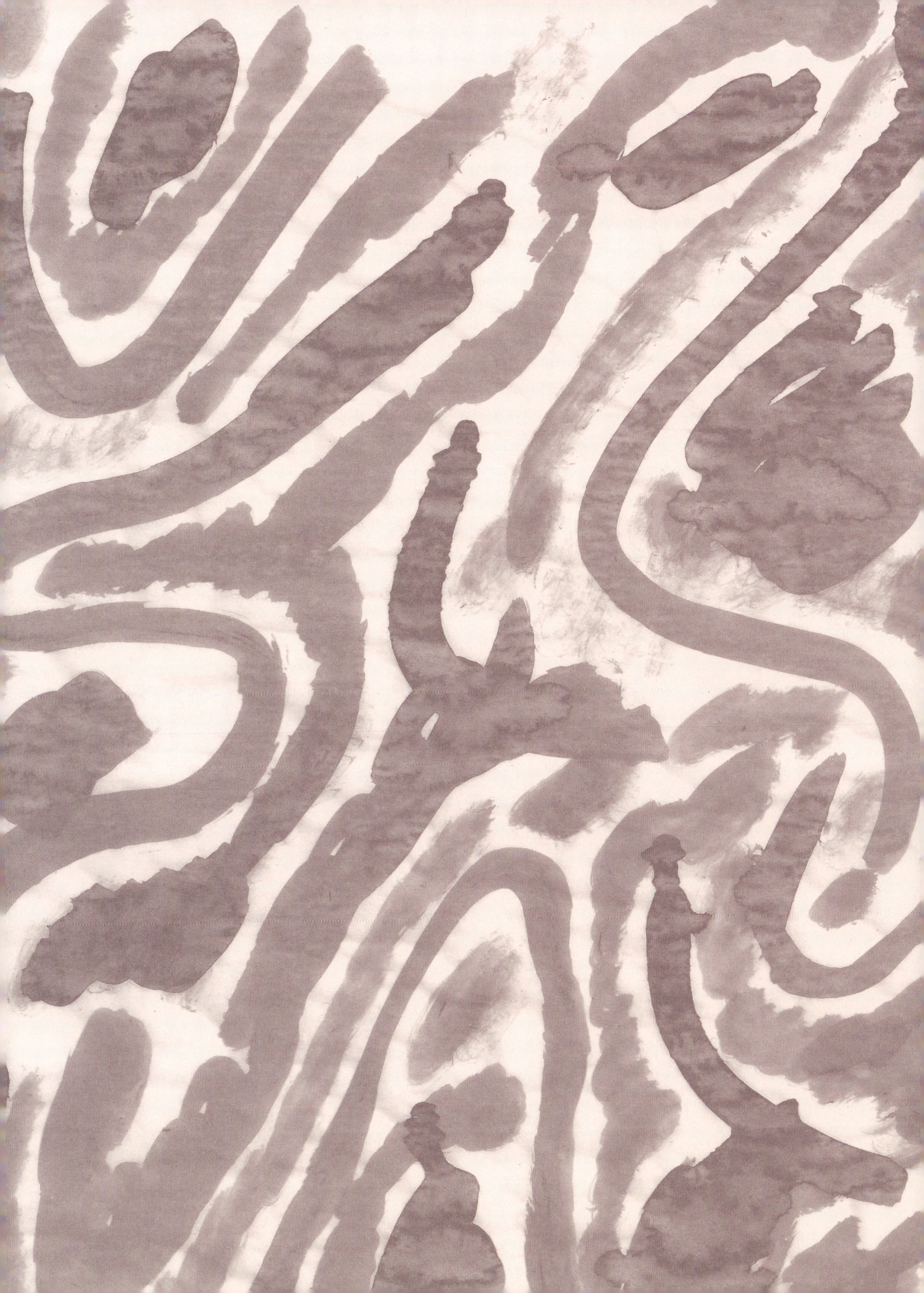

Devendra dropped by Shangri La, an apartment building in West Texas. I was on the floor working on a crossword. It was late in the day with the shades drawn and a TV on in the background. He said he had been considering permanence. It was nothing you could describe other than as a continual presence. Creature comforts seemed to be offering themselves. There was vital information but interference in the transmission. "Transmitted from where?"

I admitted I had a thought process that was temporary. There were hopes of an entertainment package that would soon be available to all subscribers. That's when he suggested we go west. But we could only follow the idea of the west. A soylent sunset over a crushed diamond delta to a place where the land reduces itself into what is. "Is it a crime to be so lonesome?"

Far above the landing strips and fairways, like a throne of earth, Monument Valley came into view. Here was a place that could demolish a century. Devendra said he wanted to find a place where nothing grows. A blank background for a holographic mindset. Instinct and ancestry were inseparable, an invisible cartography.

As night fell and the temperature dropped, we built a fire. He told me of the great Malibu disaster of 1909—the sinking of the steamer the *St. Croix*. As the crew and passengers abandoned the sinking vessel, a newborn who fell in the water was rescued by a sailor. They took refuge in lifeboats and rowed to Paradise Cove over the dark waters that were illuminated by the flames of the ship that burned behind them. They were stranded on shore until ranchers, who had seen the fire from afar, arrived with mule wagons. There were no roads to Los Angeles so they traveled down miles of beaches, all the way back to civilization. Waves overtook them along the way and overturned their wagons, injuring the already battered survivors. When they reached Santa Monica, the town took pity on them and offered shelter and relief. To this day the ship lays beneath the waters of Point Dume.

After that I heard fragments of songs he sang beside the plateau:

I live alone
However,
I am you
Now, I wait for this sacred great confusion
We sing our songs
At the beginning of the bottom, then go down
Love is no different than old medicine
Put your hand in any struggle of life
While I was talking
Many years had died
Heaven and hell is forever
I know that it is not appropriate
To contact God

I packed my business clothes
I have a good attendance record
Noting Examples of Paradise
As far as I know, it's my opinion that is wrong
I live in the war, and all the practical places

Looking up into the western skies I thought about the time I attended the anniversary party on the terrace of the Hotel Negresco wearing a bathrobe given to me by Gaston Barbelieu. Outside there was a crowd gathered awaiting the arrival of the queen of Arabia, whose luggage trunks were delivered by three moving trucks. They filled an entire ballroom. Police ran crowd control. The crowd was flagging and thinning out. I took a photo of the 16,000-crystal chandelier. I thought about the ninety-year-old woman in a bikini I had seen on the beach earlier that day, hunched over and smoking a cigarette. Her spine emerged so clearly beneath her skin, like undestructable architecture. I wanted to be indestructible.

I ate a spoonful of glass shards
there is a tattoo of this feeling
it's the voice of a billboard
CGI an Acropolis behind me per my contract
the chiaroscuro of pop is a power ballad
dads wear bedazzled jeans
The newscast named another storm after a woman
The sock puppet gave a life class
Fretless bass solos at a state funeral
Nomenclature is shrinking

Devendra pointed to the west and said we had a long way to go. I knew it just by the way it felt in the substrata. I wanted to peel back another layer of tension but it was one night at a time. You had to wear the clothes of a repeat customer before you could count yourself among the faithful.

Beck Hansen

Non-Popular Pop Art

Devendra Banhart claims to make non-popular pop music and non-popular pop art. His counterintuitive creative approach makes him one of the most engaging artists and musicians of his generation. I first encountered his work when friends who had performed with him gave me a homemade recording of his music. We listened to his songs over and over again. I was fascinated by their intricate structures, with the music and the lyrics folding into each other.

Shortly after discovering Devendra's music, curator friends who were familiar with the new generation of San Francisco artists introduced me to Devendra's drawings. I was amazed to see the same illogical logic in the structure of his visual art as in his music. Devendra is one of the unique creative talents who are equally accomplished in musical, visual, and literary media. His drawings animate the convoluted poetry of his songs.

Devendra's fluency in switching between music, art, and writing to express his vision parallels his ability to switch effortlessly between English and Spanish in his songs. His approach to art is characterized by a lack of rigidity and an open embrace of the unexpected.

Like other original artists of his generation, Devendra first connected to art and music through skateboarding. He first heard advanced music by watching skate videos when he was growing up in Caracas. It was through this aesthetic underground rather than through academic training that he developed his consciousness of art. This foundation has kept him close to an underground vision ever since. His art and music embodies an inherent freedom that remains anti-academic and anti-establishment.

Around the age of twelve, Devendra moved to Encinal Canyon above Malibu where his neighbor happened to be the artist Lita Albuquerque. As Devendra describes it, she "basically put books by the following artists in my pre-teen hands, destroying the world I thought I knew," reciting a list of some of the most radical contemporary artists, from Josef Beuys to Jay DeFeo, Lee Lozano, Bas Jan Ader, and Jean-Michel Basquiat. Devendra is still close to Lita and her daughters and remains grateful for the fortunate circumstance of his early artistic enlightenment.

Devendra then experienced another radicalizing artistic milieu at the San Francisco Art Institute, which he attended from 1999 to 2002. The influence of Barry McGee, Margaret Kilgallen, Chris Johanson, and Alicia McCarthy was pervasive. These artists and their friends did not differentiate between visual art, writing, and music and did not rank art on the street any differently than art in a gallery. There was a communal spirit with jointly organized exhibitions and artistic adventures. These so-called Mission School artists were heirs to the literary, artistic, and musical mix of the Beat generation. They were also heirs to a radical street-art tradition and enthusiasts of dying vernacular arts like sign painting and letterpress printing.

The Mission School enthusiasm for art and music that is direct and handmade as opposed to being produced and fabricated has influenced Devendra's artistic approach. His own voice and his own hand are always paramount. His work is sharp and refined but never slick. In performing a song, it is him and his guitar. In making a drawing, it is him and his pen and paper.

Devendra explains that his work "is not idea-based or conceptual," but a more open definition of "the idea" is at the foundation of his work. His ideas are not always rational ideas but instead emerge from the irrational recesses of the mind. His mental imagery is transmitted directly through his body, translated into drawing with a tactile immediacy. There may not be a rigid conceptual structure, but there is a seriality in many of his songs and his groups of drawings. He will repeat a motif over and over, with slight variations. The process builds on itself. He talks about starting in "the wrong place" and finding a path through variation and repetition. He recalls drawing a hand eight hundred times.

Ten years ago, Devendra could not finish a song without making a drawing and could not finish a drawing without writing a song. Now his aesthetic is so internalized that he can separate the disciplines although the inspiration continues to be parallel. He does not limit himself to aesthetic genres like the personal version of magic realism for which he first became known. He now works in a range of artistic and musical genres, encompassing both a personal mythology and an engagement with a modernist vocabulary.

Devendra's work is not strategized or academic, and he points out that it is not postmodern. His artistic motivation comes from "the pleasure of loving art." He is one of the unique talents for whom the personal becomes universal. Working in a range of genres and artistic styles, his musical and visual work is always immediately recognizable, embodying his own distinct signature. He evokes the inspiration of John Cage in having developed a singular body of work on what he describes as "the threshold between the aural and the visual."

Jeffrey Deitch

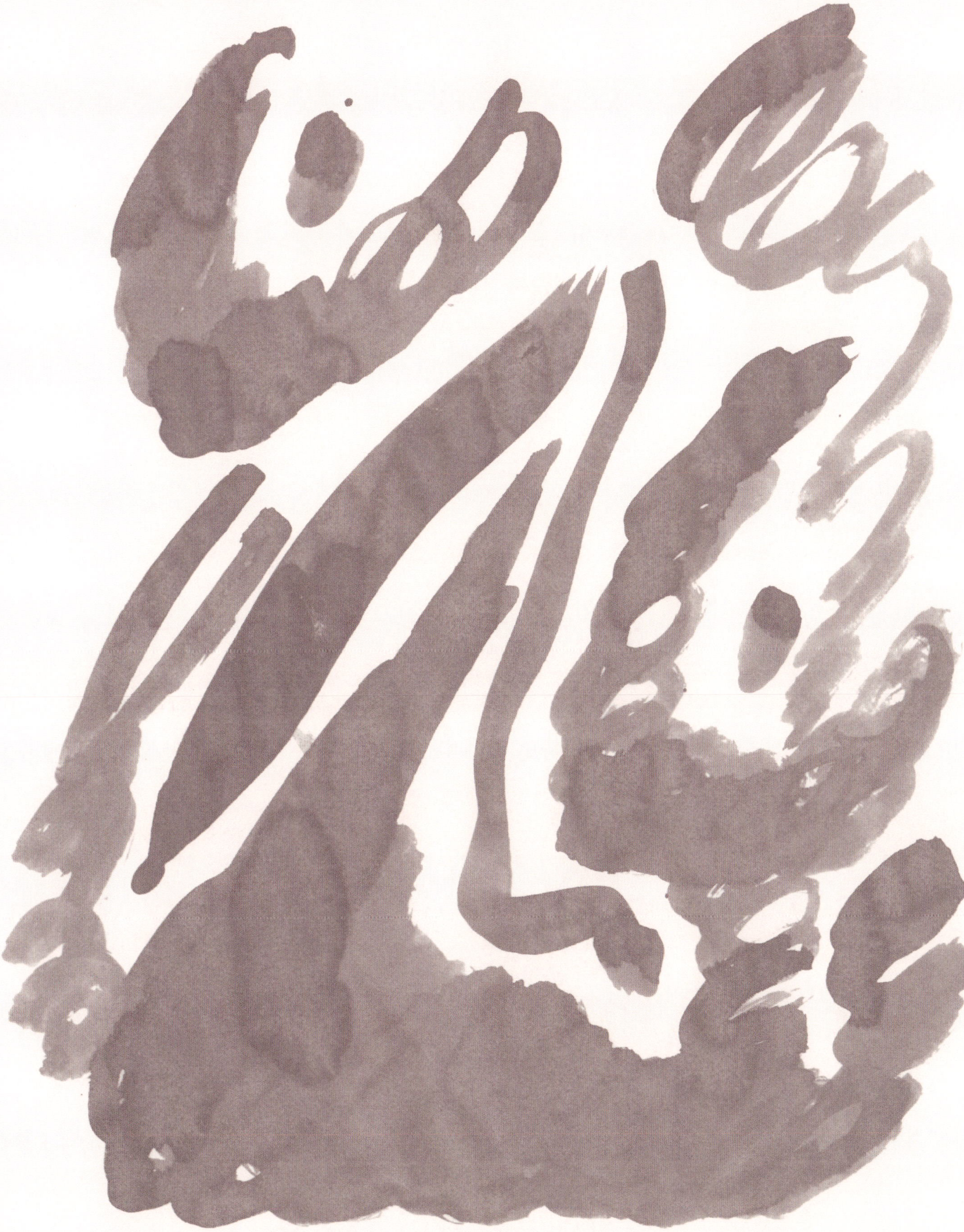

IS IT BECAUSE OF THE DOG CRUCIFIX COMMONALITY?

A conversation between Devendra Banhart and Adam Green

EDITED BY CHRIS FALLON

Devendra Banhart: "So check this out," said Adam. "I'm having a baby." And I said, "Are you pulling my chain? That's incredible, congratulations. I'm so excited," and I gave him a hug. Earlier, we were in Carroll Gardens en route to Red Hook. Driving… not driving, walking by… and on the right there's this great farmers market and Adam was drinking a Coca-Cola brewski and we just went into a Japanese—anyway, horrible story.

Adam Green: You know I actually just was in a deli and I saw a tall boy can of Coke and I actually got the chills.

DB: You couldn't get… what about a 40? Coke 40?

AG: That will make you sick.

DB: It's enough to make you sick? One time I went, in San Francisco, to an oxygen bar, and I said give me the one that's got the good stuff. He said, "Oh, I know the one you want, here's some oxygen."

AG: He gave you some oxygen?

DB: Yeah. It's the only place that still supplies them. I'm gonna bring it back. I'm bringing it to Red Hook.

AG: You're going to create an oxygen bar?

DB: Yeah.

AG: High on air.

DB: Look at this! Free tables and sculptures of…

AG: All Virgin Mary, basically.

DB: Wow.

AG: Well good, if you ever need a good mortician…

DB: Oh, I'm always in the market. That's a good question: "So who's your mortician?"

AG: A good, decent mortician.

DB: I feel like mine… see, it's just like… they don't totally get me.

DB: No, no, no. We're not recording this.

AG: Oh, great.

DB: Pause. My question to you is, "What is Lumambrian?"

AG: Lumambrian is an alien species.

DB: Said Adam as he removed his hat and stomped on it furiously.

AG: It's a—

DB: And threw his cell phone.

AG: Sometimes I get—what do they call it… aphasia?

DB: Oh sure, is that like synesthesia?

AG: It's when you have… like when your brain, like, just makes up words.

DB: Oh, like gorbading?

AG: Exactly.

DB: Well that's what they call it when that happens.

AG: But I often have a drug-induced aphasia where I write down the words. And so one of them was Lumambrian, which…

DB: It sounds like… like Namibia. And these aliens, they're very thin and, like, they're neon and it's like—

AG: They're neon, yes.

DB: Yeah, they're neon but they're… yeah, yeah, yeah, like, African fireflies.

AG: They're actually Hindu. They—

DB: Oh really? Yeah, okay, okay.

AG: They're Krishnan. They're from planet Krishna.

DB: Hindon't.

AG: "More like Hindon't" that's what Devendra always says.

DB: Every time.

AG: Every time.

DB: So that's got a Tibetan feeling.

AG: This does.

DB: That has a real Tibetan feeling.

AG: I think, you know, yeah, I feel like with these I was trying to really mess up the line.

DB: You're kind of doing a little bit of both. This one to me feels a little more… it's self-evident but it's totally your thing, you know? So it's not like you're tracing a house and making it wavy, you know what I mean?

AG: No, no, okay.

DB: This is, like, just your take on this—on a store.

AG: Well, the thing is that I—

DB: Which is a great name by the way, a strong, classic name, if you're looking for a name…

AG: Store.

DB: Adam is having a child soon and I suggest Store.

AG: Yeah, it's a girl.

DB: Even better. Store Green. Perfect.

AG: Wait, so, but then with this one I just want to… these things I think I have a different relationship with, a dry medium or something like a drawing thing, like a crayon. I've got windows like that.

DB: That's great, that's great. (Singing) "You never met me boo-oo. I'm going to do the windows like tha-aat."

AG: You never met me boo.

DB: Pop radio…

AG: Pop radio. Check out all these, like, uh… salads.

ADAM SHOWS DEVENDRA A NUMBERED LIST OF SALADS THAT HE RECENTLY ATE

DB: Salads, 1, 2, 3, 4, 5, 6, 7, 8, 9, 10, 11, 12, 13, 14, 15, 16.

AG: Nice.

DB: Dash… how 'bout 17, 18, 19, 20, 21, 22, 23. Now, it's important to note that we don't end on a period. Comma.

AG: Or maybe we should put this in the book.

DB: Comma implies "to be continued." Adam was just telling me, as he always does every time we come to this particular place, his favorite place in the whole world—

AG: Climnat.

DB: Climnat. Is… there is something particular about something, and that something is?

AG: Oh, going to the Benjamin Moore store where, like, they make the house paint.

DB: And so… oh really? So you… is that what you're going to call your daughter?

AG: Benjamin Moore?

DB: Yeah, Benjamin Moore Store Green!

AG: But they have a color, actually, that's my name.

DB: Wow, what, and… really?

AG: Yeah.

DB: No way, that's so fucking funny.

AG: I never have gotten it though.

DB: At the Benjamin Moore store there's a color that's Adam's name.

AG: All right let's have a look at it.

DB: Adam Green has his own color. That's when you've really made it. I mean, talk about making it in the art world. There's Klein Blue and there's Adam Green. I mean, that's not even, you know, you got the full name. No way, is that… was that because of you?

AG: It's not for me to say.

DB: Is there a chance that it is? Is this a new color? Let's see what it says… it says something here: "This color is part of a color preview that's… that could be you… a collection of bold saturated colors… much like you… that brings spaces to life for those looking to illuminate the world with pure extraordinary color… precisely like you… a great compliment for classic colors…" This is definitely about you. I think I just described you to your team. You are a compliment to classic colors. Wow.

AG: Like, literally just color.

DB: Wow, fuck, this is amazing. Much better than what I'm recording right now. I need a—and pizza colors live and direct from Yarmulkeville where Adam gets all his Turkish friends turkey bacon paintings from Direct TV. He's got his finger on the pulse of art… of the art beat—his life a unique blend of Eastern European mantras and spiritual pop vocal uhhh… fucking… uhhh… sutras.

AG: And then Devendra said that he had an art show where apparently Basquiat had his first art show in some obscure town in Italy called Modena.

DB: That's actually all true, that's all true, but he's also curating the show.

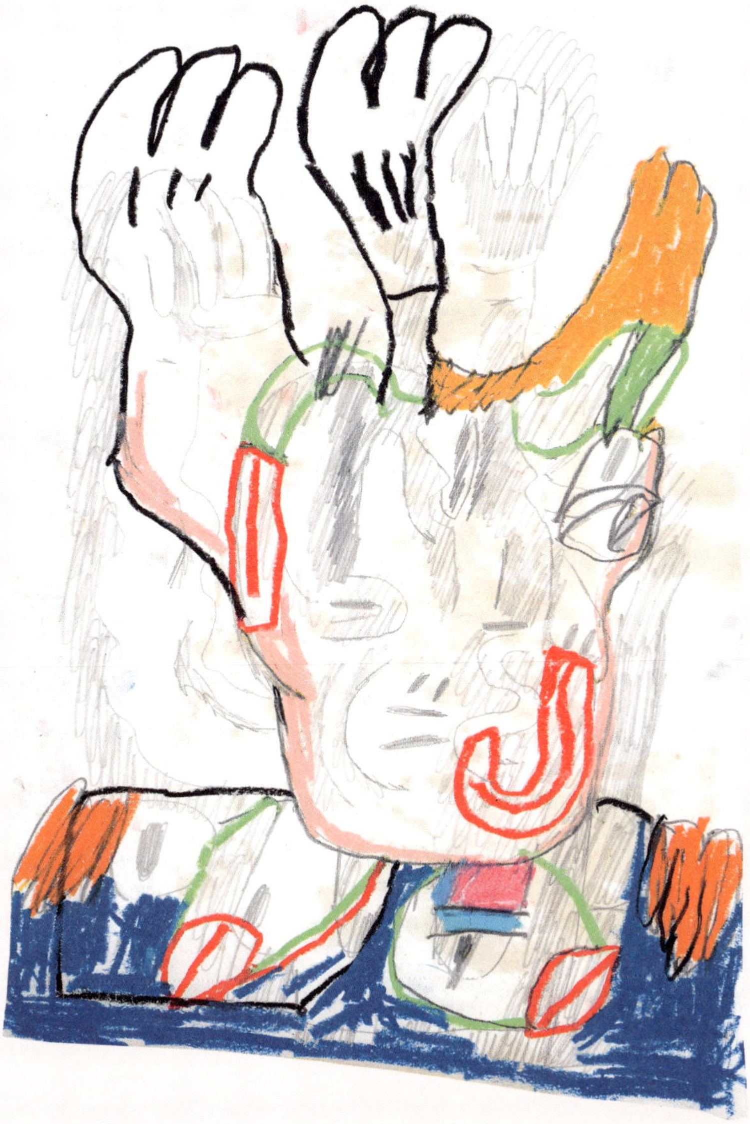

AG: Basquiat is curating the show?

DB: Him and Jim.

AG: Hahahaha!

DB: You know, I met a homeless man who decided to leave it all behind and surrender his will. Unfortunately I think he mistook his will for his identity because there is a big difference. But obviously…

AG: He surrendered his whim?

DB: He surrendered… he surrendered to the whim of anything but his own will. And the catalyst was Jodorowsky… and the Doors. But he—I think it's… it's interesting to note that he saw *Holy Mountain* and after that, in combination with Jim and the Doors, he said that's it, I'm going to walk into the desert, which he did do.

AG: Is it because of the dog crucifix commonality?

DB: It was the dog crucifix commonality—that's how it's known in academia… but for the layman.

AG: He walked into the surrealist desert?

DB: Yeah, he walked into the surrealist desert…

AG: Yeah.

DB: Kid Calamari and the Factories present Fleshy Pastel Greenster.

AG: The Flesh-Eating Pastel, even The Rubbery Flare.

DB: Rubbery Store and Fleshy Pastel present a two-man show of the mysticism of sound and music: the Sufi teachings of Hazrat Inayat Khan.

AG: Yeah, and that sounding color and everything in between.

DB: You've heard it in color but have you ever seen it?

AG: In sound.

DB: In sound.

AG: Okay so… so wait… so we're in, like…

DB: Red Robster, yeah, doesn't it mean…

AG: Yeah, Led Robster?

DB: Led… yeah, Led Lobster. Ooh, that's pretty good. Have you listened to Jahbert Ronson? I mean this is reggae. He's a reggae DJ. Jahbert Ronson.

AG: Jahbert Ronson, I've definitely heard him.

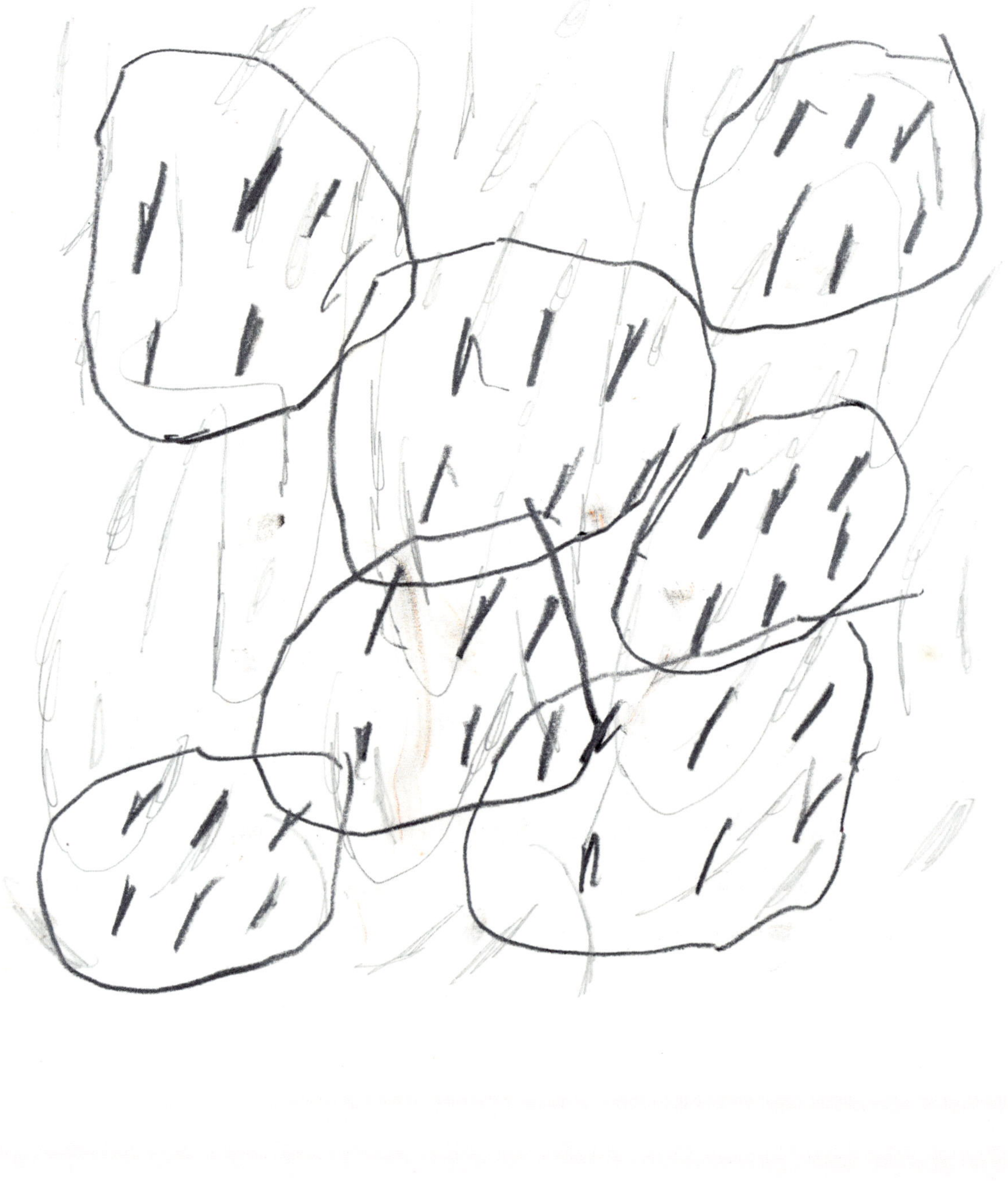

DB: He was also into the blues. He also sold his soul... to Stevie Vai, who was a good friend of mine. Anyone who I stand behind in line is a good friend of mine.

AG: Then he's reincarnated in some thirteen-year-old blond kid every, like, ten years.

DB: That's how we end all of these talks. That's the old prayer, that's the old blessing: "Please watch over this table, this family, this home, this house, and give us one thirteen-year-old kid once a year."

AG: And please inject Robert Johnson's soul into one thirteen-year-old blond kid every ten years or so. [Pointing to a drawing] So... this one isn't that bad.

DB: That's really nice, I really like it. Looks like the guy's trading my show. Looks like the bad—

AG: The bad boys club.

DB: Yeah, the bad boys club. The bat-boys club, so yeah. You were talking about the Badmobile and uhhh... something... I don't remember it at all.

AG: The art dealer?

DB: Yeah, sure, the art dealer. The art dealer and Kid Calamari, that's a...

AG: In Modena.

DB: Oh, yeah, and I had a... and I saw a solo show with them many years ago and not that long ago—relatively long ago, but we've known each other for a lot longer. In fact, we've known each other since we were both in bras for teeth. Tooth bras.

AG: You guys knew each other?

DB: There's tooth bras, you know, it's like there's toothbrush and there's tooth bra.

AG: Tooth bra.

DB: And that's your bra that you brush your teeth with, but it's also braces, which are bras for teeth.

AG: A tooth bra. Which means that's just the guy I brush my teeth with?

DB: That's a character study that we're going to be running by some people at Lions Gate and HBO. If only you could spare a couple, spare a couple of, you know... a couple of hundred thousand bras.

AG: Little bras.

DB: Bra, sir, I'm sorry to bother you, I'm tired of...

AG: I've been doing Kickstarter for weeks. Aside from Macaulay Culkin and Natasha Lyonne I have no stars in the...

DB: And there's no art-world star power other than Francesco Clemente and... um... there are no musicians other than Richard Hell.

AG: They can't get funding?

DB: Can't get foooonding. I'm having all the fun but they're taking the fun out of funding. There's a better joke in there somewhere but...

AG: That can be a lot of fun but...

DB: But I'm trying something and I'm not used to something. Kind of... I'm stepping outside of my comfort zone in the visual domain, painting something pastoral.

AG: A painting of pastel work. One of many uhhh...

DB: That's the thing, yeah, when, like, because your daughter, Store, is going to probably join the Santa Barbara nunnery at some point. So you go off to the convent into the Santa Barbra Mountains and there they will call her Pastoral, you know what I mean?

AG: Pastoral.

DB: Like Pasteur and her name, Store.

AG: Pastoral.

DB: Or she'll be a famous art heist thief.

AG: She's not a thief.

DB: Art thief.

AG: Giving birth.

DB: Giving birth to art thieves, the lives and times of McDonald's Green, Green, Green, Green... there's four Greens in there. So, Adam Green, you're... I haven't shown you, by the way, the markup of the book, but it does say "text by a list of people" and then at the bottom "with a conversation with them."

AG: Oh, no way, really? That's so good.

DB: And in fact I can show you in a moment, but I'm saying this and hoping, in hopes that it will now spurn...

AG: Oh yeah, because we had—we talked about Francis Turkey Bacon.

DB: We did, as we always do at the Kilowatt.

AG: The Kilowatt... what is a kilowatt? Is it 1,000 watts?

DB: It must be kill and watt.

AG: It's a nice place. So then we're having...

DB: It's an address in Watts, Los Angeles.

AG: These guys... Old Kilowatt. So when you move back to LA are you going to move into, like, an Aztec-type pyramid situation?

DB: Yeah, like a crystal geodesic dome made of old-growth redwoods in Laurel Canyon. Hollywood... in the H of the Hollywood sign. Oy vey. Jeez Louise, those taxicab bagels are starting to look real good right about now. Those taxicabs and bagels at the Red Robster, at the Led Robster, are looking pretty good.

AG: Are you going to make them part of the Intelligentsia?

DB: If they'll have me. I'm starting my own cappuccino store called Academia right next door.

AG: Kind of looking like a baby.

DB: Oh wow! That's just madness.

AG: Just a mad... mad baby dad and dangerous to know.

DB: Man, that's got a real second-wave British scholar Bible explosion. It's a real kill. It's a real feast.

AG: Have you seen that artist John Wesley?

DB: Yeah, yeah, I think you have some of his art, right?

AG: I don't have it.

DB: Yeah, yeah, yeah. And you bought some of his stuff.

AG: I've been buying his stuff.

DB: You can't walk down the street in the East Village without one of his collectors giving you the cold shoulder.

AG: I don't know you anymore.

DB: Well, you can't run into either his collectors or interns. Because the East Village is crawling with his collectors and interns. Oh man.

AG: It's the village, the downtown scene.

DB: Look out East Village, there's a new bon vivant in town.

AG: Yeah, so...

DB: But he's leaving us, he's leaving us. The Greenster is moving to Tinsel Town.

AG: Like, *you're* moving to Tinsel Town.

DB: Oh yeah. You're moving to midtown.

AG: I'm moving to midtown.

DB: You're moving to midtown. Midwifery in midtown.

AG: When you go, will you start doing films?

DB: To midtown?

AG: Are we going to, like... can we collaborate on that?

DB: Yeah, we definitely can.

AG: Are you open?

DB: It's been seven minutes and thirty-two or three seconds. You know I don't... one of the things that I despise is ticking clocks, ones you can hear ticking... I mean when they're very, very loud. Of course if you really listen closely there's something kind of beautiful about that. But if you need to—

AG: I grew up with that.

DB: I mean if it's the loudest thing when you start speaking, its tick, tick, tick, it's maddening and it's off when I always turned it off. But if you hear it... for a moment to hear it... it's a different way of experiencing time and it's a rhythmic wave. Time is being measured out in rhythm. The relationship between time and rhythm becomes really apparent and there's something worth investigating there. And beautiful but, I mean, this is something that you can enjoy thinking about for two seconds.

AG: Yeah, well...

DB: Then turn it off.

AG: No, I think about it, like, you know, rhythm is like uh...

DB: A dancer.

AG: Yeah, a dancer.

DB: And it's gonna getcha too.

AG: Yeah, and it's always going around.

DB: Is that a song, rhythm's going around?

AG: Yeah.

DB: The rhythm's goin' aroouuund!

AG: Rhythm's going round.

DB: You know what's goin' round? The rhythm.

AG: The rhythm.

AG: There's a website called New York Sunglasses. You want to go out?

DB: Oh really?

AG: Yeah.

DB: Well, there you go. It's a shame, people used to just talk bullshit all day, now they can just—

AG: So you know, actually, the guy that sold the... that rented me the apartment? Me and Yasmin were, like, looking at the place and he throws in at the end, "That writer used to live here."

DB: No.

AG: He goes, Allen Ginsberg.

DB: So are we talking about—?

AG: So we looked it up and he didn't live there at all.

DB: No that guy, that's what they always say. Every apartment in New York City is Allen Ginsberg and every fucking house in LA is the Doors: "You know the Doors lived here, the Doors lived here."

AG: Even if you order a couch.

DB: That's what they say about every couch—no... couches are a different story. If somebody says this is a Door's couch, it's a Door's couch.

AG: This was definitely Jim Morrison's couch.

DB: Oh yeah, but house you've got...

AG: Devendra owns Jim Morrison's couch.

DB: You know why? Because I collect musical artifacts. What the fuck, you know what I mean? Somebody writes some weird shit on Wikipedia and that's it, that's your identity. You know, a lot of music journalists go only as far as Wikipedia and then they go, "So... I hear you collect musical artifacts."

AG: I think I might have started that one.

DB: Oh man, it was you all along, huh? I gotta say some shit about you then: "They say that you're an ex-Nazi that's trying to get kids back into it."

AG: No, "He's trying to get whiter kids."

DB: No, you're an ex-Nazi who is, you know, trying to be worse than a Nazi.

AG: Yours are pretty good. I'm not really adding good stuff to your good ones.

DB: Well, I'm trying to make up for this dumb shit I'm saying while you're the one that's supposed to be talking. I think the cool thing about this is that we can—by the way, while we're speaking right now we're drawing. We're doing these collaborative drawings and we're going to do an amount where there's an equal division between pieces and there's another way of saying that, which is that it will be even numbers and we'll split it.

AG: Thanks very much...

DB: You know you pick the five you like, I'll pick the five I like, and we can throw them away when the other one isn't looking.

AG: Yeah, my daughter just did a film...

DB: Get on the way of the bank. That's good, that's a good title for...

AG: My daughter's little private drawing.

DB: Yeah, that's great. Can we hear the contender for the title of this, other than "Send my..."—whatever we said, uh... "God's gift to Chinatown?"

DB: Or... my garbage disposal collaborative drawings. My garbage... not my garbage...

AG: My garbage disposal collaborative drawings. And so is my garden. My garbage is my garden. But can you remember the drawing one... or it's just so busy doing the hotelier.

DB: So busy making a... hit picture—a picture.

AG: A little hit picture.

DB: A new hit picture, featuring the new hit picture *TV*.

AG: Oh yeah, that was good.

DB: *TV and the Rico Case*, starring Mildred Sunflower and Emilio Estevez.

AG: Emilio Sisyphus.

DB: Emilio Sisyphus and the Socratic Oath present: one night of—

AG: Trojan.

DB: Trojan hedonism in hot steamy...

AG: That's 100% because we need a good door name. Yeah, Aphrodite, Eros.

DB: Aphrodite, Eros, Delphi!

AG: Jezebel.

DB: Jezebel, clam. I think, you know, you should go with a Hindu name. I think the time is right.

AG: Maybe go with a Hindi name.

DB: I think so.

AG: These are the *worst* drawings.

DB: Often glacial water comes up when we're discussing… umm… gender reconciliation facilitators. Particularly when Adam and I start scheduling when to work on our screenplay. A combination of—

AG: It was *I Was Up So Close*…

DB: *I Was Up So Close*, which is a sequel to *Cliffhanger*.

AG: Yeah, as you said.

DB: And it's called *Some Kind of Everest*.

AG: *Some Kind of Everest*.

DB: What did I say earlier? Fuck! There's so much… it's, like, immediate. I can feel the art of it… that's like the—

AG: There I was, so close to the picture. I couldn't even see the edges, but from what I could tell she had hepatitis. What is that, some Egyptian goddess?

DB: Hahaha. Fuck, that's really good. What is that?

AG: Those are her nipples.

DB: That was from our noir piece, right?

AG: Those are her nipples.

DB: Oh shit! We'll have to put that in the book, okay? We gotta put that in the book. Wow, that's really good. What's the name of the book?

AG: I don't know. I thought a zebra.

DB: And out with a zebra print papyrus.

AG: I like how it sounds.

DB: Faced with the challenge, stuck between two hieroglyphs…stuck between two glyphs.

AG: Stuck between two glyphs. Or, yeah, I'm trying to, like, trace out…

DB: Trace out…

AG: Trace out a space.

DB: Trace out.

AG: Between two glyphs that are half-seen.

DB: Ooh, that's nice.

AG: Yeah, New York Yanks. And New York Yankles.

DB: Uni York. Uni York. Making all your brewskis come true.

AG: Yeah. What's the day? Is it…?

DB: I googled "art jokes" and there's a whole thing like "you might be a redneck," but for artists. It's like, if your house is empty, but there's a $2,000 easel, you might be an artist.

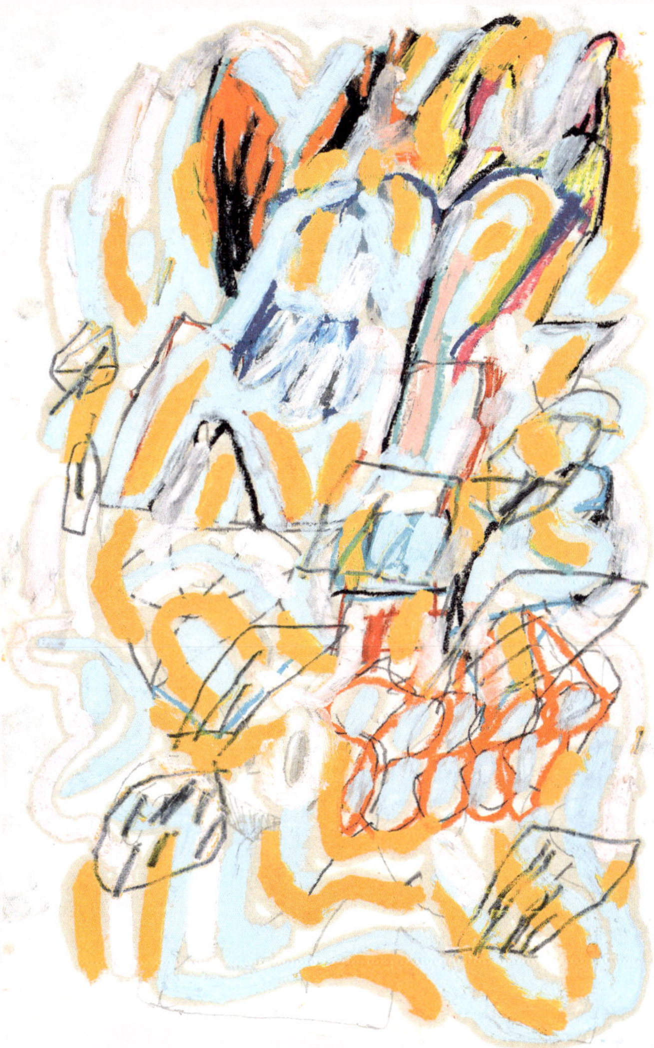

AG & DB: Hahahahaha!

AG: Yeah.

DB: He's got his eye on the prize. He thinks it's Fourth of July.

AG: Yeah. I got four Broadway shows and I read none of the reviews.

DB: I'm here with writer, producer, director, and star of…

AG: I'm here with…

DB: Barney Green

AG: I'm here with legendary songwriter Desmond Childs, author of such hits as "Dude (Looks Like a Lady)," "Livin' on a Prayer," "You Give Love a Bad Name," and "Angel."

DB: And the breakthrough R&B album *Electric Lady Lamp*.

AG: And "La Vida Loca."

AG: Who do you think is the most famous Japanese musician or rock star?

DB: Not in Japan but to the whole world?

AG: Yeah…

DB: Melt Banana? The Boredoms?

AG: The Boredoms

DB: Yoko Ono probably, what do you think?

AG: Yeah, it's probably Yoko Ono… when I was growing up I was really inspired by Masaki Batoh from Ghost.

DB: Yeah! Ghost!… You know what? Yoko Ono might be the most famous Japanese *person*… to the rest of the world.

AG: Right, right.

DB: To the rest of the world. I mean in the rest of the world.

AG: Yeah, that was actually…

DB: Everything, everywhere but Japan.

AG: Thanks for fleshing out the point I was intending to make.

DB: You're welcome.

AG: I feel like you're a puppet to my thought strings.

DB: My God, I've been played the whole time. The whole time you've been using me for your own… devices.

AG: Yeah.

DB: Adam could do that—keep getting in your head. And you find yourself thinking about the most famous Japanese rock star, you know?

AG: I think it's like it was with Harold and Kumar, you know? They said in the trailer, "the Chinese guy from *American Pie* and that Indian guy," and that was the joke they had for the trailer. That's how they introduced the actors.

DB: I was talking about that earlier today. I was at Antony's house and he was saying how there's a big backlash right now in the—I suppose you could say transgender or gender-unspecific community—it's a little bit of a gray area at the moment because the backlash is toward big members of that community, particularly RuPaul, who has embraced that word forever and uses it often on her TV show. And a lot of members of that community are saying please stop using that word because it's completely, you know, it's totally disrespectful at this point because people don't use it in the way that we use it. It's an affectionate term that we use amongst ourselves, much like other words are used by different other groups or whatever, you know what I mean?

AG: What's the PC word for it now?

DB: I'm not sure, I think it's kind of being debated at the moment, but tranny isn't it.

AG: Not, like, transgender?

DB: Transgender is closer to it, yeah. But that's not the same thing as a transvestite. It's not the same thing as that but it's transgender. It's complicated, and the decision should—it can be discussed by us but not made by us. Ultimately, it should all get to a point where it's just "human being." That's the whole point.

AG: Yeah.

DB: But at the moment, because the world is kind of opening up to there being something other than just, like, a white guy, this has become a discussion because suddenly people have a voice. And once they have a voice they can say, "Yeah, I'm a human being. I'm not a caricature, I'm not something for you to sexualize or to—"

AG: This is something that Axl Rose thinks.

DB: This is what...

AG: This is what Axl Rose is trying to tell us.

DB: Yeah, and what is Axl short for? Axl.

AG: Umm... Axl. It's his name.

DB: Axl short for Axel. Talk about a guy who's the conduit.

AG: Right now, I don't know... yeah.

DB: That's really nice. That drawing's real good.

AG: Axl...

DB: That's real nice because your drawing's real good. That's real nice because...

AG: Wait, now Axl is a... it's a...

DB: Well, his real name is something else.

AG: You don't know his real name?

DB: Guns.

AG: His name is William Bruce Rose.

DB: Billy Rose.

AG: William Bruce Rose from Lafayette, Indiana.

DB: Oh yeah, sweet kid. So, as we were saying... yes, in terms of minorities in the United States there's a tremendous amount of reduction and caricaturizing and sexism and racism and misogynism. It's insane.

AG: Yeah, resetting sexism. Resetting sex. Resetting...

DB: Resetting sex... it's, like, anything we do is resetting sex.

AG: They are resetting sex.

DB: I got a painting studio in LA.

AG: Oh, you did?

DB: I did.

AG: When are you leaving?

DB: In... in late July. Well, that was the worst of our conversations. I apologize. Matchmaker to the stars, the guy is like freaking King Midas. Everything he touches turns to Oscar gold.

AG: So, how do you feel going back to LA?

DB: This guy, the Greenster, he's like Sisyphus. What's the story of Sisyphus?

AG: That he... he has to push a boulder.

DB: Oh yeah, yeah, he's, like... Sisyphus gets the boulder, and the boulder he's pushing is... an Oscar! So... Adam and I think it's clever to paint drawings. We call them prawings.

AG: Prawings.

DB: Or... or draintings.

AG: Draintings.

DB: And they are inspired by Adam's childhood, which was mostly spent in the water. He's a beach culture kind of guy.

AG: I was an aquatot.

DB: He was an aquatot. He was an aquatic army brat. His father was in the Navy. Mom: marine biologist. Both of them were poets.

AG: And slaves to the blues?

DB: Slaves to the blues but free, free... free to dance. Yeah, free to dance, right.

AG: Free to Kahlo.

DB: Right, free—

AG: I'm Frida Kahlo.

ADAM MAKES A CHANGE TO THEIR DRAWING

DB: Friiiida Kahlo! That was one of the jokes! It was a *Black Adder* art joke, which was in El Salvador. Do they have a newspaper called the Salvador Dalí? Ooh, I like the neck. I like the neck.

AG: Yeah, it was that—is it too much?

DB: No, no, it's fantastic.

AG: Fantastic.

DB: Adam "Fantastic Neck Giver" Green—

AG: Even better than that, you have a life.

DB: The guy can give a neck.

AG: No, no, you know, the No-Neck Blues Band.

DB: Oh, yes, sure, we were both very big fans and still are. We were following them around back in the day.

AG: No neck.

DB: Right, right. I will never forget playing a festival with them, the De Stijl fest in, I believe in Minneapolis. They were throwing plates at the audience yelling, "This is the psychic frog versus the astrodome." It was haunting. At the time it was... majestic... horrifying and... titillating. Seen any good movies lately?

AG: Not really. I saw...

DB: Building any good movie sets, lately?

AG: Everyday. So that—

DB: So what we were saying earlier about gender... gender...

AG: Politics?

DB: Politics. Jeez, what are they gonna call that movie, *Transformers*?

AG: Transgender—

DB: Non-gender-specific machinery.

AG: It might seem pretty good, right? So, what's going on here?

THEY LOOK AT THEIR DRAWING

DB: No, that's nice. It's got this, like, Garfield producing sort of these nebulous egg fields… through the foggy egg fields.

AG: You could give it a Garfield—

DB: Like Garfield-meets-Geiger.

AG: Garfield-meets-Geiger. Garfield. Did you… did you like Garfield?

DB: I did. I even had his game on a floppy disk, you know what I'm saying?

AG: You had his game? What kind of game?

DB: Like, "Garfield the Game" on a floppy disk.

AG: Wow, cool.

DB: The floppy disk was invented by a Japanese inventor: Nakamatsu.

AG: Is that true?

DB: Yeah, he's a great guy.

AG: He gave him, like, a little yarmulke.

DB: Nice, that's a really great yarmulke by the way. Love your yarmulke.

AG: Yeah, I was reading the article about the guy… the Japanese guy that invented *Mario*. Also *Link*. He was like… *Link* was inspired by his memories of playing in, like, a cave near his house when he was a kid. No, actually… now I believe the part where they said that going through the labyrinth in *Mario* in the back of the levels were, you know, methodically organized. Like, level one, two, level one, three. Like, save the princess, go to the second floor, like, level two. It was the ultimate bureaucratic nightmare and they compared it to Kafka's *The Castle*. You know, but when I was doing a lot of ketamine I used to call it "Josef K."

DB: Wow, wish it were Campbell.

AG: No, like Josef K, the protagonist in *The Trial*.

DB: Oh, right, right.

AG: So there's something… a video game, like, about ketamine.

DB: I don't… I just didn't really dive deep in my explorations with ketamine… actually I think I only did it once… certainly I didn't go as far as you did… I think for you it became a daily thing.

AG: You know I had a mound of it on the kitchen table.

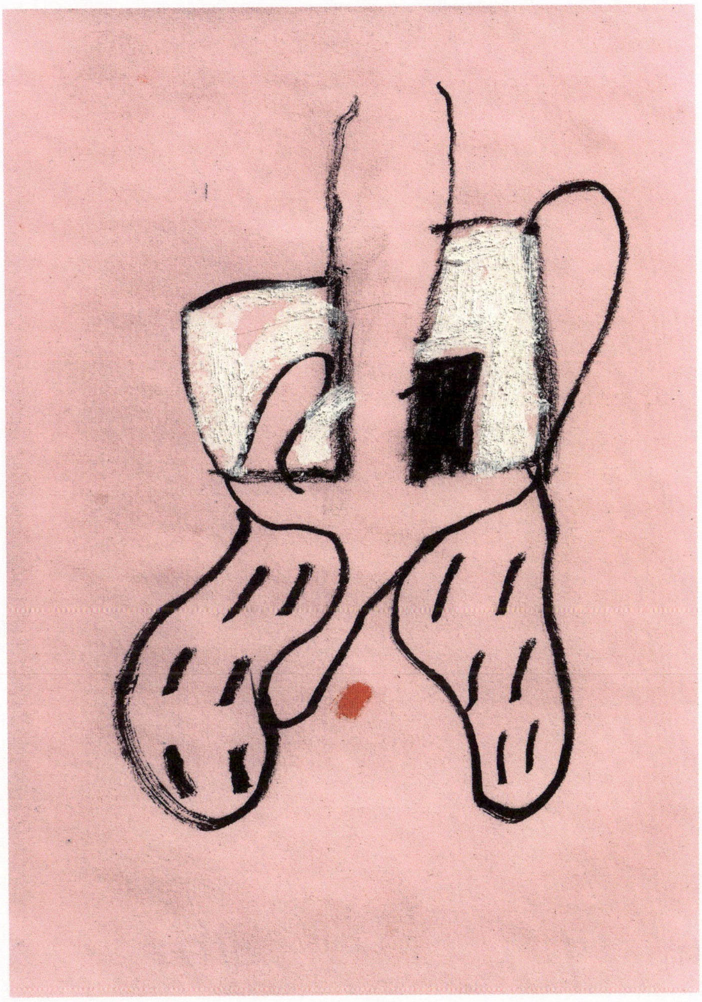

DB: I'm trying to draw something, by the way, that's going to really resonate with you.

AG: Oh yeah, yeah, that's nice. How do you feel about, like, going, "We're trying to land this showbiz?"

DB: Well, one day I looked in the mirror and said "Dev, Dev-dog, you're not getting any younger. It's time you made it," you know what I mean? Opportunity doesn't knock.

AG: You do.

DB: You bust through the door when opportunity doesn't knock. So, you know, I used to say I need to go to Hollywood like I need a shot in the head, but now I think I'd better go home and get some head shots.

AG: If you—when you live in Hollywood, as you often do, do you feel that it's run by movies people?

DB: What kind of people?

AG: Movie people.

DB: I don't know. I never go to Hollywood. My experience in Hollywood is not experienced at all.

AG: Wait, it's not through Har Mar's eyes, your experience?

DB: It's a shock, the very whole thing.

AG: Your experience with…

DB: Get Har Mar on the phone and tell him I haven't lived—I haven't seen them go through it yet, and I haven't lived.

AG: Okay, so basically you are trying to… you go to Hollywood and, like, if your life is not like your soul… is not manipulated by…

DB: No, like, how can they manipulate a manipulator like me?

AG: By Hollywood, by the showbiz.

DB: You know what I mean? Besides you've got to have the right 'tude, which is, "I don't live in Hollywood, I just live in one of the boroughs. I live in the sixth borough," you know?

AG: Where is that? That's…

DB: I live in New York City, it's just very far away.

AG: Where is your house?

DB: Hollywood. I don't have a house. The art studio is downtown.

AG: What's also downtown is, like, the museum, right? The one… not the LACMA…

DB: The MOCA…

AG: MOCA, exactly.

AG: So, you know, I was thinking the most valuable... if there was a person that just knew everybody's name, and could just go up to everyone and know their name, that person would be, like, one of the most valuable people.

DB: There are people like that.

AG: Who just know everyone's name? Like, let's say you had a concert and you got—

DB: There's some guy who does that. He's got, like—

AG: What's his name?

DB: I don't know... Johnny.

AG: And then he just goes... let's say you have a concert, and then that figure goes up to, like, 5,000 people? And this dude is like, "Hey Frank, Devendra's playing tonight," you know?

DB: Yeah, people would go, "How do you know my name?"

AG: But he's just like, "What? I just know everyone's name."

DB: But he's an app, that's the thing. Is that what you're trying to sell me here? You're trying to sell apps?

AG: No, he... that's what I'm saying.

DB: I'm trying to make an art book here. Are you trying to sell apps? Amidst a book of art? Adam is trying to surreptitiously insert his apps.

AG: This is off the record.

DB: You might have recorded that.

AG: That was it. It was my idea.

DB: Oh man, so nice to hang out with someone that I really, really love... on the record—a dear, dear old friend.

AG: I told you about squatter punk reform, right?

DB: Spider skunk reform? Oh yeah, I was going to text you about that.

AG: Squatter punk reform...

DB: But I thought twice.

AG: I know you thought twice.

DB: So, Adam's been working on an app about squatter punk reform.

AG: Squatter punk reform like...

DB: Squatter punk reform in the UK.

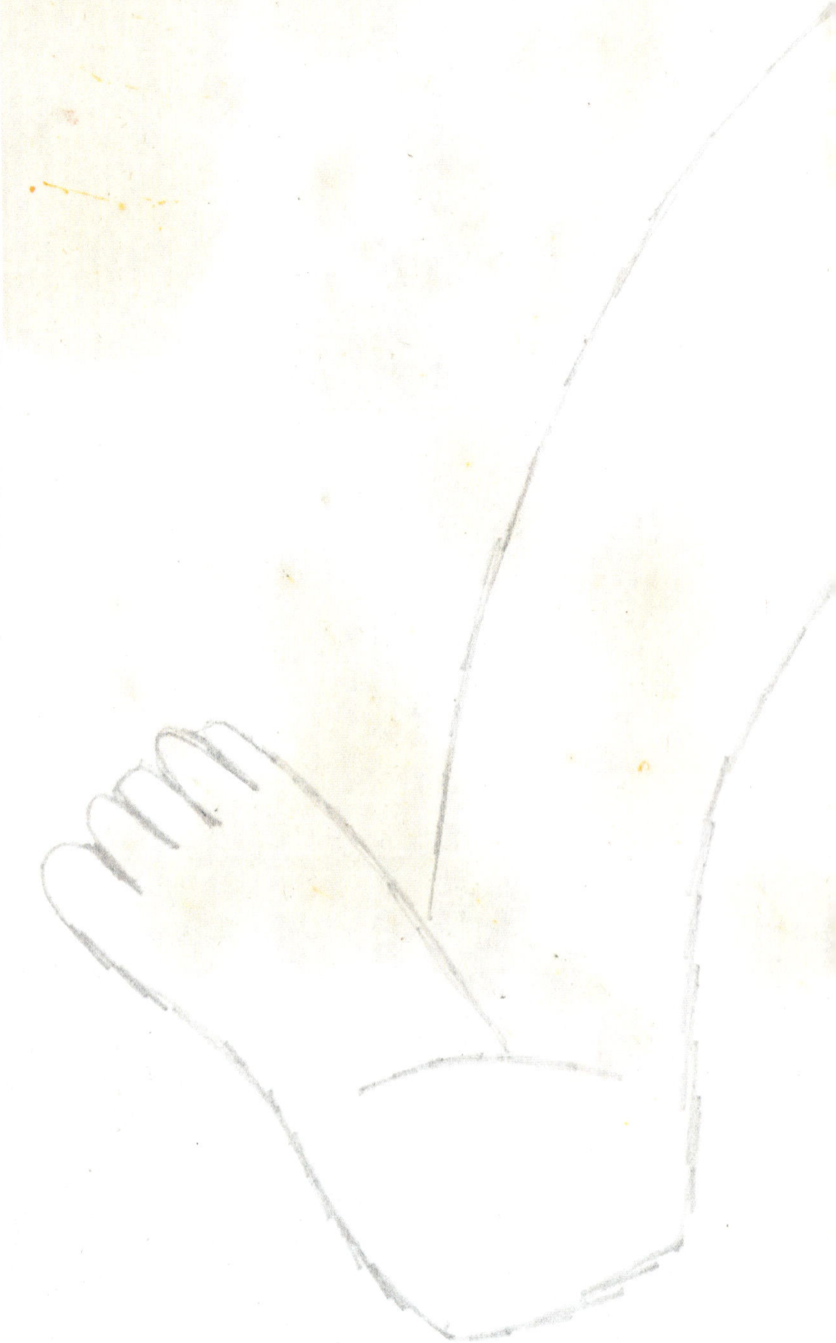

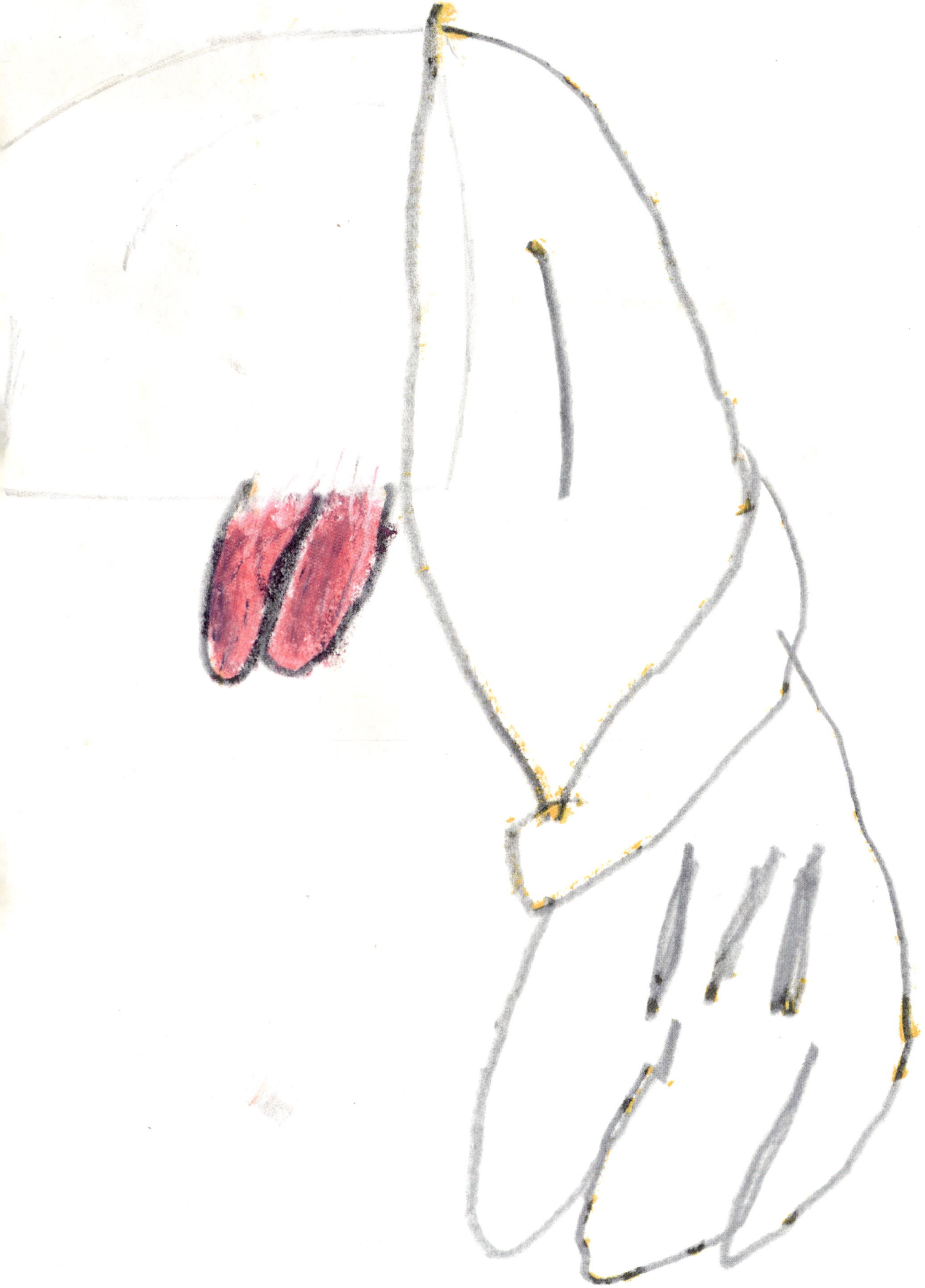

AG: Yeah, you can get people that have been through it help get kids out of it. You know, because they… they will listen to a former—

DB: Yeah, but those guys are all… they made a million dollars on their apps, on their squat apps.

AG: So what do they do? They show… they tell them where is the squat.

DB: They squat it all the way to Silicon Valley. They made a cool mil.

AG: Yeah, I think by that point they had made a cool mil. No one could say how much exactly, but a cool mil was possibly suspected.

DB: A cool mil is… well… after they got the news of the shutting down of the mill… they weren't as distraught as others. After they had made a cool mil.

AG: There was like hot millions that was, like, jizzing out of their, like—

DB: Things were jizzing out of every financial orifice in the Inland Empire, and you try to stay in the area, but…

AG: You know there was… they found a hooker in a Roman phone book…

DB: There was a game of Presbyterian cat and mouse.

AG: *The Da Vinci Code* and a self-portrait, man. You know, all his cohorts that were down at the cathedral trying to descramble, like…

DB: Descramble.

AG: That's some kind of Christmas cipher. But it was, like, an Italian Vatican Christmas. It was a Garfield Christmas.

DB: Oh yeah, it was pretty good. What do you think about adding some pencil on that?

AG: Oh, pencil?

DB: Yeah.

AG: I believe in pencil.

DB: Oh, I think this one's maybe done, yeah. Mmm… maybe one little thing you ought to do.

AG: I always think about souls, like… they're probably at some point just kind of quaint, rustic… they're quaint rustic things that just interact with our feelings or whatever. You know like…

DB: Like somebody has the cojones to say that—

AG: Like, did you see how quaint and rustic and retro souls are?

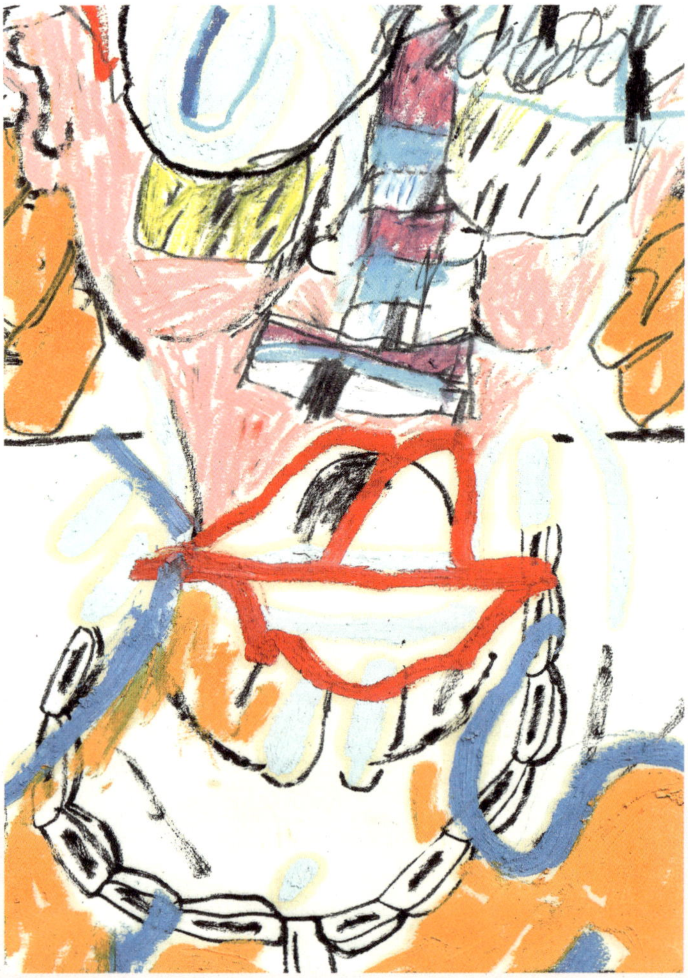

DB: Quaint and rustic?

AG: Yeah, yeah. It's like… you're so old.

DB: Where did you get yours, on Etsy? Like that?

AG: Yeah, but I believe there is a spirit economy.

DB: Oh, that's nice. This is good stuff. Ye-ess?

AG: And then the traders of the souls trade the souls in the spirit economy without… they send our egos down the line and we don't even know that they did it.

DB: They just send 'em all down to the Rio Grande. That's where they end up.

AG: They trade egos like traders, Wall Street traders.

DB: Like Trader Joe's sells carrots.

AG: A lot of the ego is a part of the soul that represents the goal, because it allows the people to… like, their will is sort of transmuted through it, so they sort of trade in pure ego, which is like a crack—soul crack. And they have to study down at the Rio Grande.

DB: I hear what you're saying.

AG: Looking for a—you know what, it's basically because our bodies are the feces of the spirit realm. Just, like, gangly, out of our souls' assholes is our rubber soul flesh.

DB: That's beautiful, that's amazing. What are you, the Jewish Alan Watts?

AG: I will use some rubber fat factory.

DB: It's a good question. The thing is, the soul—okay, to quote the Buddhist adage, "The finger pointing at the moon is not the moon," and the word soul is not the soul but merely pointing at it, and that IT is the definition of transcendental, as a word it's just a word. Just like "God" is just a word, just like "anything" is just a word. These are things that just point.

AG: Does that… is that what you were talking about, pencil, or did I ruin it?

DB: No, it's great.

AG: What about to the left, do you think it's unbalanced?

DB: I know what you mean, yeah, but I think it's kind of nice—it gives it a weird city-of-the-future dimension.

AG: Yeah, you don't want to unbalance, because it's just like a color field painting.

DB: I like it a lot. No, no, no. It's much better than that. It looks like you can call it "The Wild Fires." You can call it "The Santa Ana Wild Fires." The wild fires, brush fires, towers.

AG: Greenberg. Leonard Greenberg hates it. Leonard Greenberg tore it apart.

DB: Leonard Greenberg, director of the Red Bull Museum. Oh wow, that guy had a rough time.

AG: And stern. Do you want to work on it?

DB: No, sure, but I've got a couple of… you got a bunch of challenges there in front of you. You gotta just finish those little touches and then we're good. I like it. It's got a roadrunner aura… emanating real roadrunner energy.

AG: I was reading a book about Yves Klein.

DB: Master of judo.

AG: The section I started to think about is that, like… as far as utopias are concerned, I think there is a sort of… architectural staples in utopias are usually globes, like geodesic dome centers.

DB: Oh sure, I explained it there for you.

AG: That's the centerpiece of the utopia, like from *The Garden of Earthly Delights* to, like, Epcot Center. You know, they always have the geodesic dome.

DB: Yeah, I know.

AG: But then I was reading this book about Yves Klein and he was interested in trying to design a utopia.

DB: But didn't?

AG: And he traveled to Disney World to check out Disney's ideas on the subject. I started to think that it would be a funny future kind of world where Disneyland is a sort of archeological tomb site, and it's, like, all mapped out in accordance to… like its roads are mapped out like in Rome, with a Palatine Hill. Like, then it's actually considered to be the tabernacle of utopia and people are, like—

DB: That's because over time the concept of what is entertaining is relative, and entertainment shifts. What if entertainment changes and so, over time, Disneyland will be observed as this architectural oddity—an attempt to make some sort of…

AG: Yeah, like a futurist…

DB: Yeah, exactly—paradise on earth. Not just a symbol of our excess and obesity and cheap, tacky, kitsch entertainment, you know what I mean? And that's mostly where I worked it all out. That's our mission statement.

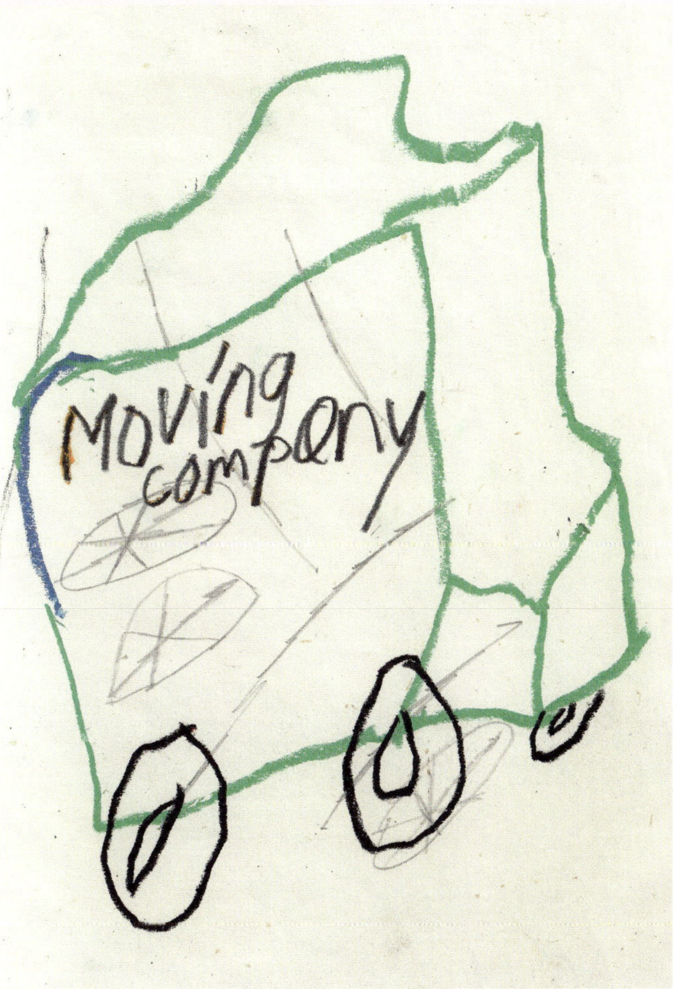

AG: Do you consider Walt Disney to be sort of like a Jodorowsky type?

DB: That makes sense. It makes sense. I don't know if I can, but sure.

AG: Is Walt Disney considered to be one of the greatest artists, like, of all time?

DB: For sure, I think so, definitely.

AG: I feel like people don't normally list him in their lists. He's like a Norman Rockwell. Like Norman Rockwell he's a stupid genius. Norman Rockwell is like… I feel like he's a guy that is possessed with virtuosity and genius, but he uses it to express these kind of stupid ideas.

DB: But does Norman have some… isn't he just… I don't know, lets talk about what these people are. Okay, so Norman Rockwell…

AG: Versus Walt Disney versus…

DB: Versus Norman, yeah. I think I'm going to go with Walt. He's a lot closer to Jodo than he is to Norman.

AG: Okay, now, of course.

DB: And the thing is, it's almost like Norman and Jodo equals Walt.

AG: Okay, right, there you go. Yeah, yeah, I like that.

DB: Well, this'll be edited out, but we didn't talk about the fact that we're both musicians.

AG: Oh yeah, yeah. I know.

DB: And we've really divided our time between disciplines—you're venturing into making films and I'm going to get into ballet. I'm not kidding. I'm going to take ballet when I get to LA. Ballet in LA.

AG: No… are you?

DB: Ballet in LA isn't it… it makes sense.

AG: No… are you going to be doing it?

DB: Yeah, Adam, I'm going to do it because Bob Hurwitz sat me down and played me a DVD of… of…

AG: Merce Cunningham.

DB: No. I did see Merce, though, before he passed away, over at Lincoln Center, but this was the great—oh fuck… this'll make a great interview. By the way, I'm jet-lagged. Balanchine! George Balanchine! Thank you so much, yeah.

AG: Okay, okay so—

DB: He's my buddy…

AG: I gotta turn this music down 'cause it's gonna mess up the transcription. Can I turn it down?

DB: Oh yeah, turn it down. Sorry about that. Turning down the great Shintaro Katsu—Hanzo the Razor, and of course Zatoichi… he made some great albums too! So… Adam and I were born a couple days apart the same year. We have all this time that we've been speaking and while we've been speaking we're making these collaborative drawings, but also we hadn't talked about it… about what it's like to be a musician.

AG: Yes, okay. So you were talking about this—the guy I was telling you about. Sitting on a chair with… like, I'm sitting on a chair Indian style. I feel like… like when I started to make noise music when I was really young, I had, like, a drug experience where I, like, smoked weed and recorded some noise music with some friends. We were about…

DB: What did you—what did you call each other?

AG: The band is called Neep.

DB: L-E-E?

AG: N-E-E-P, Neep.

DB: What does that mean?

AG: I don't know, it was made out of a reference like… like extraterrestrial communication or something.

DB: Like, "We are speaking Neep." Or when you communicate with an alien it's like Neep…? Or it's the language that they speak.

AG: Yeah, all of that. During that particular drug experience I felt a really strong relationship between sound and texture, in terms of, like, sounds that appeared to me to be, like, fibrous. And I made certain connections between certain sounds and line styles, and I think ultimately, like…

DB: You connect fiber and lines, that's so interesting.

AG: I think I did ultimately come up with the way that I'm drawing lines through like a blocky wooden sound concept. And that to me the line became like… like, my hand became a thing with which I felt emotions that were, like, vibrations. So I definitely feel like, in a way, my drawing style is kind of, like, noise drawing.

DB: Yeah, that makes sense. It's so cool.

AG: Do you feel like you connected your music and drawing when you were younger?

DB: Yeah, absolutely when I was younger.

AG: Tell the recorder.

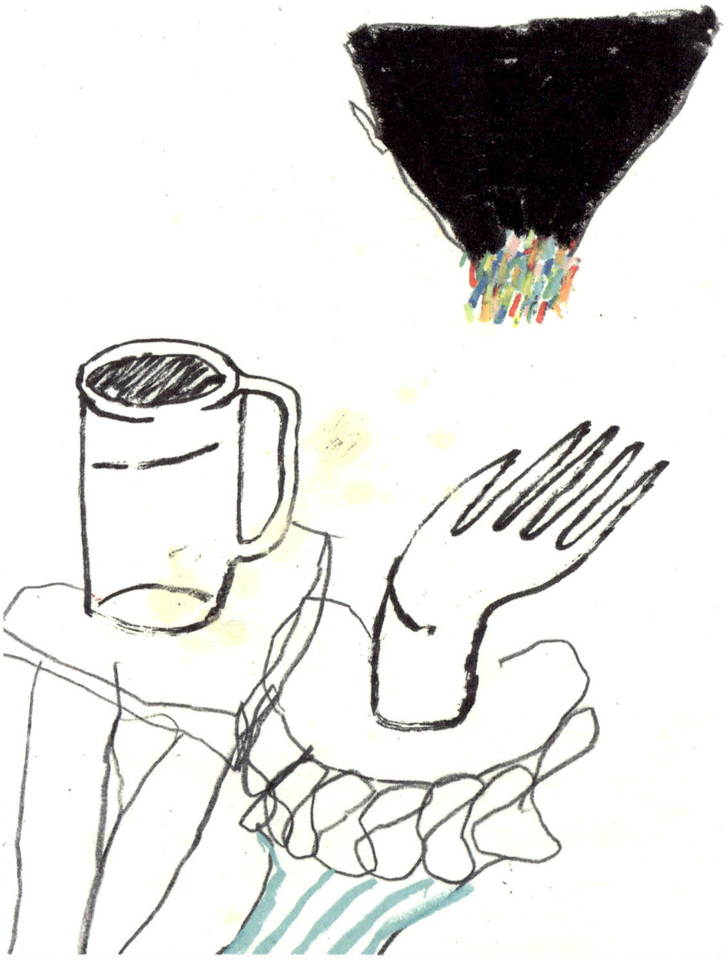

DB: Yeah, hey recorder, I've got something to say. It's really how I felt when I was first starting out writing songs and drawing. I really always—it was this thing of, okay, the song doesn't have to start sonically. I can start it with the drawing. And I'm going to finish this drawing and that's the song.

AG: Right, that's cool.

DB: And it felt just like these completely—because it was kind of clear that the source wasn't a place or a thing, wasn't tangible. So however I choose to have that be manifested or become tangible, who says it has to be through one vessel. So it could be this amalgamation of different disciplines and that just seemed really natural.

AG: And there was, like, a fluidity at the time where you were drawing things that you were singing about.

DB: Yeah, for sure.

AG: Can you give some examples?

DB: Well, corn and teeth. I did a show—my first ever show was at the Canada Gallery—and all the work was just drawings of corn and teeth and hands, and hands.

AG: And hands.

DB: And then I made a record called *Rejoicing in the Hands*, and most of the lyrics were about teeth and corn.

AG: So they were feeding into each other, and there were actually specific times where you, like… where you had a drawing for this before the music.

DB: Yeah, drawing before music or music before the drawing or, like, how do I solve this puzzle? And can I finish it with another verse or a line?

AG: Right.

DB: And then… when I put out a record that's why it's so important to have the visual element…

AG: So the visual elements in your records actually correspond to the drawings…

DB: Completely…

AG: That's really interesting.

DB: They were, like, inseparable to—

AG: Yeah, so excellent fluidity between, between the image and the—

DB: They were just this unified whole kind of thing, then they totally split for a period of time, and now they feel pretty separate. Let's say it's a bifurcated path. Let's say it's a dual narrative.

AG: That's right, because I feel like I had the opposite—well, not the opposite—I think… I was really interested in visual art and it didn't connect into my music at all for a long time. I think I just had opinions about it and I would read about art history. I was interested in reading about it and I was just kind of, like, an information store, and had a lot of information in my brain, but I had no one that I knew to talk about it with, so I just didn't talk about it until recently.

DB: Maybe also at that time you had… you had a pretty successful band really, really early on and probably the visual—there's just no time. You're constantly on tour. And there's also the fact that the visual element gets… maybe the visual is being manifested through writing so much poetry, because you were the only one that was actually printing up books of poetry…

AG: Well you remember I did do some drawing on tour and I showed them at Loyal Gallery in 2005, and that was, like, my first art show.

DB: Where was that gallery?

AG: It was in Stockholm at the time and, like—

DB: Where is it at this time?

AG: Malmö.

DB: Is that a cool way of saying you don't know?

AG: No, Malmö, yeah. Malmö, yeah. Malmö. And so, like… but, you know, that was cool because then I think I got to show that aspect of…

DB: What was the name of the show?

AG: *Animal Dreams.*

DB: Wow, that's so good.

AG: I actually I think that phrase almost applies to some of the work that you were doing at the time.

DB: Sure.

AG: Because there was kind of an anthropomorphic approach to…

DB: I did the first record and the lyric, oh, that was a part of the first title, "the dogs are dreaming."

AG: Because I feel like you were, like, drawing from some sort of myth. You know what I mean? Like during that period…

DB: Diego Cortez told me this story about how Patti Smith was watching a band going, "God I hope they just stop," and Diego is like, "Come on Patti, you play rock and roll." She goes, "I may play

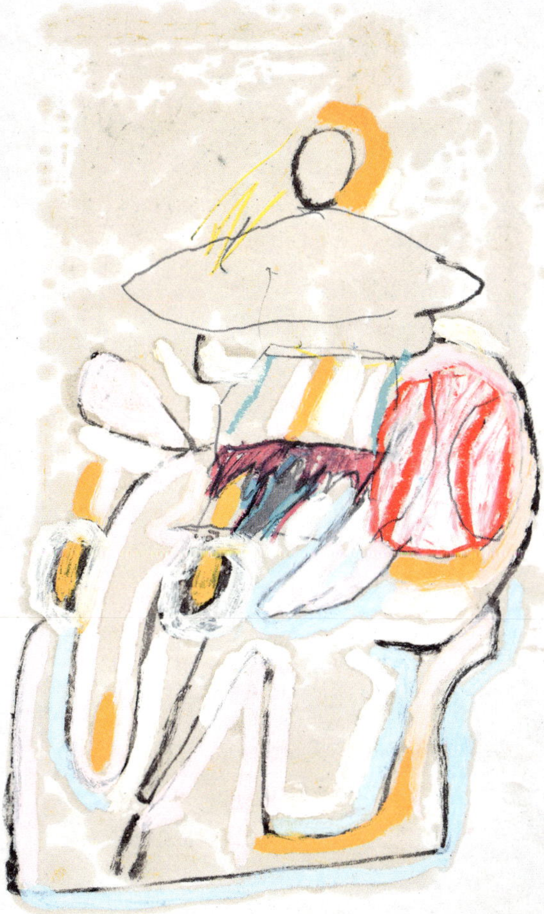

rock and roll, but I think opera." And what I was looking at then was what I still love now, but the formative artists for me were Cy Twombly and Joseph Beuys and Jean Arp. Even though I was drawing these figures and these animals, they're all made up of these little repetitive lines, and that was what got me going. It was the meditation of it… like the serialism in Agnes Martin's work.

AG: Agnes Martin, yeah. So you did develop a symbolic alphabet and then you produced it to this small, fine level where you could make other shapes out of it and—

DB: Yeah, and then the shapes were the thing I was trying to figure out… it was like a final verse that I couldn't find. It was like writing a song for someone or something…

DB: You were saying you had your first show and it was called *Animals Reduce.*

AG: But, can I say something? So you had your period. You had a lot of work that was comprised of a symbolic alphabet of stuff that you had, like, repeated, and then you had command of this particular thing and you were expounding on it to make all these different images, you know? And then you eventually—like that time you exhibited some stuff next to Paul Klee at the San Francisco Museum, right?

DB: Yeah.

AG: So there's a… I also feel like that has a commonality. Or that was like…?

DB: That was kind of where it was coming from early on, because I didn't have… I don't have a concept and I don't have, like… I don't know.

AG: Yeah, I think it's a cool mission statement.

DB: Yeah, that was coming from earlier. In the picture now, I mean, I was in that fucking squat and I painted both covers for the first two albums in the squat that was right under the bridge… you know, it was near your place.

AG: Yes, we were neighbors…

ADAM AND DEVENDRA LIVED A BLOCK AWAY FROM EACH OTHER IN BROOKLYN IN 2002

DB: We were neighbors. I mean fuuuck… I remember. Ben Goodman once goes, "You know what, man? I went to Adam Green's house today." Long silence. Lets it sit in. "I was in his fridge. He has a mason jar full of vodka."

AG: You gotta be shitting me.

DB: No, I was like wow... this guy... fuck, he's like a grown up. I mean, he can just put, just a mason jar full of vodka in his fridge? It's amazing.

AG: I feel like I had that and like one thing of, like, Romano pecorino cheese.

DB: We never think to photograph our fridges. Wouldn't it be great, just fridges through the years?

AG: Yeah, I love the cheese because I thought it reminded me of Matt Romano...

DB: It's a pull quote—maybe the title of this chat! So... fast forward. They're naming a house full of paints after you.

AG: I think... no, I don't think so. I don't know. There's no way to tell. I think it's like Adelle. The thing is like a tradition.

DB: Adelle Green? You mean you misread it?

AG: That's actually...

DB: How you really say your name?

AG: Yeah.

DB: For years people...

AG: No, no, no, no, I'm in somebody's phone as that.

DB: You finally made it, when you're in someone's phone.

AG: He's making an assess like he's... basically I'm like... I've basically been extending my outfit choices to only the things I want to ruin, so it's like my life is a permanent laundry day.

DB: Your life is a permanent outfit extension.

AG: An outfit extended. I have, like, six different velcros with six different outfits hanging out of the window right now. And some of my outfits are even in the subway...

DB: Oh my God, this is so good. Wait... they're in the subway?

AG: Yeah, they're dangling...

DB: Dangling in the subway? That's how much your outfits are extended?

AG: I'm like an outfit Rapunzel on laundry day.

DB: That's better than the Romano line. I didn't think it could be beat, but that's the best title: *I'm Like an Outfit Rapunzel on Laundry Day*? Fuck! Oh man, I'm so sad to be going. These are the moments. Most of the time I'm just so happy to enjoy the city before I move, but then when we're hanging out, I really... I really... I'm going to miss being able to just hang every couple of days, you know?

AG: You managed to be in New York and be so reclusive here that, like—

DB: That's not truuue.

AG: Well, pretty reclusive because, like, I tell people you're moving and they're like, "He was here?"

DB: I live here? Well you know, socially, yeah, I guess I'm pretty reclusive, but, you know, in terms of leaving the apartment and doing things, I do plenty. I go to Chelsea and I take a boat...

AG: Take a boat?

DB: I take a boat. I do the Architectural Institute of America's tour of the island. Yeah. I go to the museums...

AG: What island?

DB: This island.

AG: This island?

DB: This island. And I do, um... and I go on... you know, on whatever.

AG: I wanna go back to something we were talking about before. The connection of this thing, like, noise versus—I was thinking about this today, like, getting exposed to noise music and stuff. It made me feel like... that...

DB: Maybe it was the perfect kind of intermediary between painting and the kind of music that you write...?

AG: Yeah, maybe, yeah.

DB: Just because there was that clear fabric or textural...

AG: Yeah, it was definitely art and not anything else, so it helped me see music in a pure art context. And then I think that from there, I think when I withdrew from that deep focus, I retained seeing pop music—or whatever I was going to write—still in terms of the noise aesthetic, and so what I was connecting it with my mind, was that the... like, I kinda see the textures of different kinds of noise, in a way. Like, it came to me like a spice, like, you know, I sort of realized that the noise itself was a context.

DB: Yeah.

AG: Like, noise gives things context, like we know that we're here because we are hearing this music and we hear the sounds of the city.

DB: Right.

AG: And so to listen to pure context like that, it made me realize that that was like a powerful spice, and I think that's something that you understood really, really, really, you know, better than anybody. Like, when we were so young, I thought you had a tremendous grasp of how to present, like... for example, like, in a way that Twombly does. You know, where you present, like, a worn thing and your art appeared to be on these yellowed antique things that were part of something ancient, you know? And I think that, in that way, like that kind of context and that kind of noise that you put on to your own work... you know, in some cases like, really different from like a formalist, uh... you know... thing, where somebody just draws lines on a plain piece of paper just to be able to show you a diagram, you know? Like, your stuff, like, told the story through just how you presented it, you know?

DB: Well, I don't know, I mean, the artwork that I started making and sharing and the stuff that you've seen and were talking about, the really early stuff, that was much later when we were living so close to each other almost ten years ago—actually over ten years ago. Over ten years ago, dude. Fuck! Over ten years ago. But... it's kind of like how David Byrne has that whole—he wrote that book about it and also did the TED Talk on how the architecture or the context in which the... the society the person lives in or the space where the person resides or works in, that's what shapes the music, and music serves this purpose based on the kind of context in which it's in... it was more of like a practical reason—not purely, because aesthetically I like those old papers, but there was an old bin where they would have free books, and so—and also in New York, you know, like, summer and winter at one point people were moving and there's just books on the street, so you always look for pages. New books don't waste paper like that anymore. But all the old books, which was the only paper I would use, they do. There's always like five blank pages before you even get to the title.

AG: Right, right, right.

DB: So, that was it. For me it was free paper.

AG: Yeah, right.

DB: But then it's, like, what kind of work can I make that's going to look good on this paper? And so, there's this one type of watercolors, Lukas watercolors, that were, to me, the best and the most, kind of… earthy, and they blended the best with that old antique paper, and just making work that is going to fit the medium. You know…

AG: Yeah, yeah, yeah. Because that's, like, distinctively you. Most people don't think like that, you know what I mean? I feel like the way that you use indigo ink for some reason looks like Asian art, like—I don't know if you were looking at Asian art at the time?

DB: It was more, like, snippets I'd get from different people—Matteah Baim… she had a really big influence… You know Matteah, right?

AG: Yeah.

DB: And yeah, Matteah would be a huge influence, and also… I don't know, I mean… Colter Jacobson, Sarah Cain, and you know, Colter has a band called Coconut and he also makes incredible beautiful art, stuff like that. He actually has an art opening right now here in New York.

AG: So…

DB: But I want to try to—now let's jump to something that I am curious about, which is the trajectory of having *Animal Dreams* at Loyal in Stockholm. I feel like it was relatively recently that you've really been showing so consistently.

AG: Yeah, well, since 2010. In 2010 I did a show called *Teen Tech*.

DB: *Teen Tech*?

AG: Yeah. Well, the thing is, I was doing a lot of, you know, touring, and so I wasn't really, like, focusing on, you know, doing any kind of visual art. And then for whatever reason the girl I was with at the time was not encouraging me, so I was drawing and, like, I don't know, like, she really didn't like—she really just didn't feel that I was any good, so I was just sort of like…

DB: Sounds like a keeper.

AG: Yeah, so I was kind of feeling, like, not too great about my visual art. You know, like, whatever. It wasn't… it wasn't an important part of my life.

DB: Have you noticed that, like, your significant other… when they don't support what you do, you don't have that drive, like, "I'll show you…"

AG: Yeah, you've tried it, like, five times and if they still don't like it, you're like, "Okay, well, I guess I give up drawing."

DB: Yeah, like, if they're friends you can be like, "I'll show you," kind of. Or it can be a slightly driving force of like, well no, no that's not gonna deflate the balloon, and then parents, definitely, that can be a force of… it can be an impetus to actually make more if you're not being supported.

AG: Yeah. So anyway, when we split up I came back to the apartment we were sharing and it was totally empty except for, uh, there was a bunch of cardboard so I just started to make paintings on it. And I made like twenty paintings on it, and like huge paintings and, like, you know, I just started to make sculptures there and I just filled up the whole place with art. Then from then on I just kind of, like, you know, I just became engaged in a dialogue about it, but, like, with myself, you know?

DB: But you might have just demystified a fallacy, which, the fallacy is, make art or make something to kind of work through the pain of the relationship having ended, which is the typical—that's the kind of thing…

AG: Right, right, right.

DB: Ohhh, you're going to write such great songs, or you're going to make some art. But it's more like, now that this relationship is over you can finally make art.

AG: Right, right, yes.

DB: It's almost like, okay, now this thing that was kind of not supporting me working on my work is out of the way, now I am going to make some shit.

AG: Yeah, now I can actually do it.

DB: How much time went by after *Animal Dreams* before your next show?

AG: Five years.

DB: So, yeah, it's so similar, man, my trajectory. So similar. I had the show with Canada, Andrew Roth, Mazzoli, and then the Klee show, and then it was, like, seven years of…

AG: Nothing?

DB: It was little group shows, you know what I mean? I curated a show and I did a little this and that, but I was just… I hadn't found that space where I just—you know, whatever, it's just a question of growing and…

AG: Yeah, yeah, but you did actually end up, like, I mean, in the last year, you've kind of started avidly drawing and developing, like, all these new avenues of art.

DB: But it seems new to really fully be… dedicating an equal amount of time to both things.

AG: Right, right.

DB: But it's only because a lot of the things—a lot of the distractions have been, you know...

AG: Yeah, lifted.

DB: Transmuted or, you know, lifted or, or... done away with... and made peace with. I think that's the best way to put it. But, it's so similar where you had five years after *Animal Dreams* and I had a similar stretch of time between—

AG: Well, let me ask you. I remember you were getting very into Arthur Russell, and you actually ended up finding a place, like, two blocks from where he lived.

DB: Right now we are two blocks from Arthur's old place.

AG: Yeah, and I was wondering if that also had an effect on your visual art.

DB: Wow, that's a cool question. I haven't thought about Arthur's affect on my visual art, although he had such an effect on my music that I think that later ended up affecting the way I started drawing. I was starting to get really, really into Arthur... actually, I don't know. To be honest I don't know. I don't even know how Arthur has affected my music. I just... like, there's no way that he didn't because when you just love a musician or an artist they're gonna inspire something. So maybe it's not some explicit influence, but it's certainly gonna, you know... sometimes we also don't know, and then when we hear something, like, two years later, you're like, "Oh man, it's so clearly that thing I was listening to at that time."

AG: Yeah, and if you're carrying around somebody's soul with you or whatever, you know, you're kind of—it's like your buddy.

DB: I mean that's even—other than oil paint and the fact that the band lives in LA, having done this Arthur song and having met Tom Wilson, and having had this experience with Arthur through rerecording one of his songs for that AIDS charity, *Red Hot*, like, that was the kind of, "Okay, it's okay to go now. It's time to go."

AG: Interesting.

DB: Yeah.

AG: So, in a way, like, I feel like you did sort of carry on that, though...

DB: You know it might have affected the art only in that he... like the way John Cage has that line, which is, "I have nothing to say and I'm saying it." When I first read that I was relatively young and it was, like, "Oh my God, thank you." I feel that way. I have permission. I've always had that feeling of, "I don't know how to do these things, but that's not going to stop me." And then Arthur, also, you know, like other—like Yo La Tengo, just people that are clearly not defined by a single genre and are experimenting with a variety of disciplines and styles, forays and cultures, tunings and timings, and on and on and on. They're playing. They're playing. Like, Mike Kelly is a good example. Like, "I'm just gonna try all these different things." Sigmar Polke, all these artists...

AG: But you know that's why I was feeling like what really defines an artist at the end of their lifetime is the commonality that these things had with each other. You know, a common thread. You know, like, I guess there's a commonality to things, I think, and you can see it really well once you see a lifetime of somebody's artwork.

DB: Yeah, I mean that's kind of one of those things where if you're lucky you get to see it at the end of the whole kind of...

AG: Yeah, you're like, "Oh, this guy's still drawing a sneaker."

DB: Today, I actually read about a German painter named Peter Dreher who's been drawing the same glass for, like, thirty years. He just said he was planning on doing—he teaches at an art school in Germany now—but he said he was just planning on drawing it three or four times, but he got so into that experience and he's just drawn that one glass for thirty years.

AG: That's crazy. So let me ask you...

DB: It's something like a ring. It's going to be the new thing.

AG: And then it turns to juice.

DB: And I'm going to dance ballet in LA. You're making a big Hollywood picture while I'm dancing ballet.

AG: Wait, ok, so I was gonna say one more thing about my idea. Humor me here... can you describe the difference, for example, let's say, like, we started drawing together last year right? You were working on a series of stacks of urns and things...

DB: Oh yeah.

AG: And it was very minimal and it did seem like it was a... what do you call it? Like a clean slate for you, you know? You were drawing album art that was almost like a cutout. So how would you describe the differences in your thought processes versus when you were taking little elements like that or repeating elements and then building these things out of all these different elements, like the tooth and the corn, from experiences you had last year where you kind of did have a clean slate for some reason. Could you describe some of the feelings of, like... what you were thinking for that work and where have you gone with it, you know?

DB: Well, as opposed to... maybe it's an effect of to some degree both of us kind of having had things that probably shouldn't have been public be somewhat public, relatively public. So instead of kind of going through a period of, like, hibernating and kind of working through what the next phase would be, which I kind of feel I'm at, doing visual work, it felt like doing all those urns, vessels, or receptacles was my way of drawing the blank slate.

AG: So, that was actually pretty cool, you know, that you could look at this series as, you know, as you drawing, like, a blank slate for a receptacle for what's to come.

DB: But yeah, and I love that you said urn, man. And that makes so much sense. It was just an urn. Drawing the... the... the old face.

AG: Yeah, that's cool.

DB: It was a receptacle to put the last phase in, to put the ashes of the old in.

AG: Yeah, yeah.

DB: Yeah...

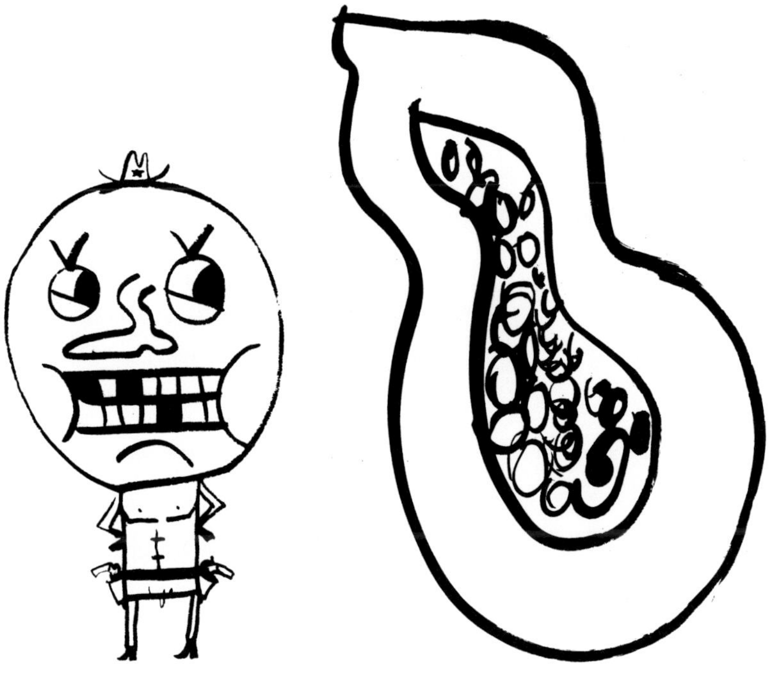

and suddenly everything that is not happening
is not happening ...

For the most part ,

misunderstanding is my primary medium .

While the variegated void ,

floating off into who knows where ,
my primary process ...

and

like so many before me ,
six flags magic mountain .

Polychromed gelatinous zooplankton skin is nothing to me , I've got plenty of it ...
right now
out there
where
outer space
sits

my motto's always been :

Never be prepared !

and my two favorite words :

Who Knows

(begin again

and

start over

are pretty good too ...)

My vocabulary doesn't expand ,
I'm only trying to say one word well

sí mi pana , sí ...

I think of Bas Jan Ader and Houston Airport in the rain ,
the red tiles on an unmopped floor ... of Joe Brainard ... I remember *I Remember* ...

now
Hong Kong Charlie looks at the empty page ,

a little space goes a long way ...

while working ,
I am often guided by the suspicion
that I haven't started making my actual work ...

my advice is

try to be as soft-spoken as possible
and with everything else ,

lighten your touch .

further simplify the simplified
and once you learn to draw ,

learn to draw .

two things I believe to be true are :

gratitude is the essence behind any worthwhile offering (it's what gives it any true value)
and when all words fail , thank you is always a good way to go ...

qué más ?

art is mostly
people who
just tried

and though it says many things ,
one of those things is this :

close your eyes
and look at me .

that's it ,
que disfruten
queridos y queridas
chamacos y chamacas .

Devendra Banhart, 2014

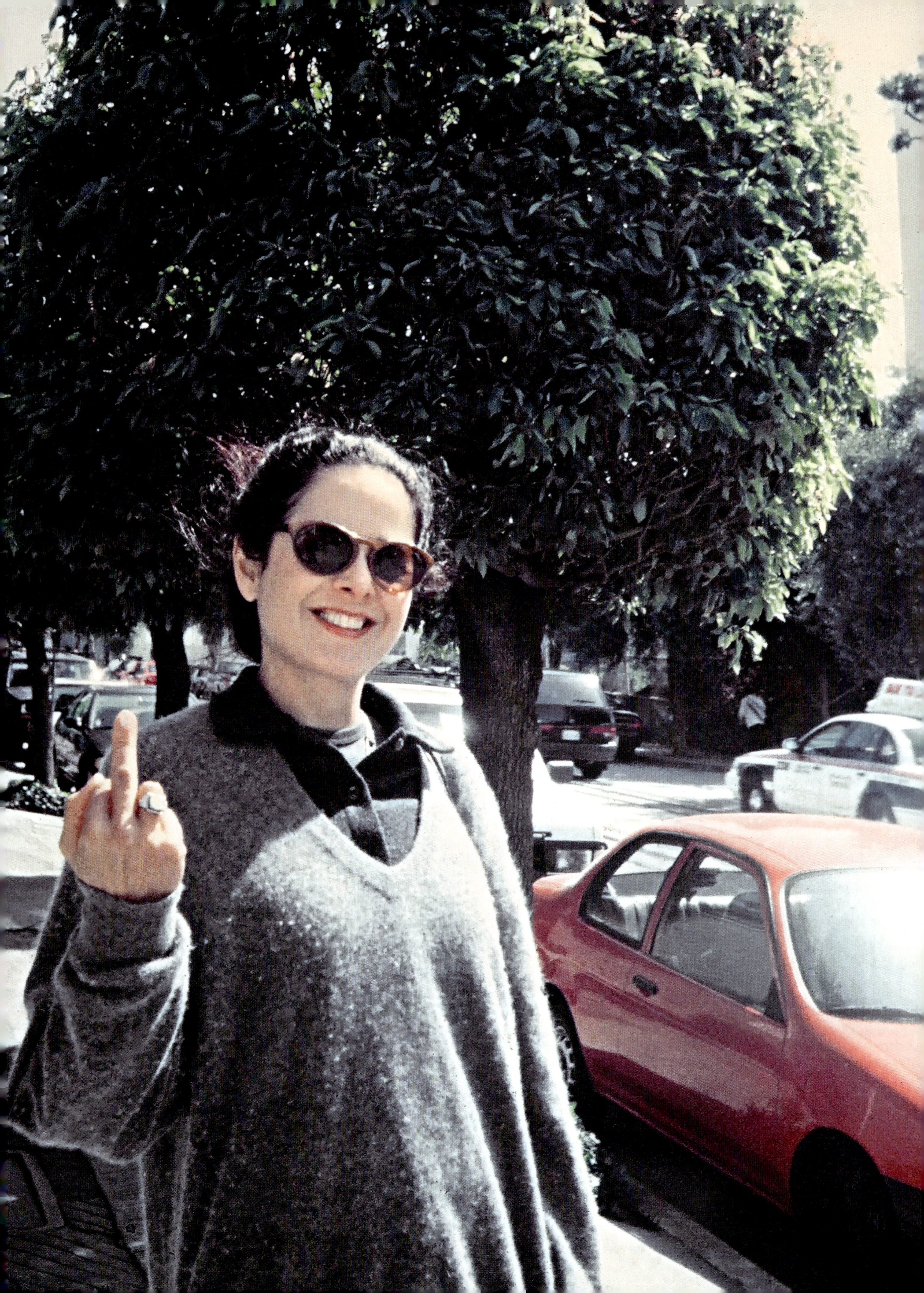

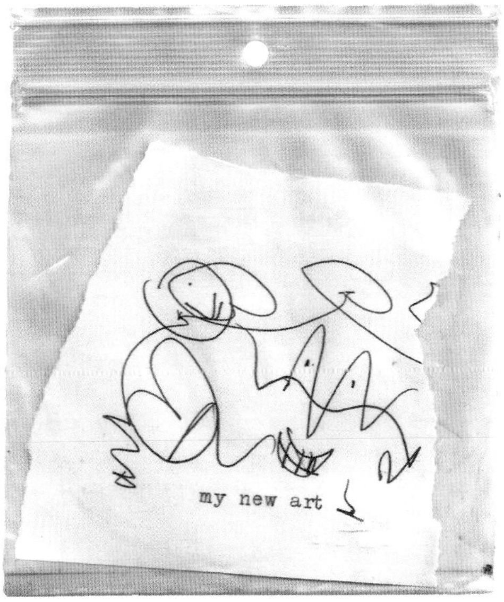
my new art

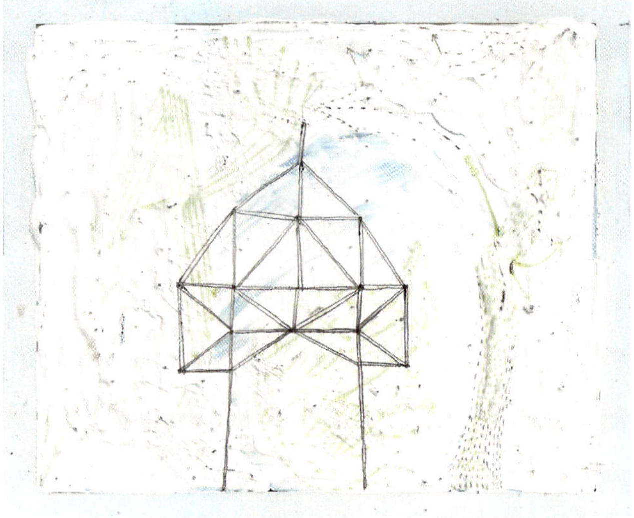

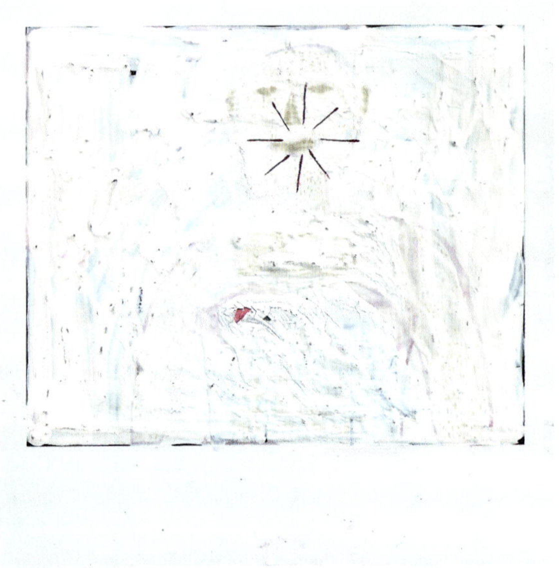

80,
80,

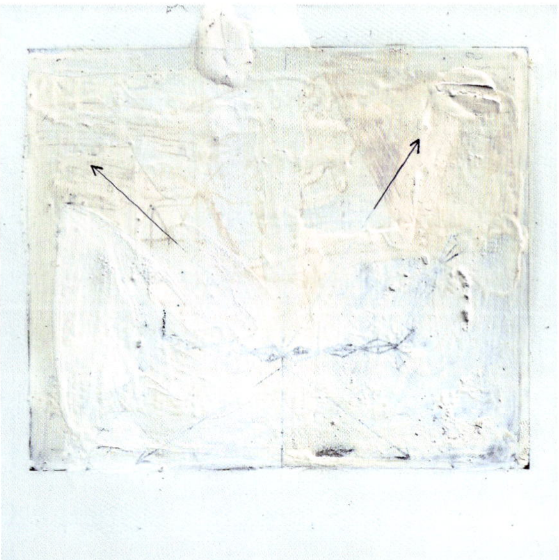

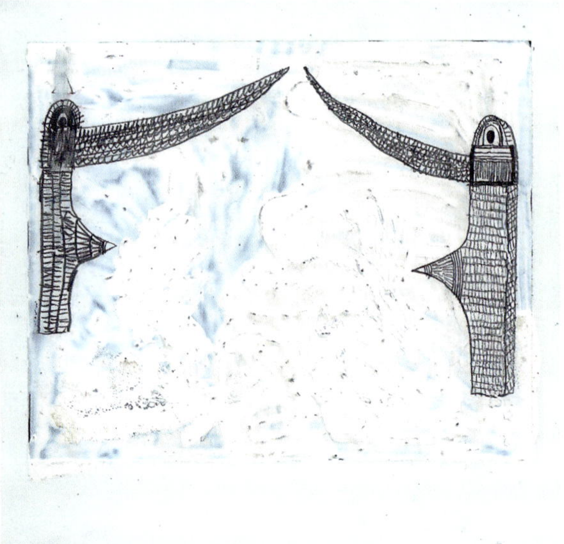

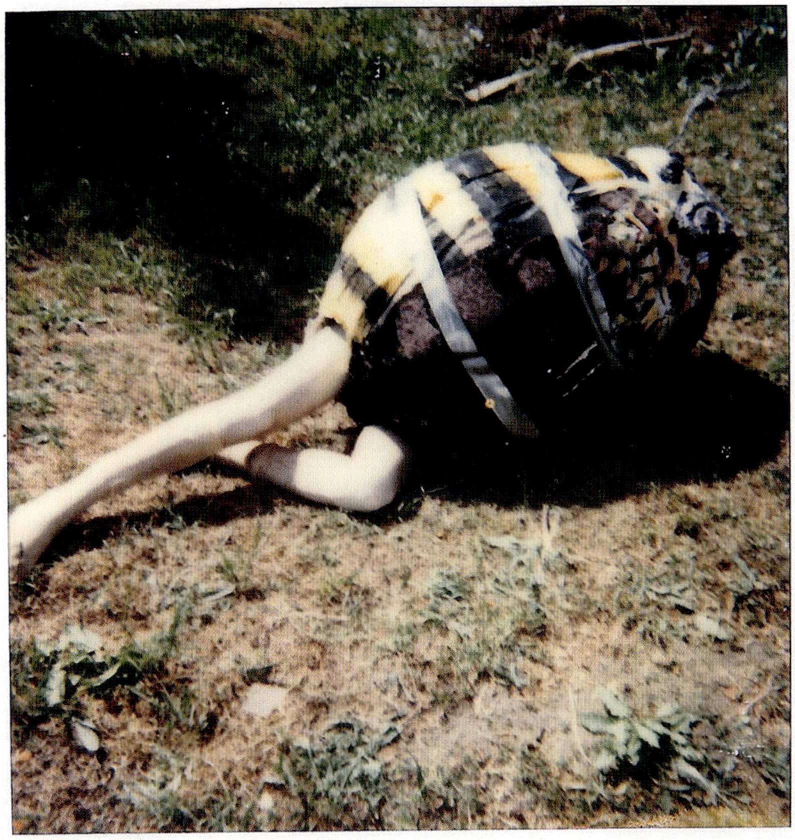

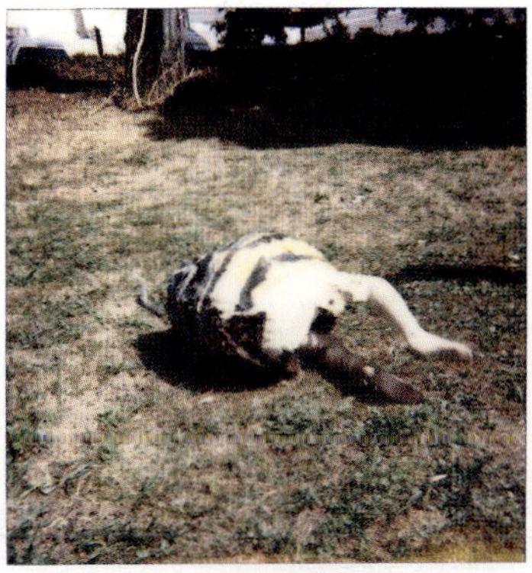

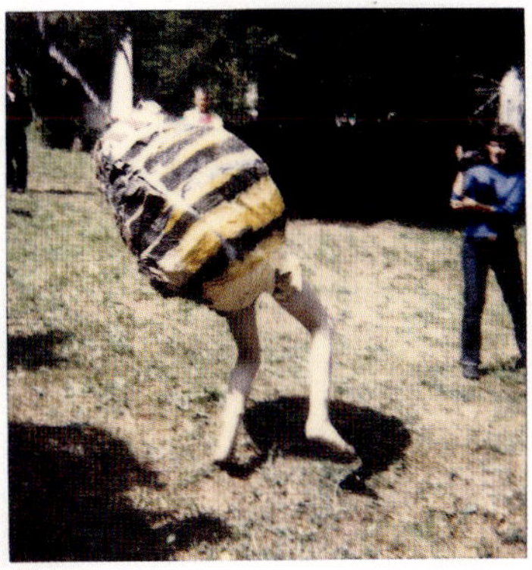

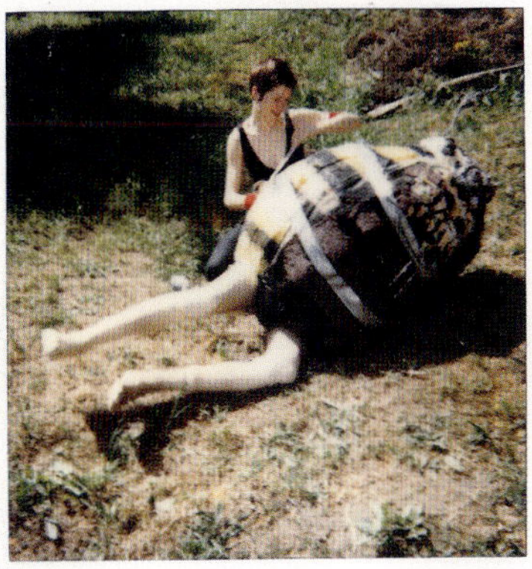

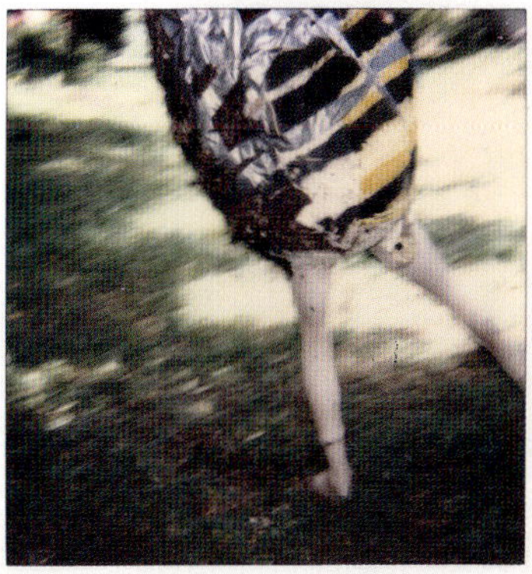

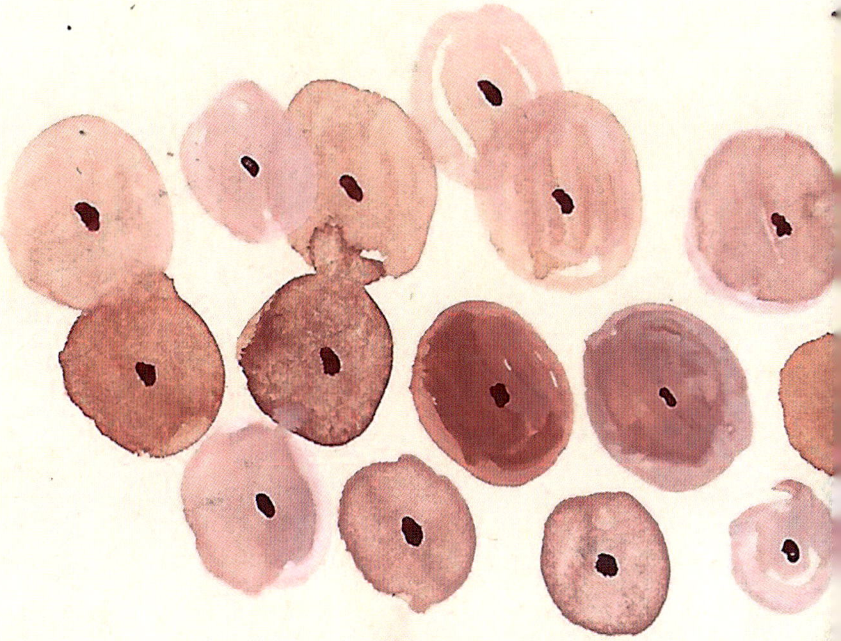

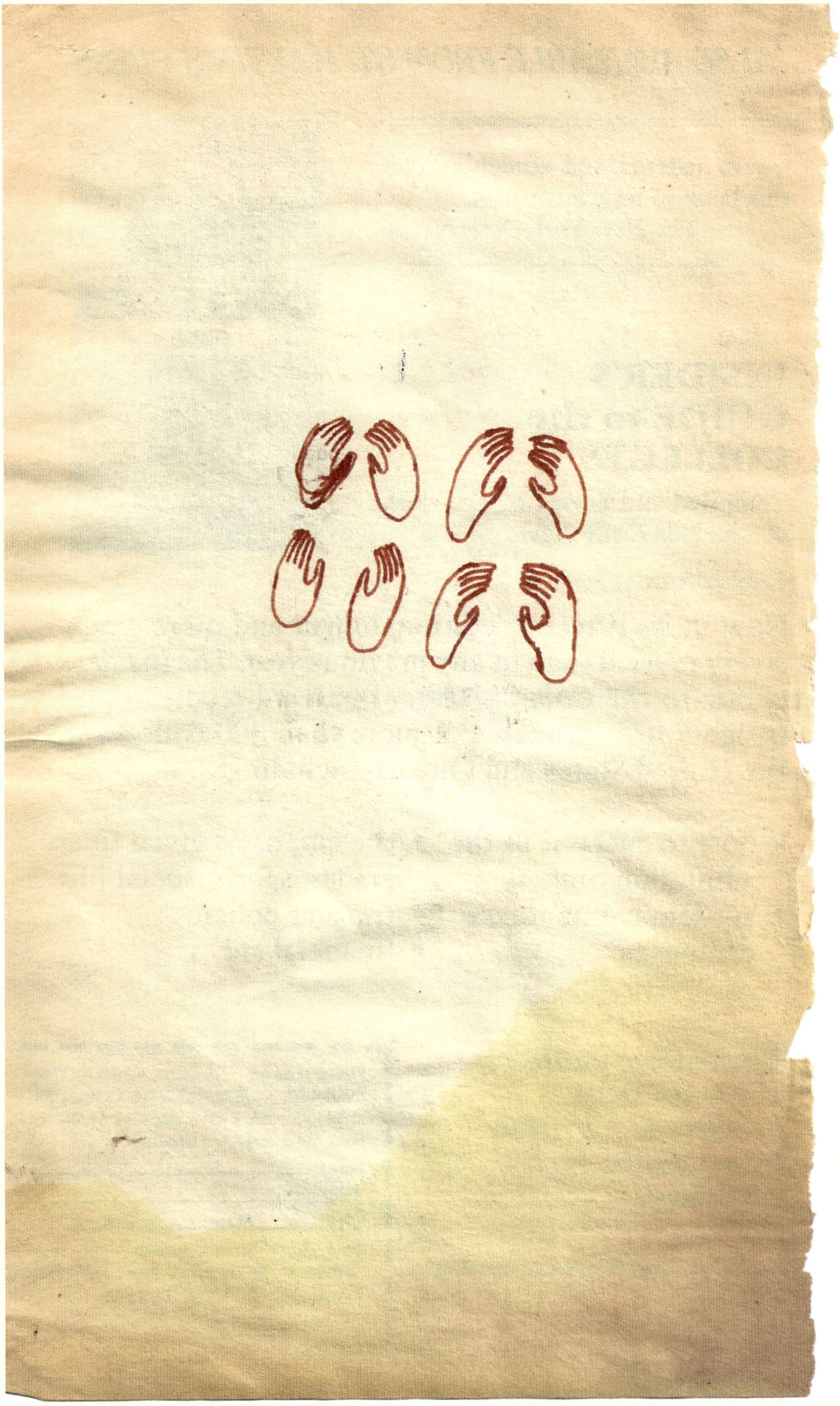

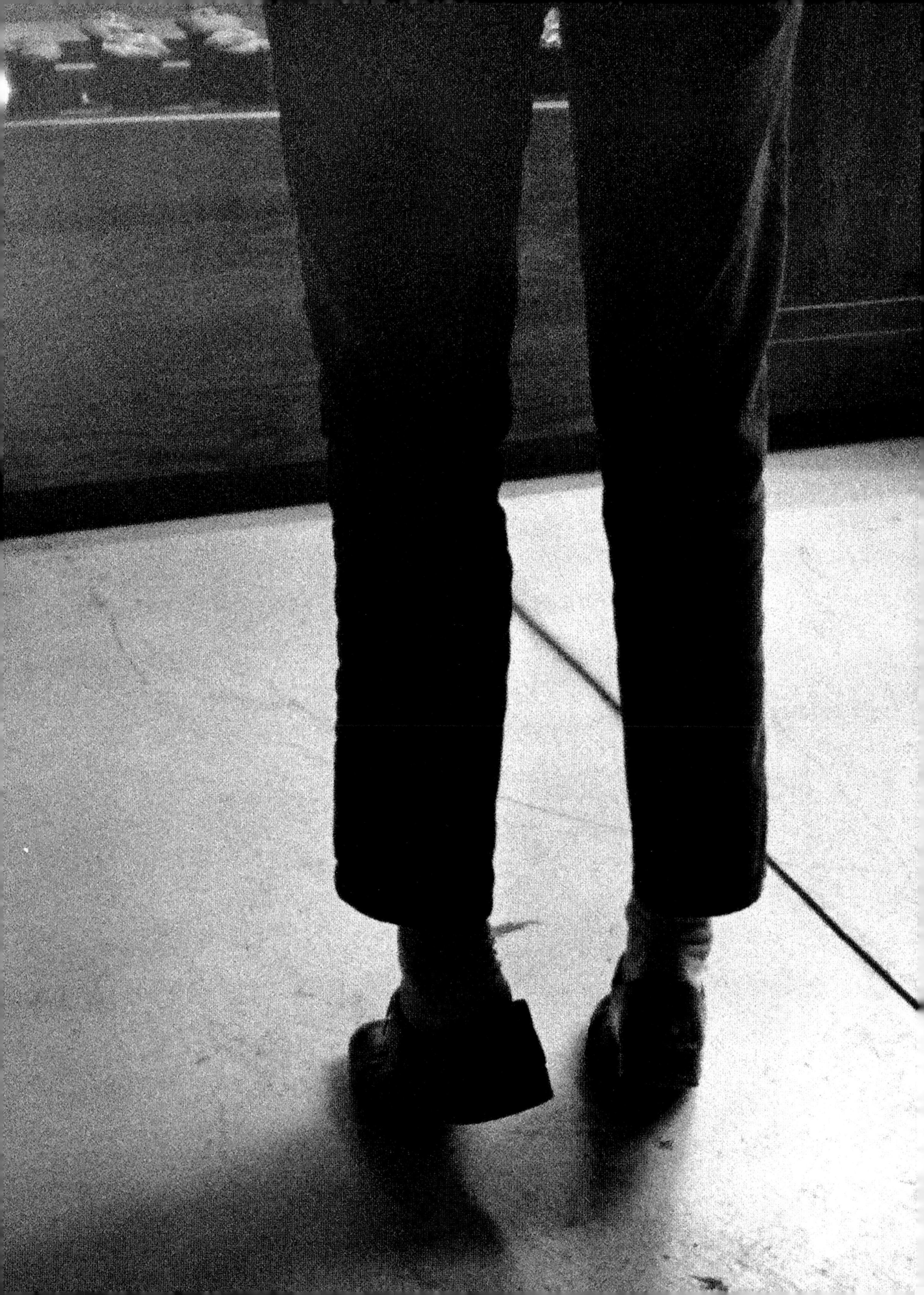

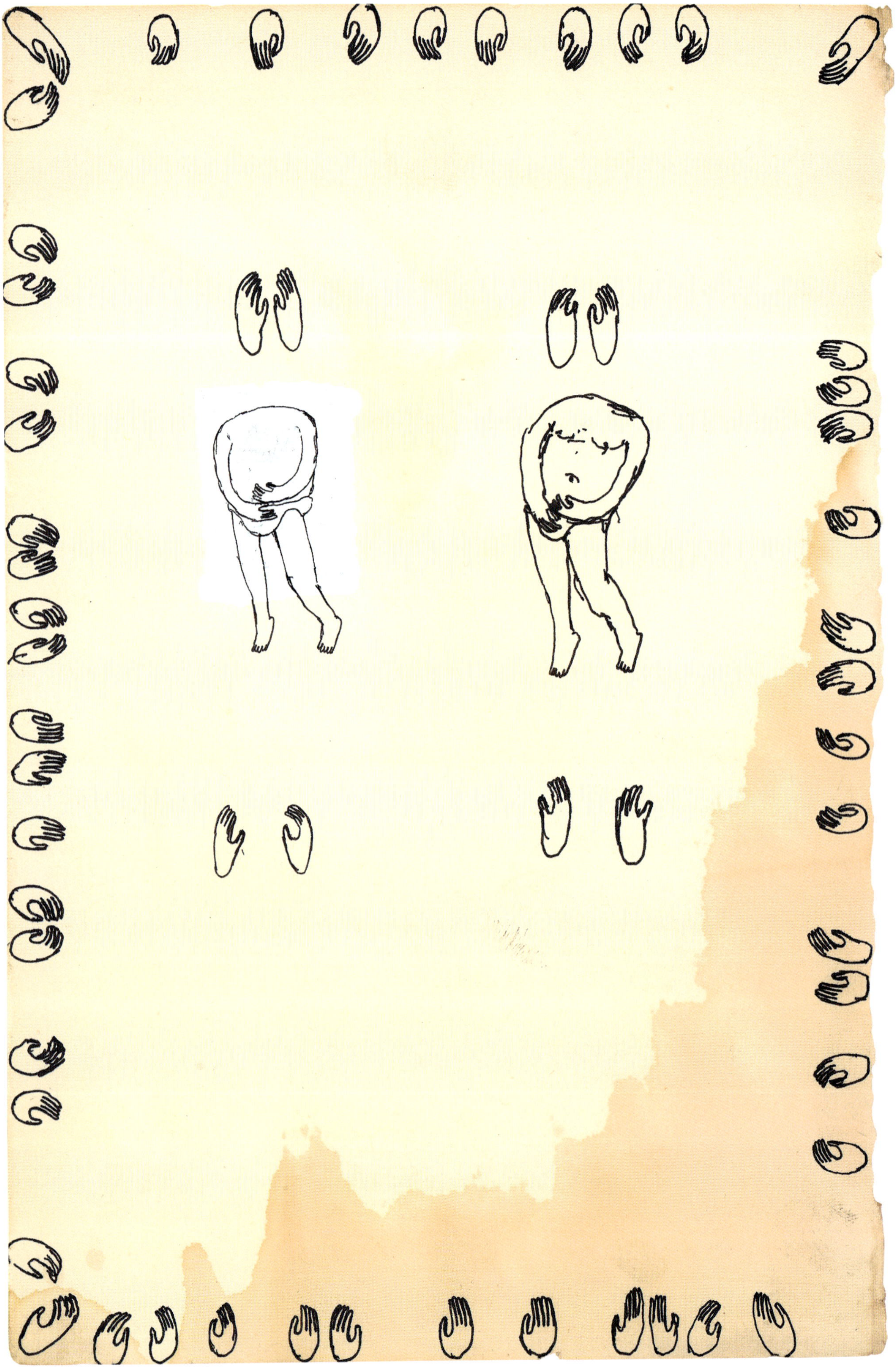

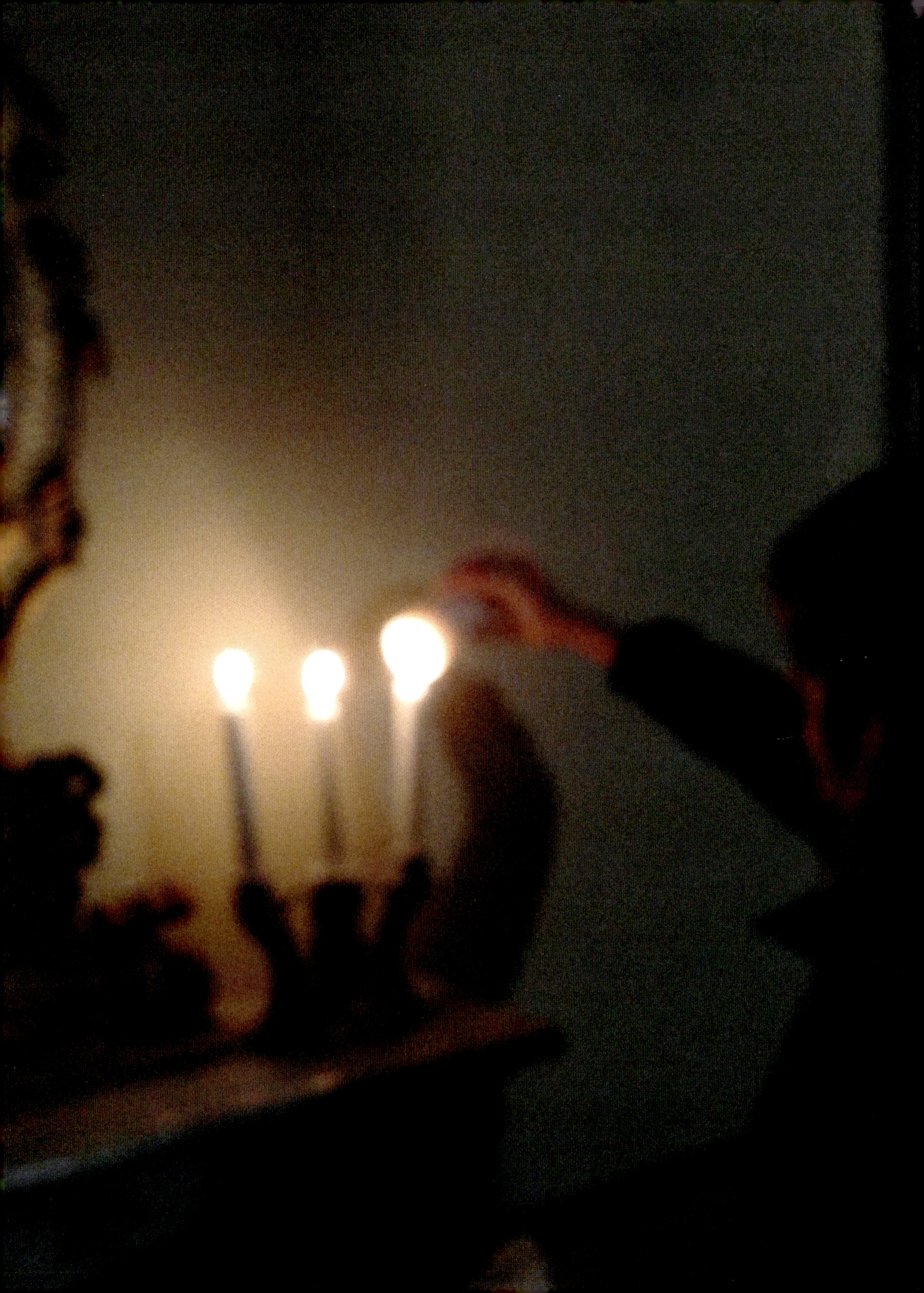

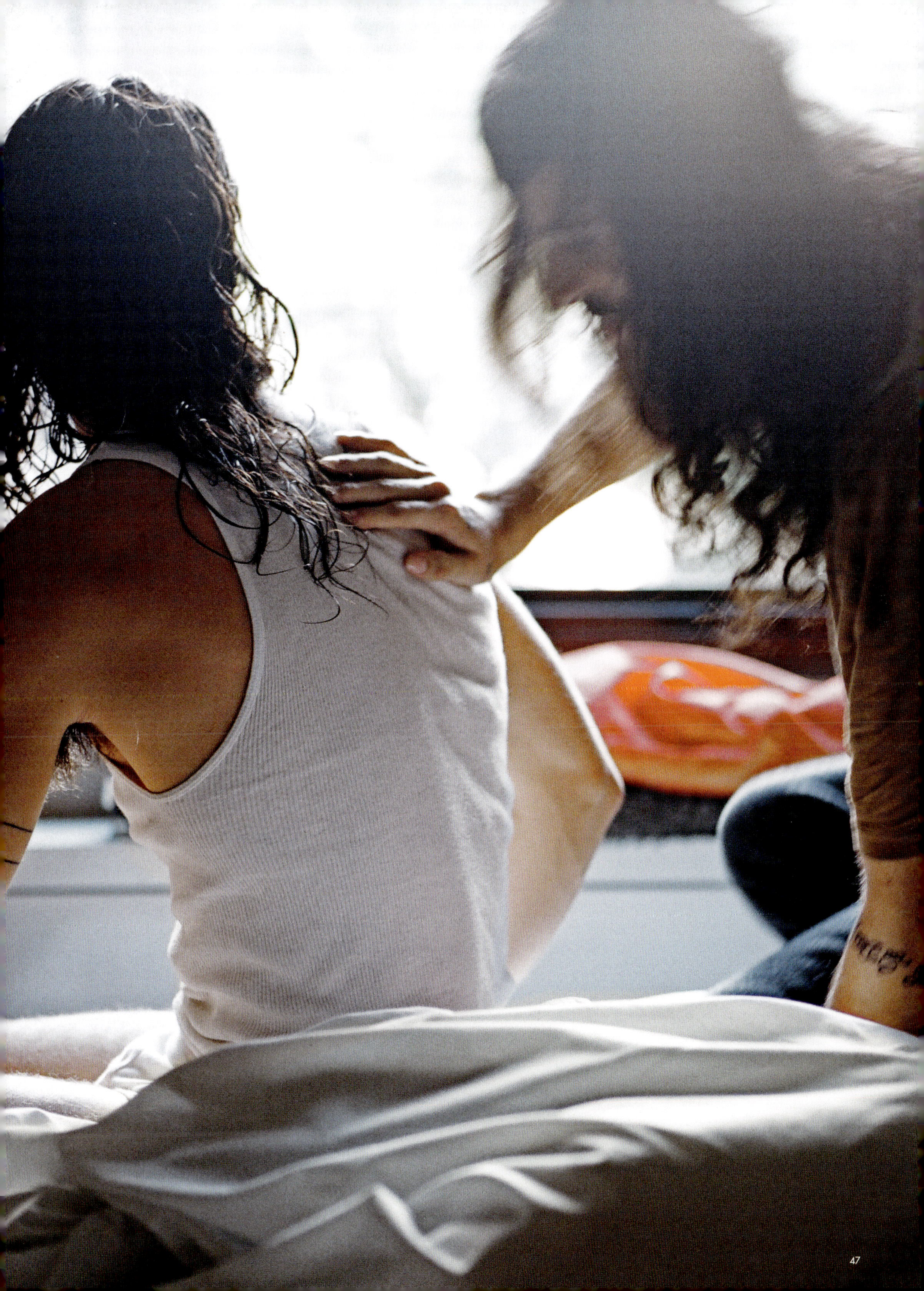

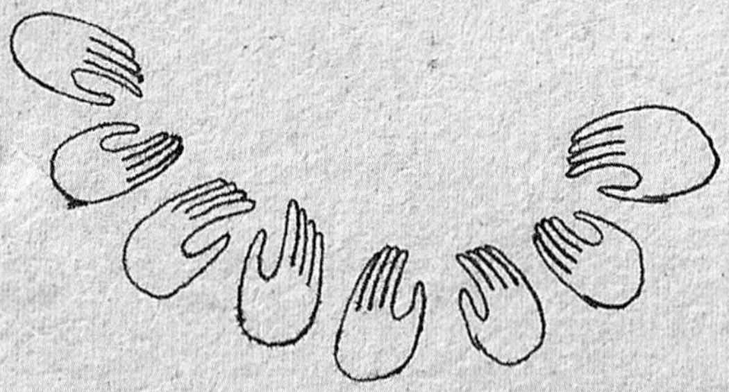

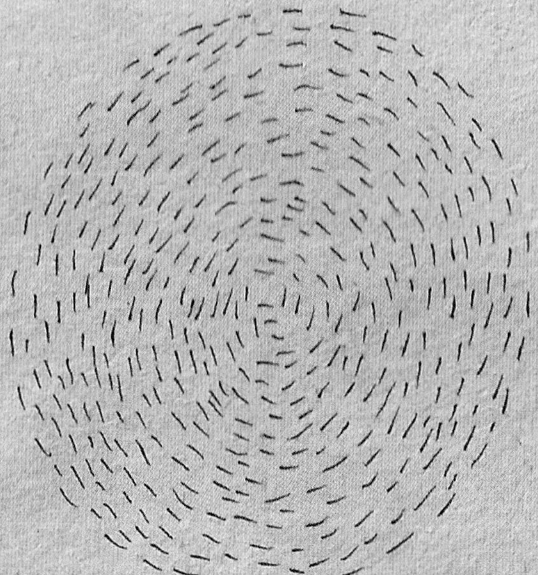

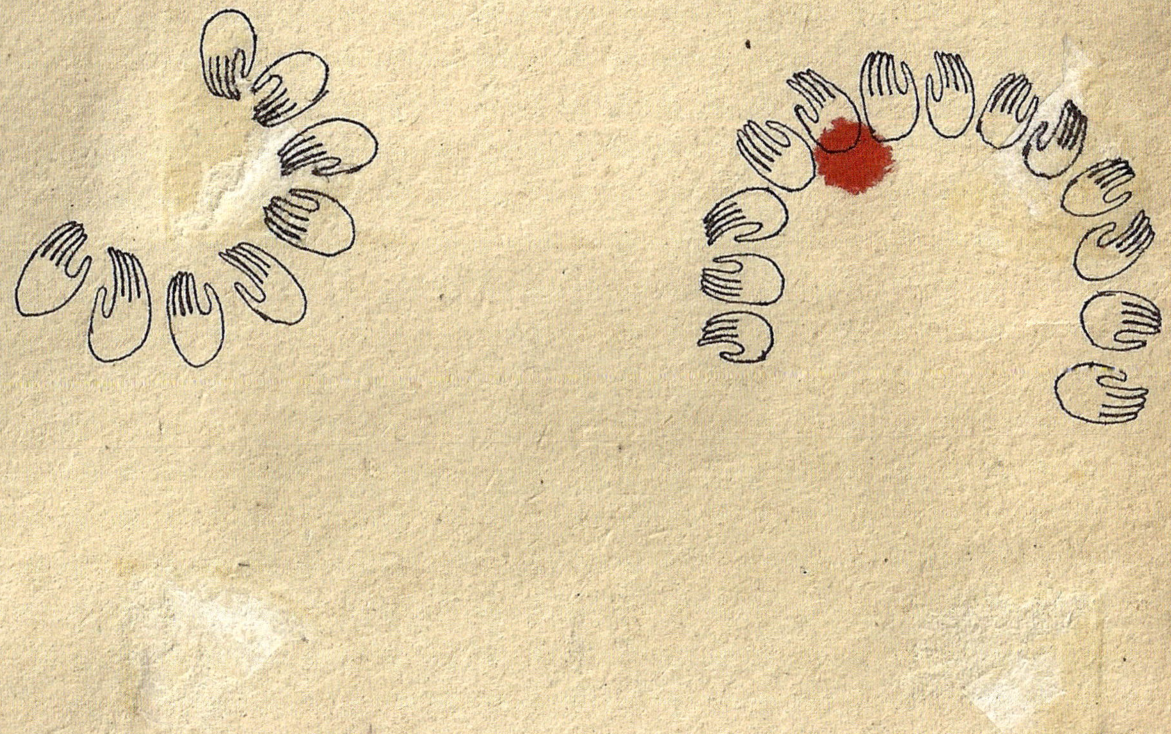

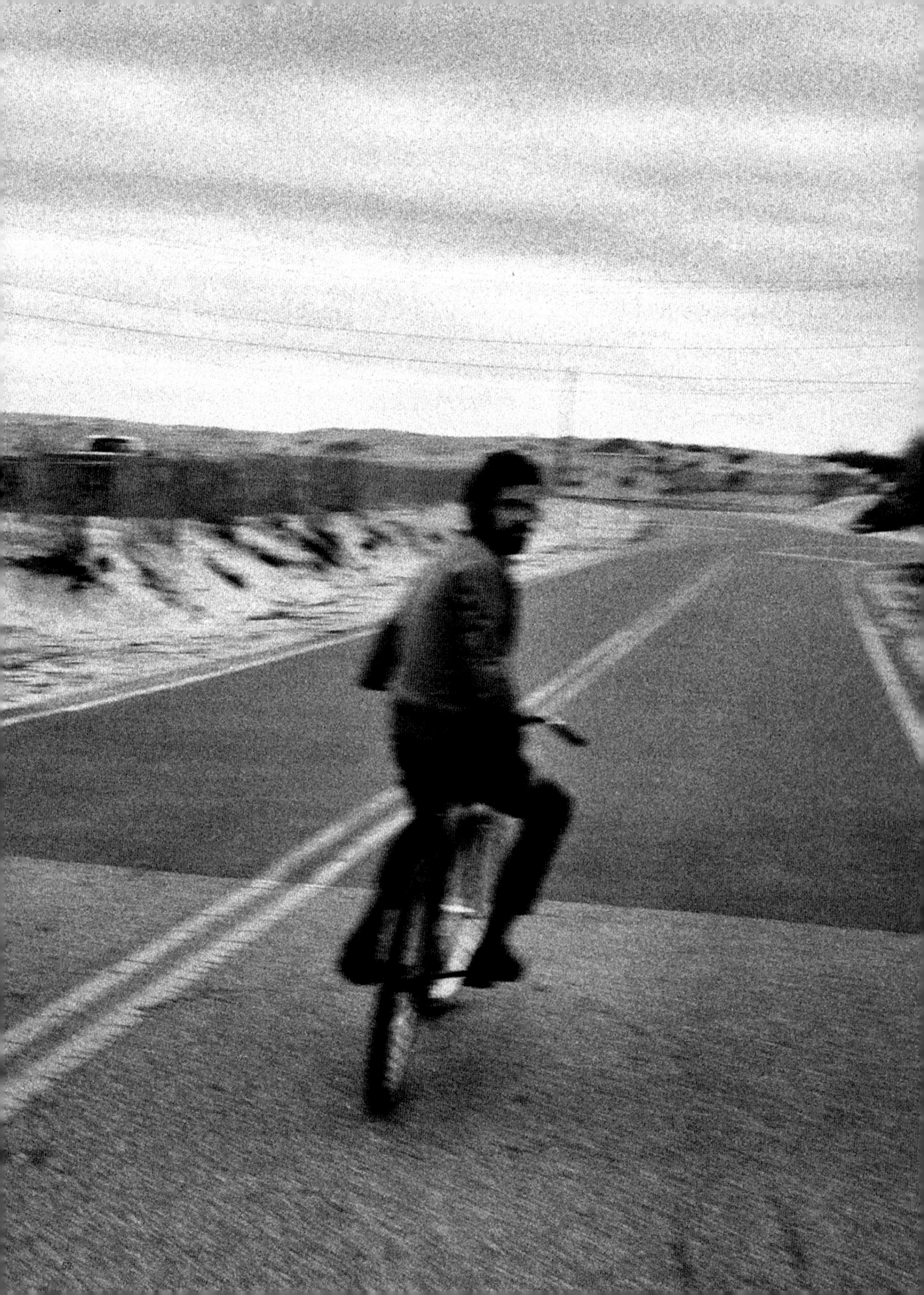

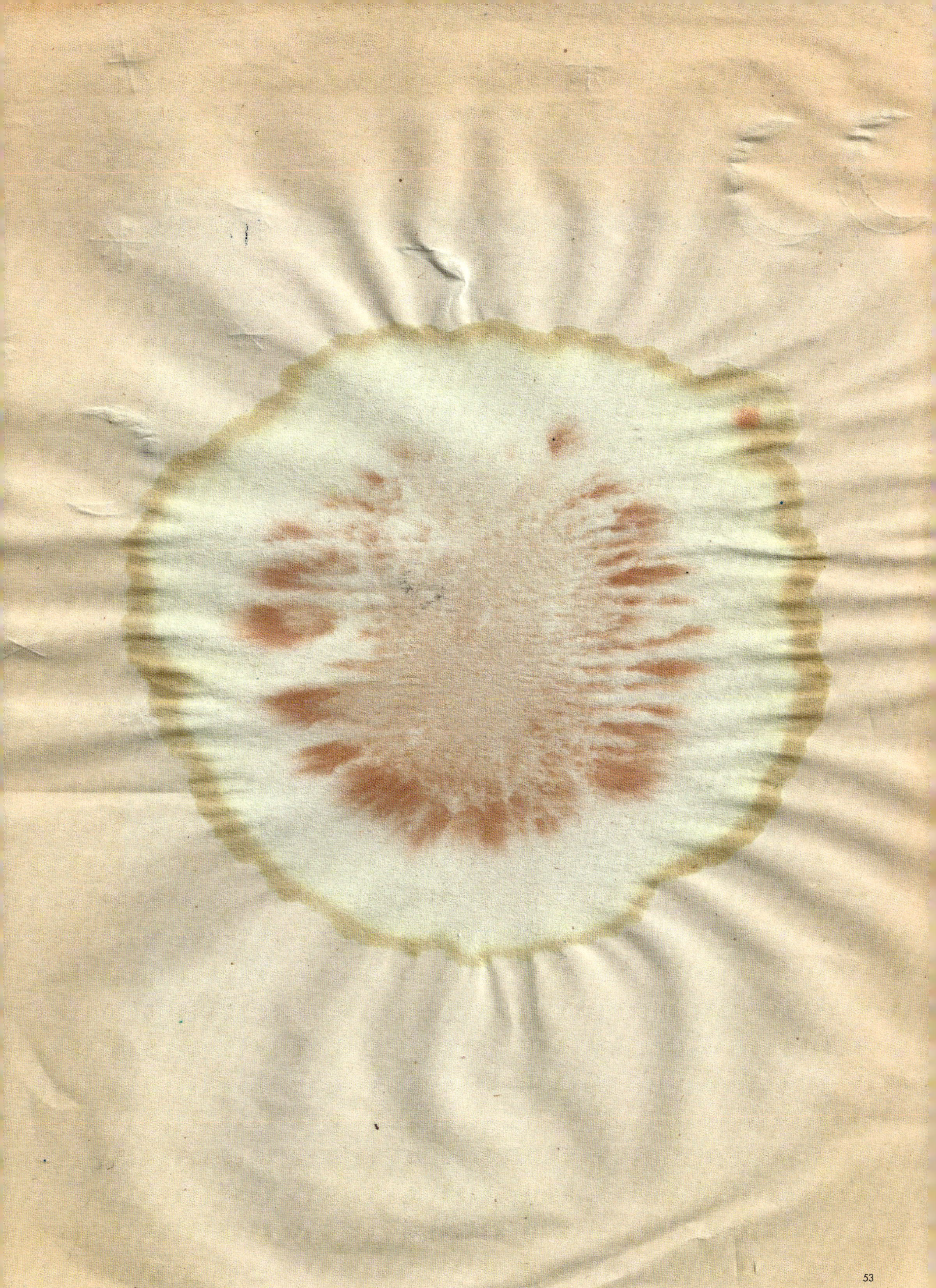

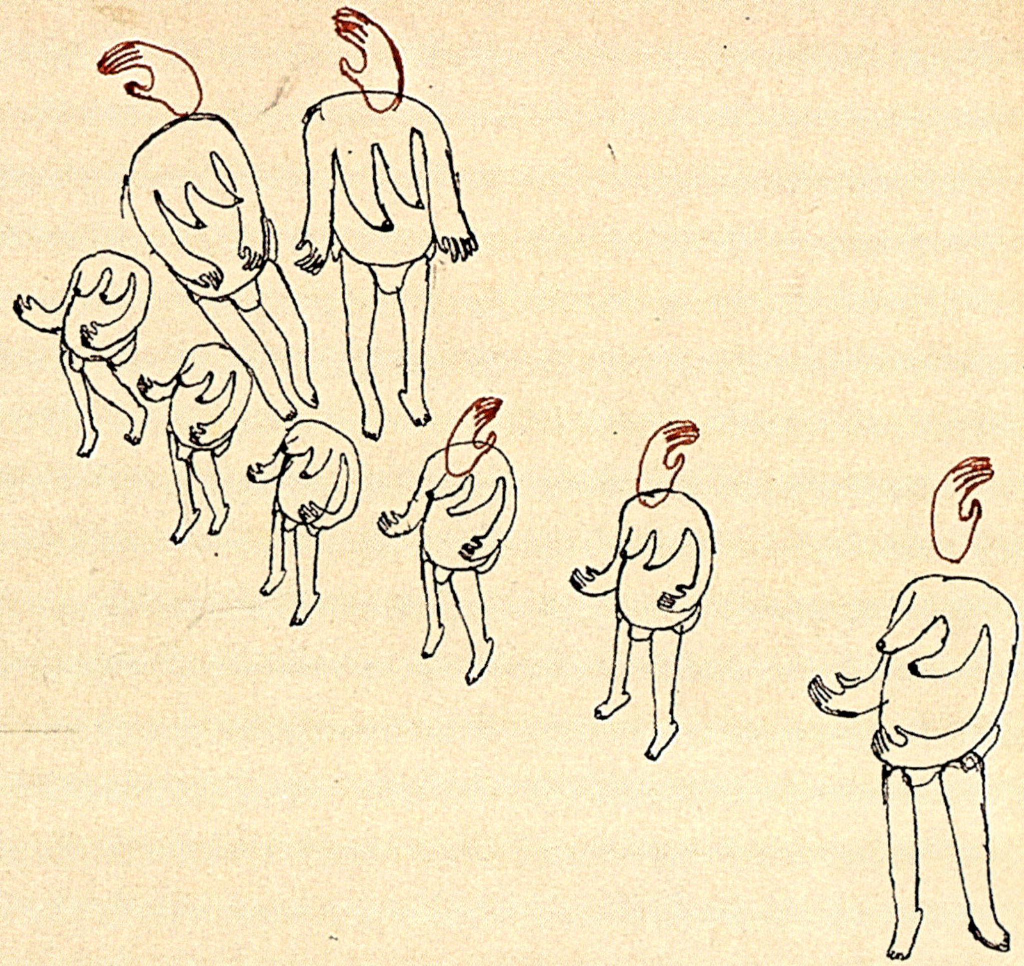

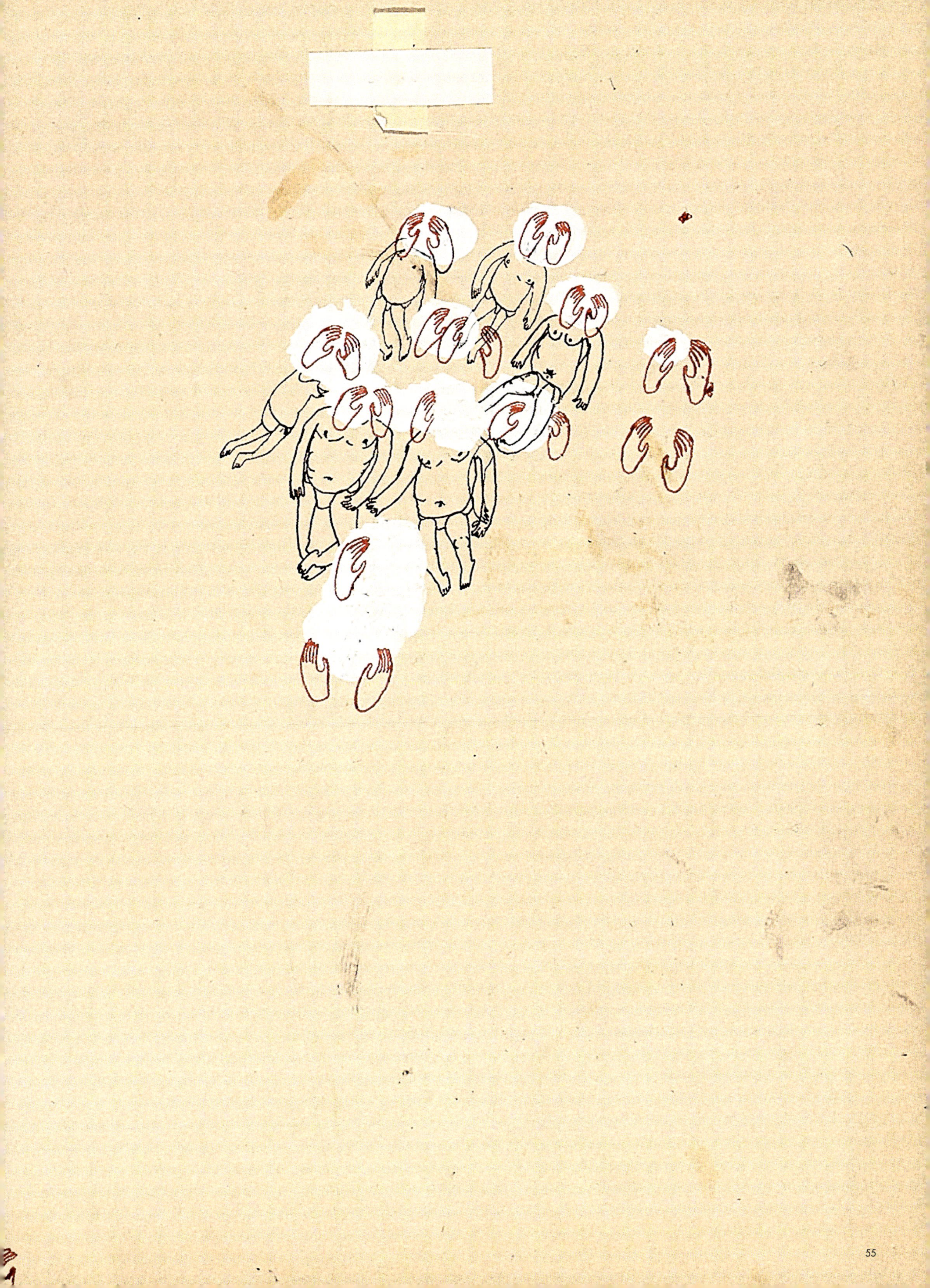

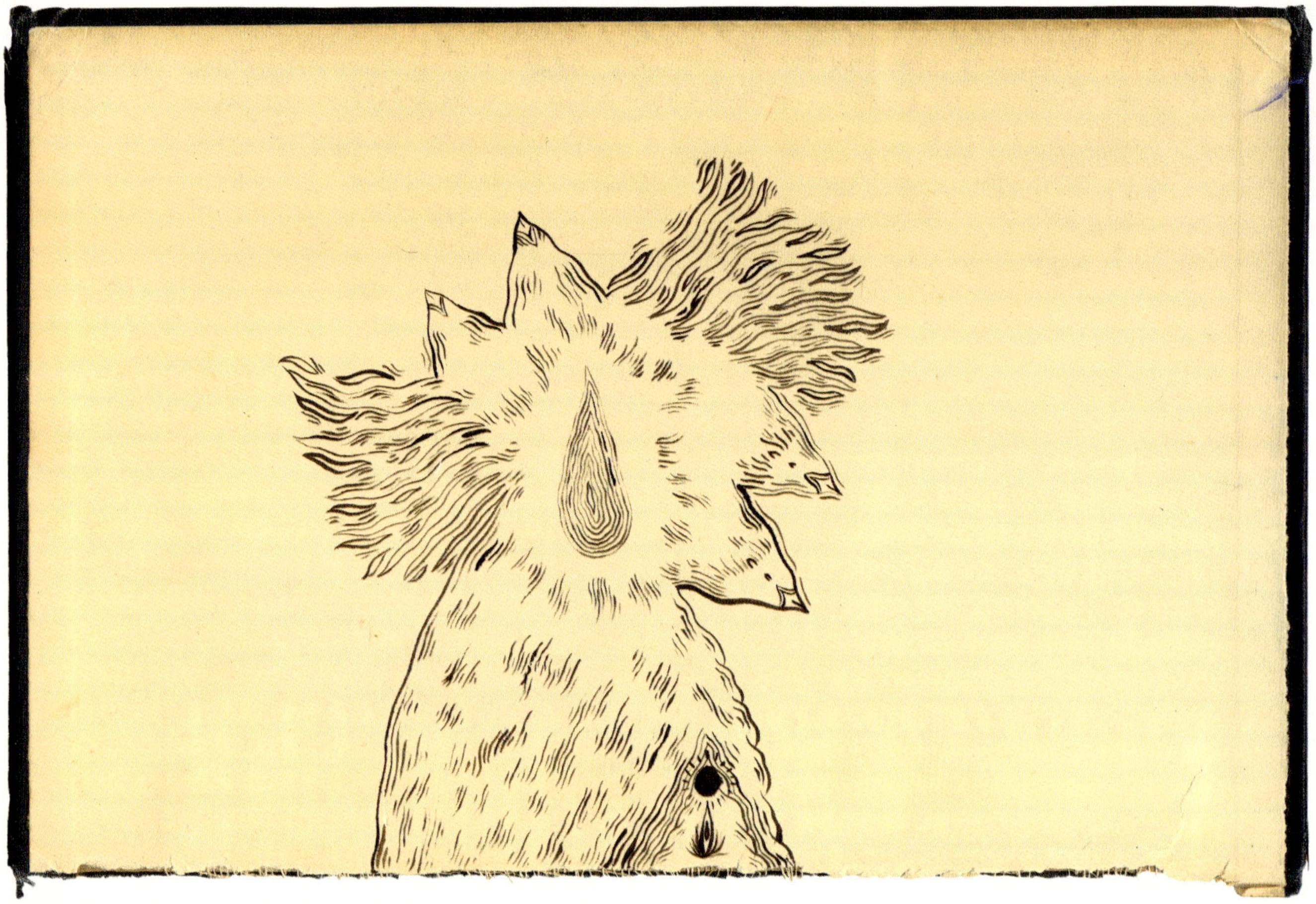

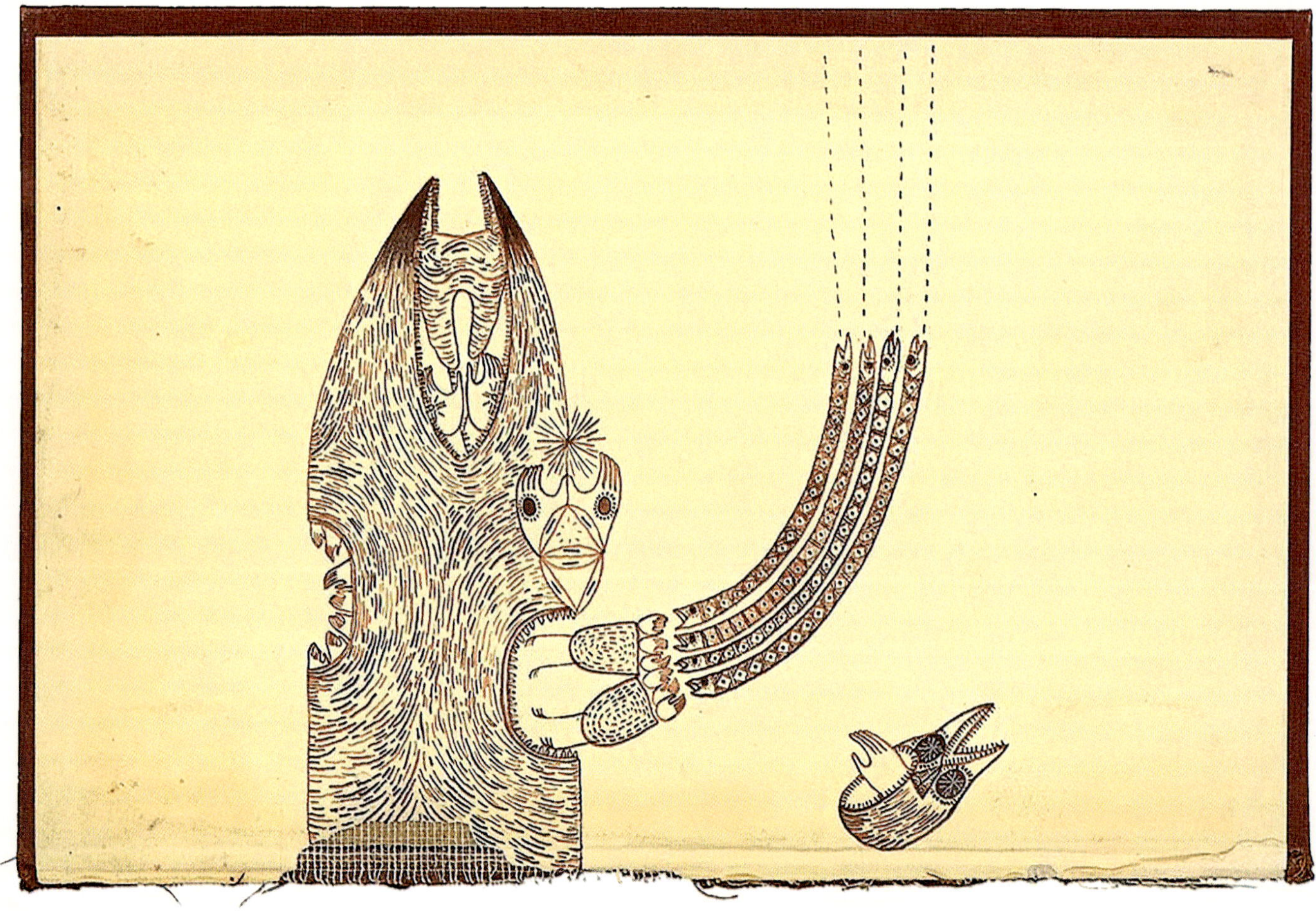

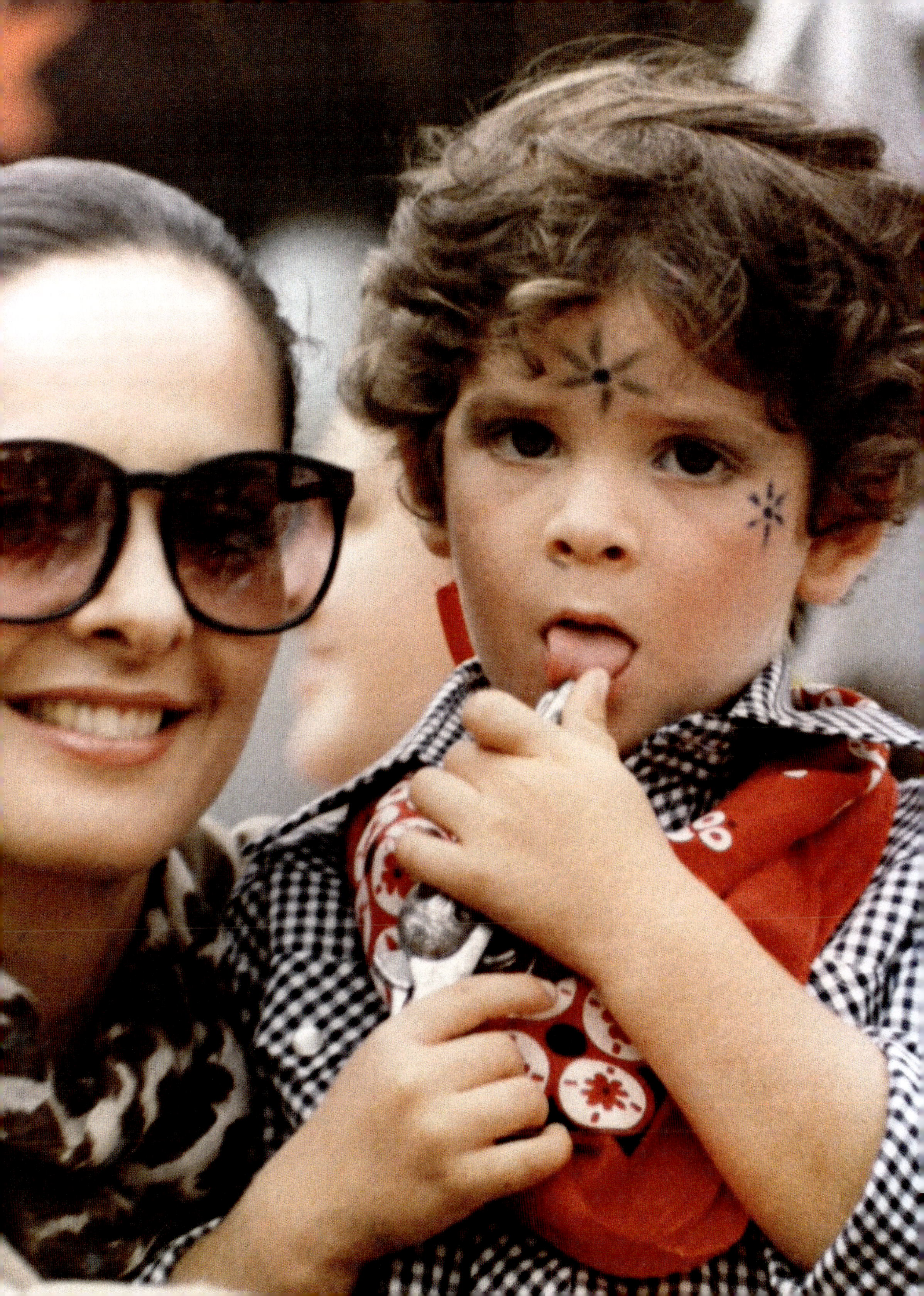

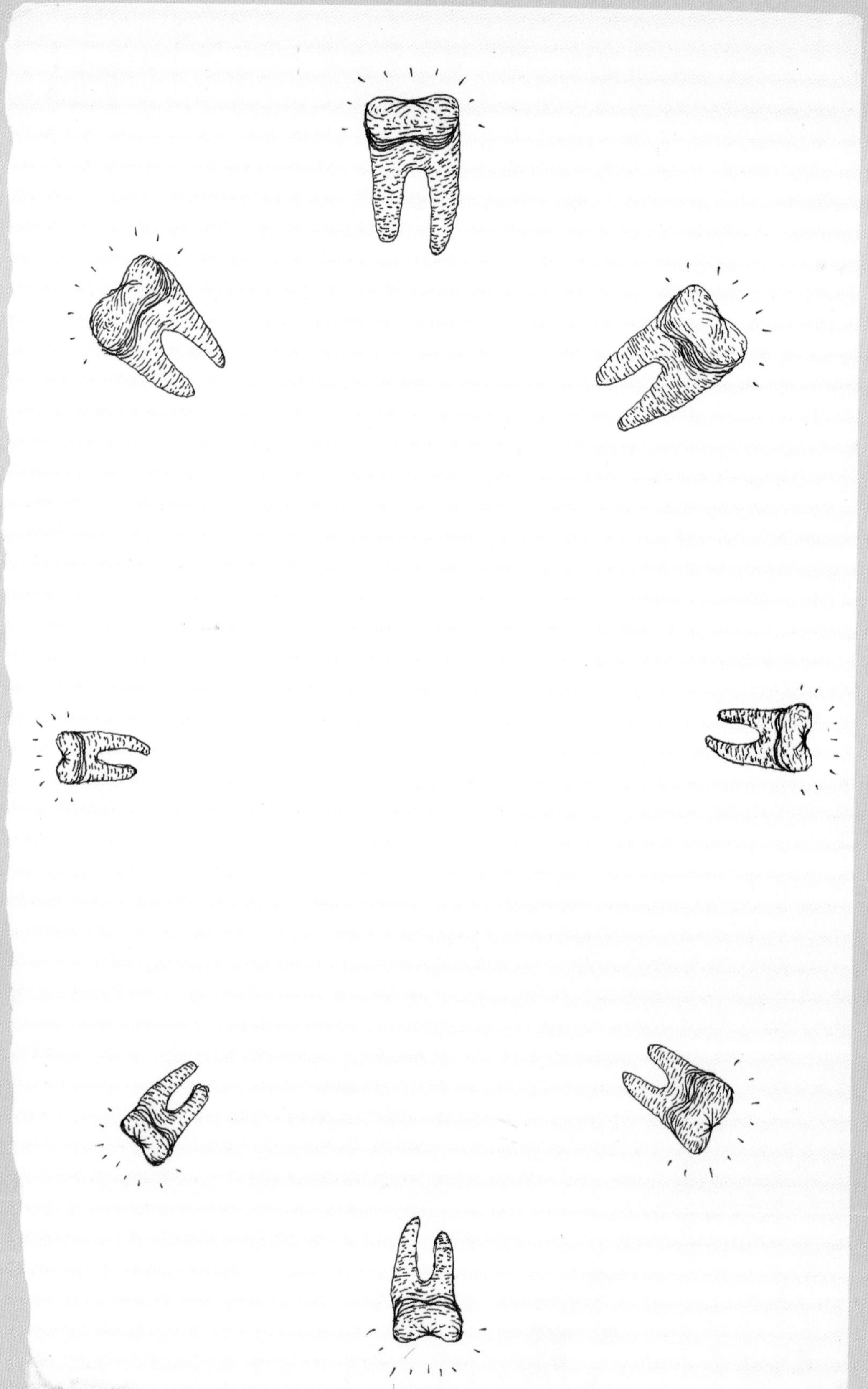

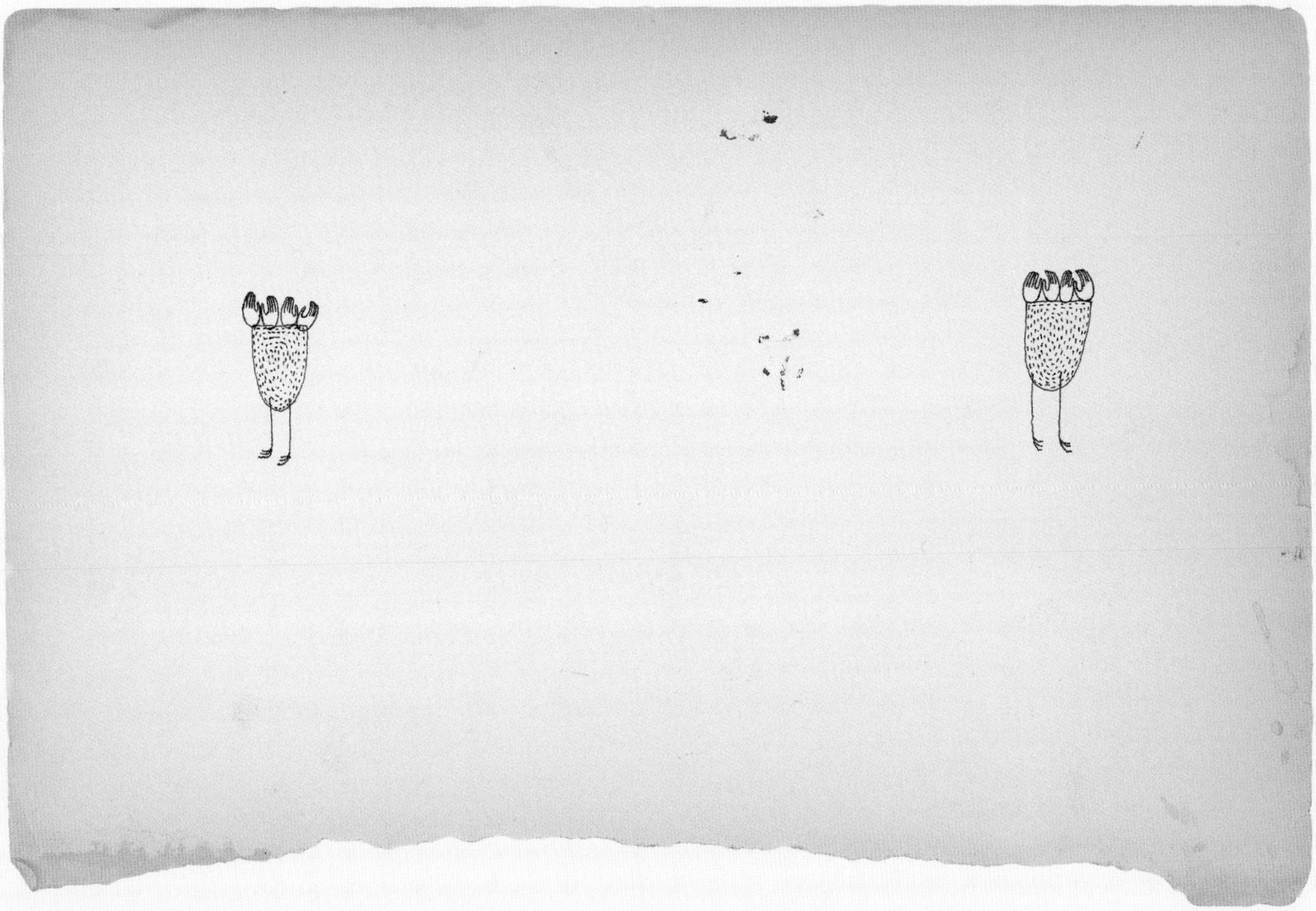

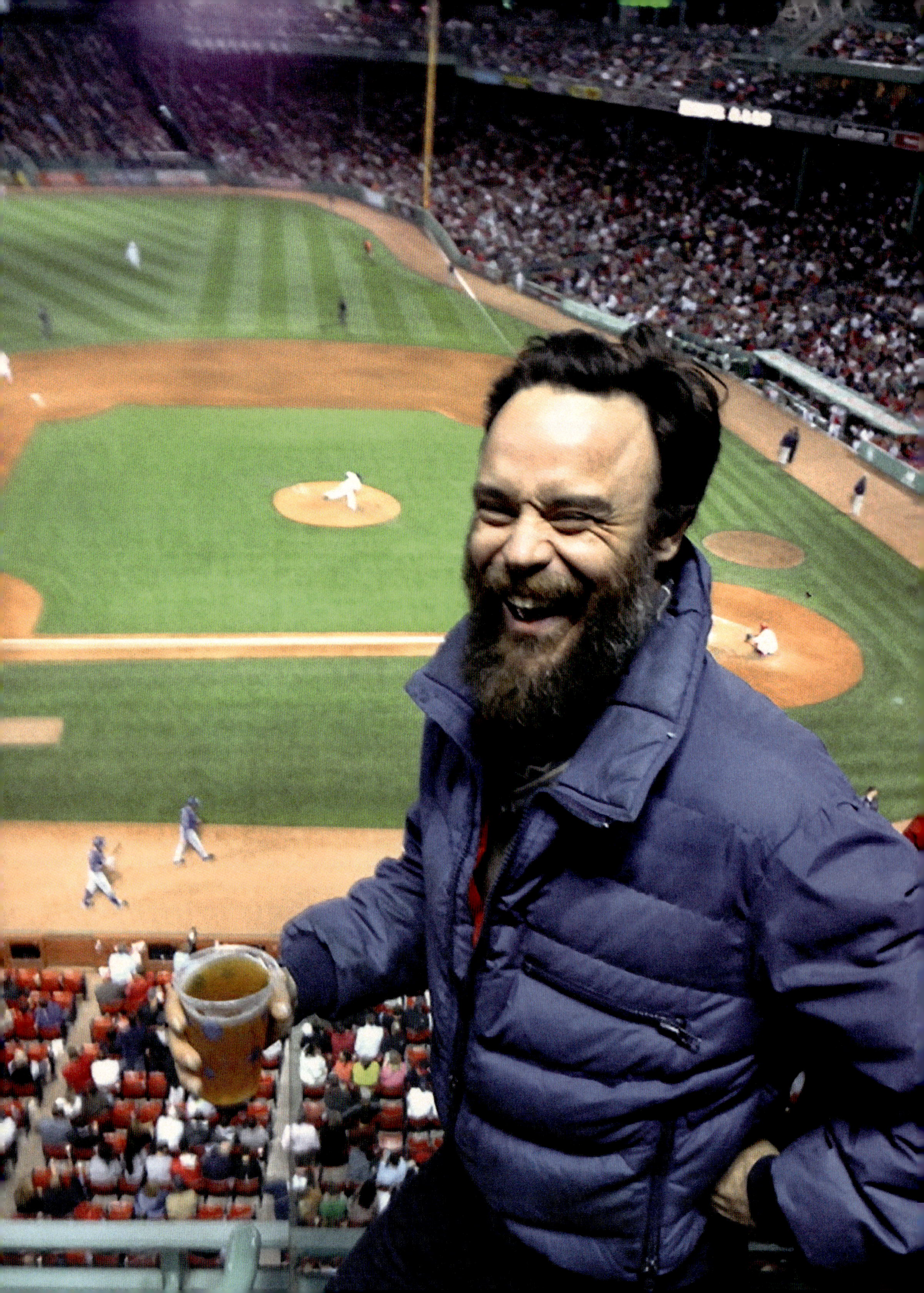

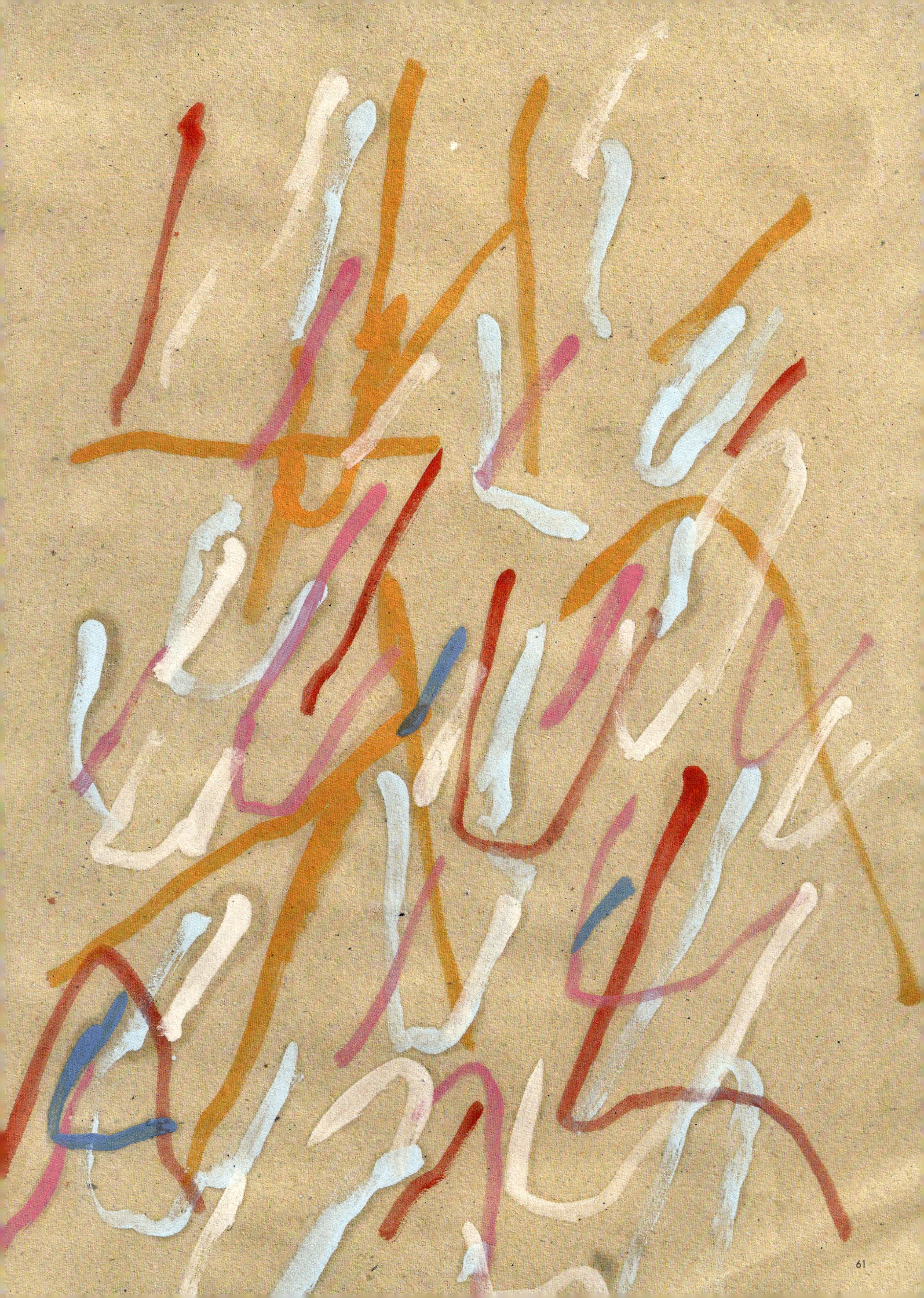

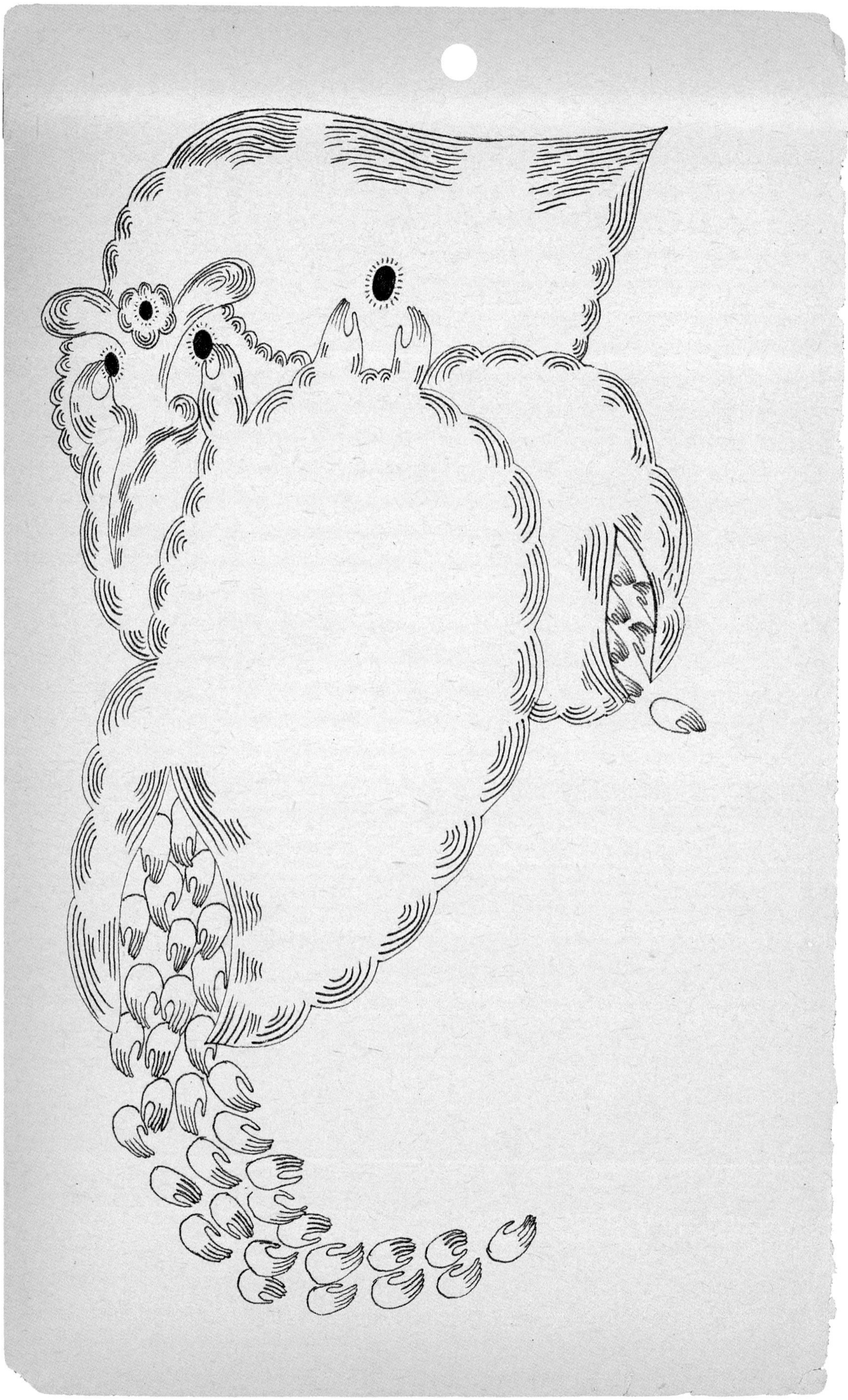

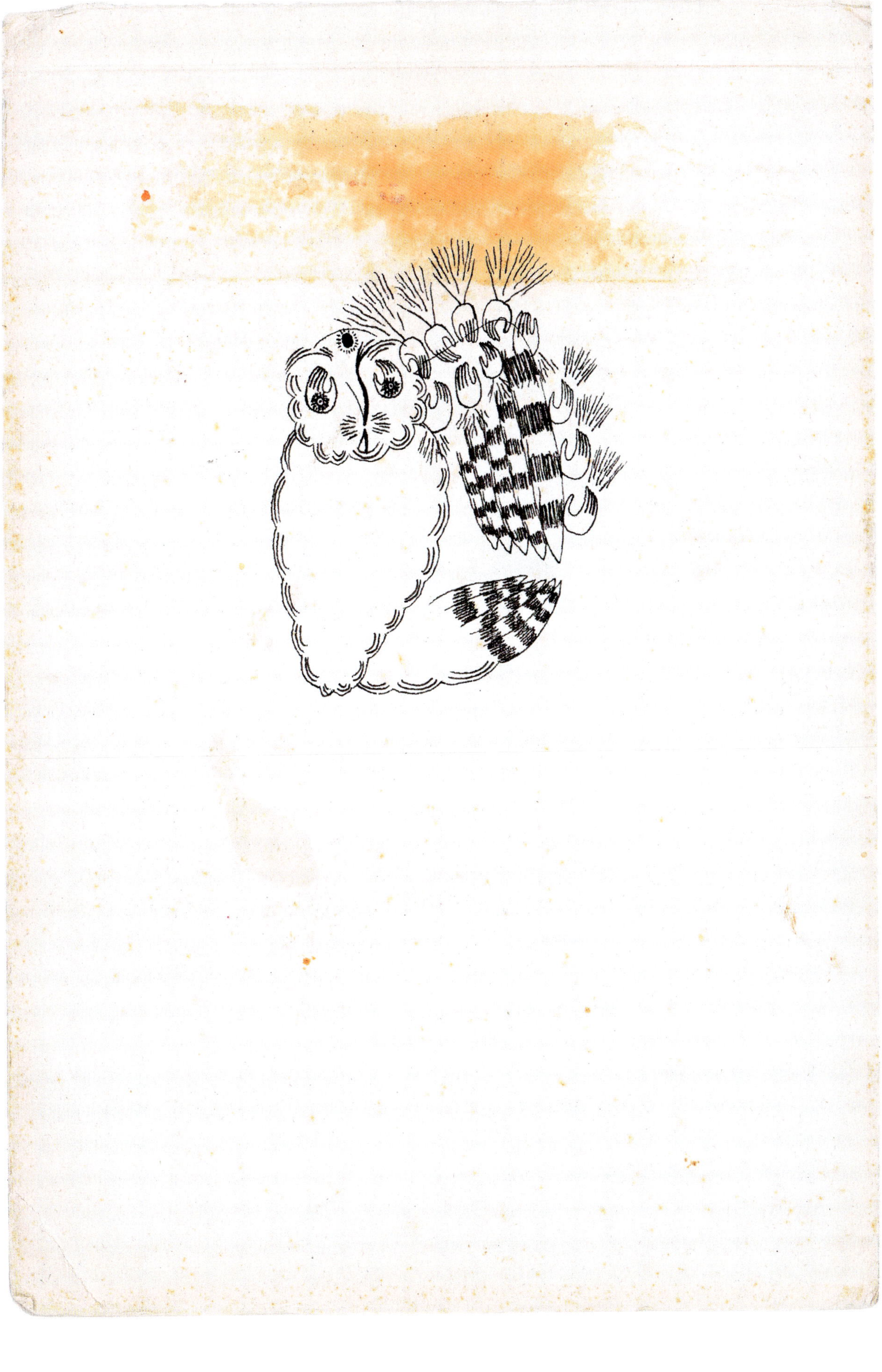

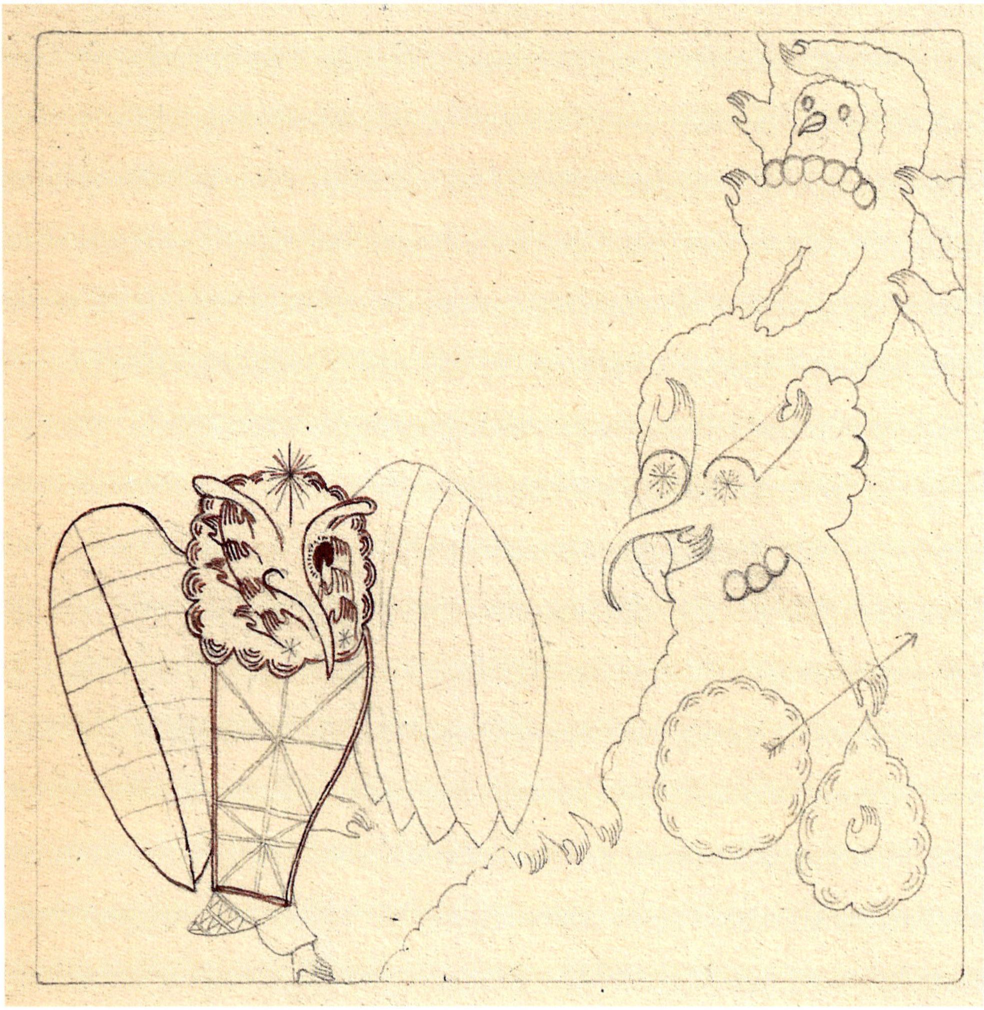

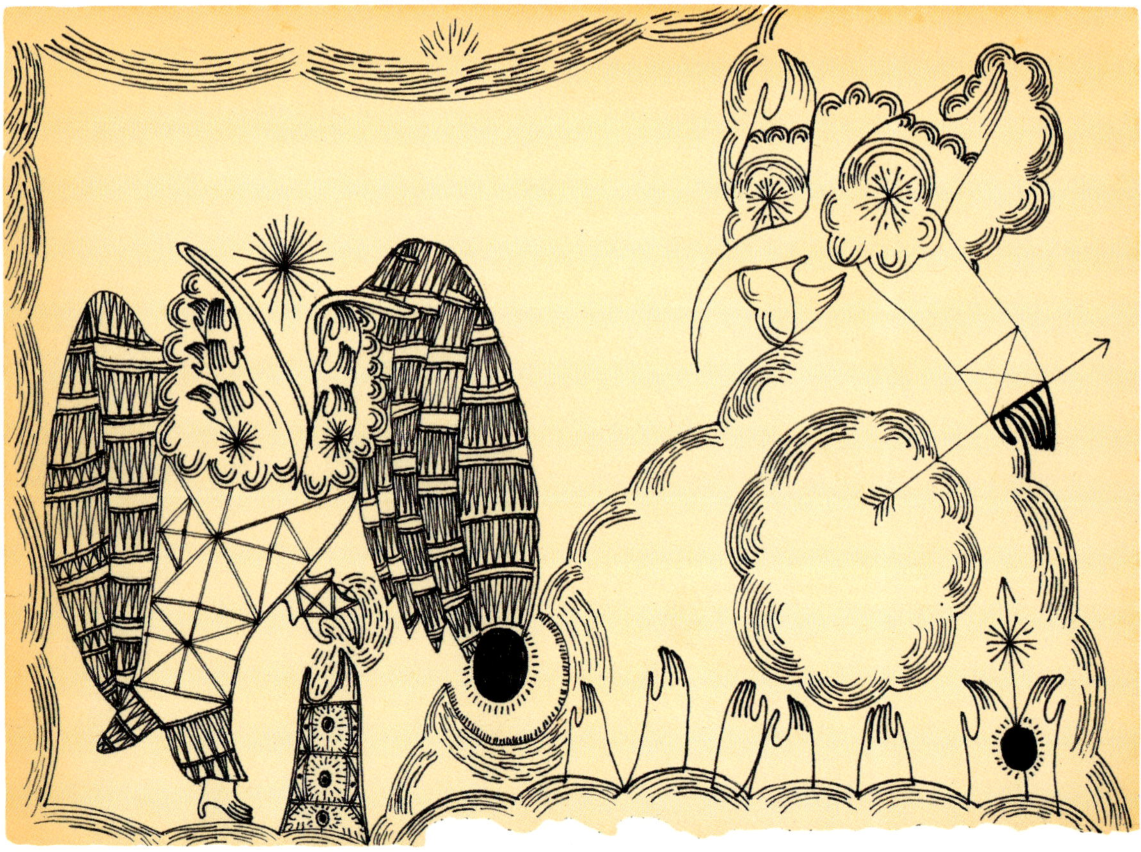

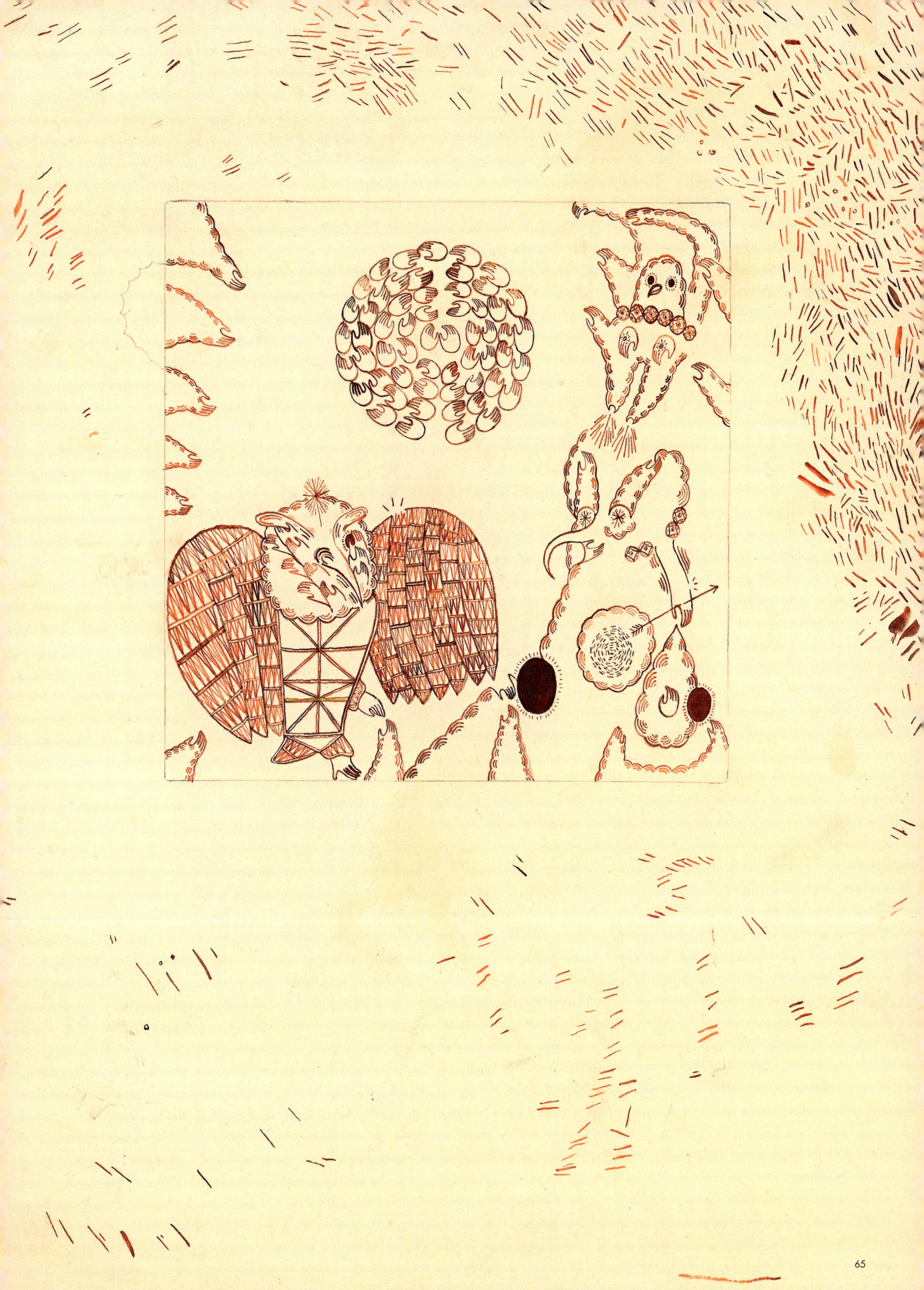

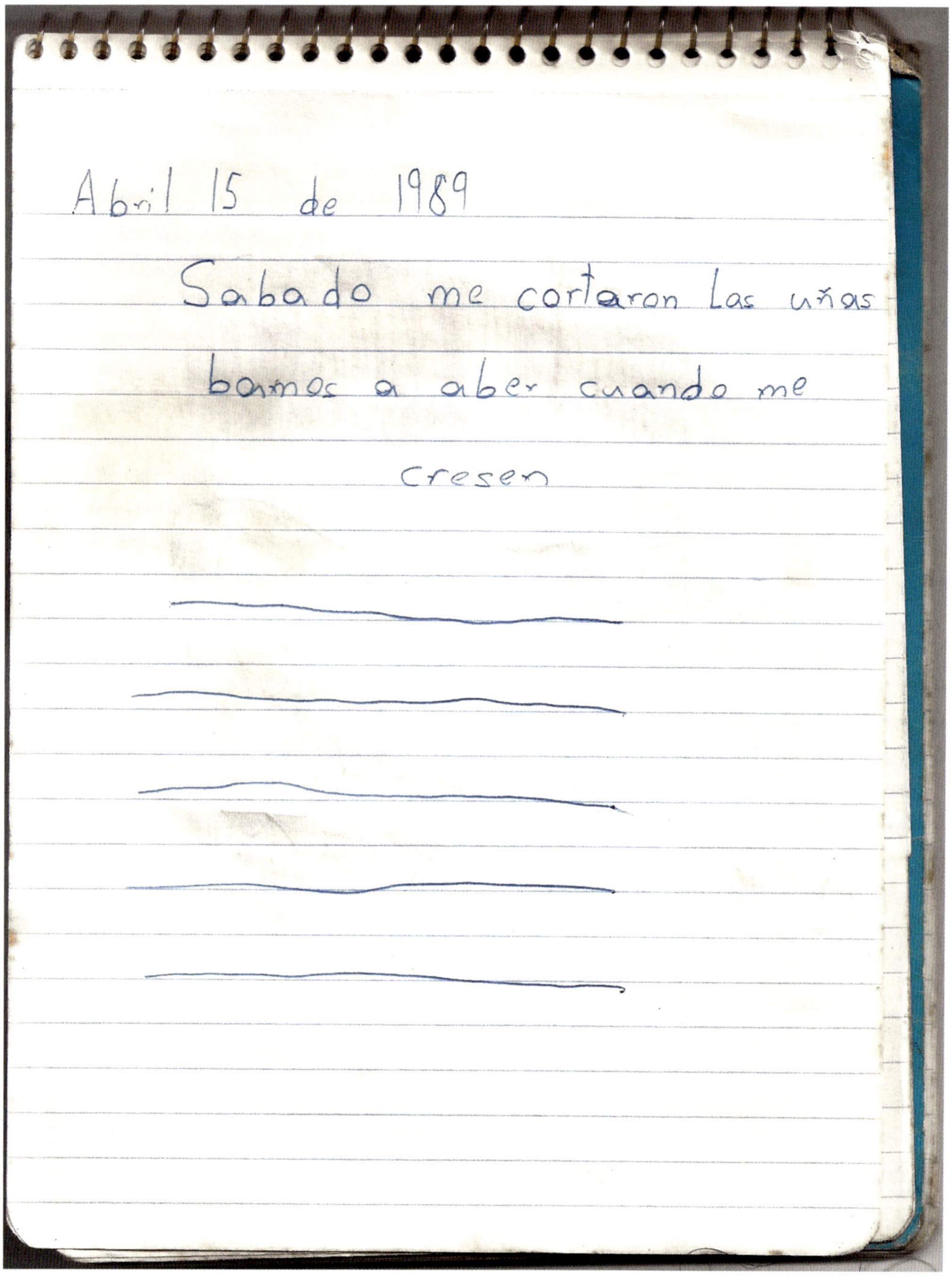

Abril 15 de 1989

Sabado me cortaron Las uñas bamos a aber cuando me cresen

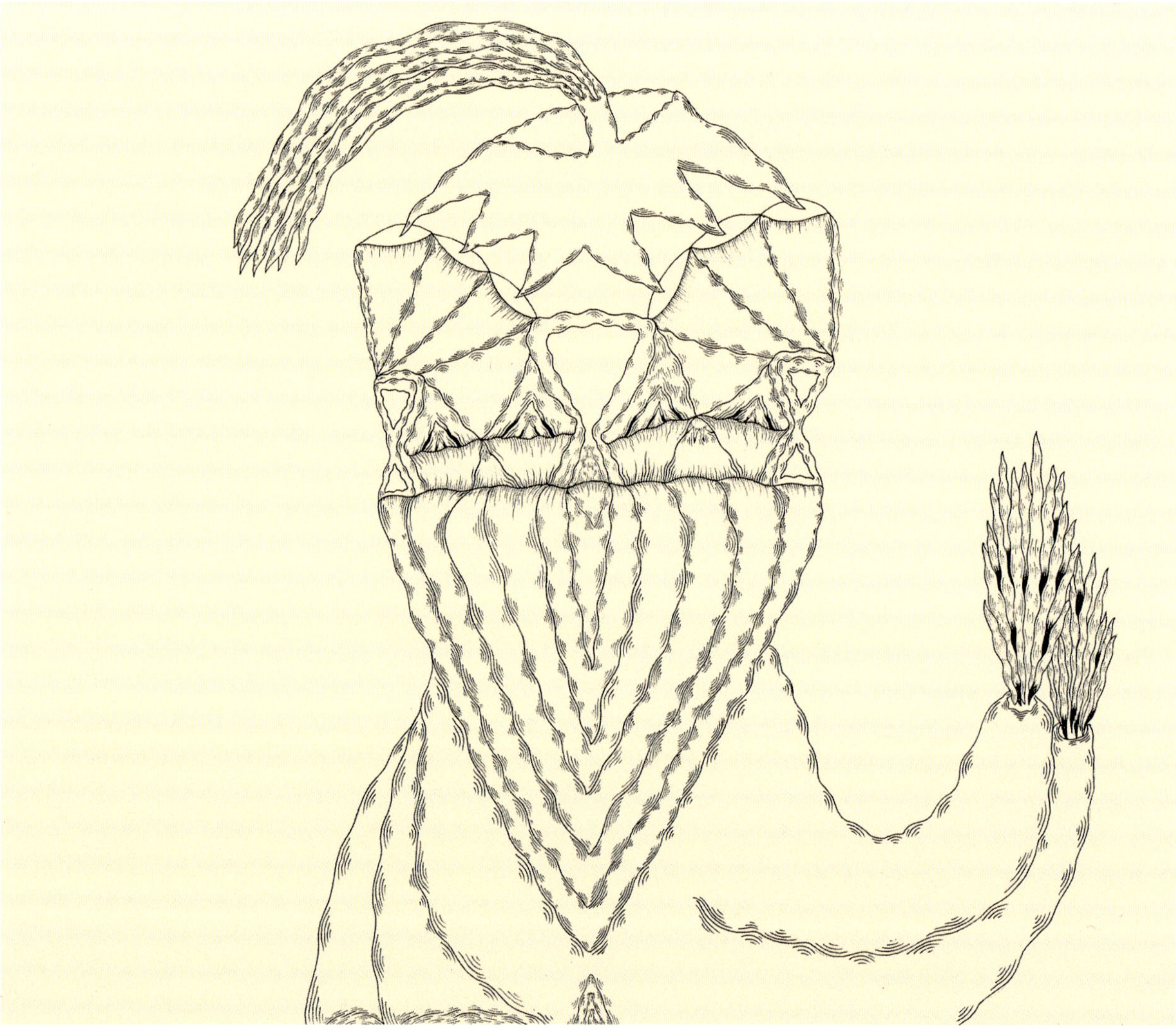

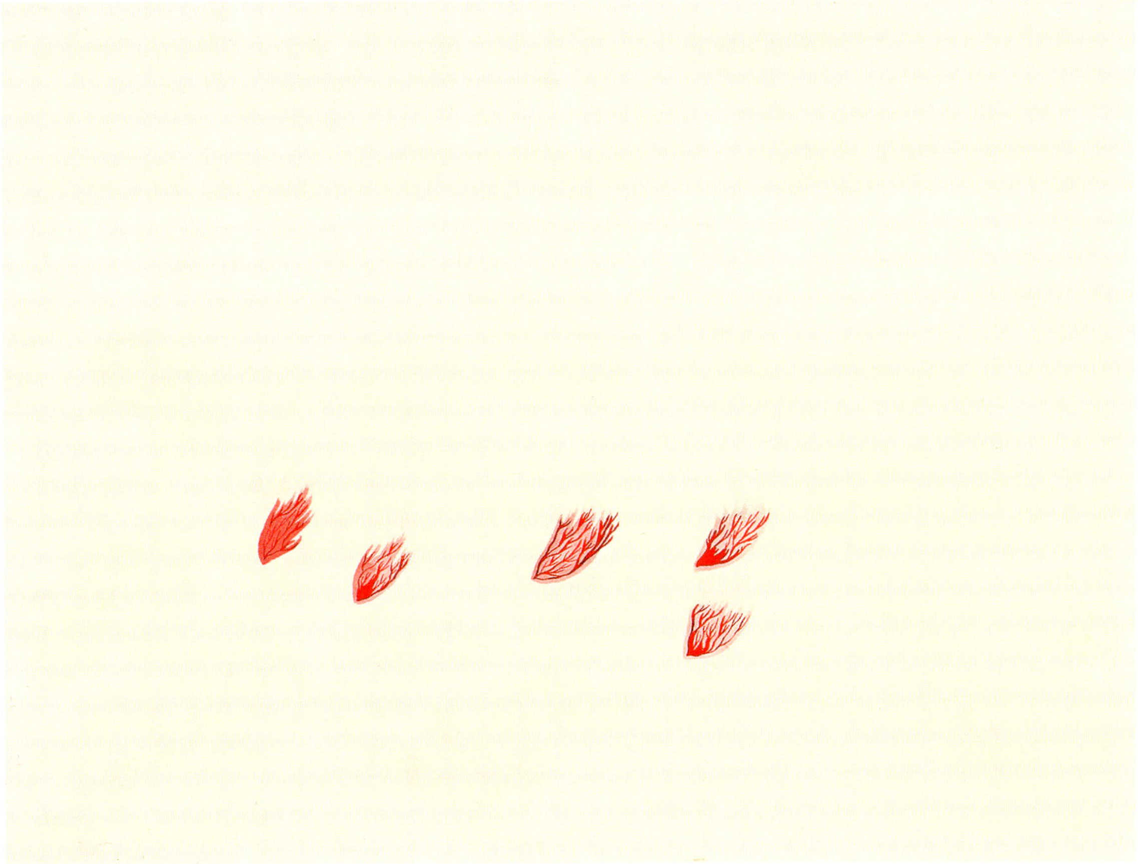

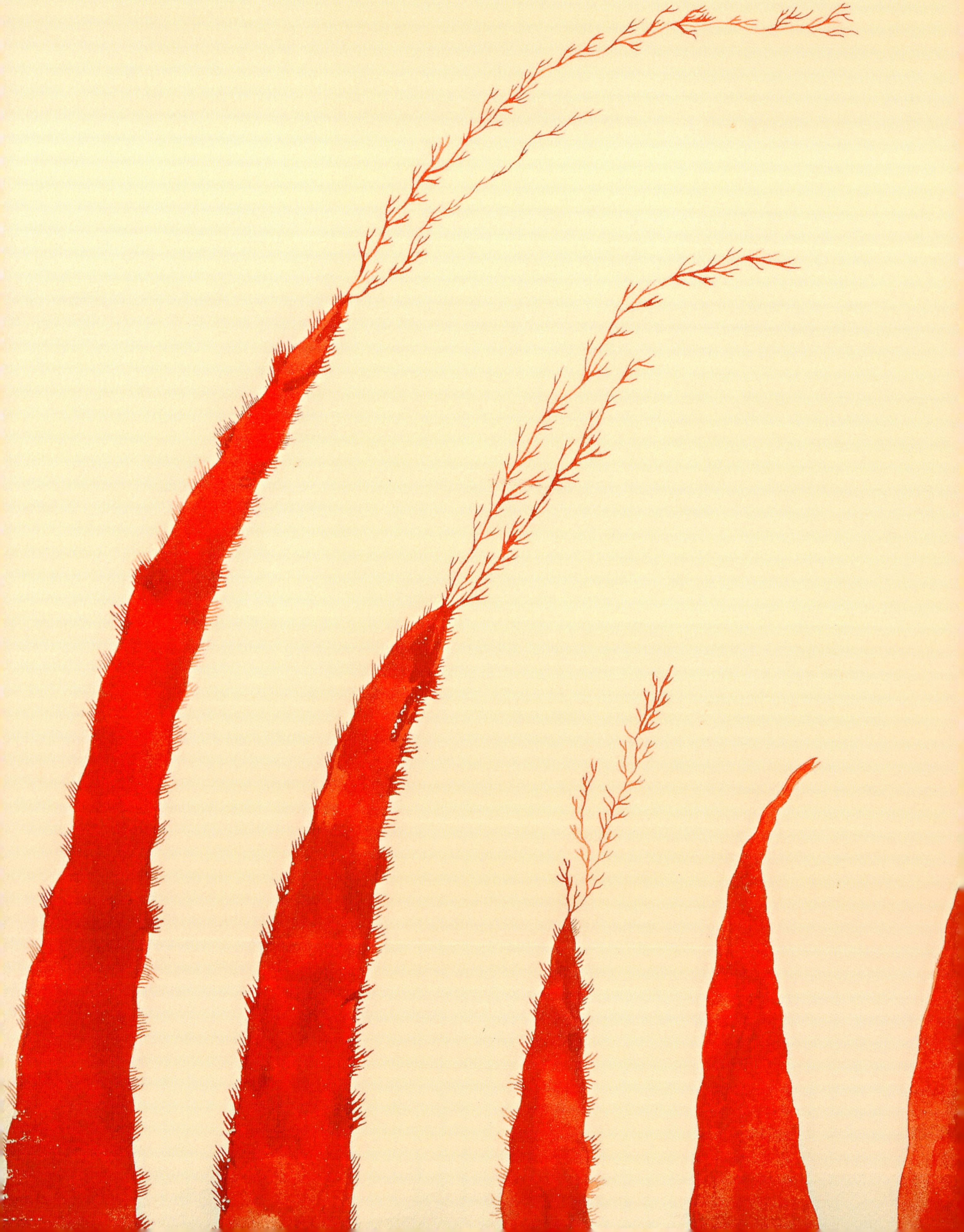

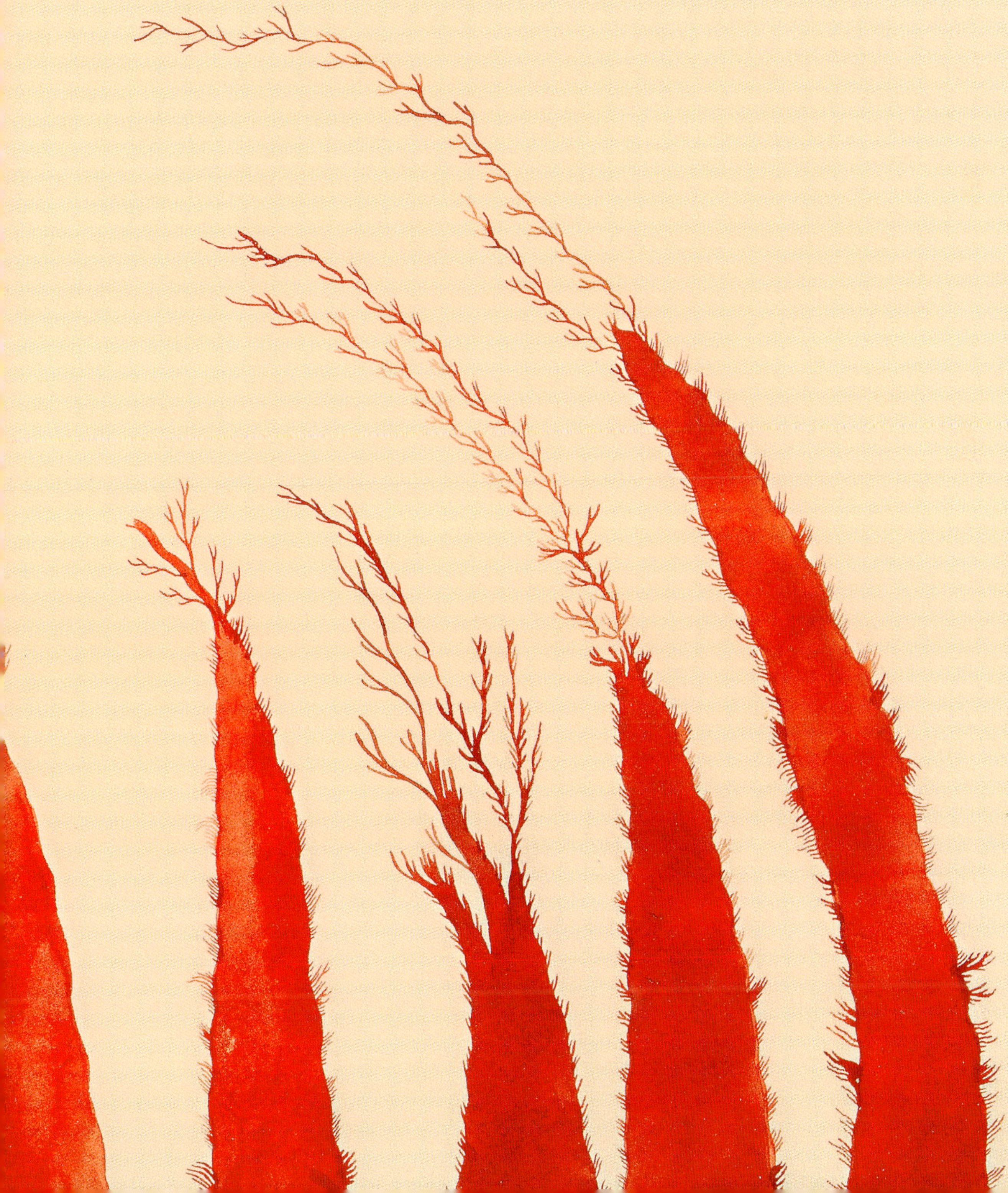

Light Aligns

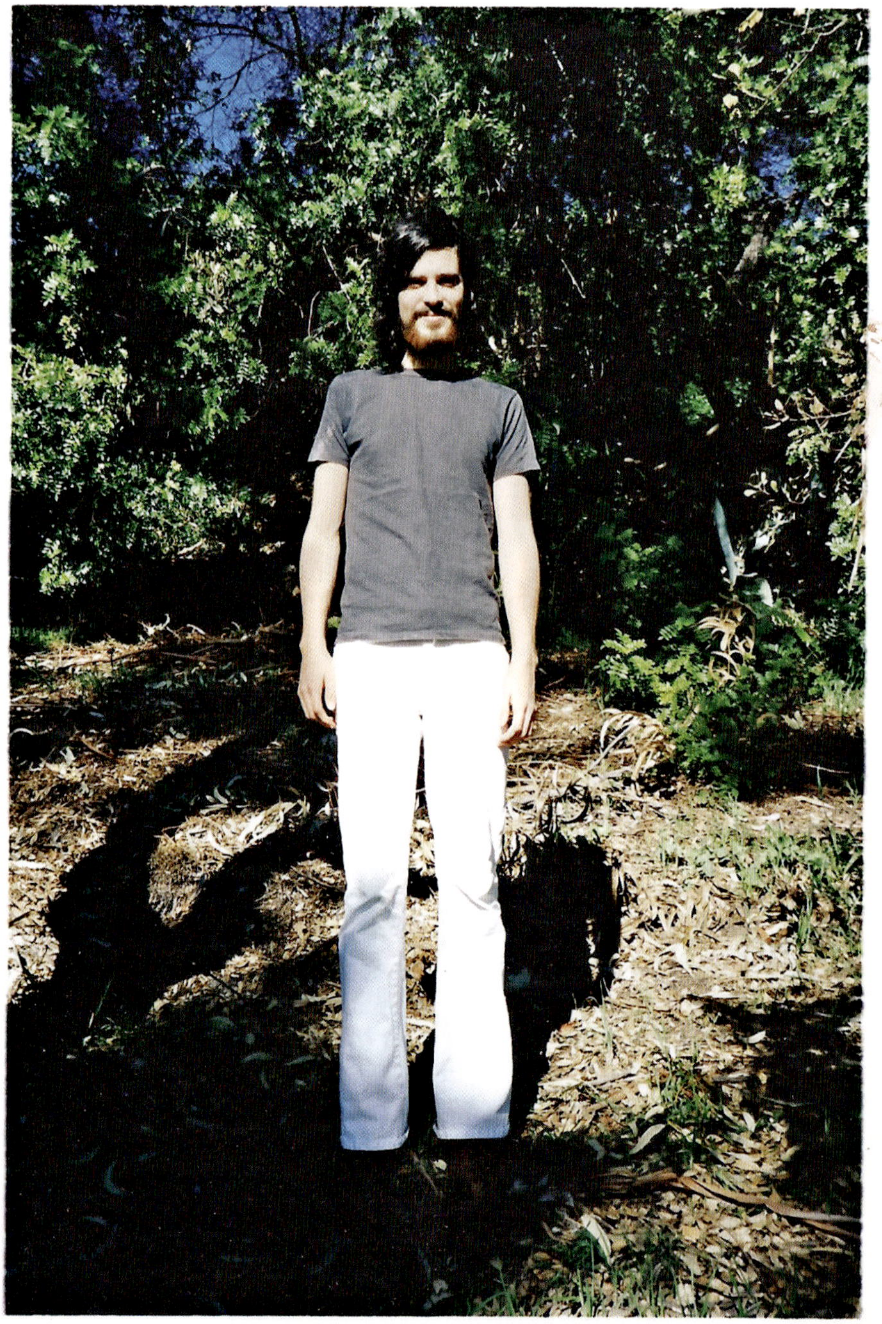

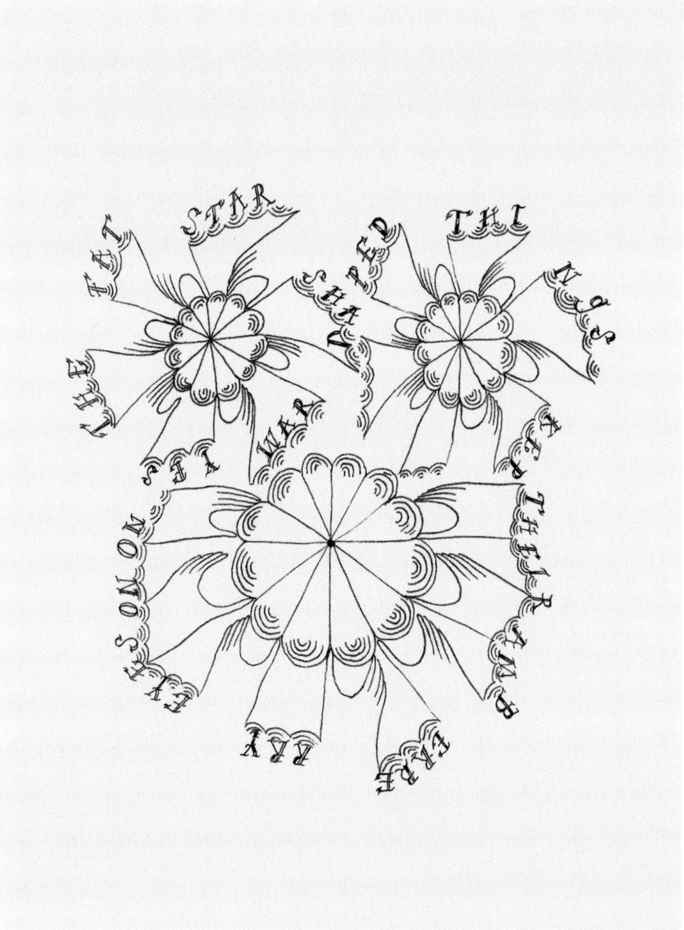
THE FAT STAR
SHAPED THINGS
KEEP THEIR
EYES ON
WAR

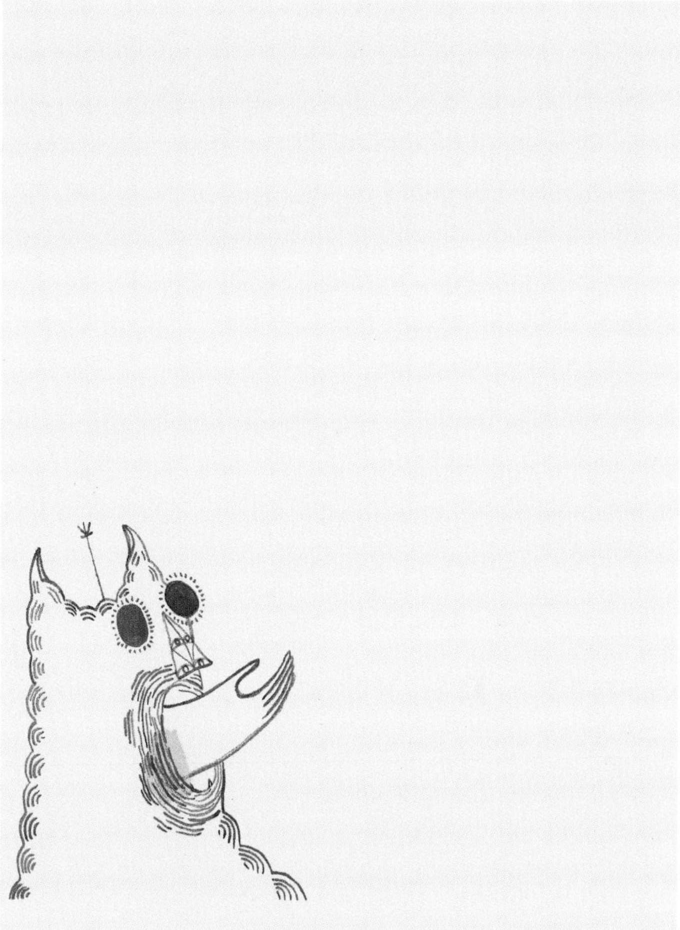

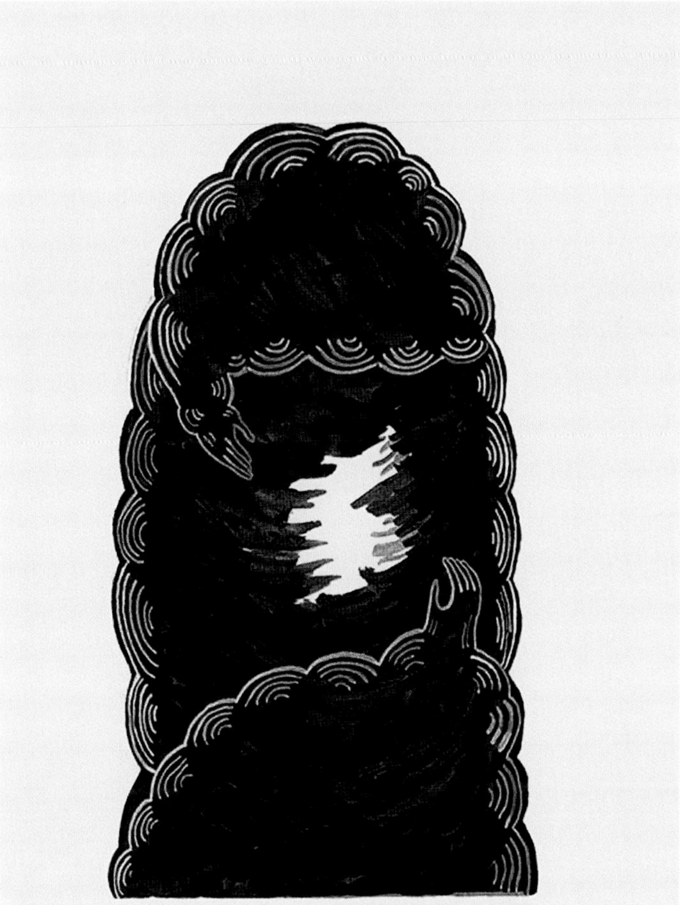

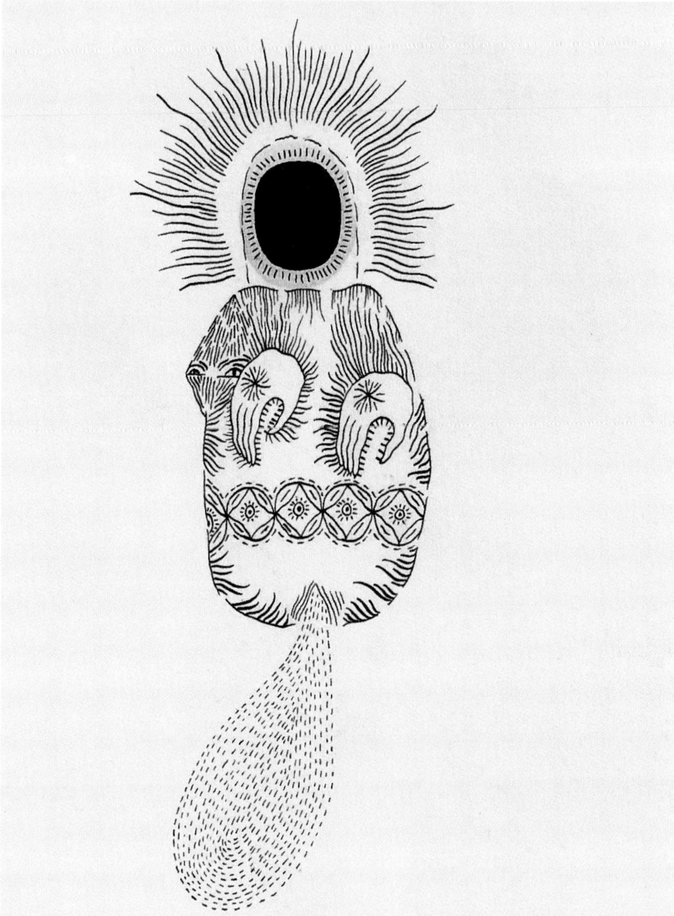

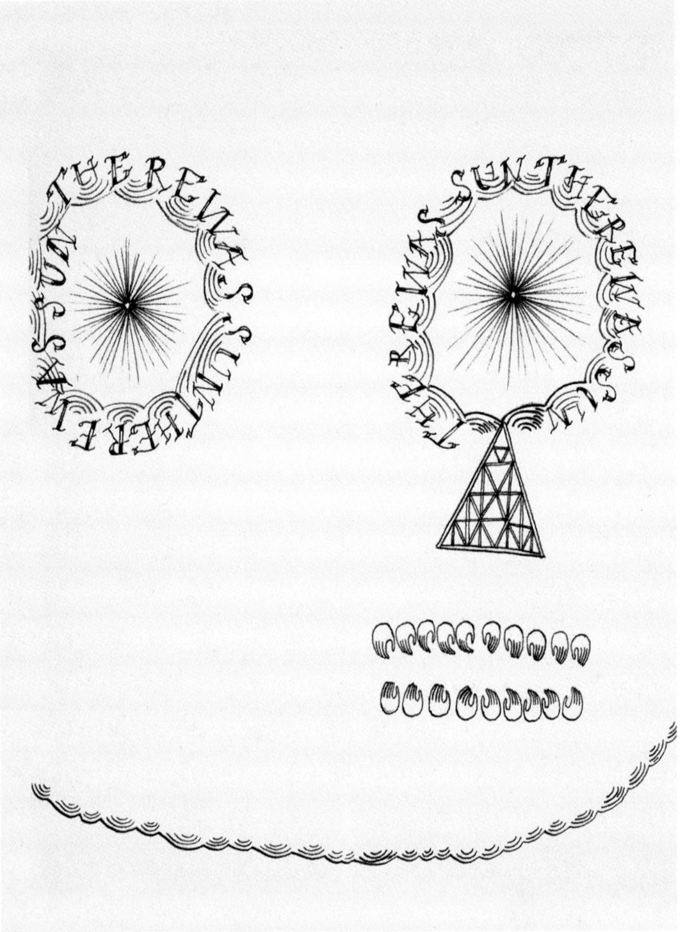

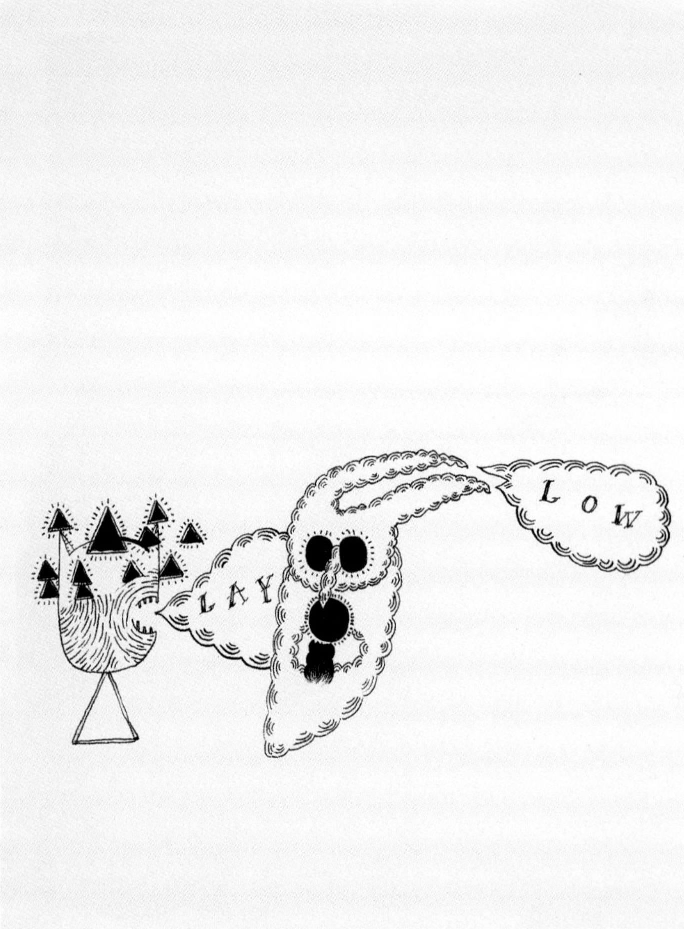
LAY
LOW

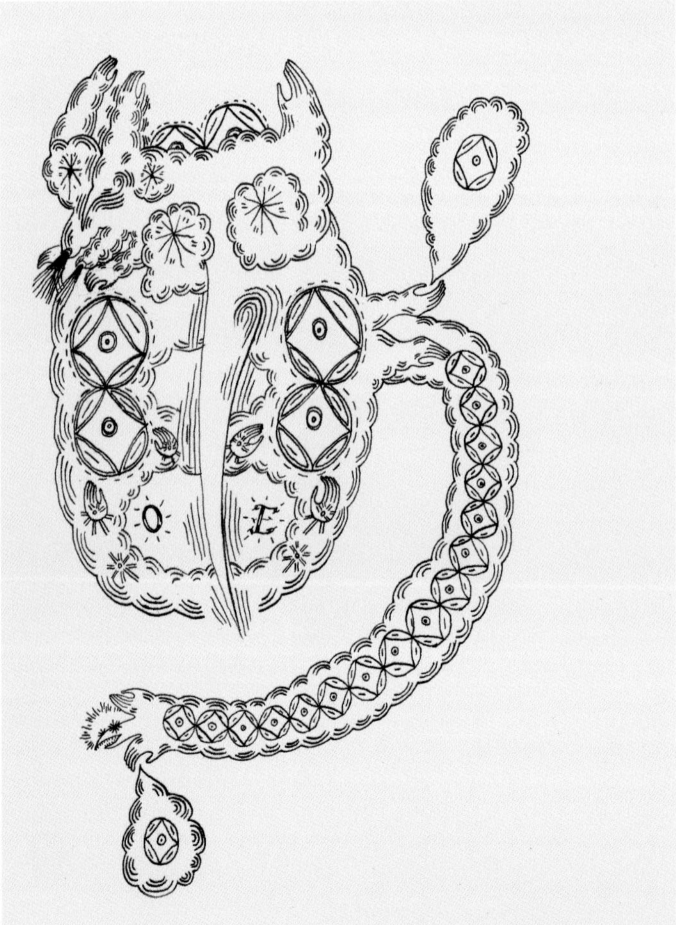
O E

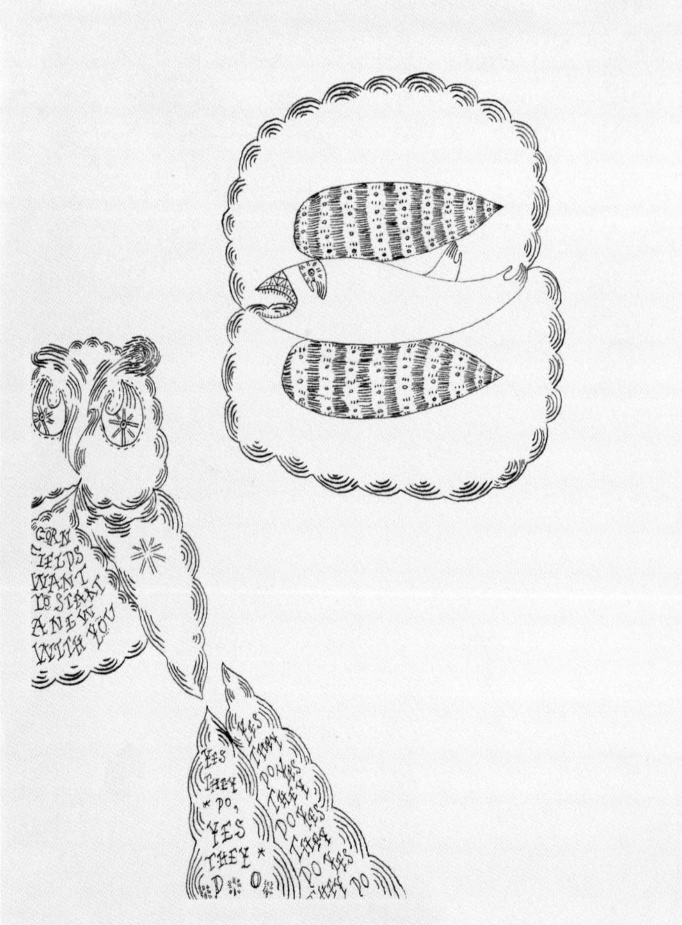
CORN FIELDS WANT TO START ANEW WITH YOU
YES THEY DO, YES THEY DO

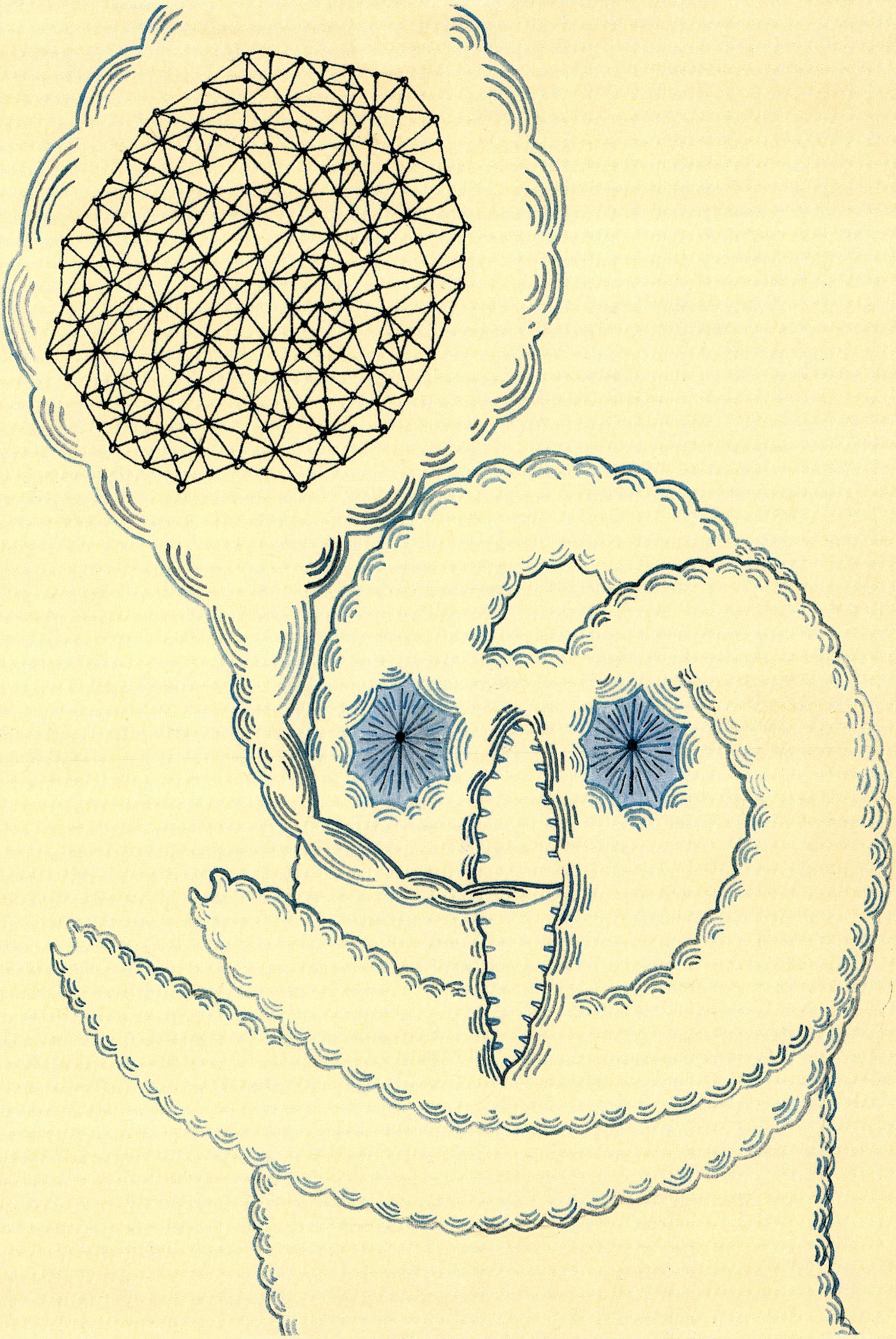

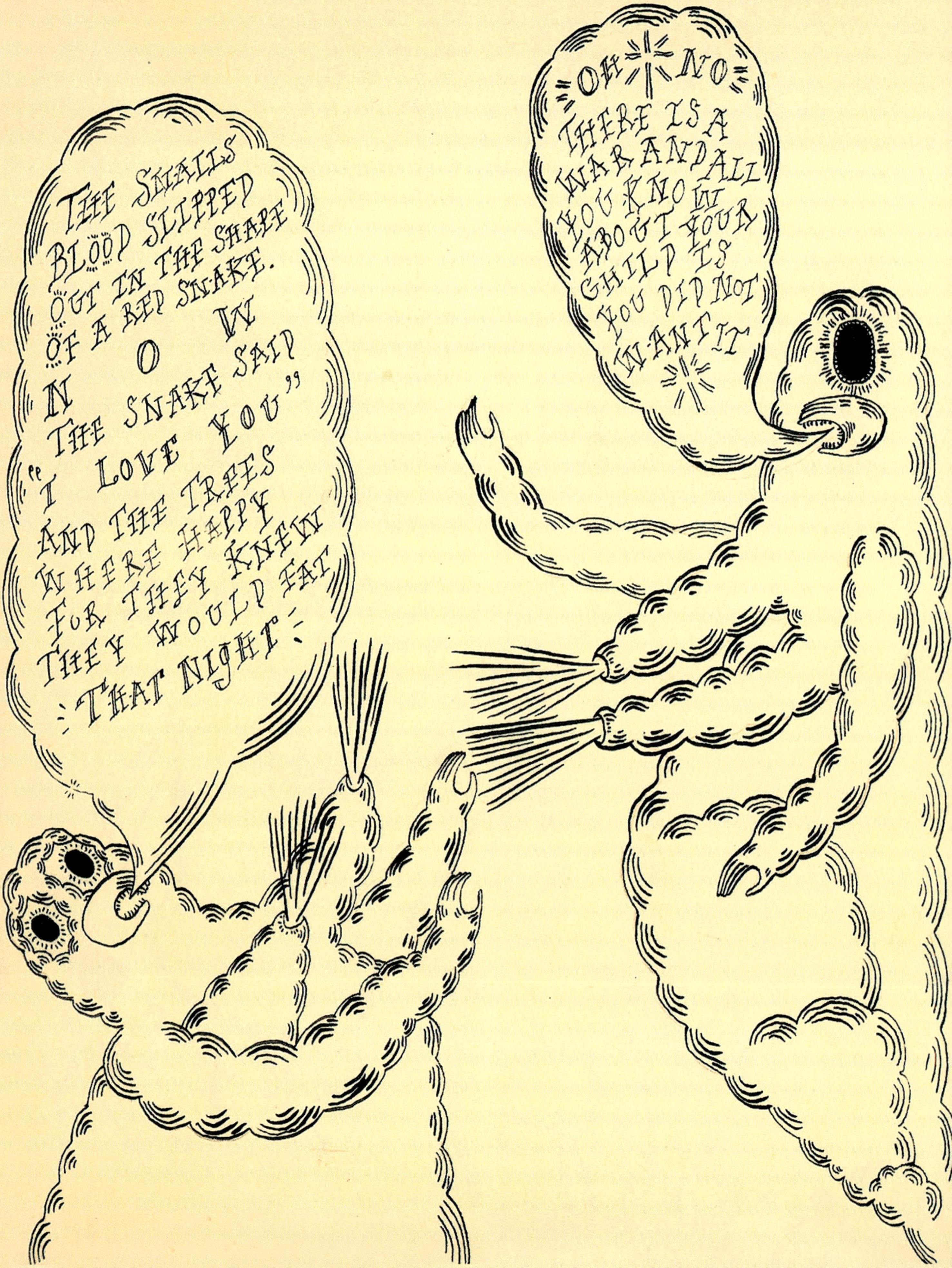
THE SNAILS BLOOD SLIPPED OUT IN THE SHAPE OF A RED SNAKE. NOW THE SNAKE SAID "I LOVE YOU" AND THE TREES WHERE HAPPY FOR THEY KNEW THEY WOULD EAT THAT NIGHT
OH NO THERE IS A WAR AND ALL YOU KNOW ABOUT YOUR CHILD IS YOU DID NOT WANT IT

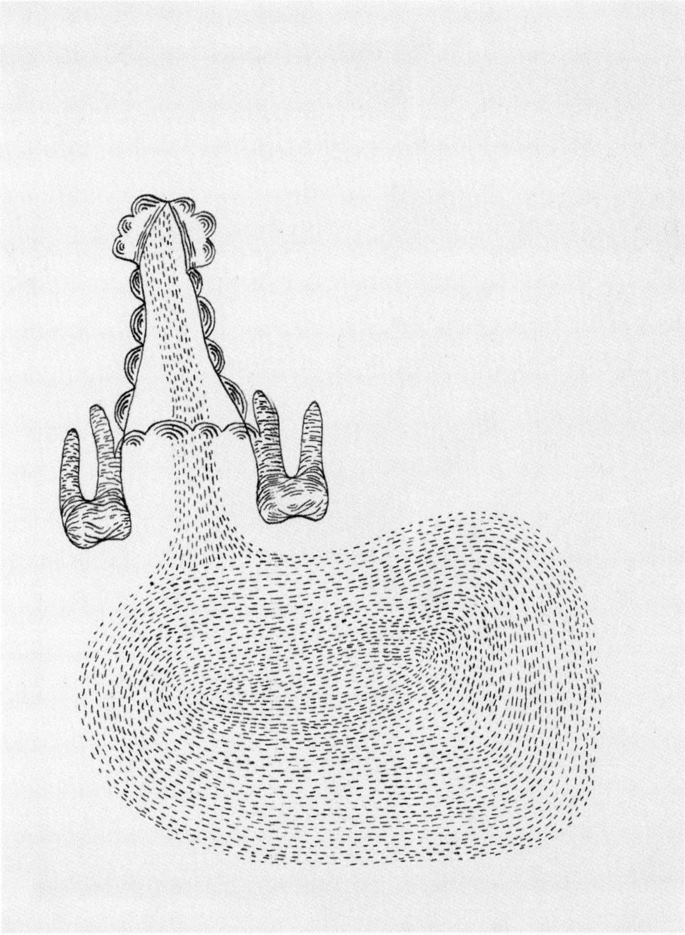

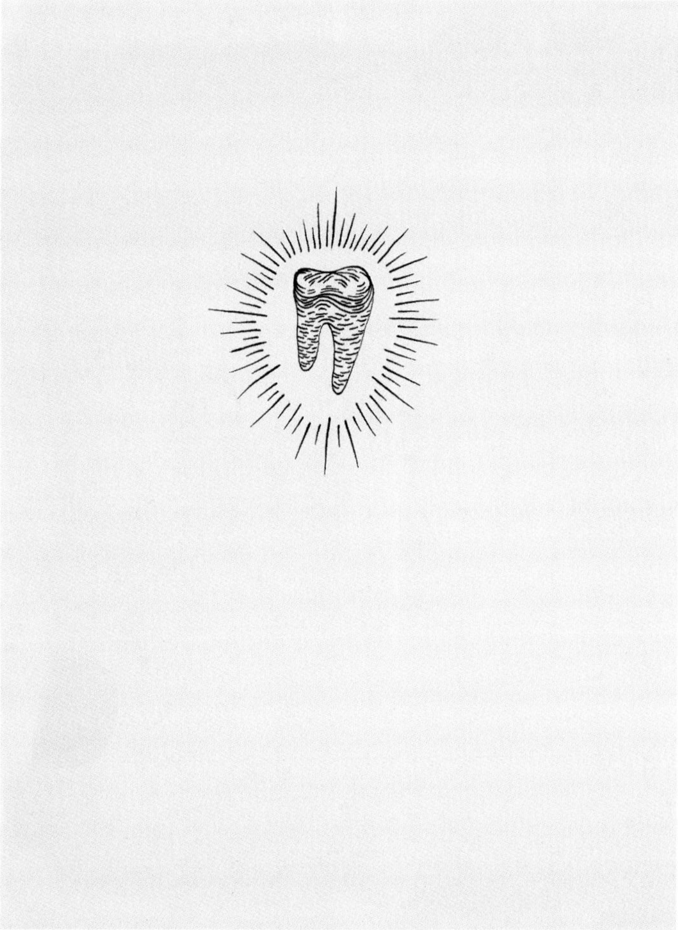

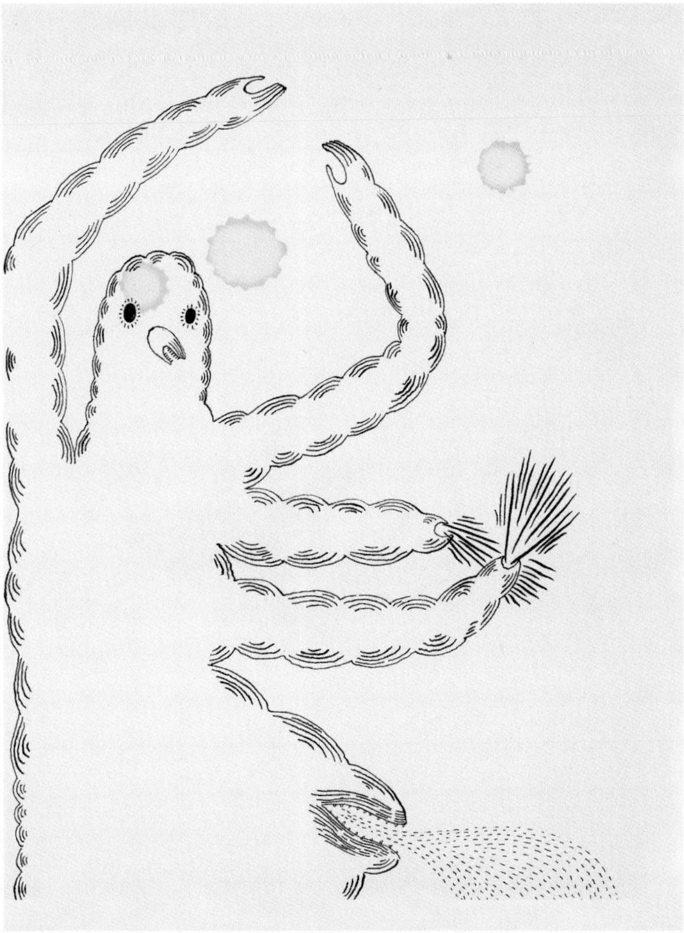

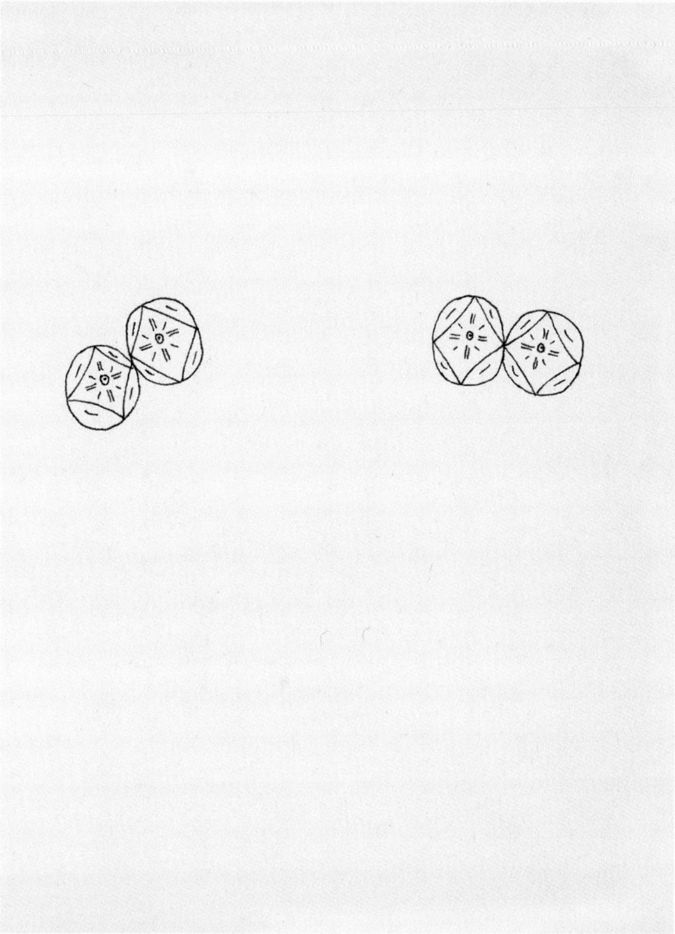

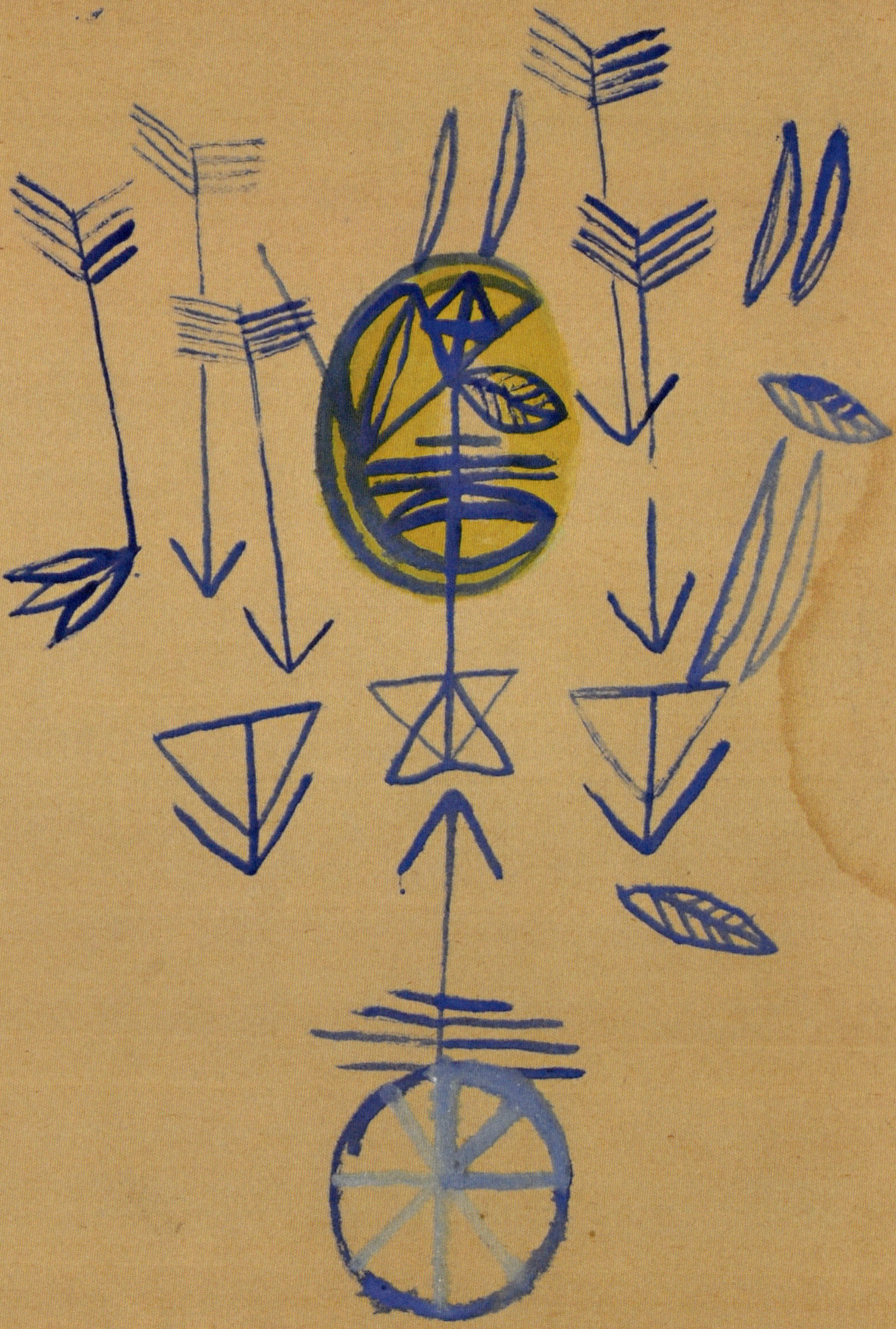

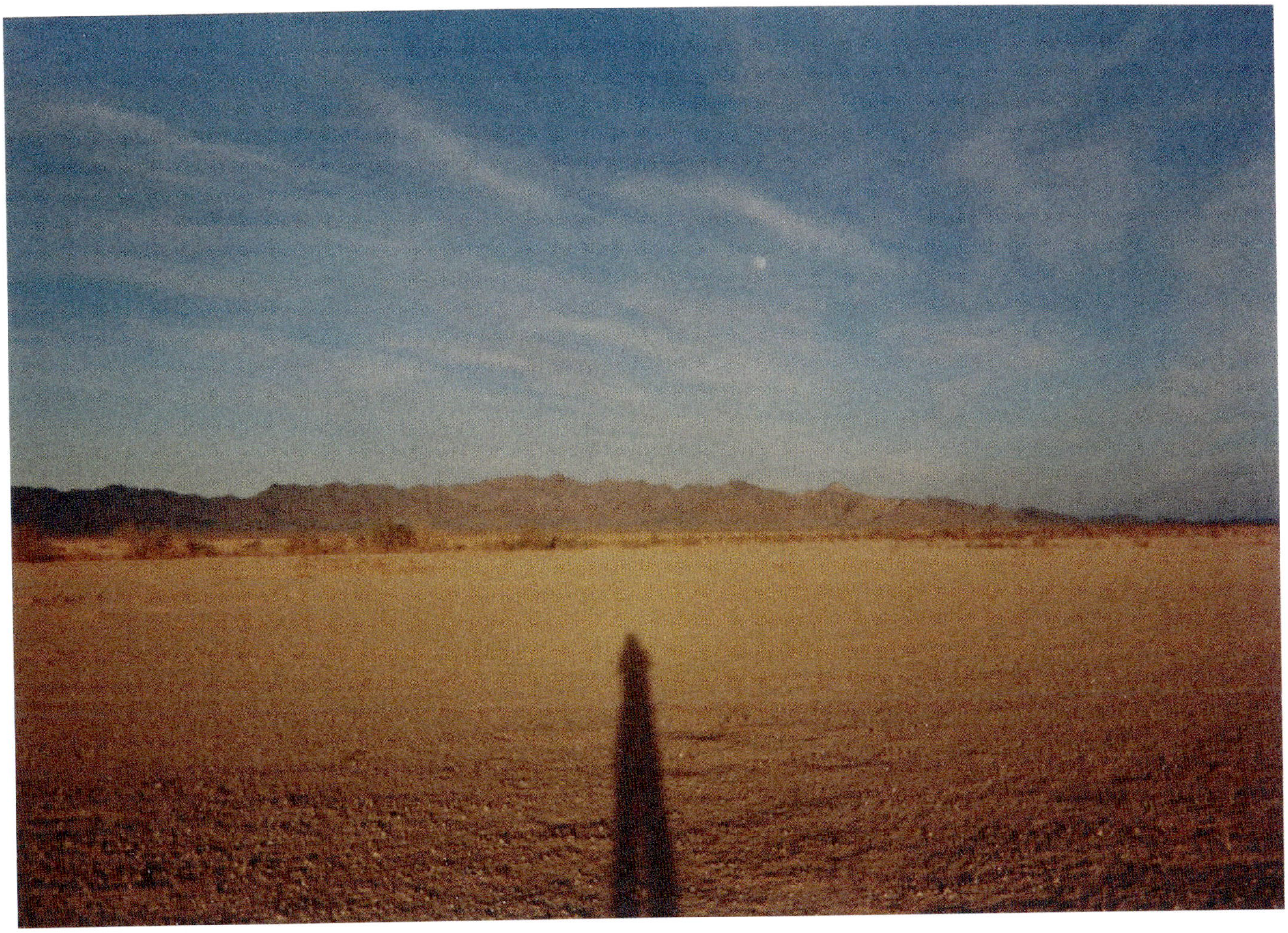

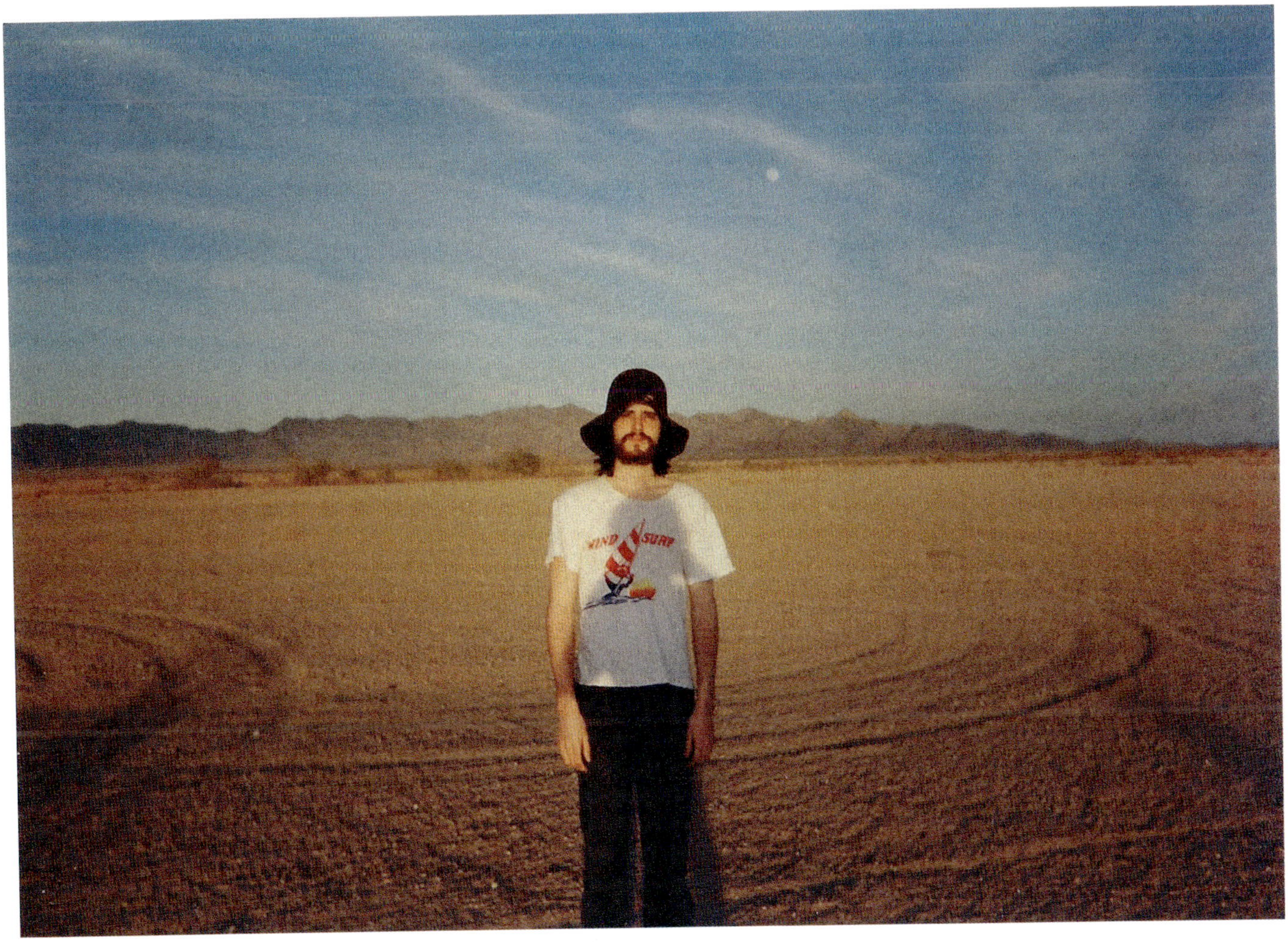
SURF

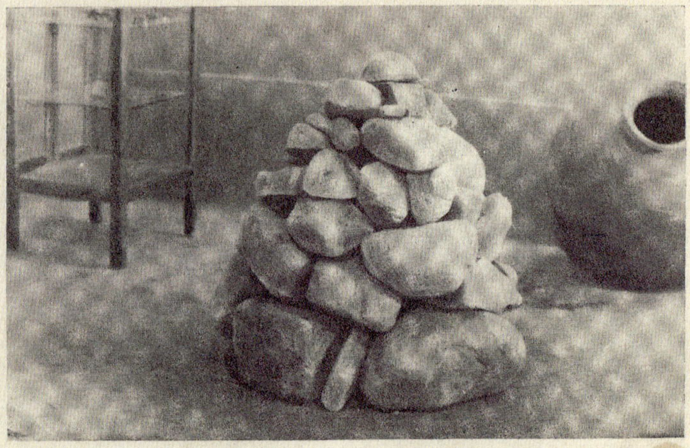

Apacheta.

41

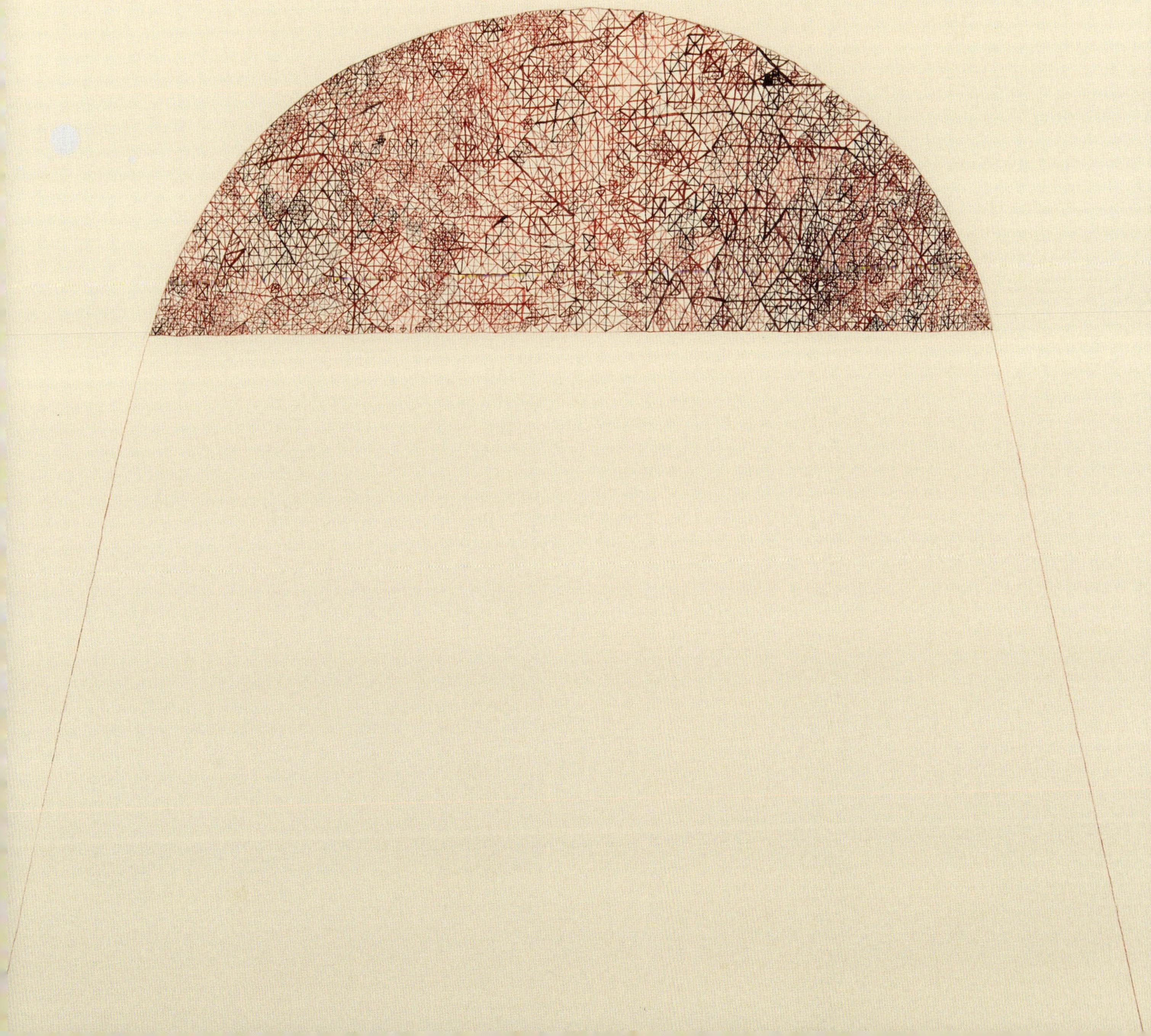

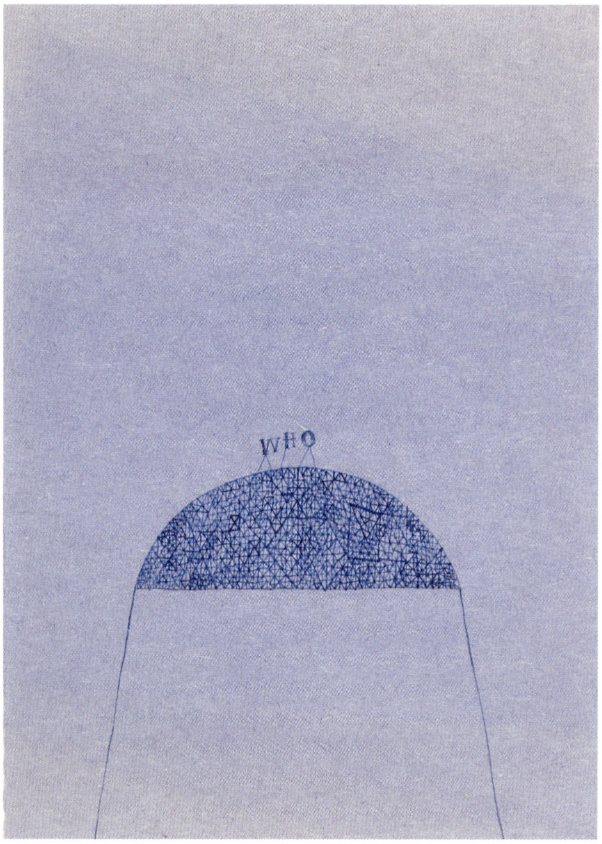
WHO

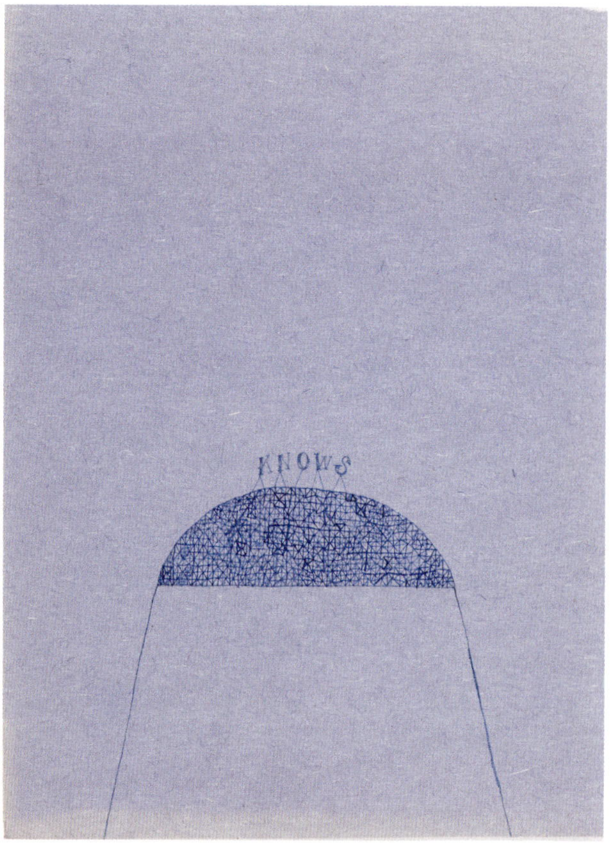
KNOWS

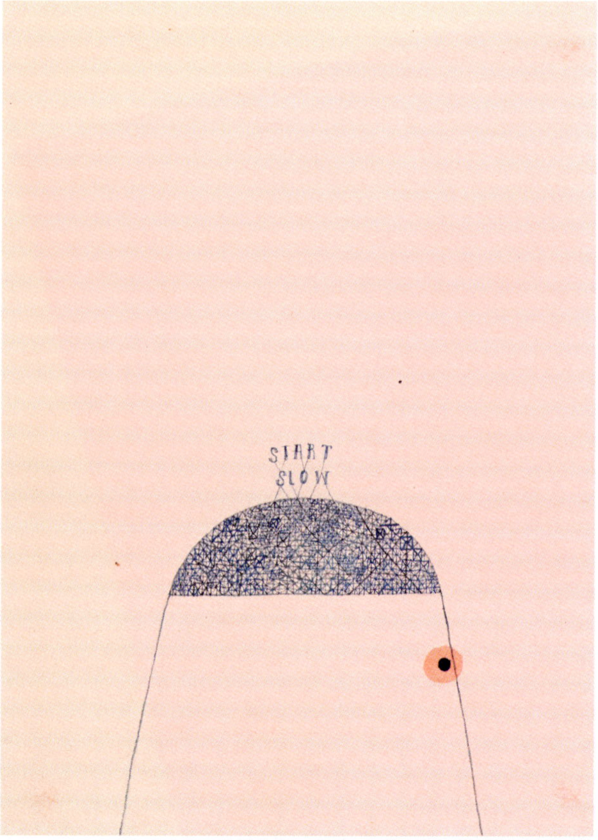
START
SLOW

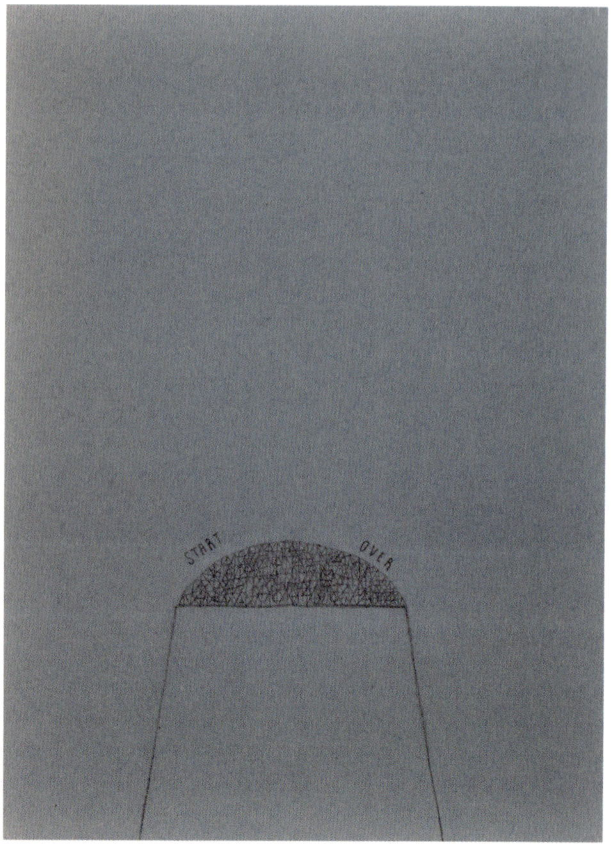
START
OVER

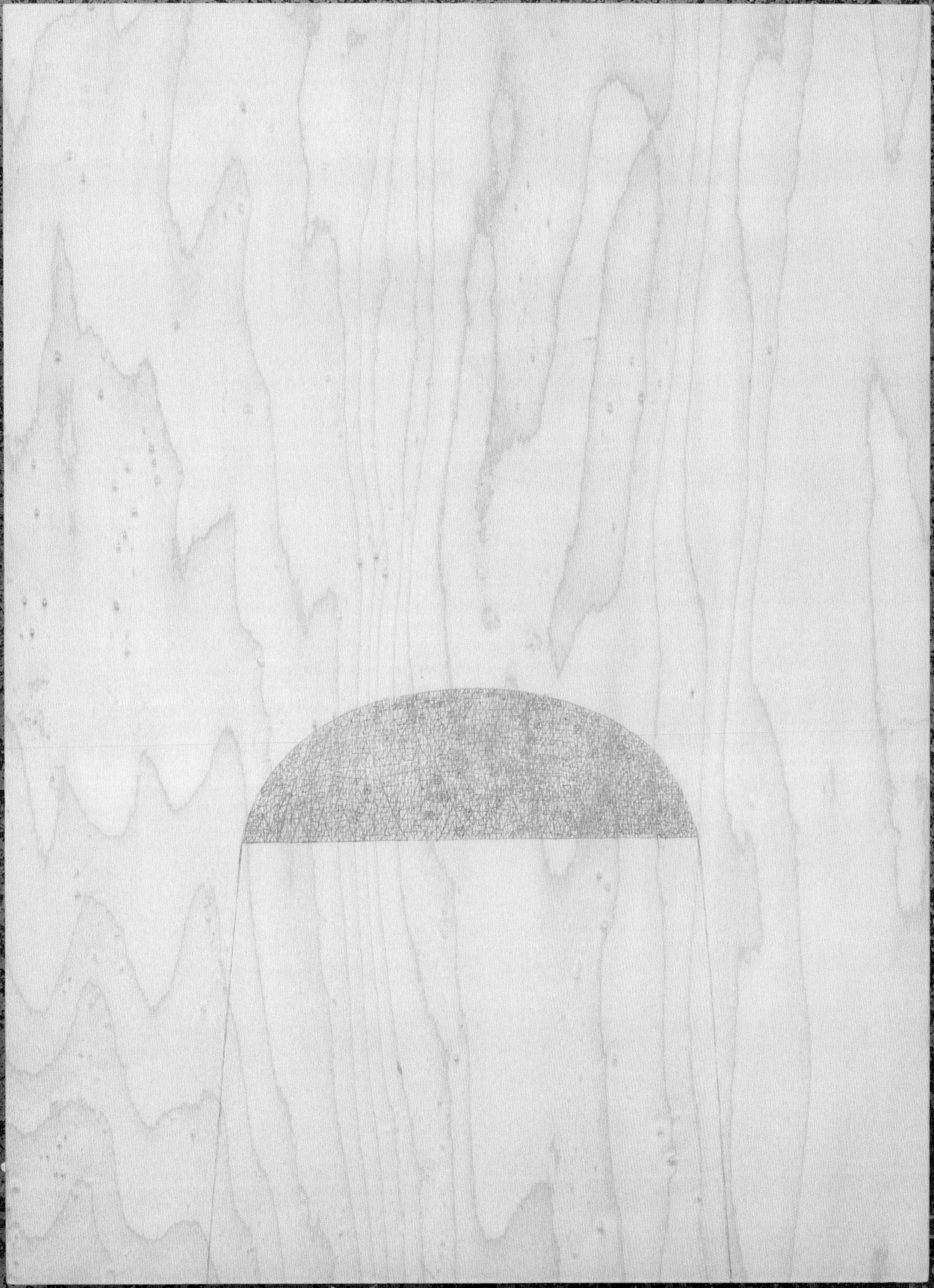

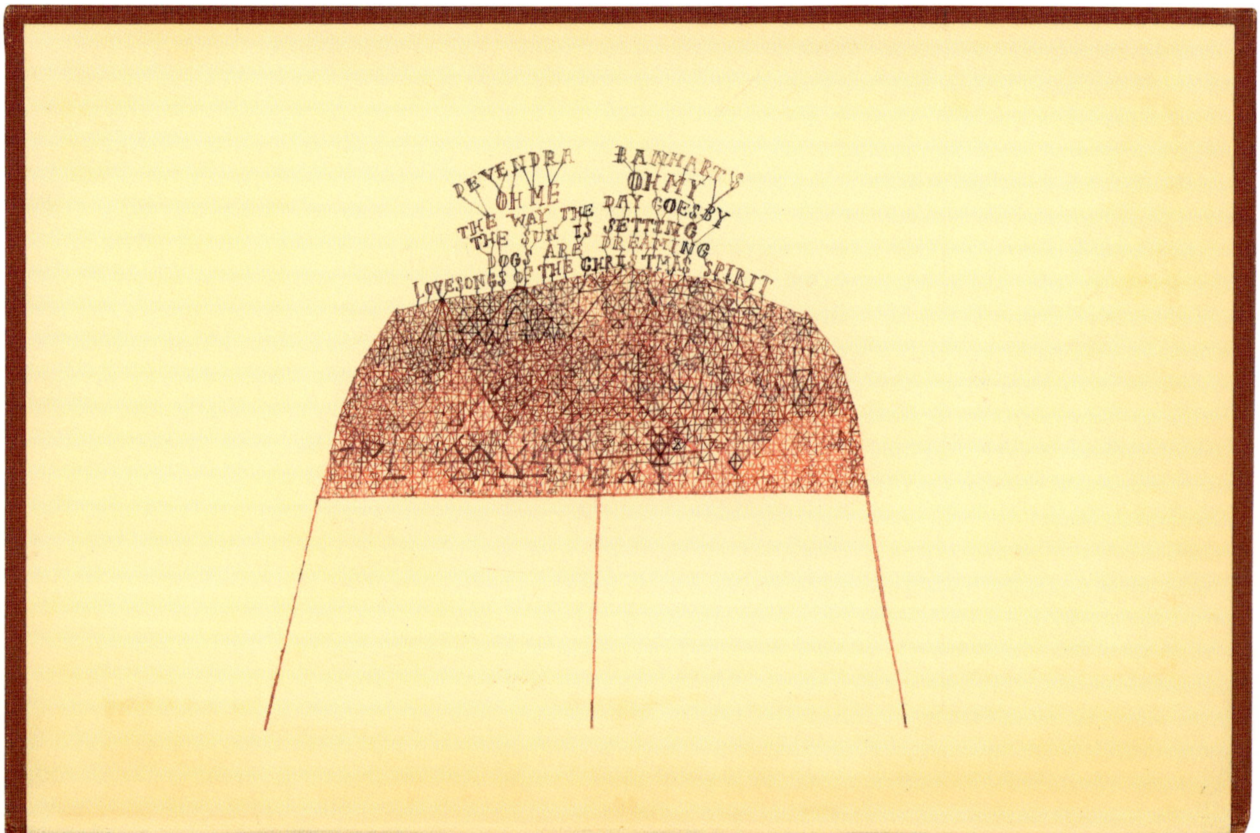
DEVENDRA BANHART'S
OH ME OH MY
THE WAY THE DAY GOES BY
THE SUN IS SETTING
DOGS ARE DREAMING
LOVESONGS OF THE CHRISTMAS SPIRIT

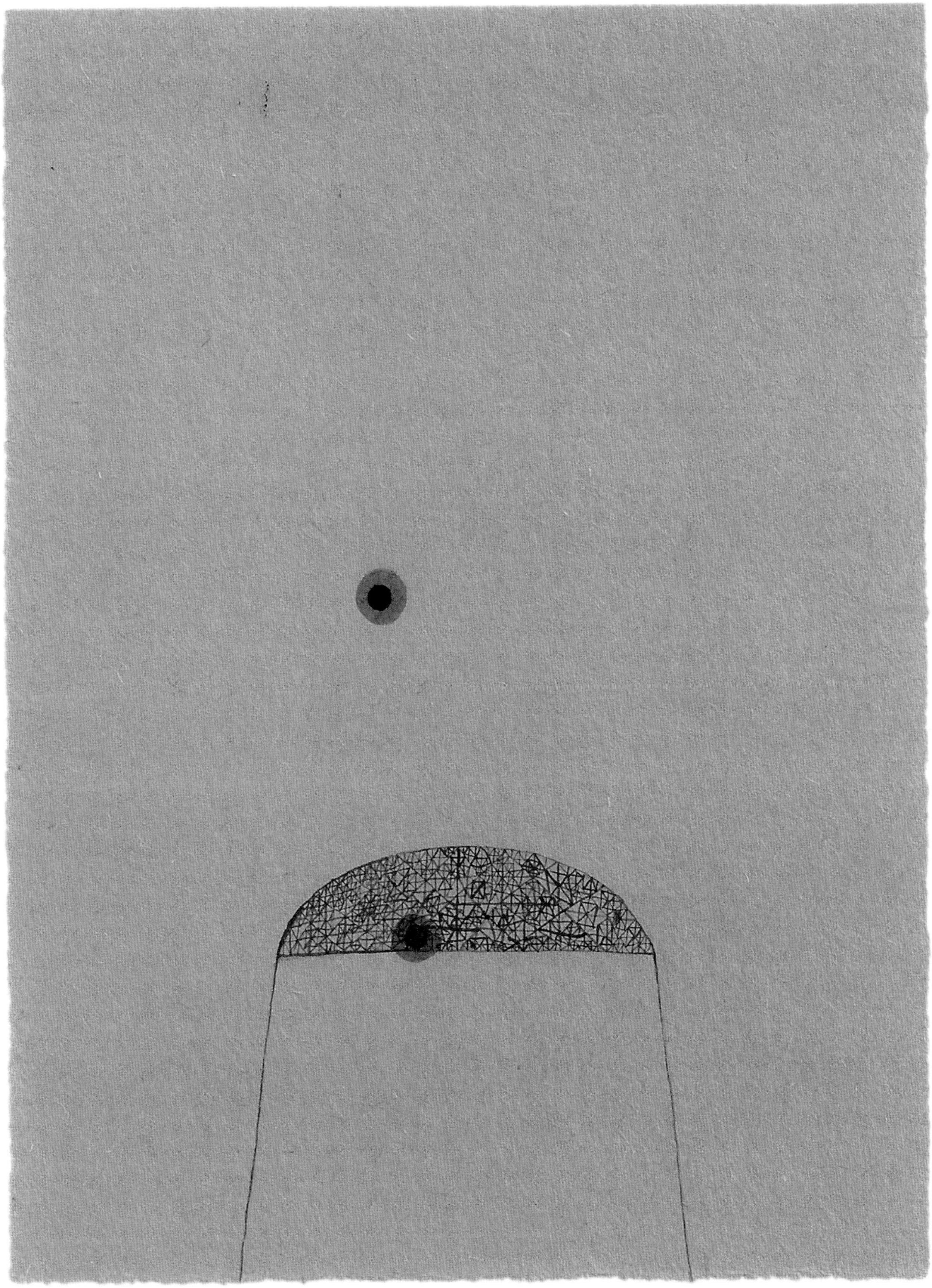

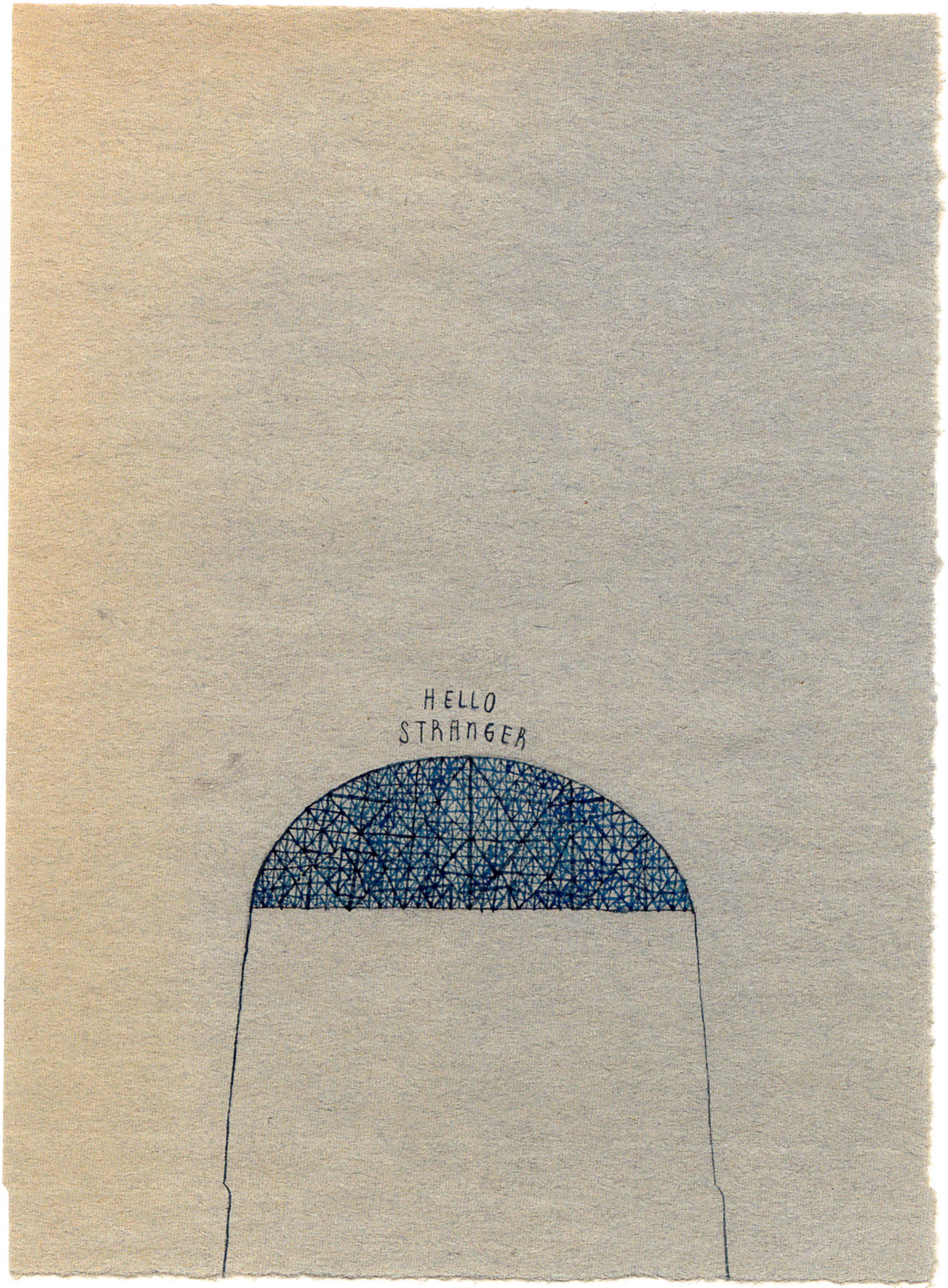
HELLO
STRANGER

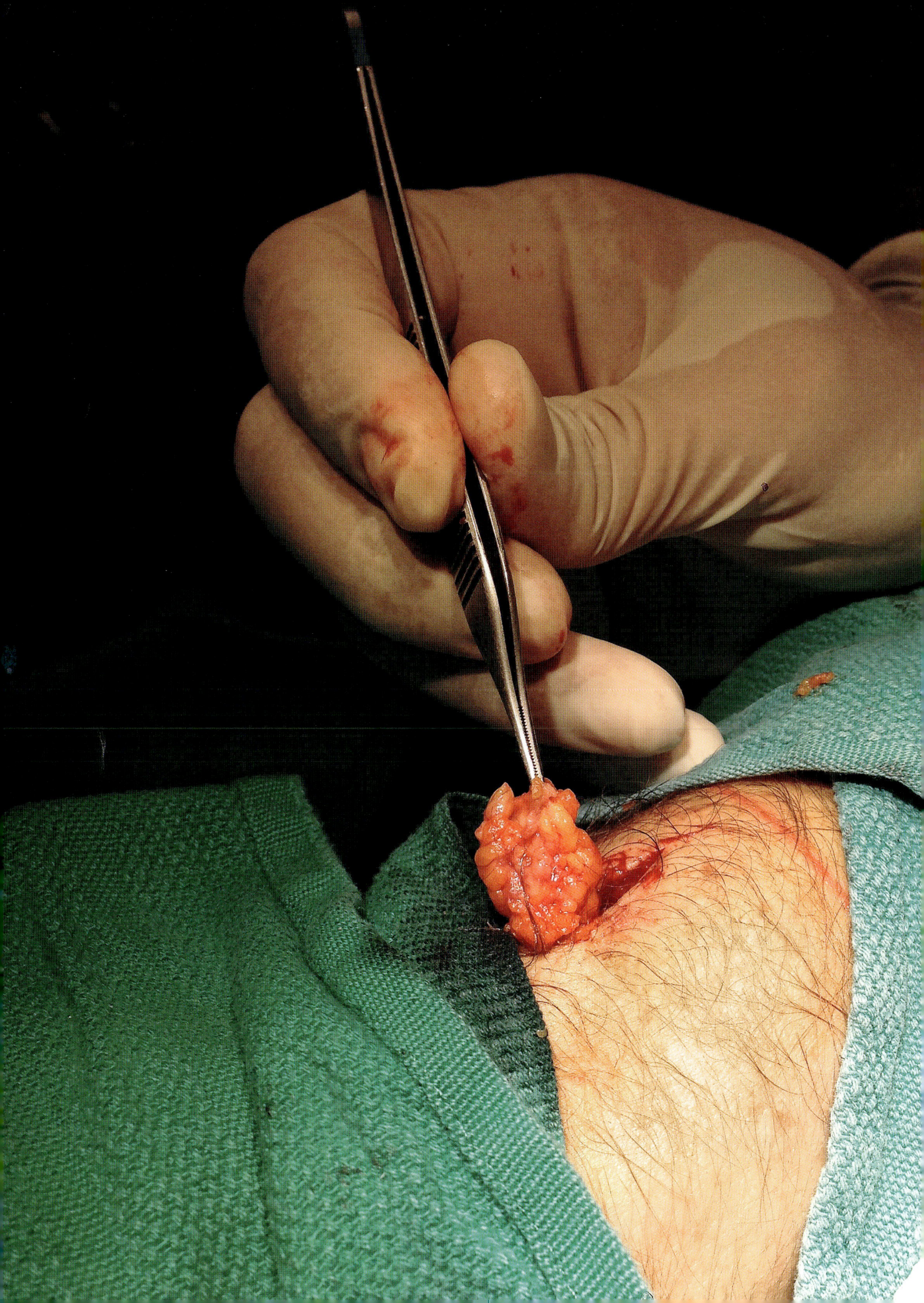

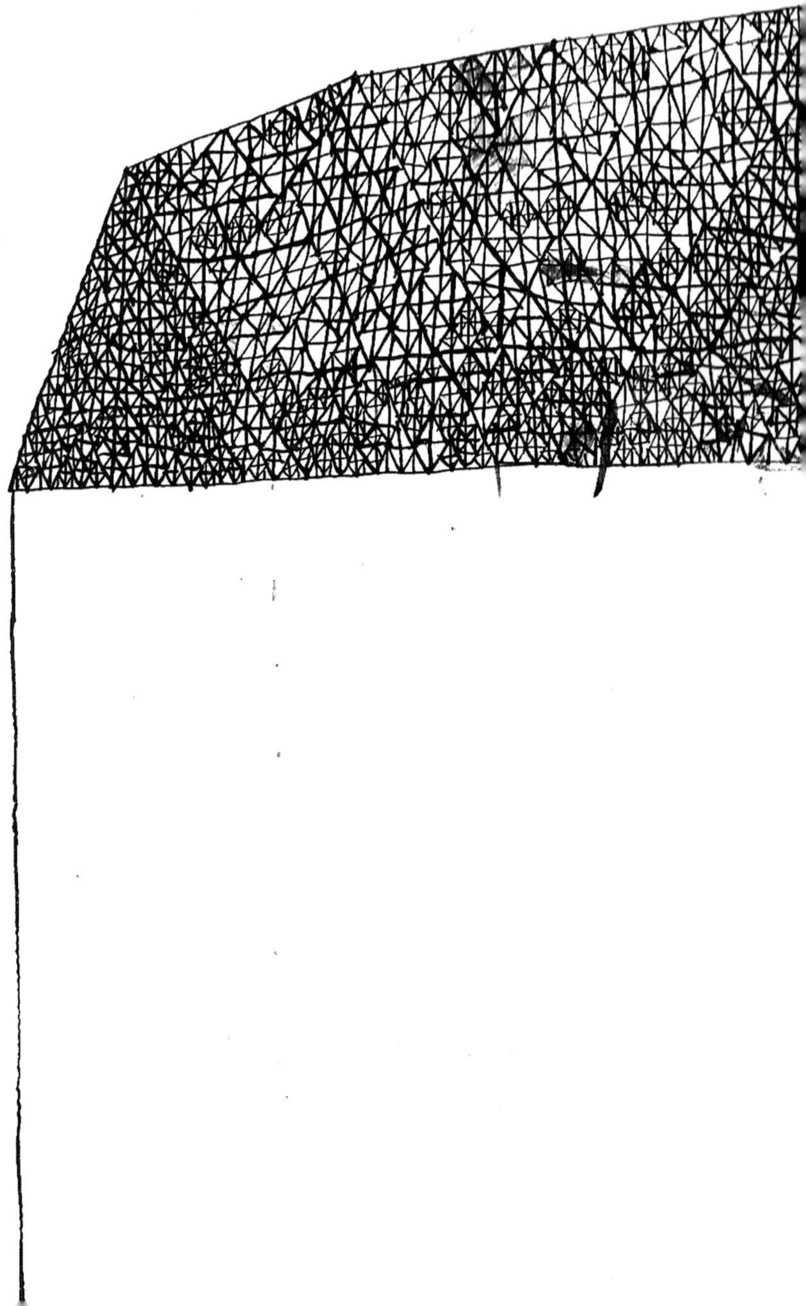

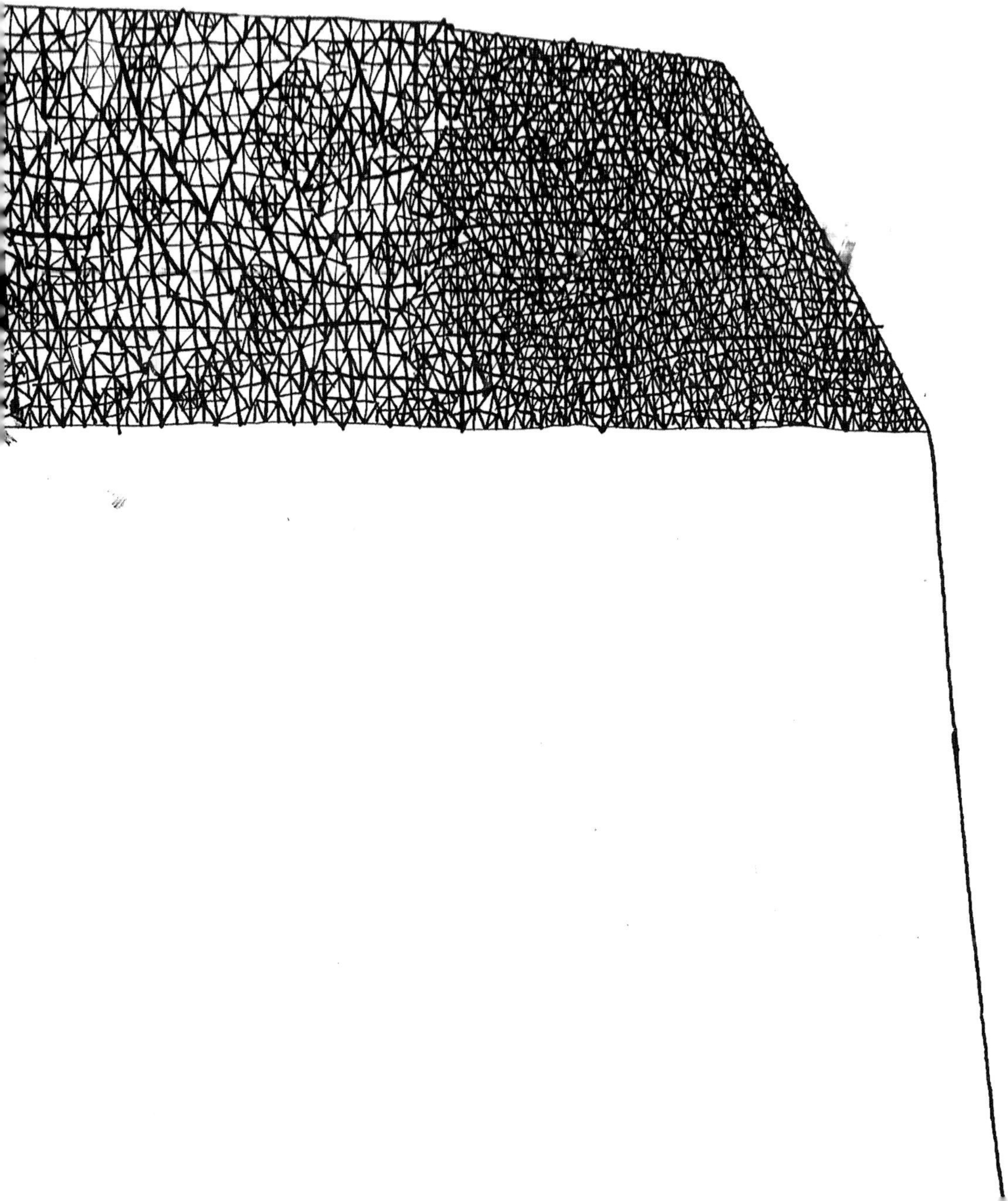

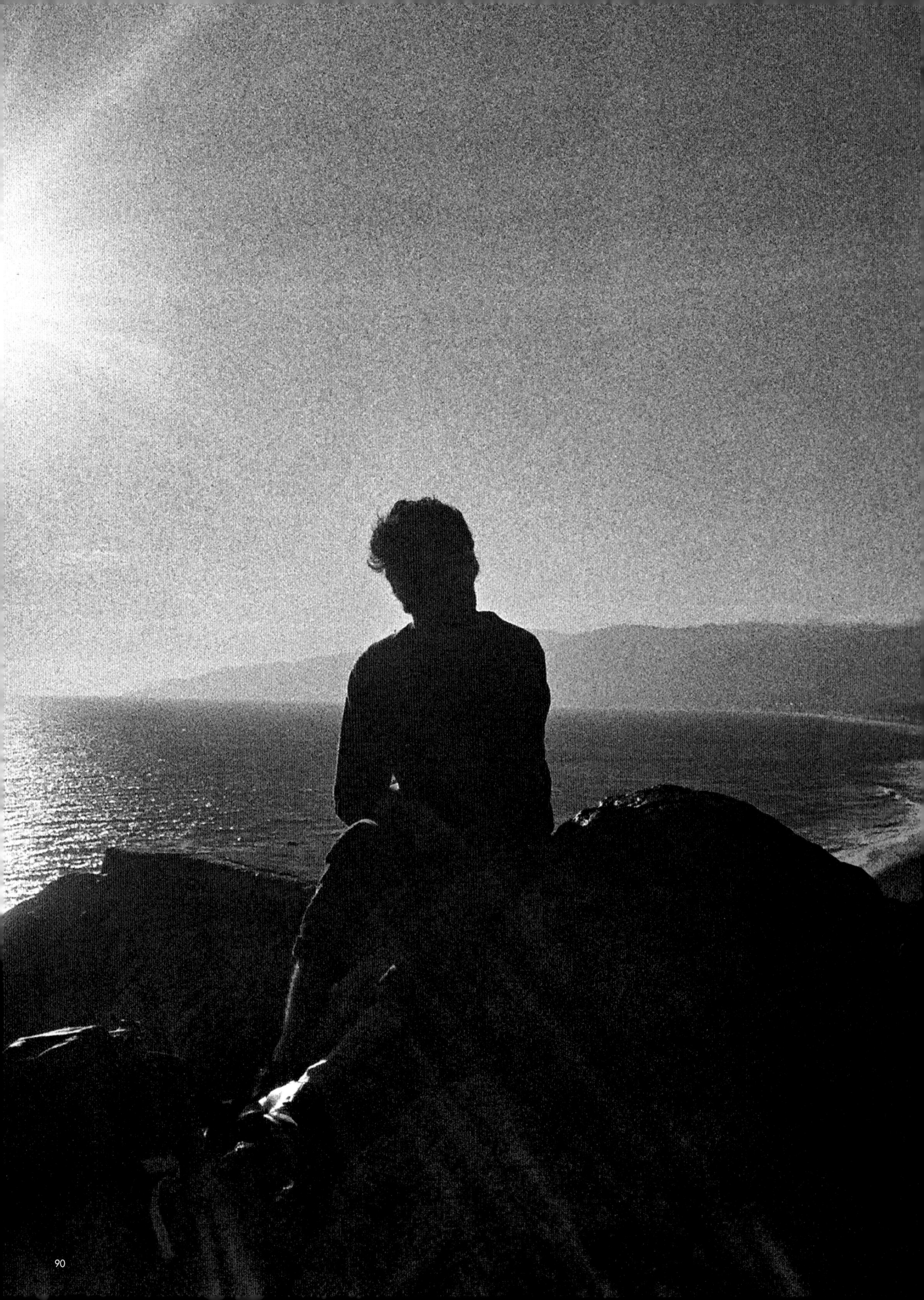

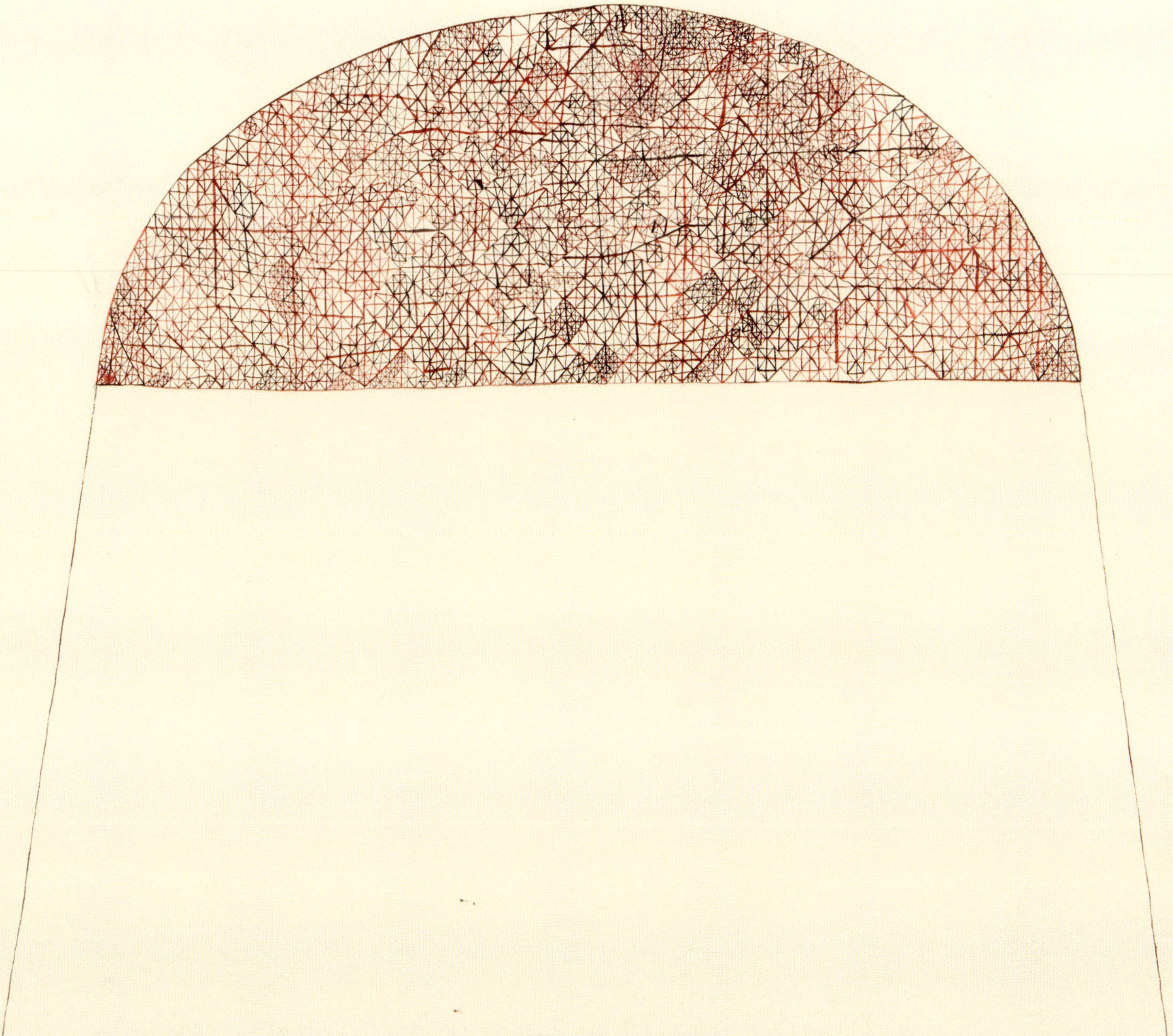

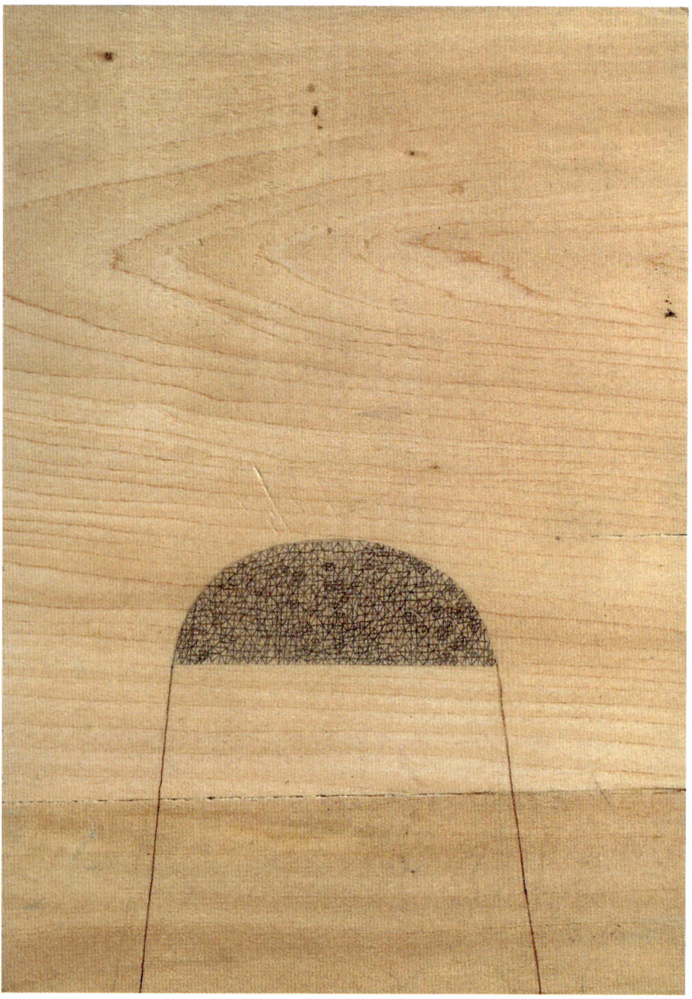

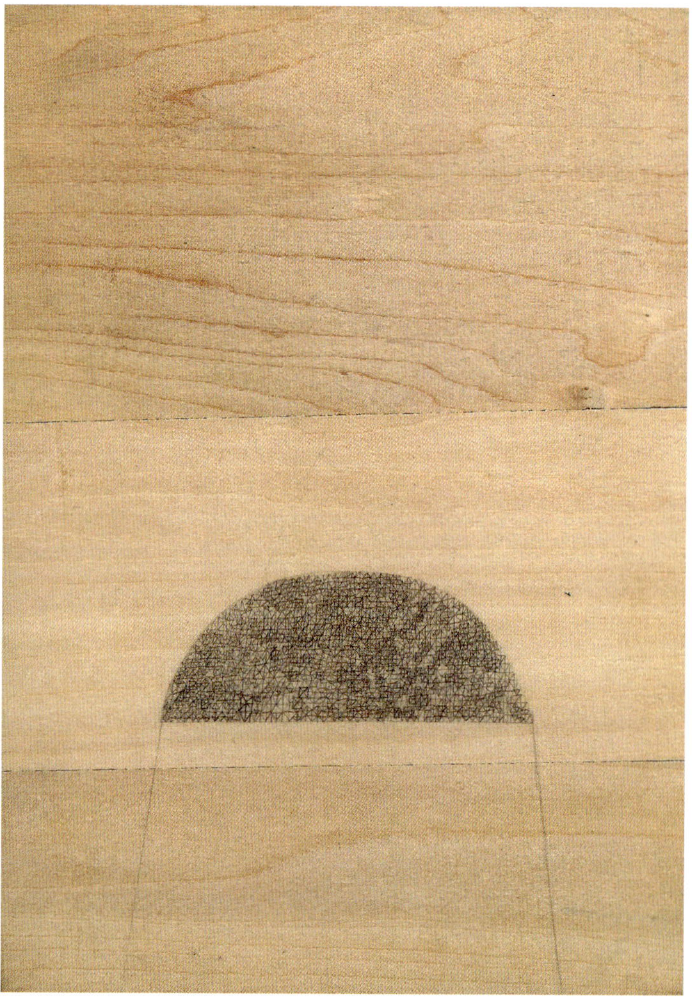

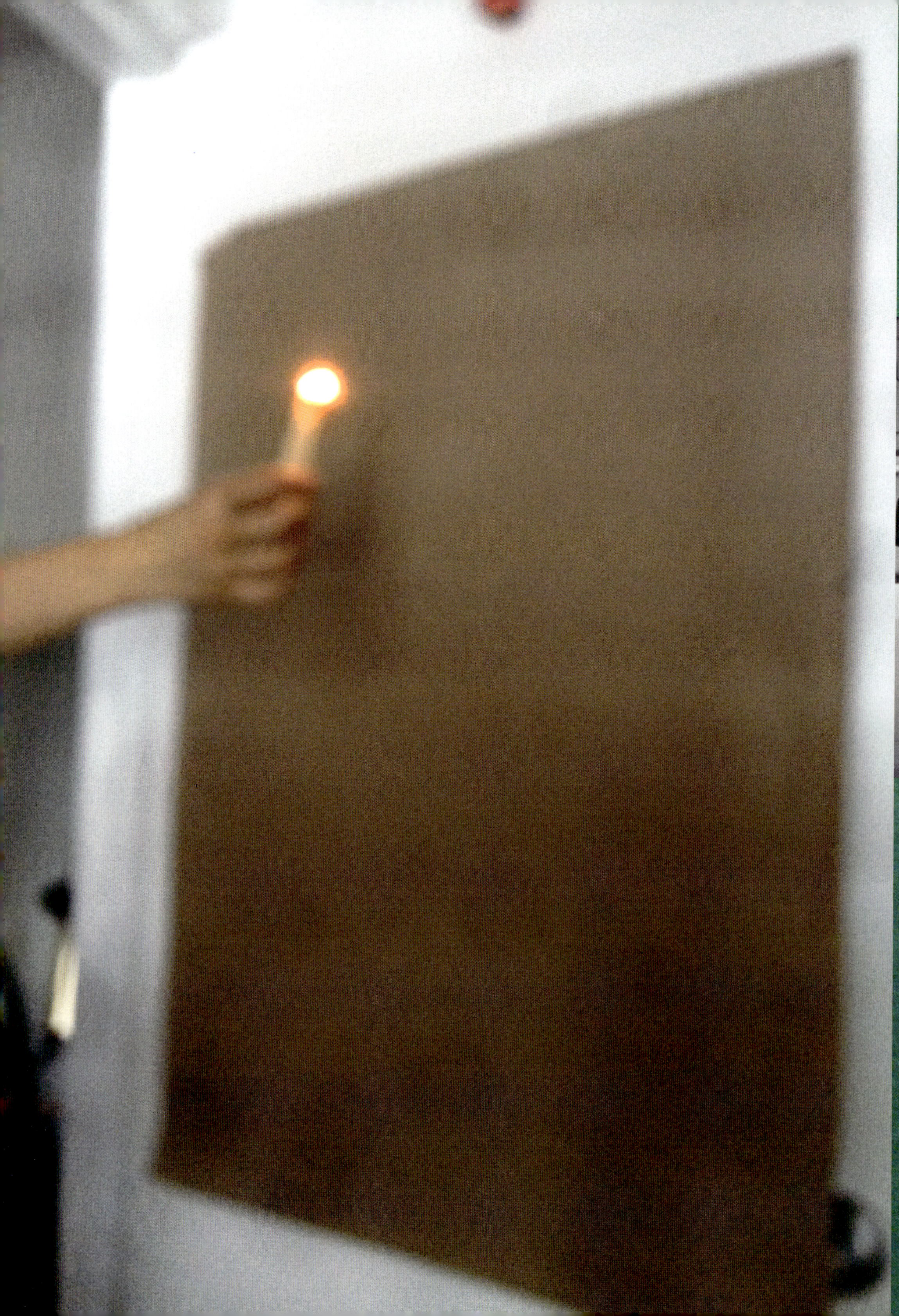

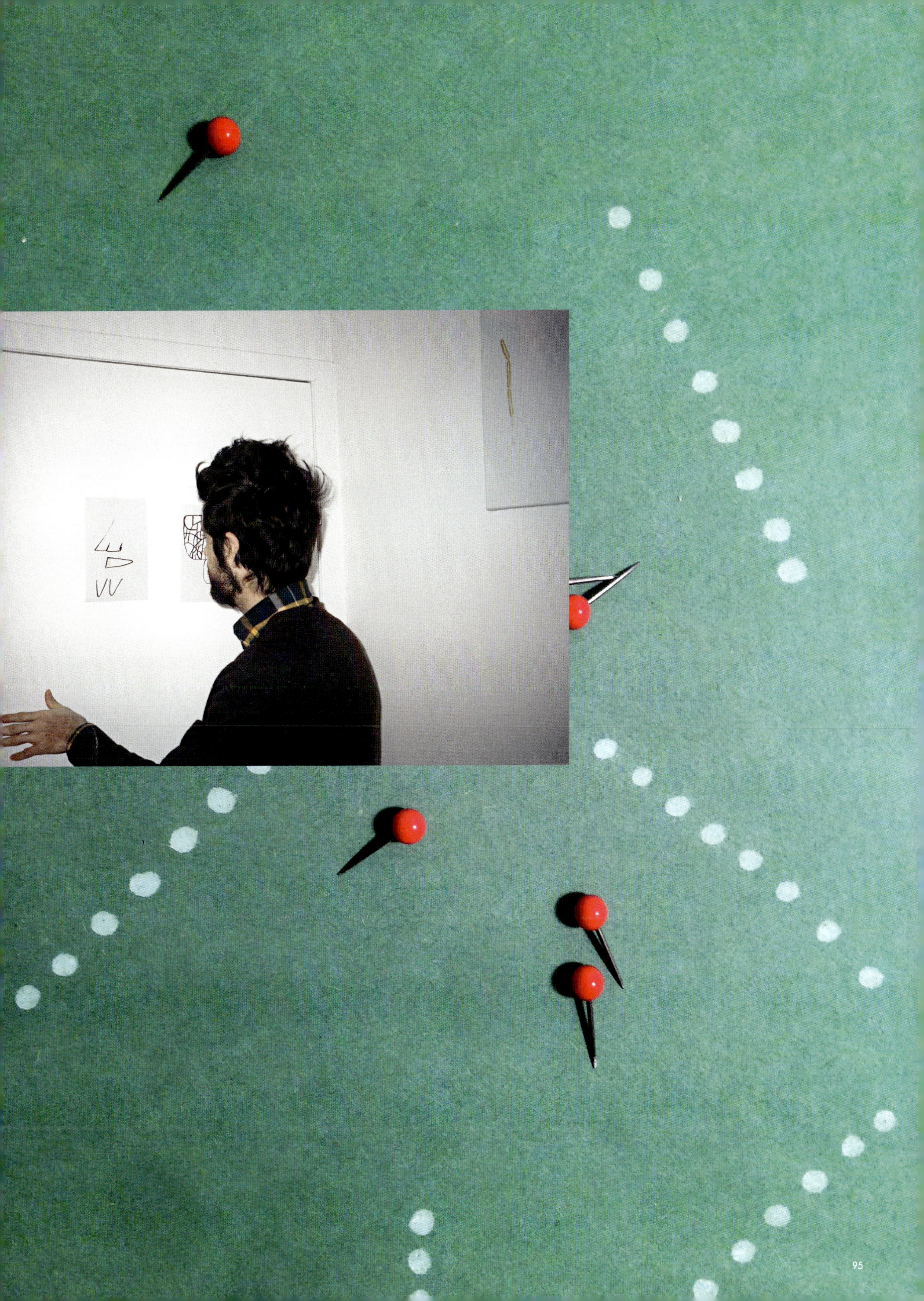

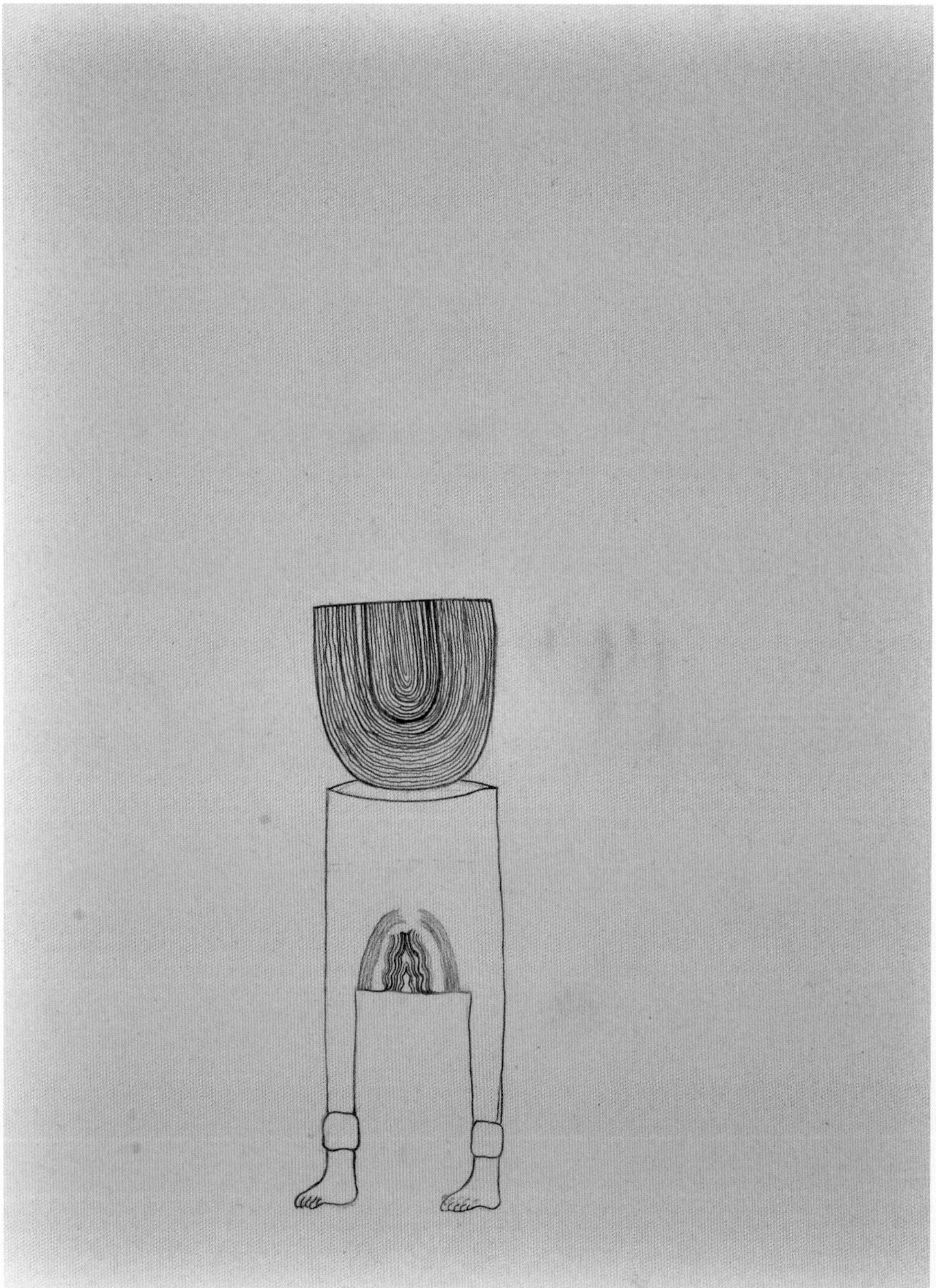

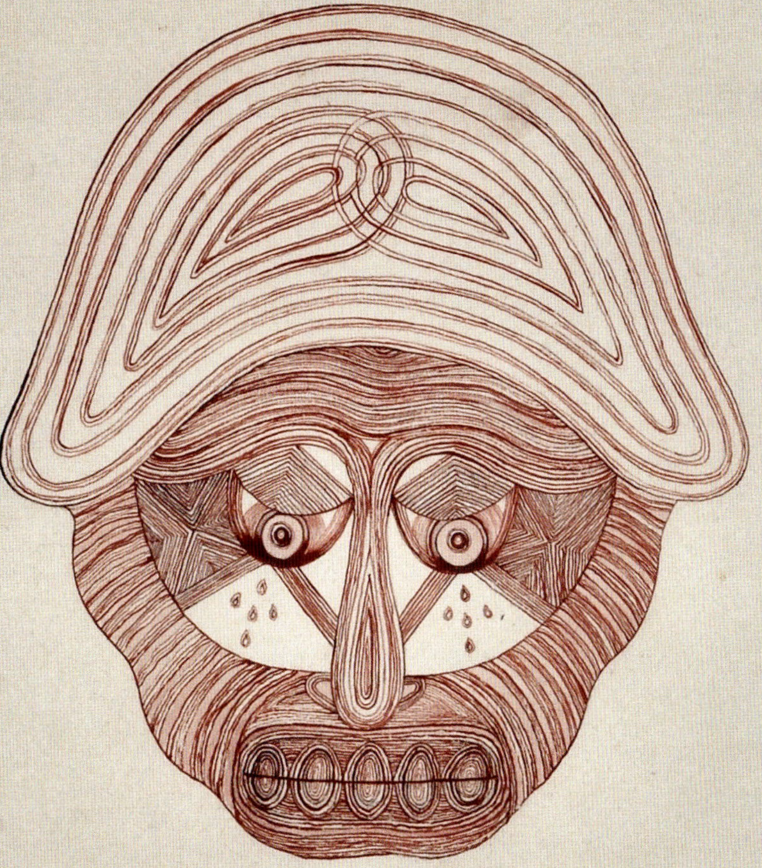

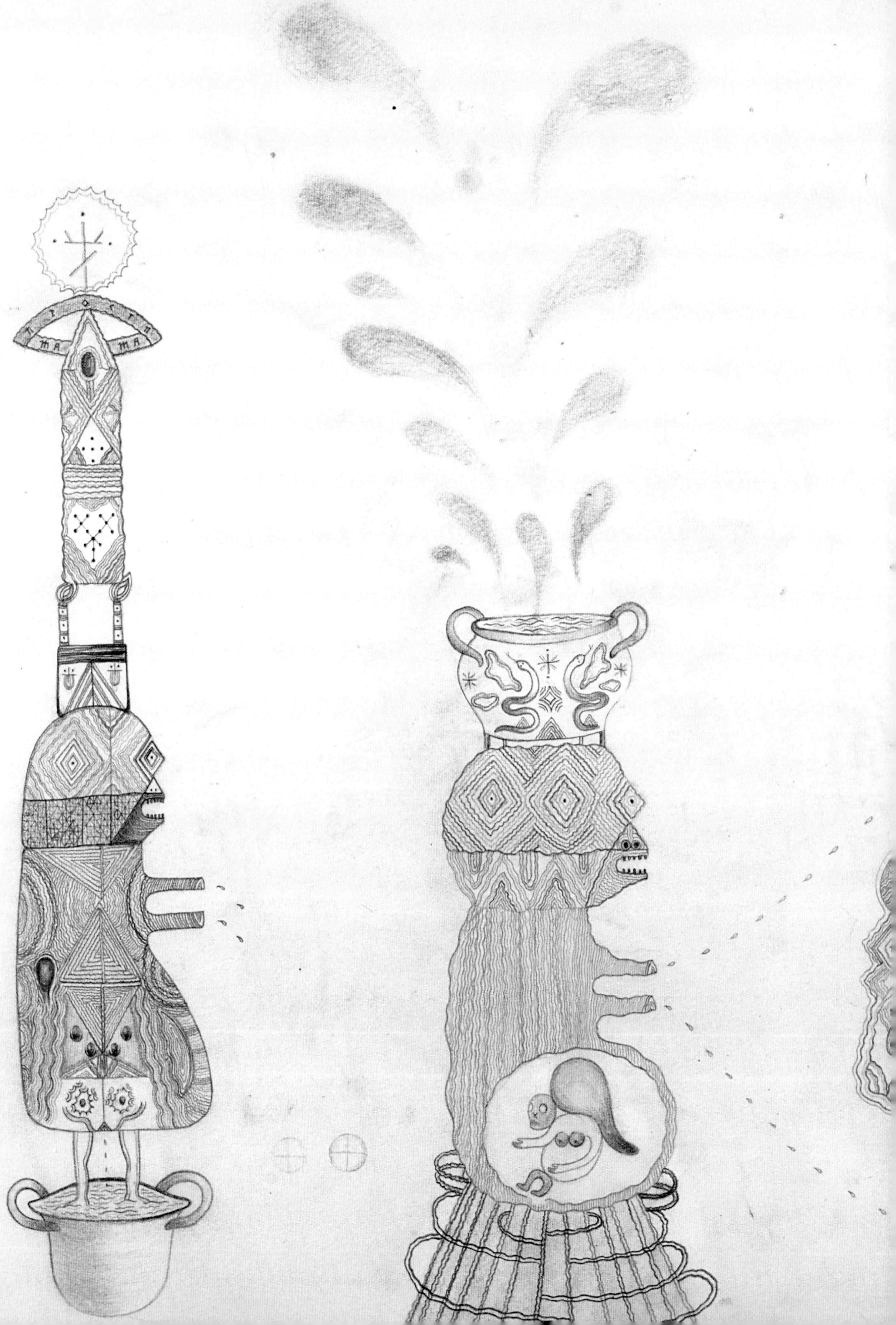

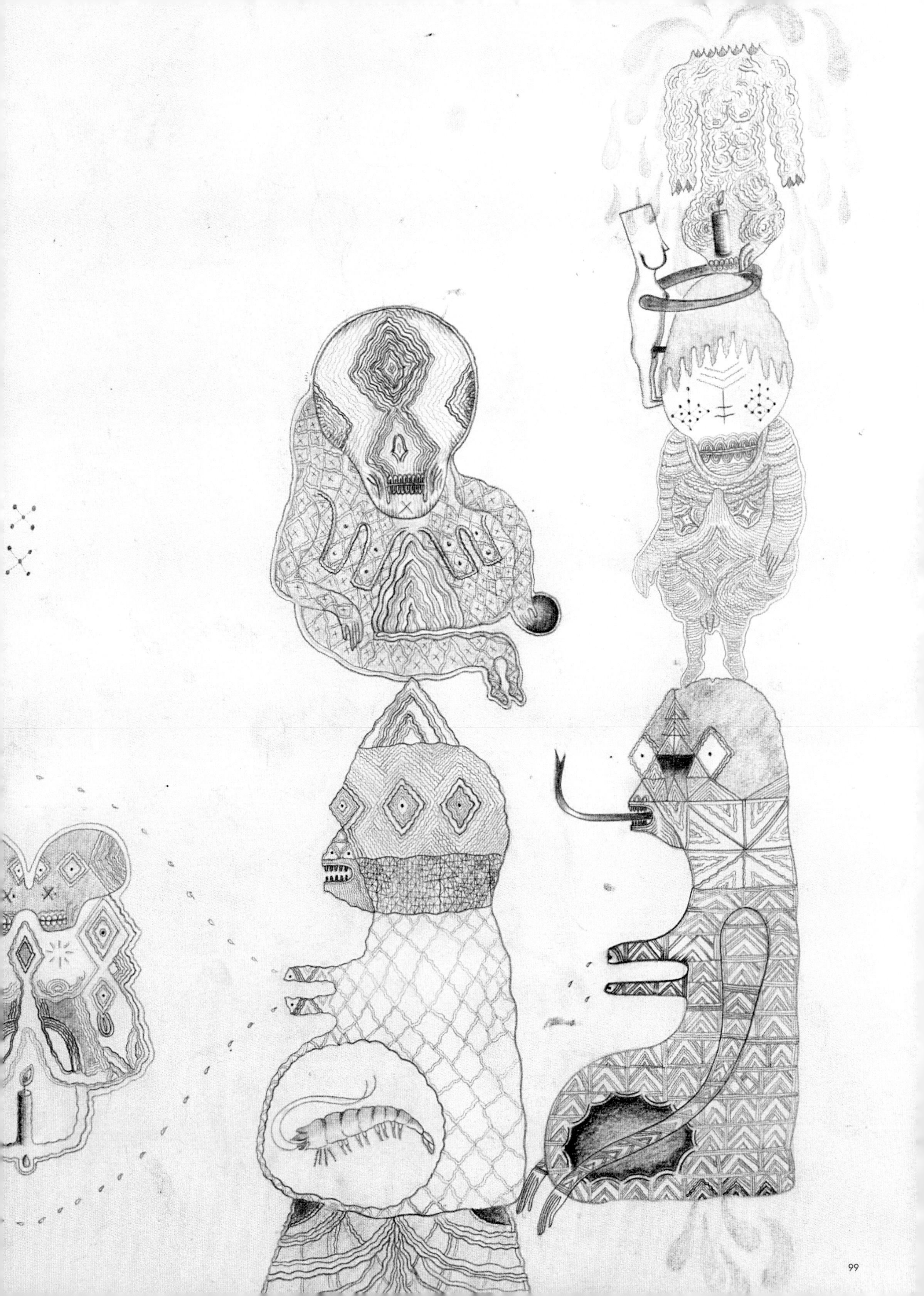

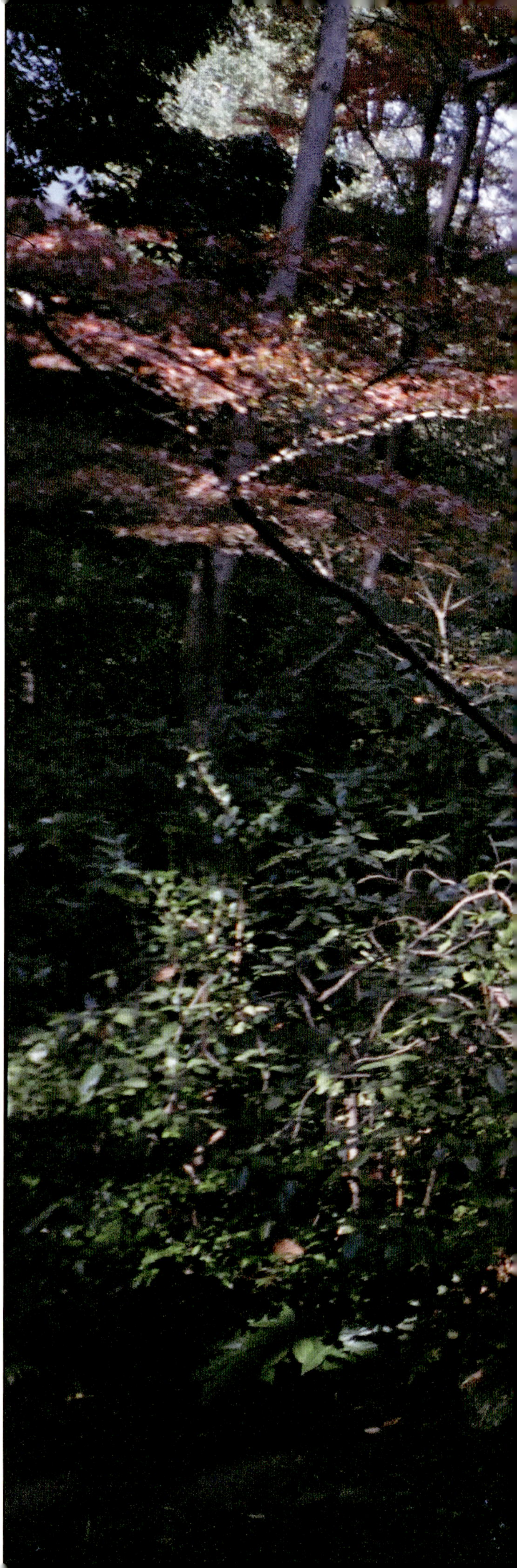

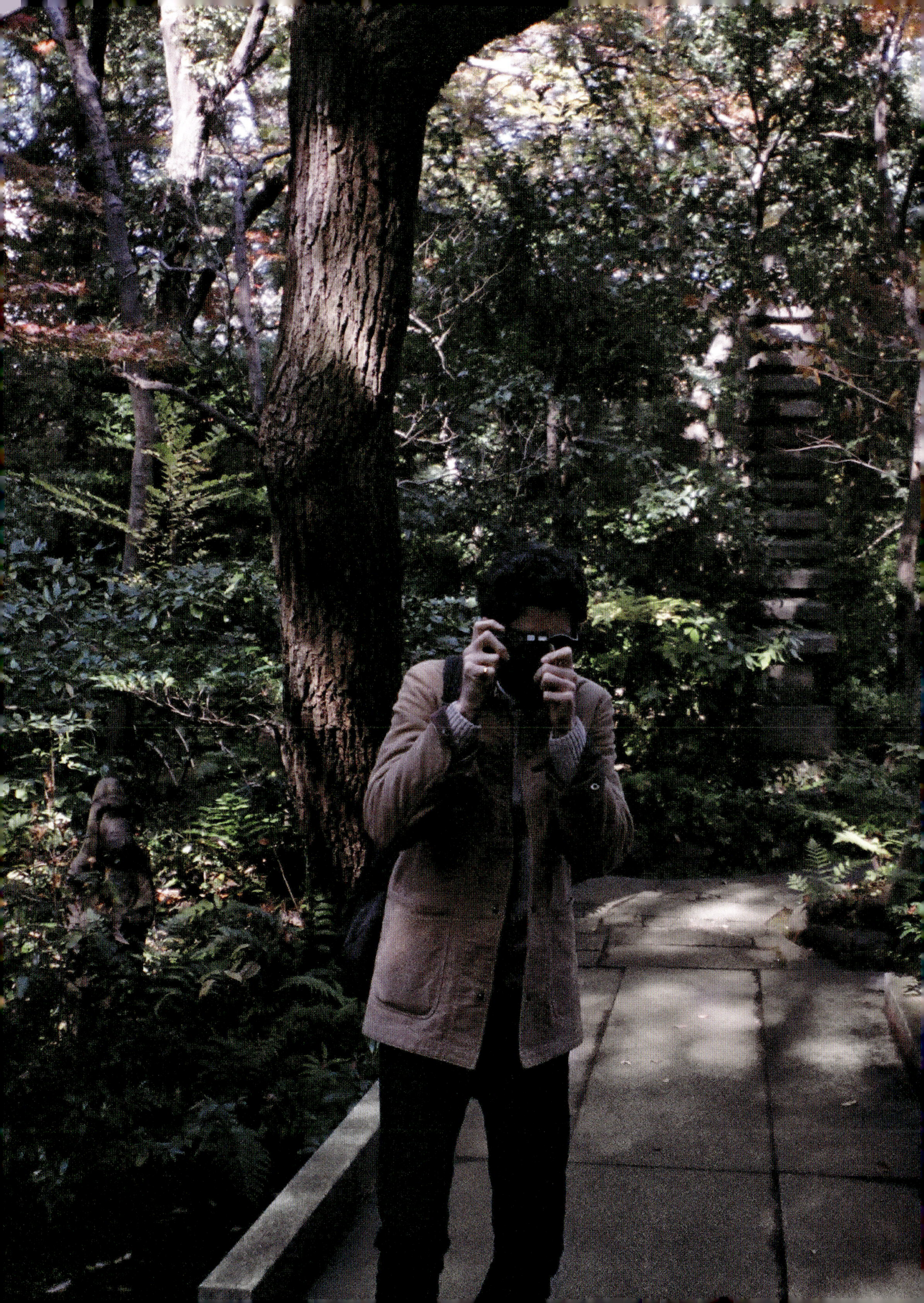

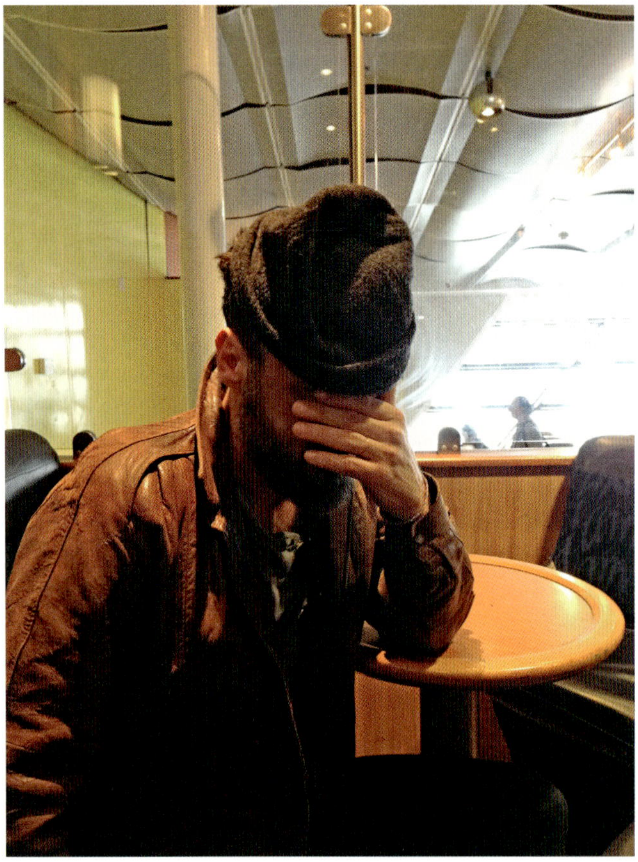

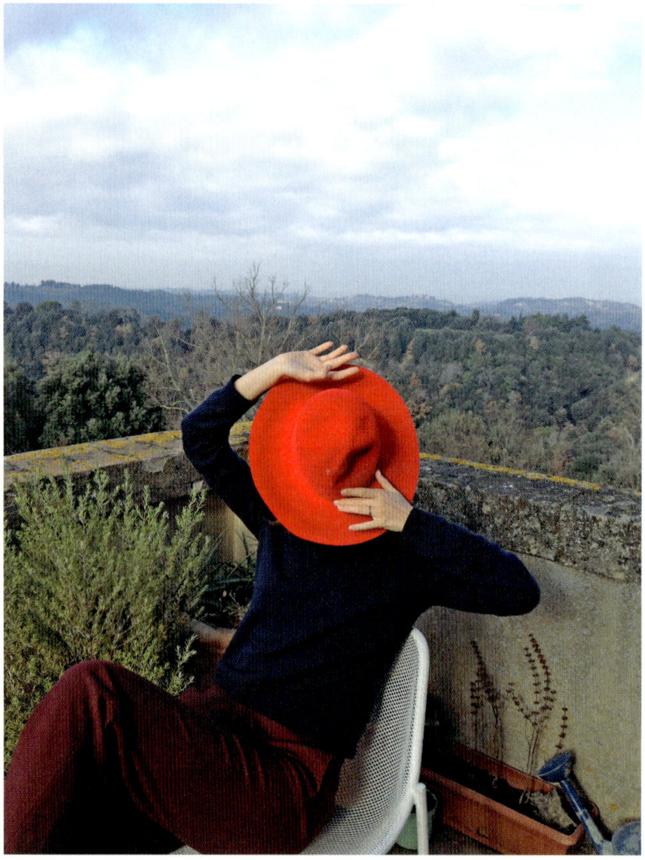

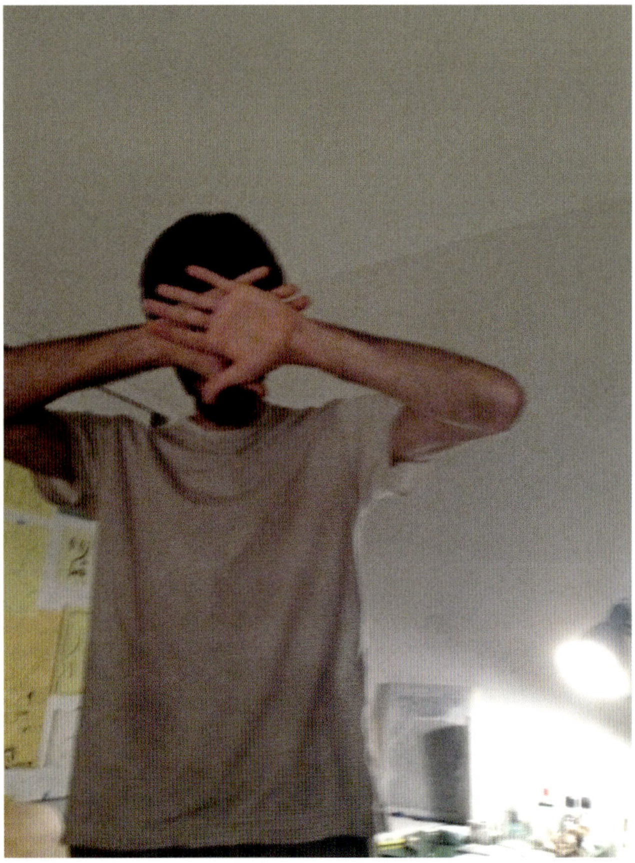

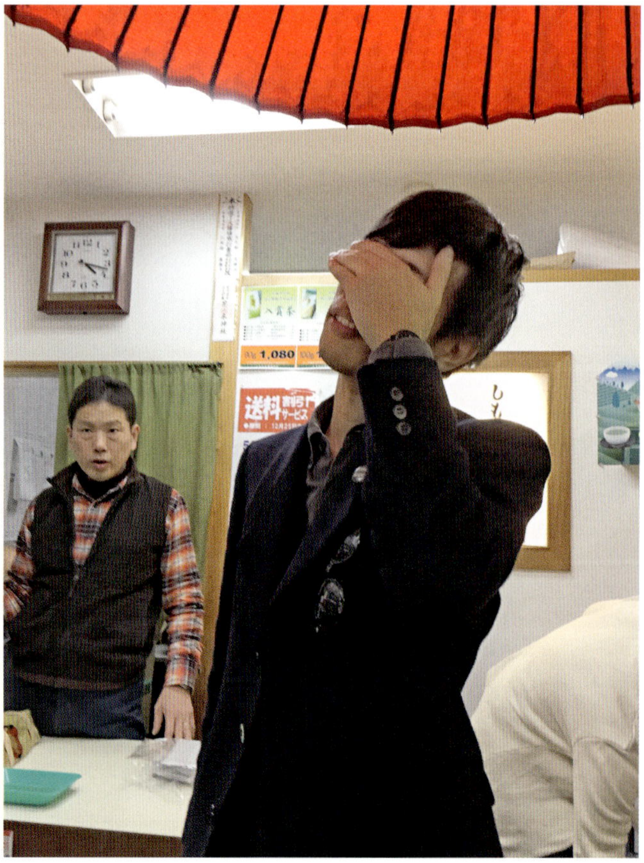
1,080
送料
サービス

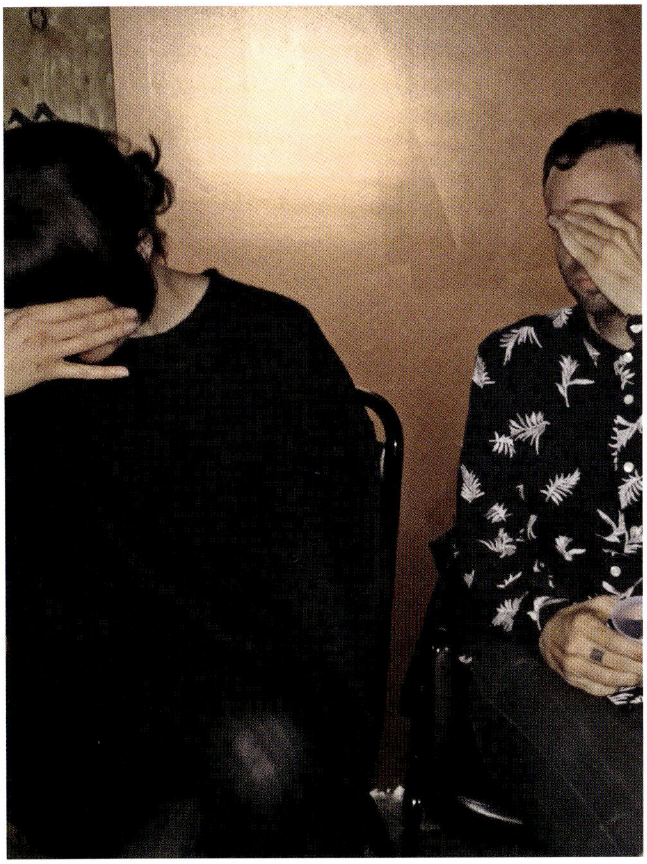

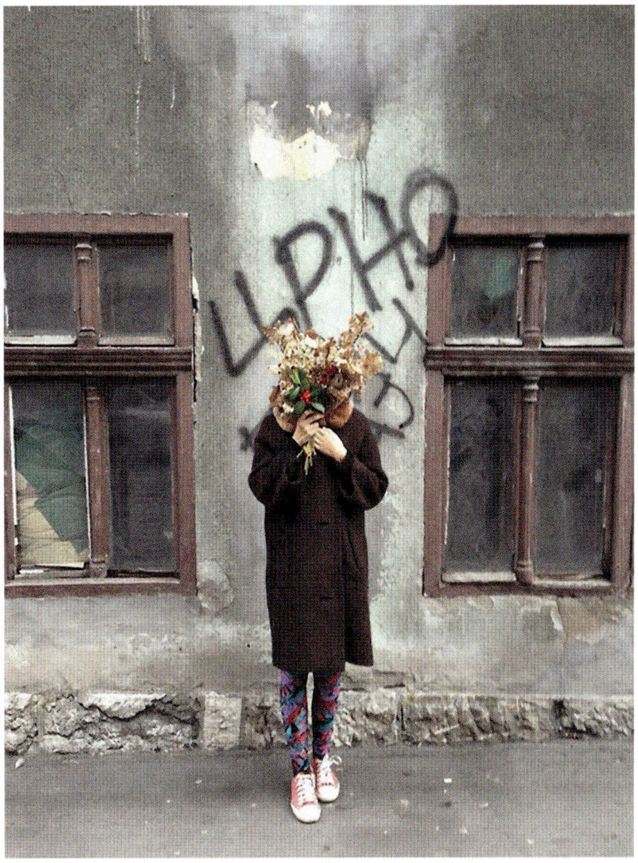
ЦРНО

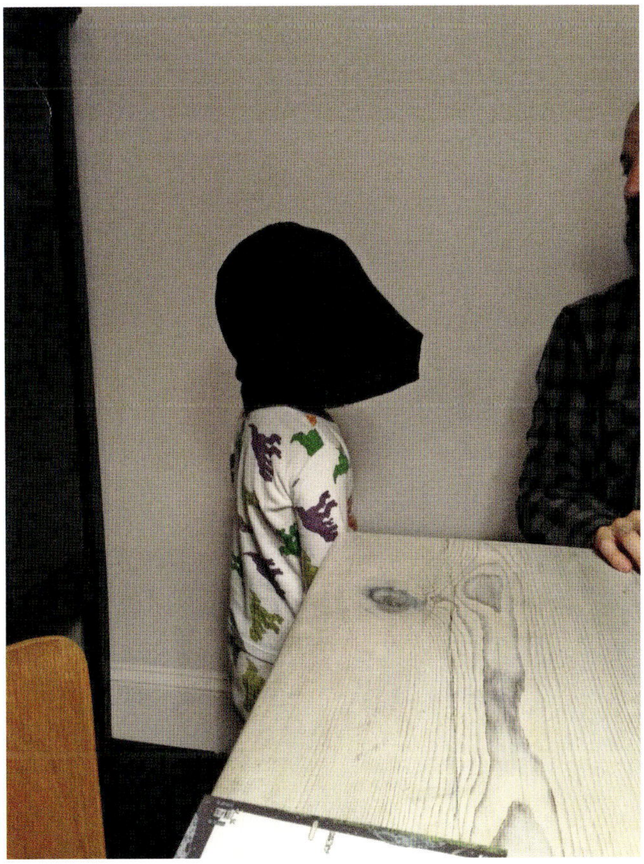

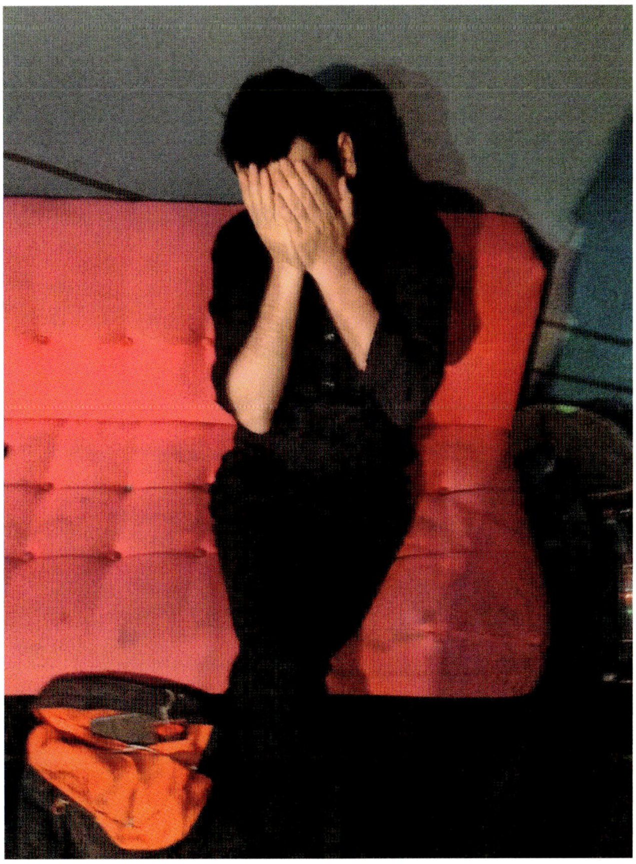

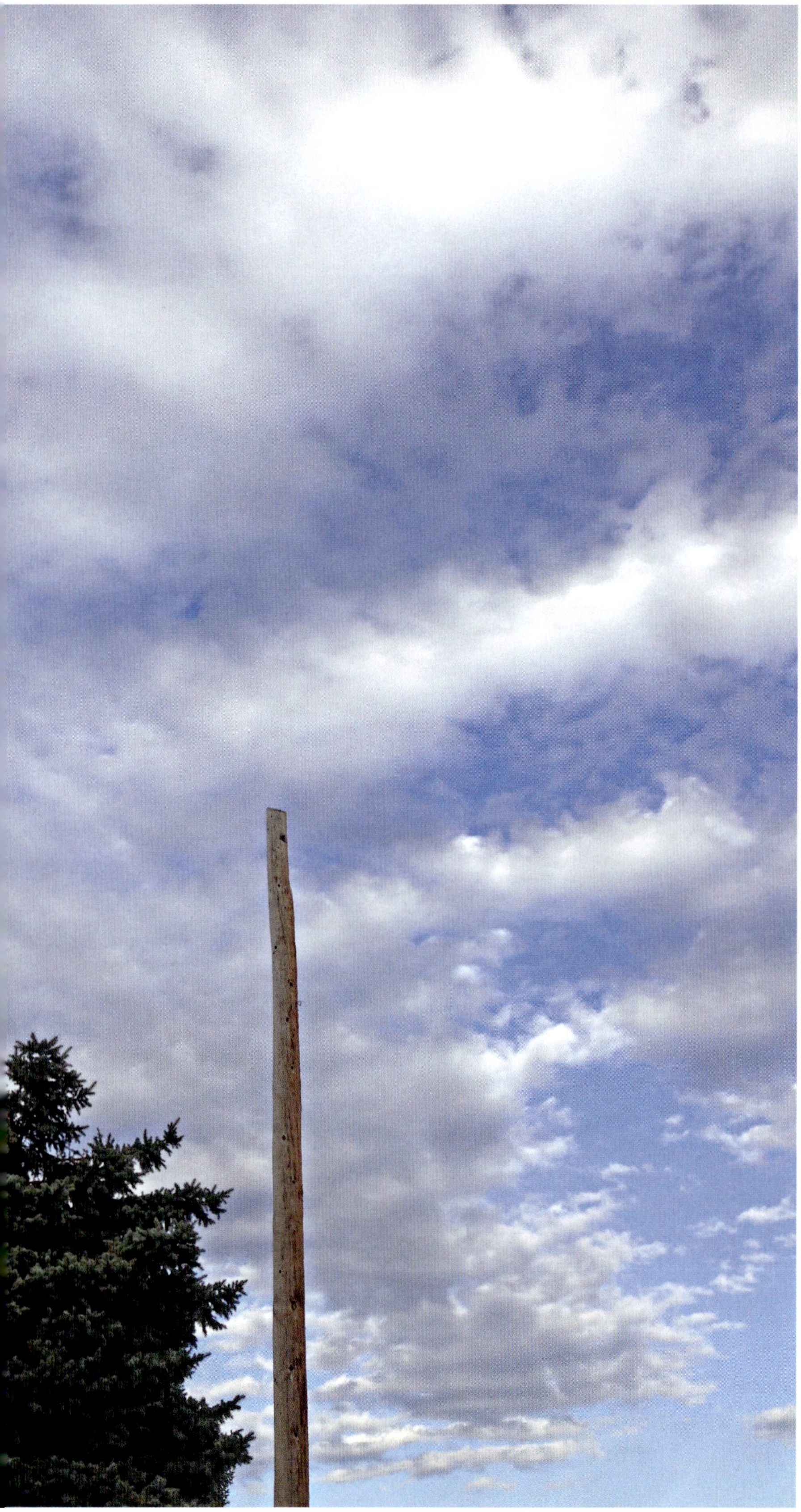

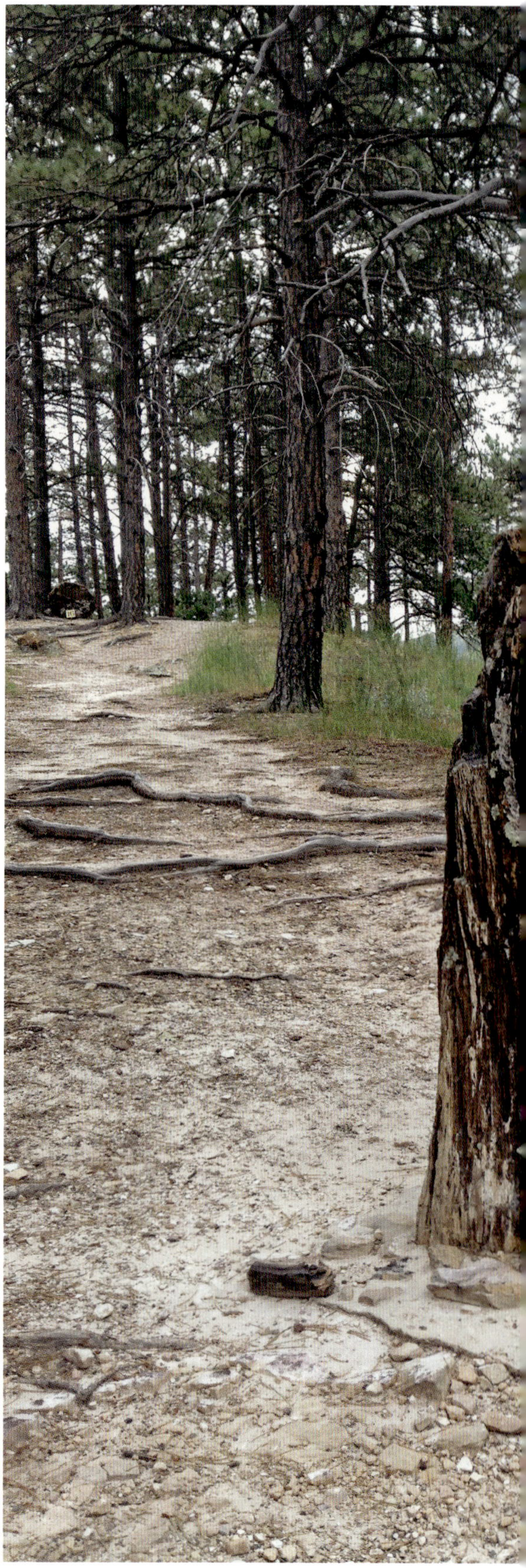

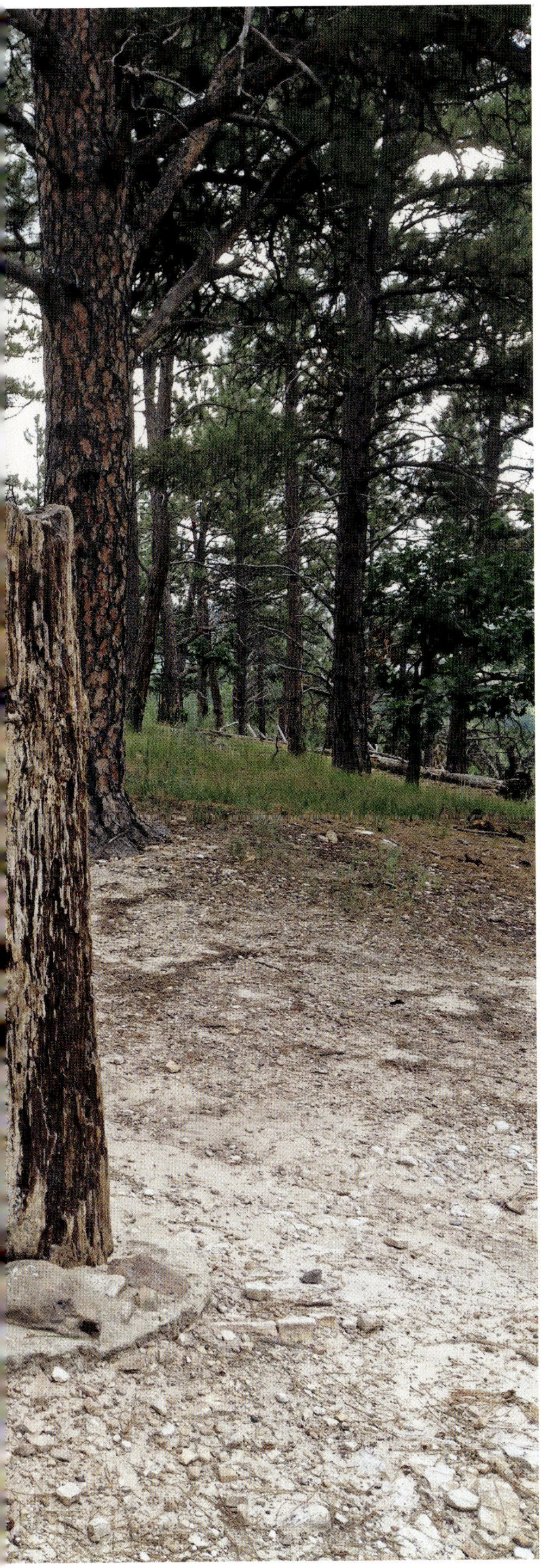
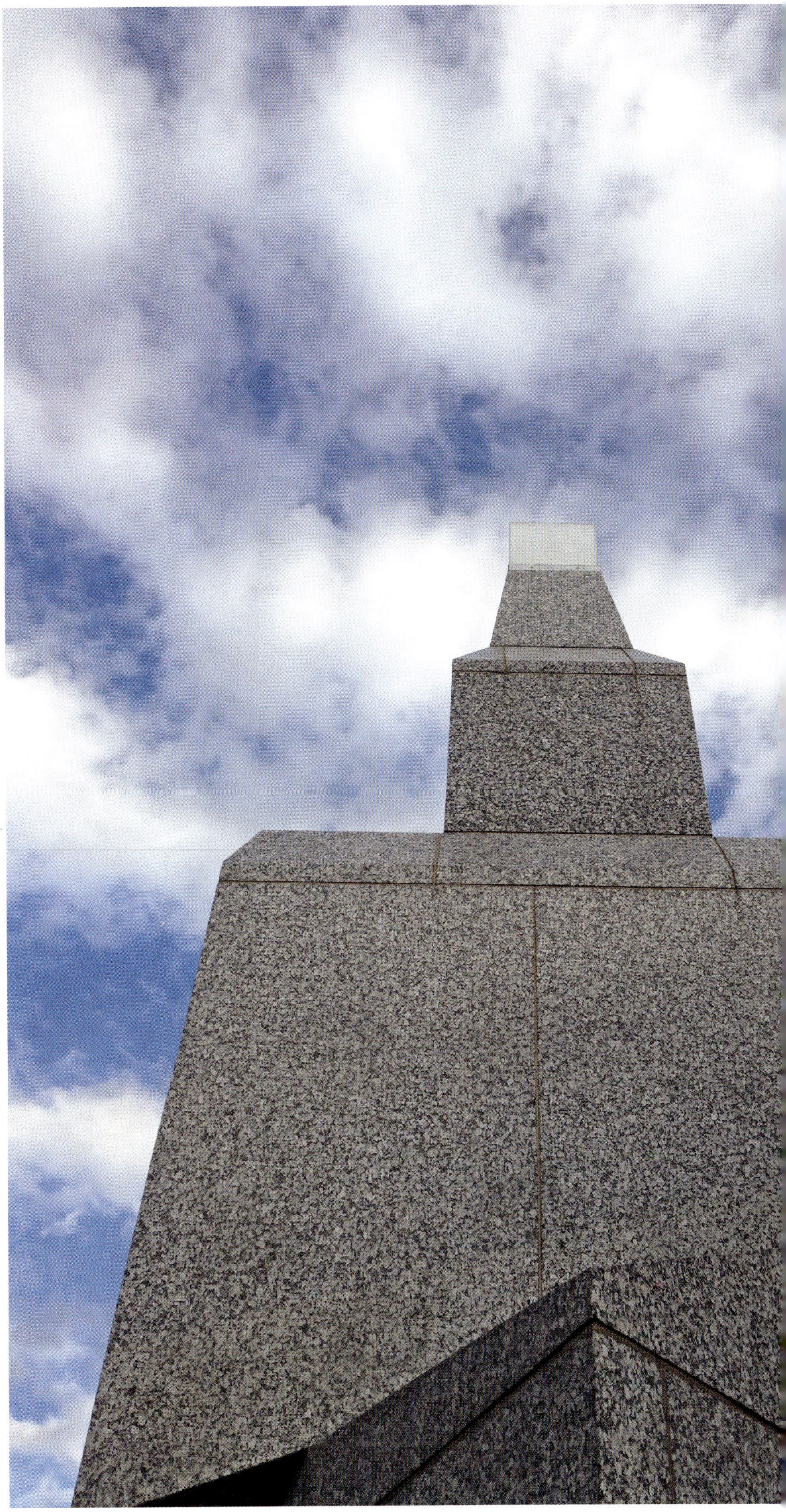

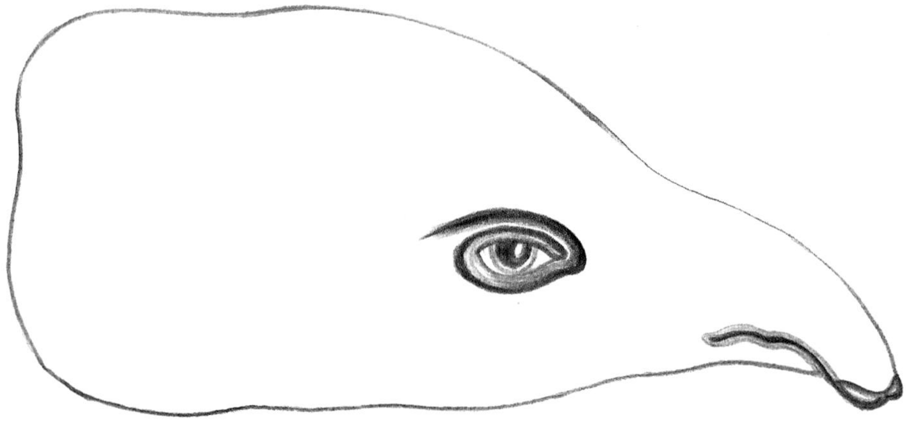

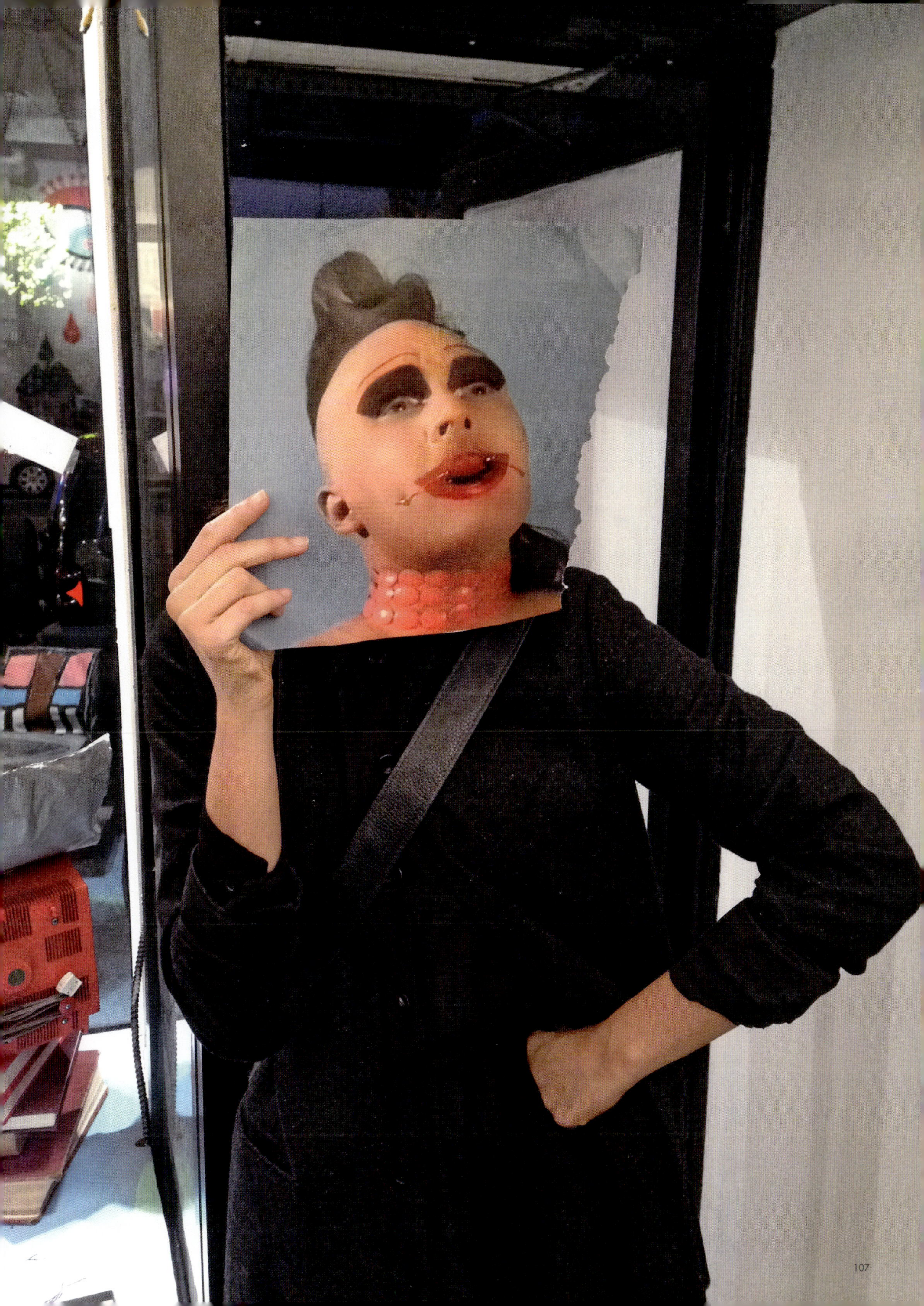

I HAD SUCH A

GOOD TIME

AT WALGREENS

WITH YOU.

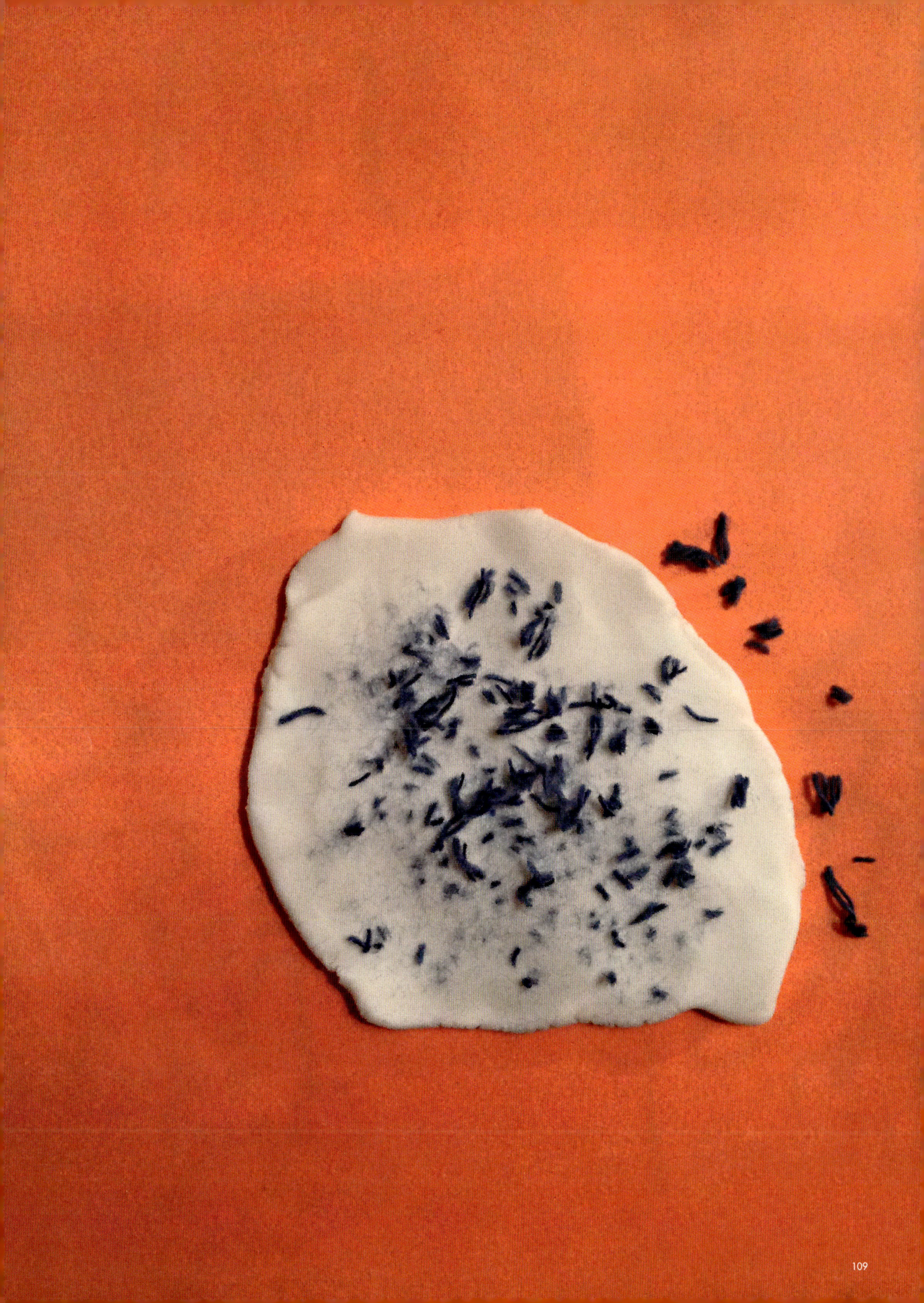

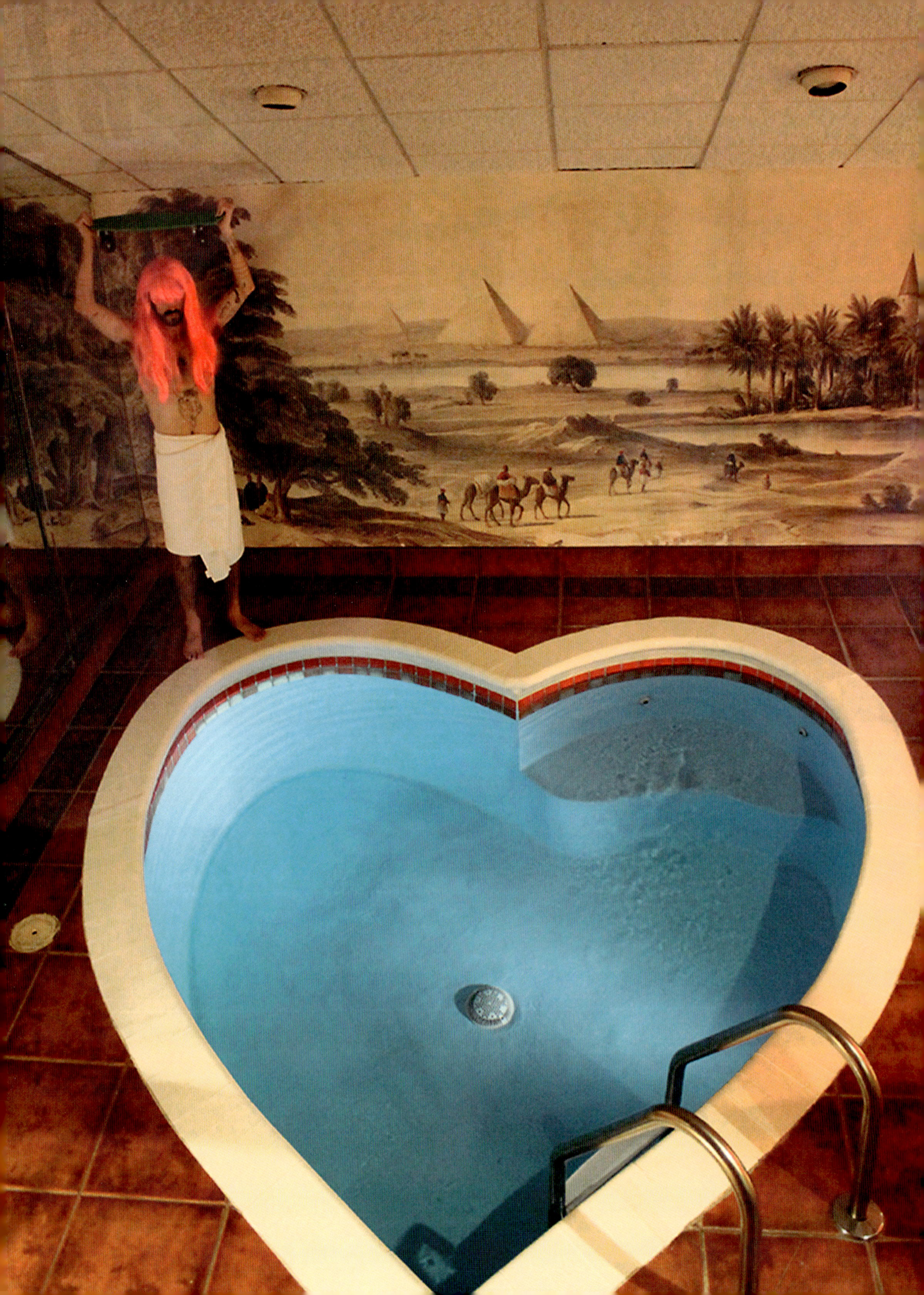

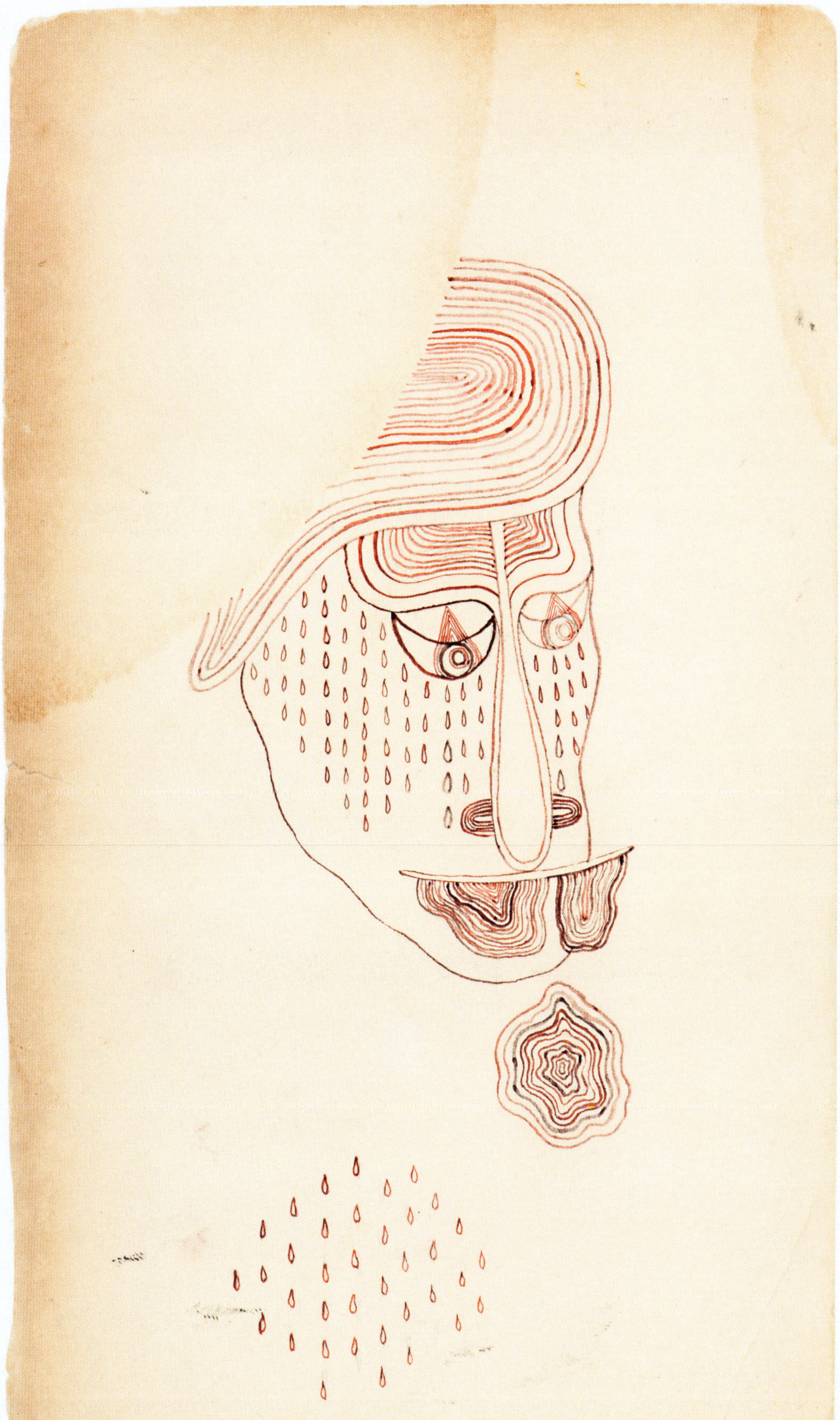

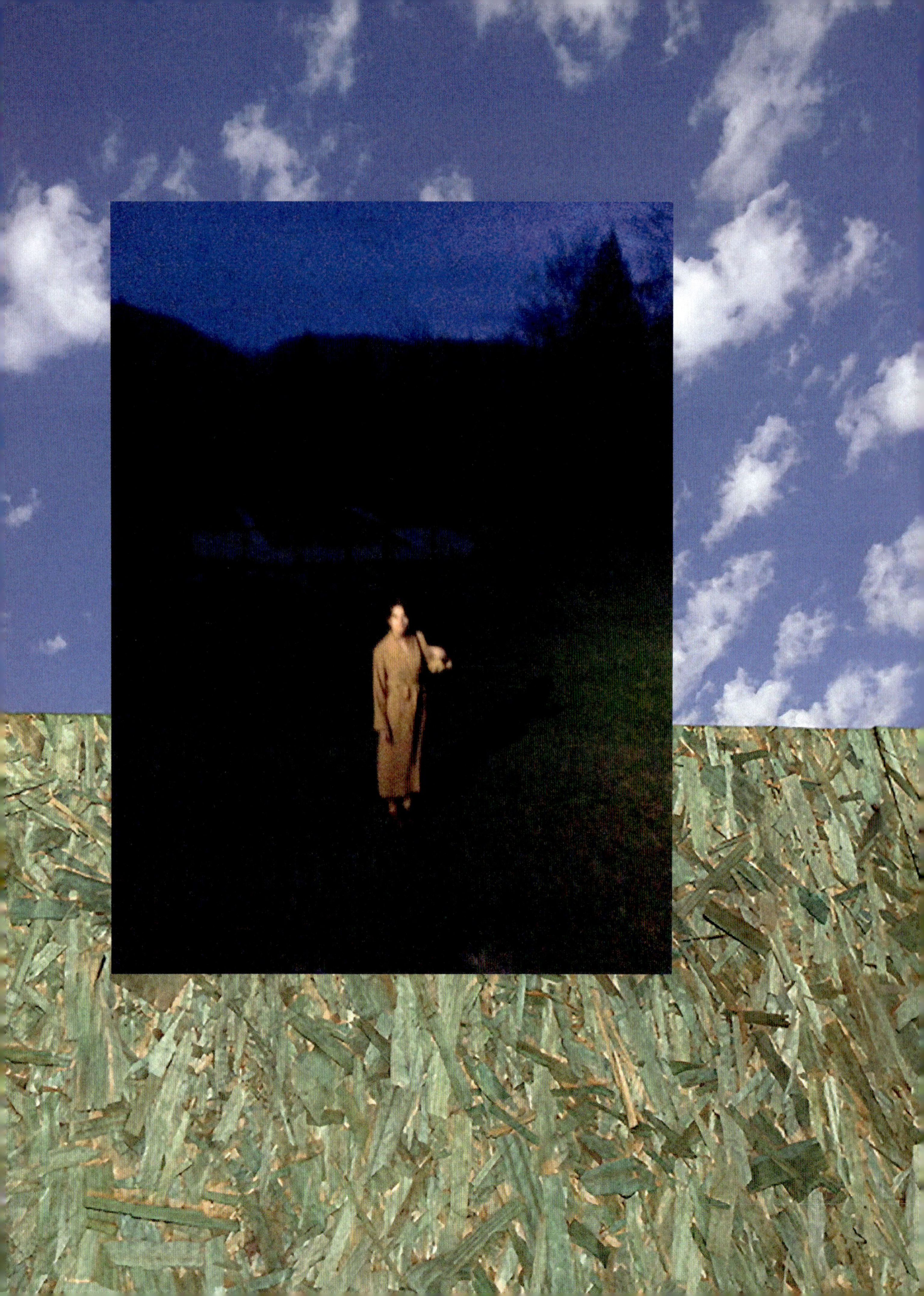

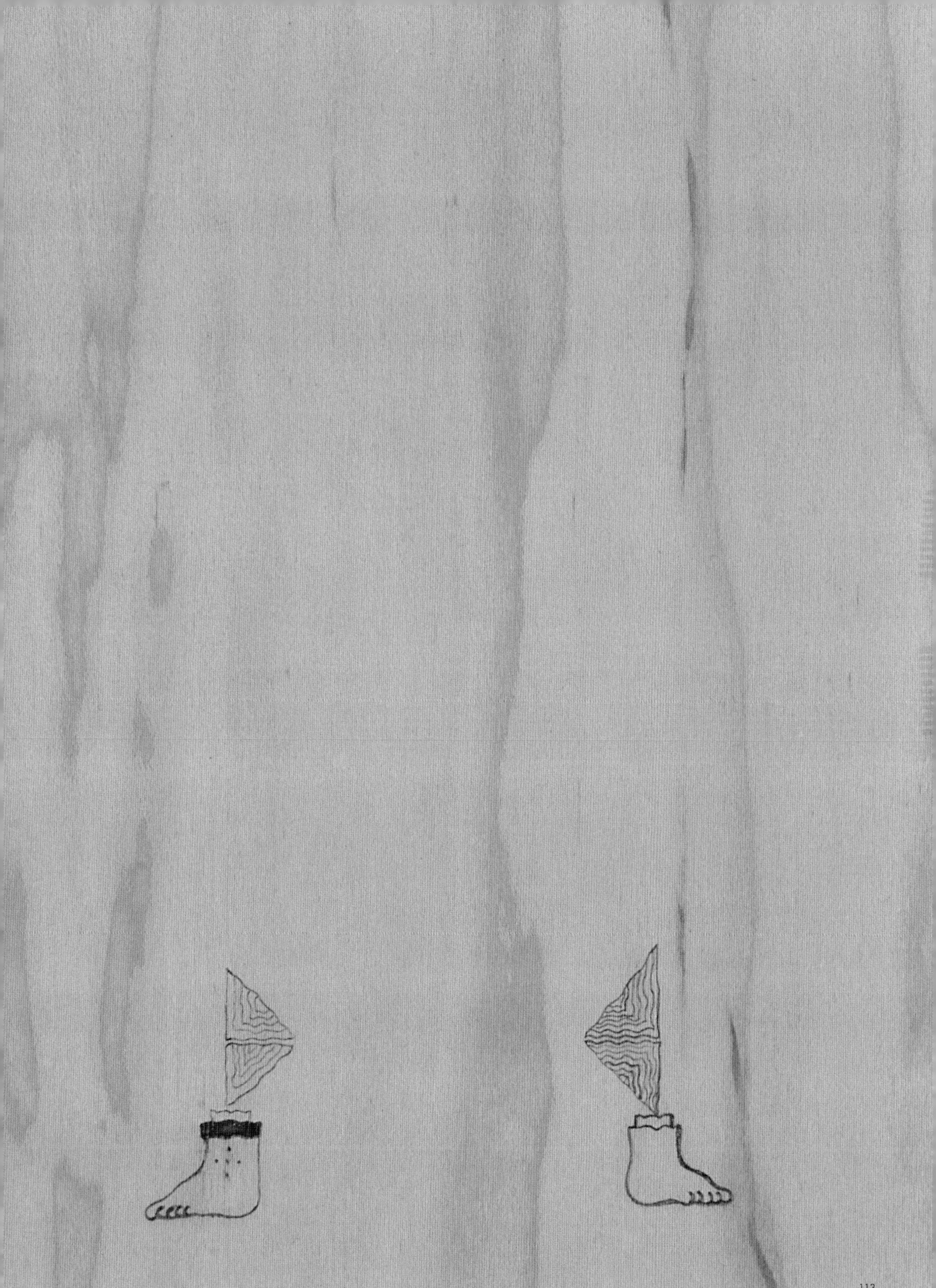

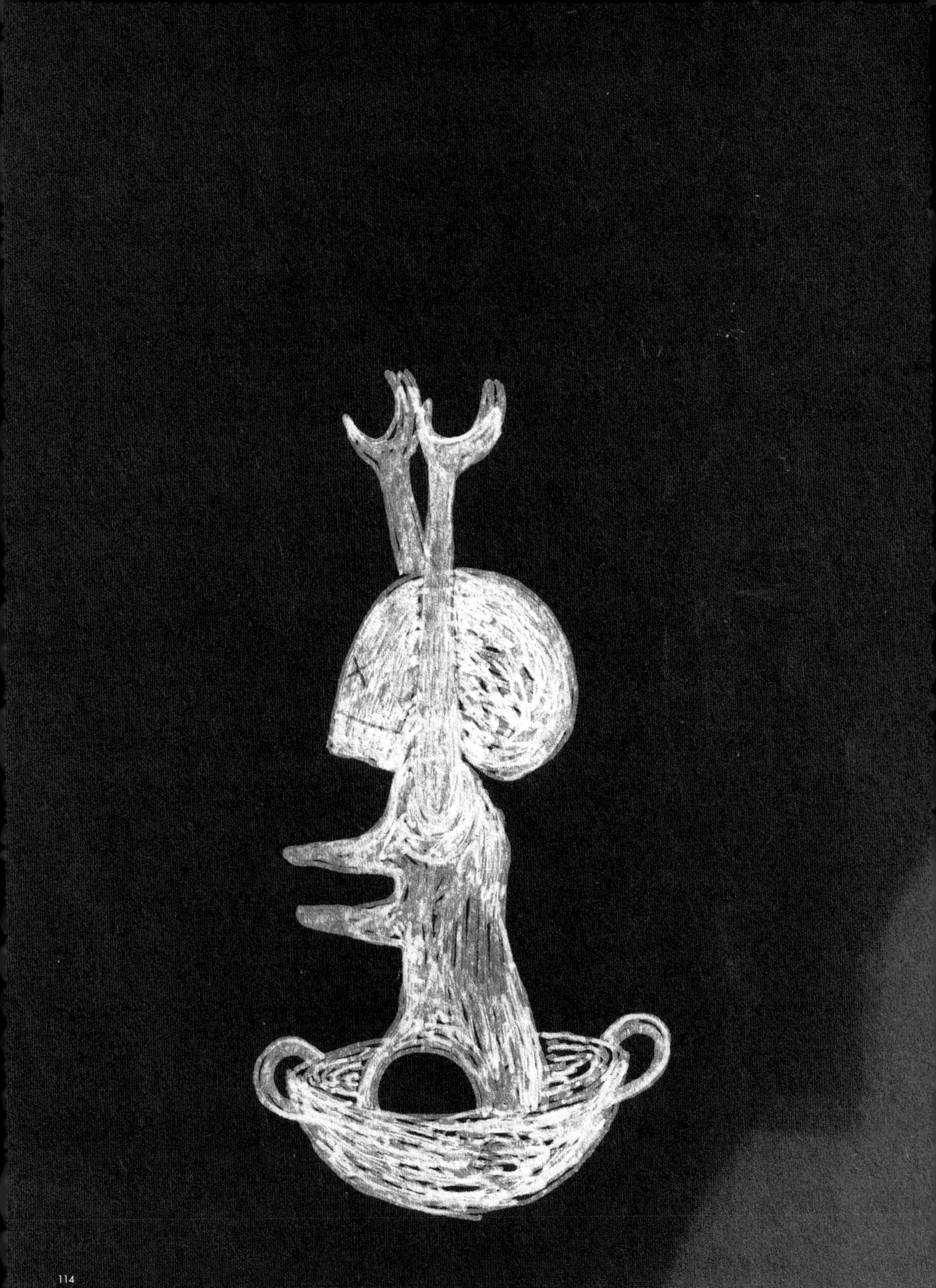

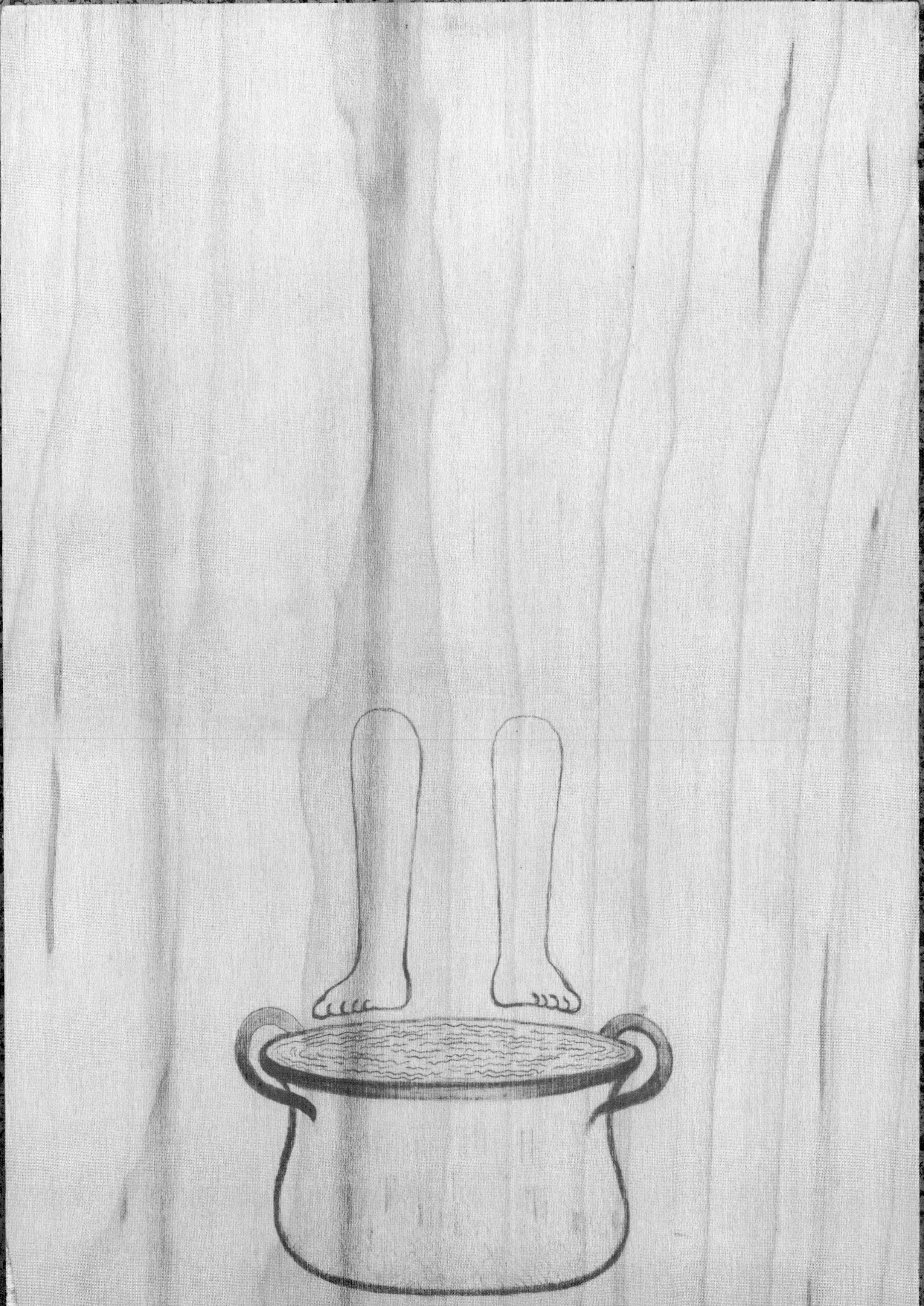

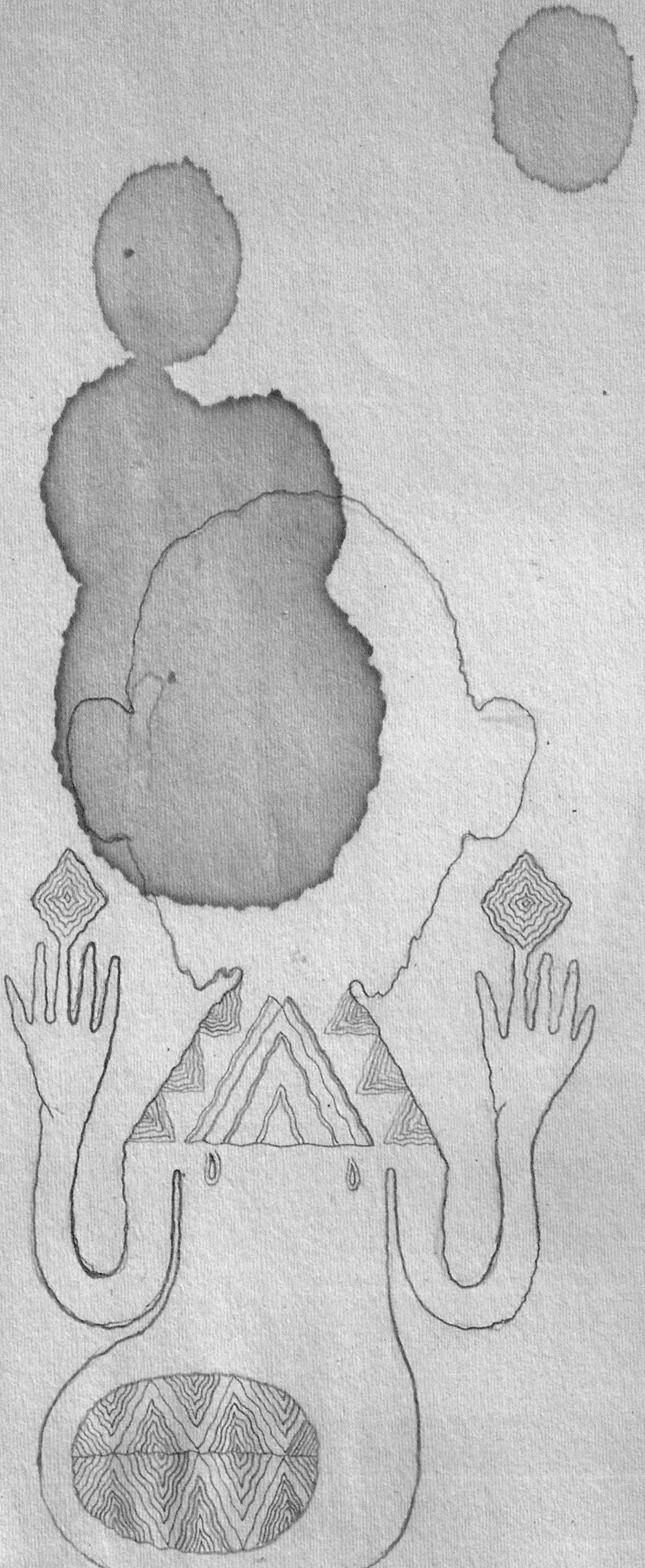

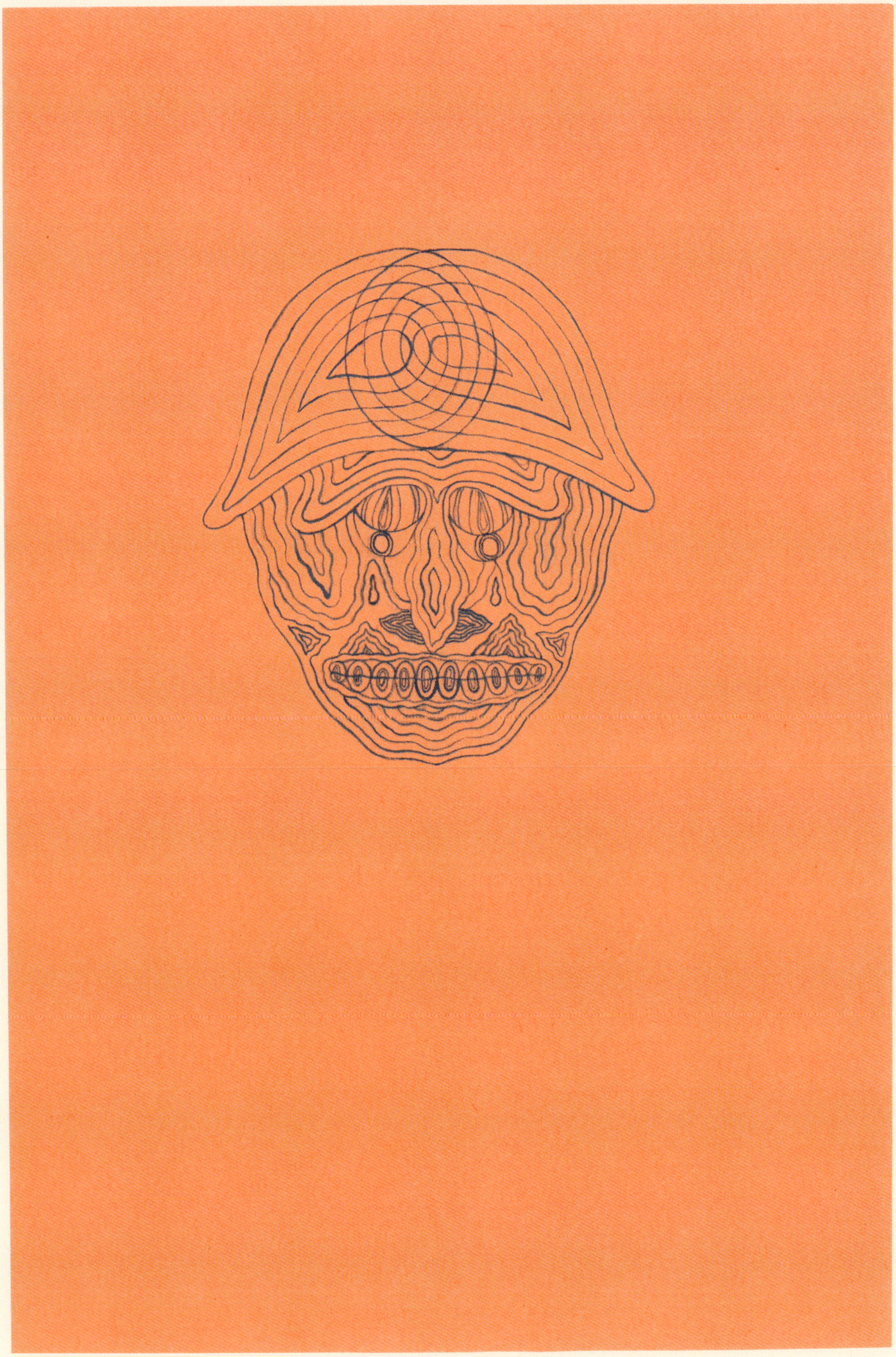

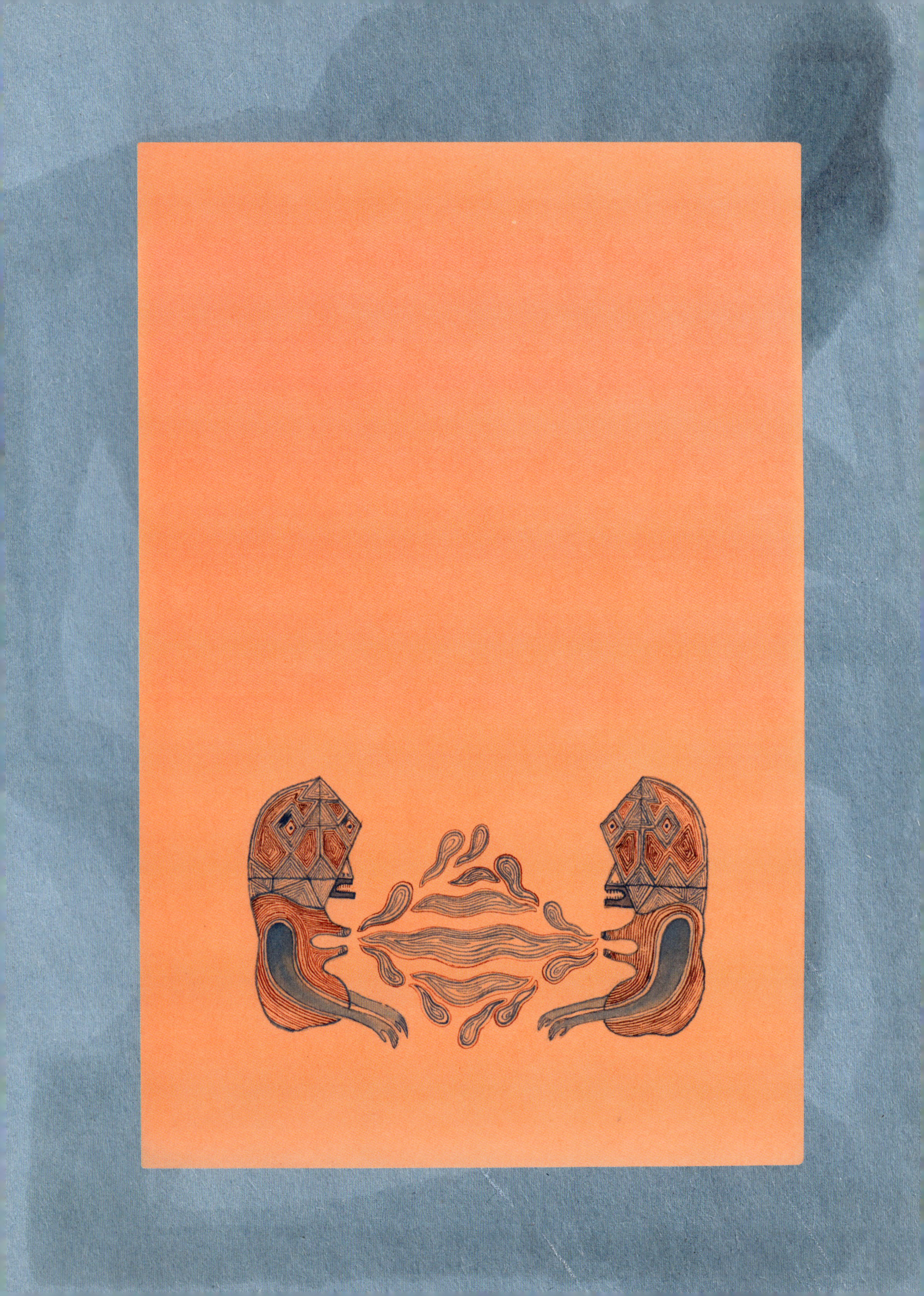

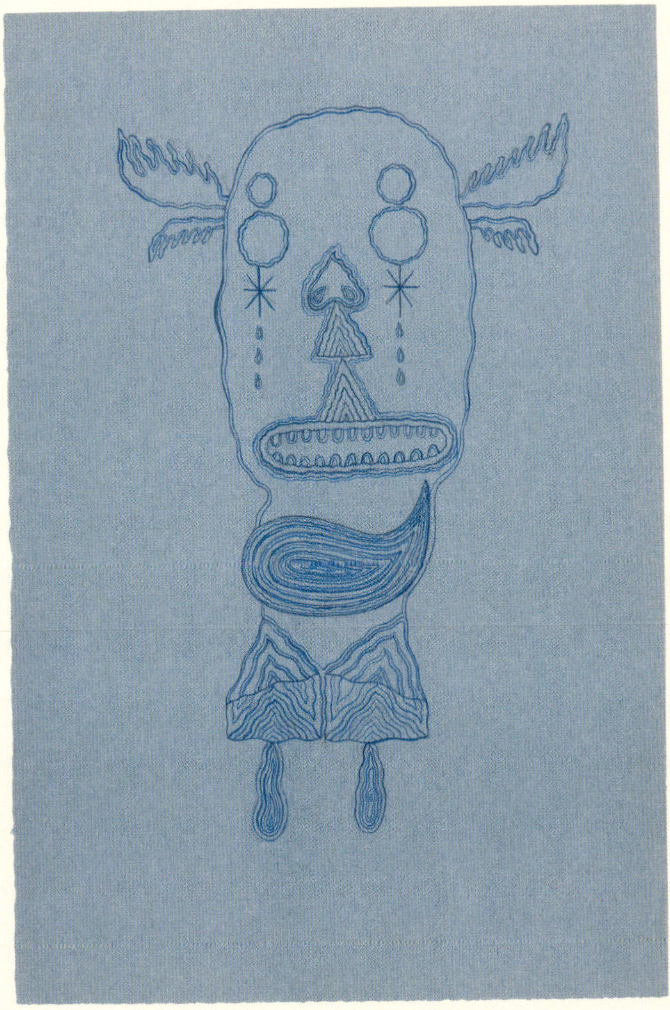

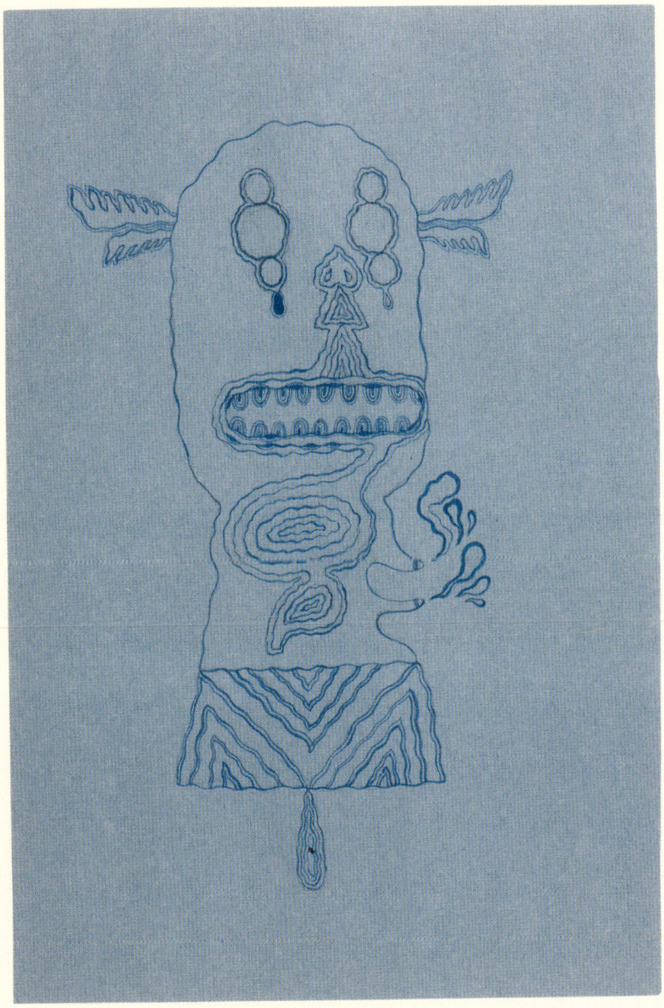

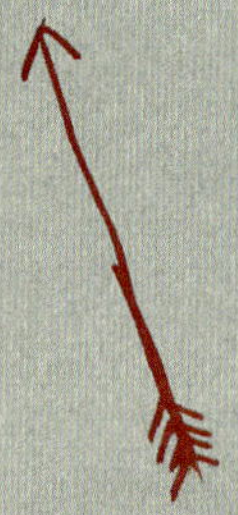

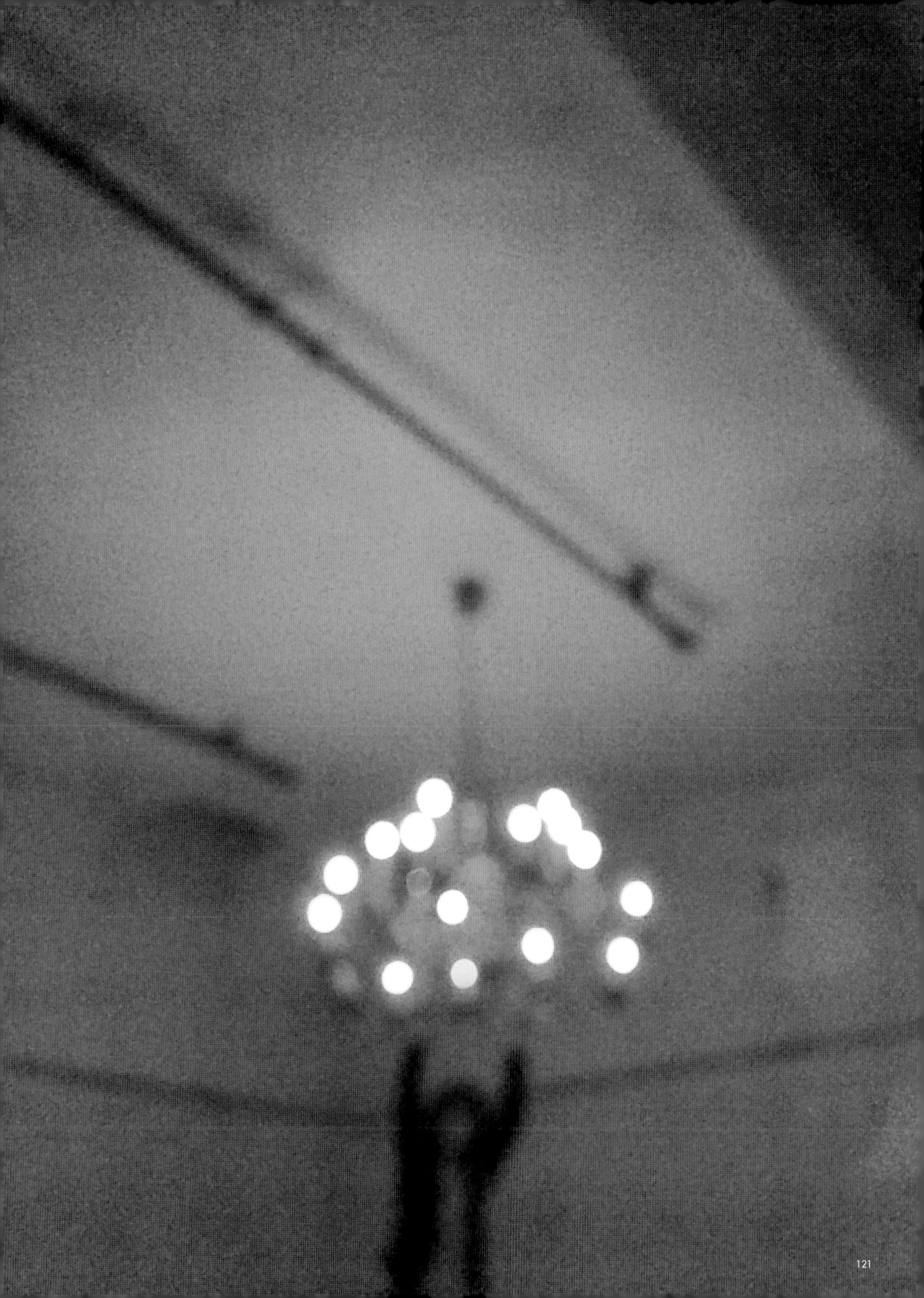

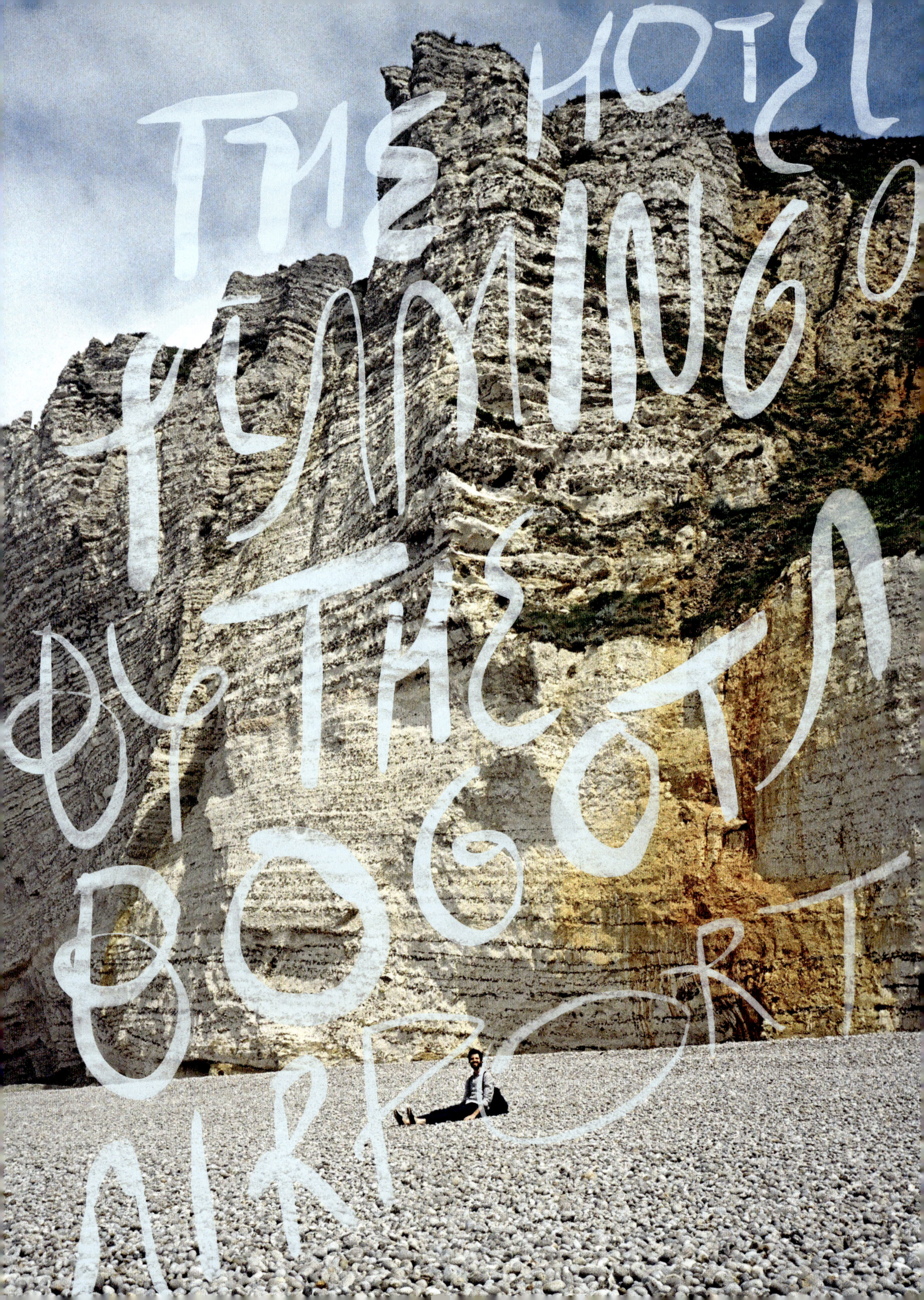
THE HOTEL
FLAMINGO
BY THE
BOGOTA
AIRPORT

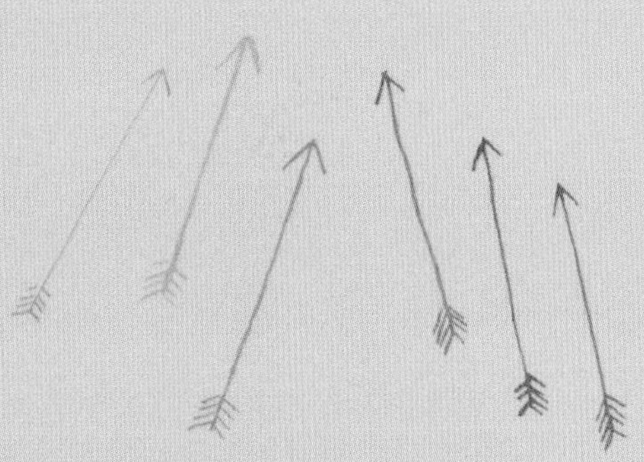

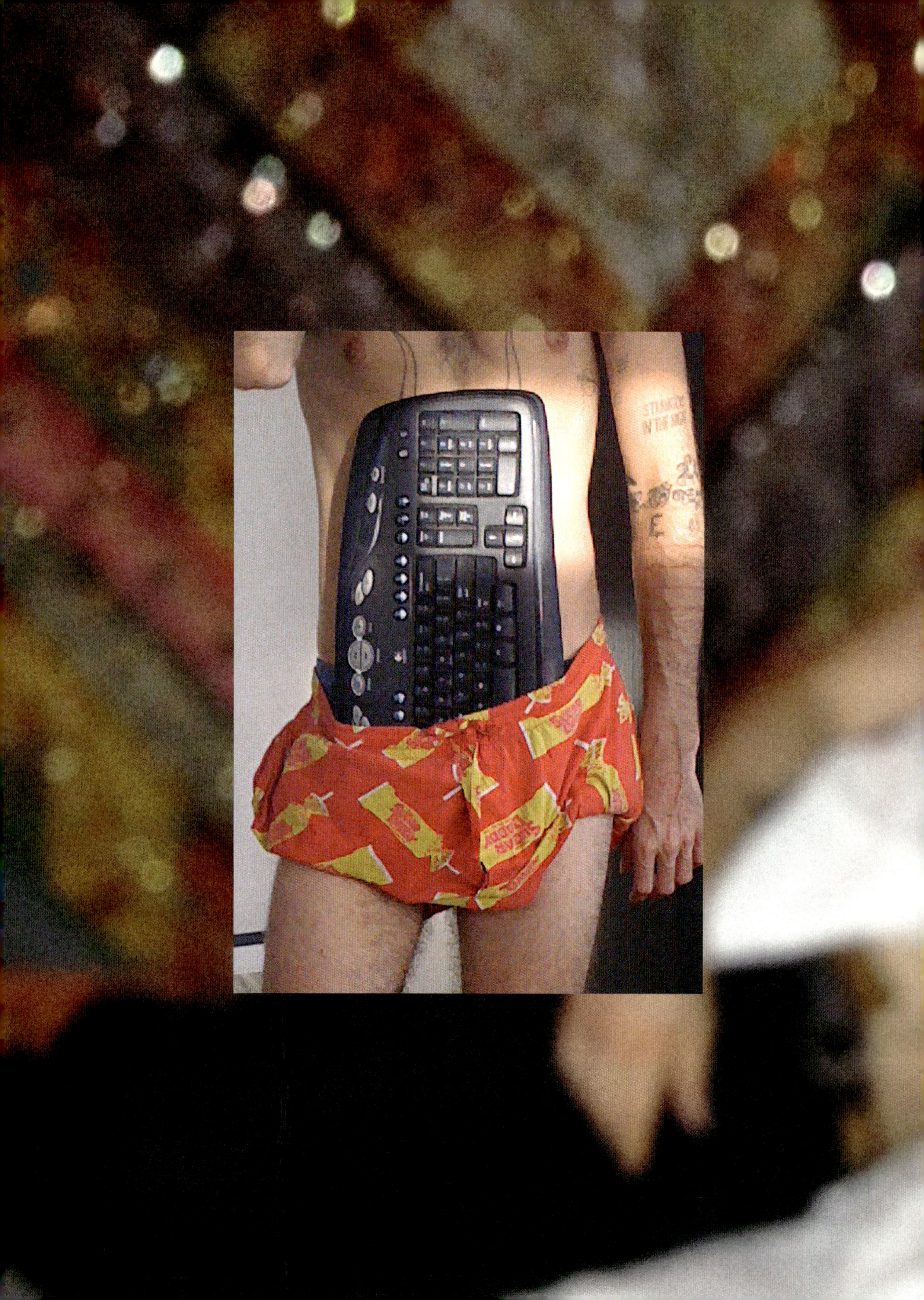

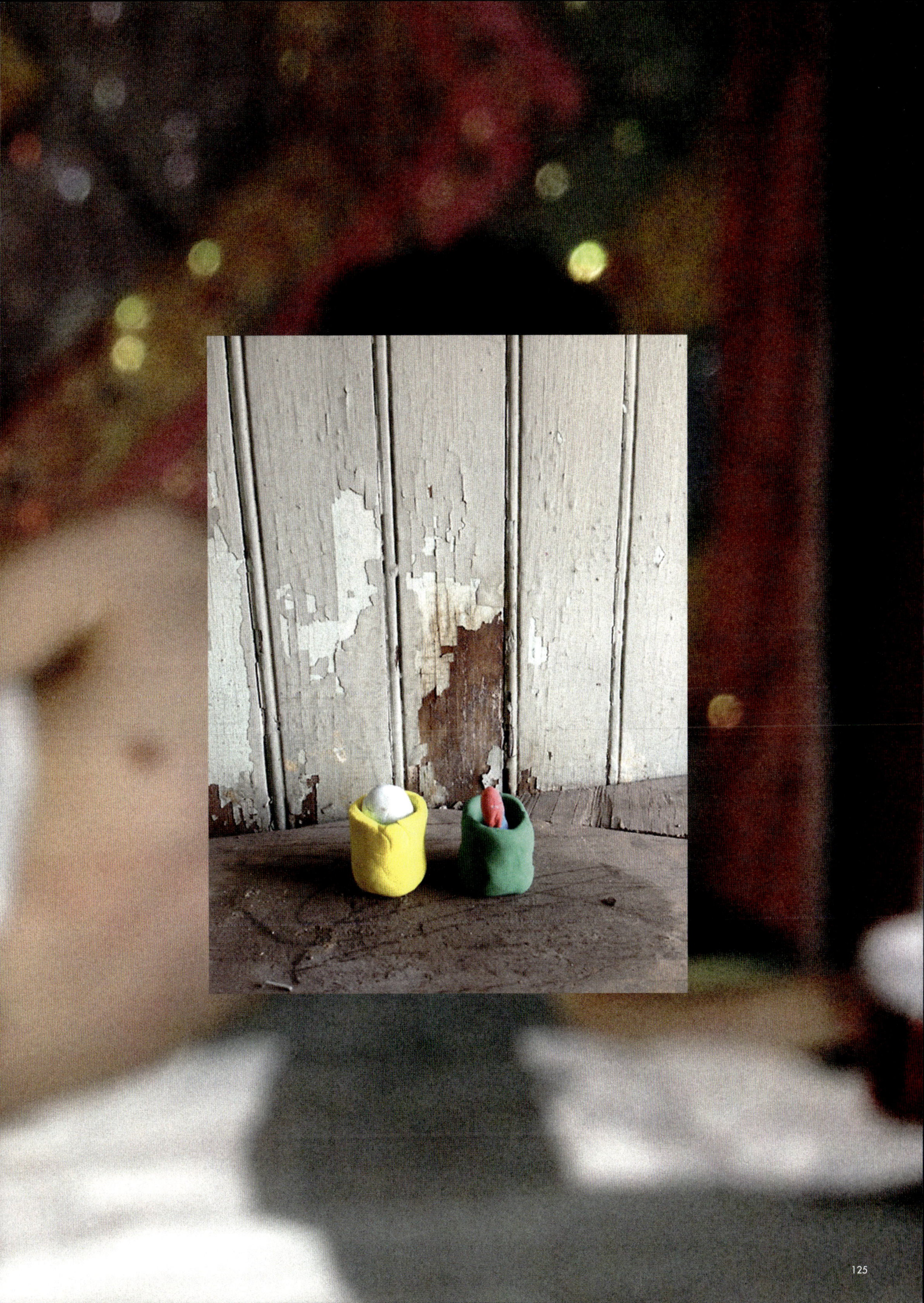

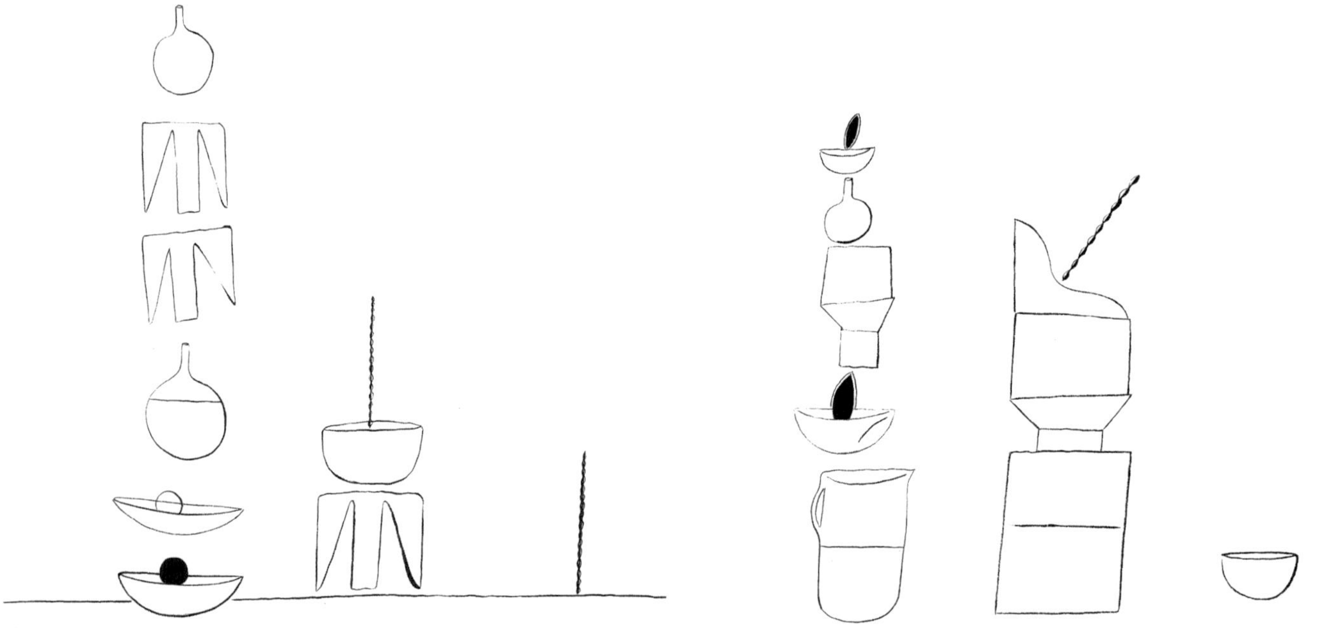

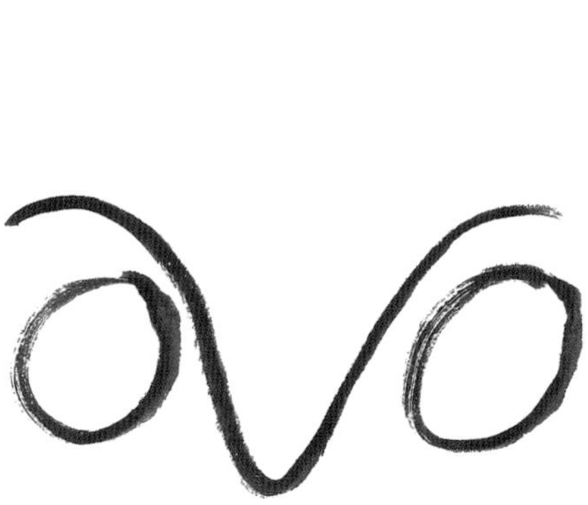

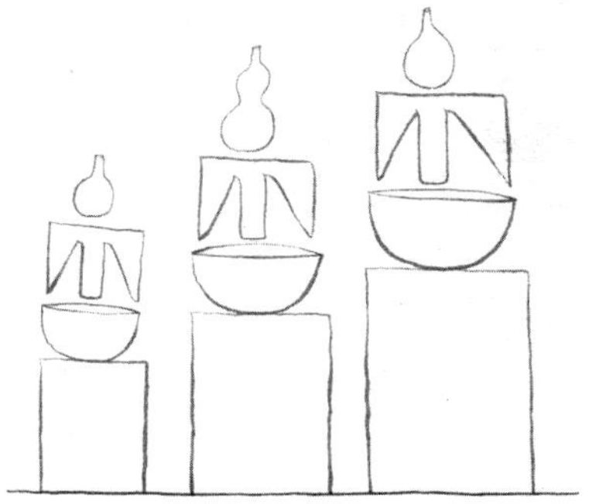
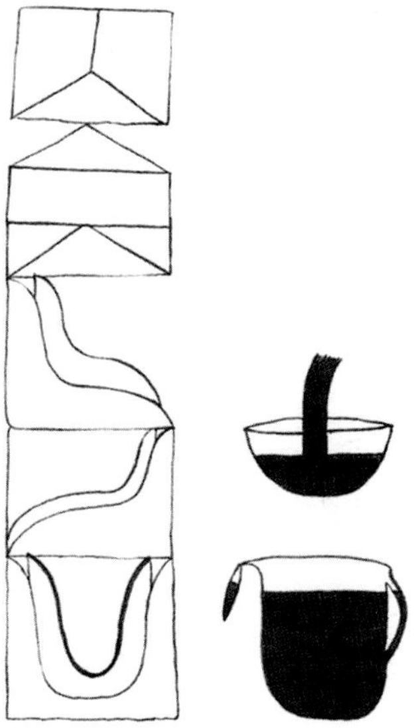
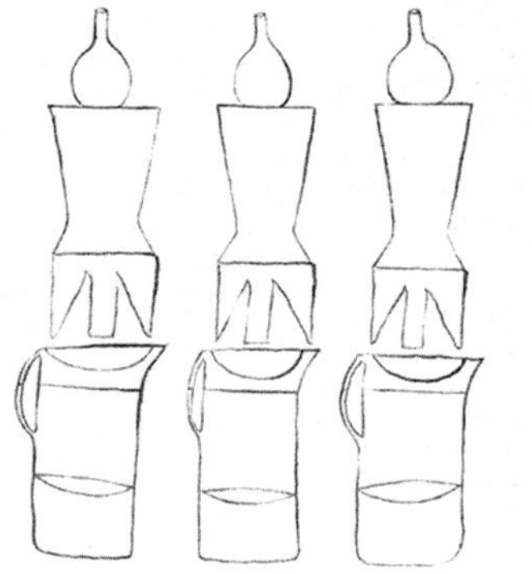
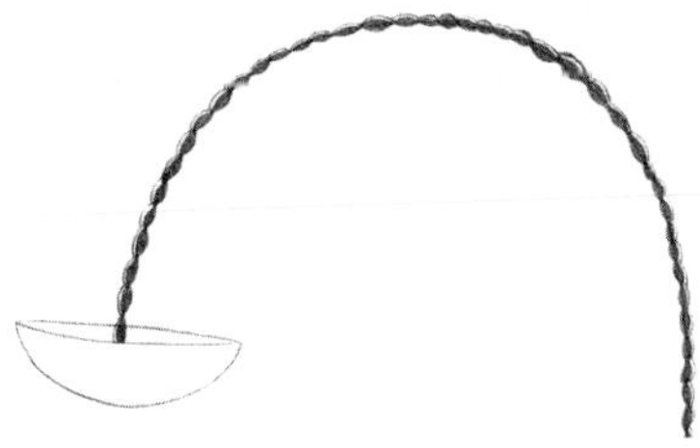
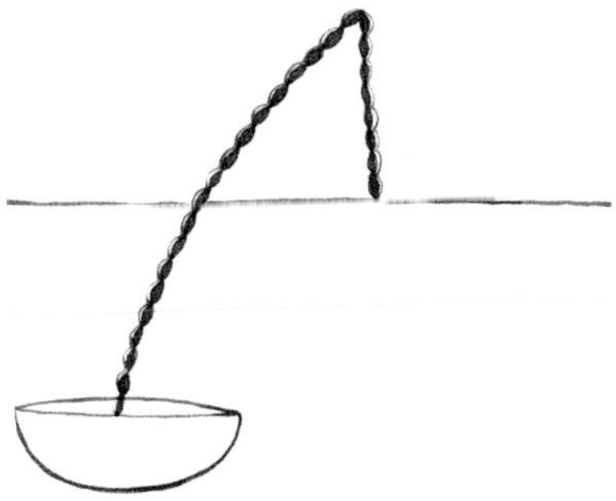
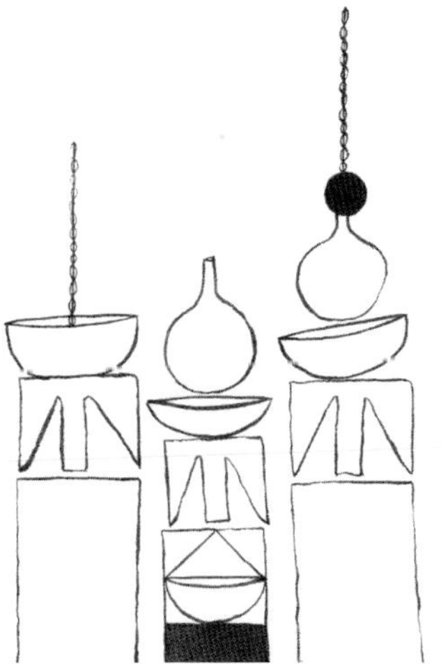
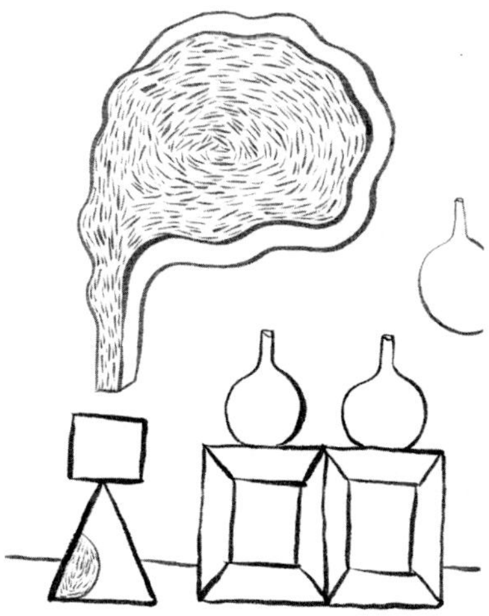
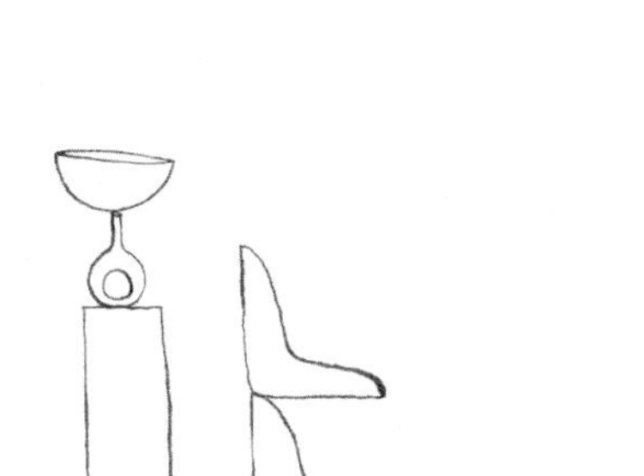
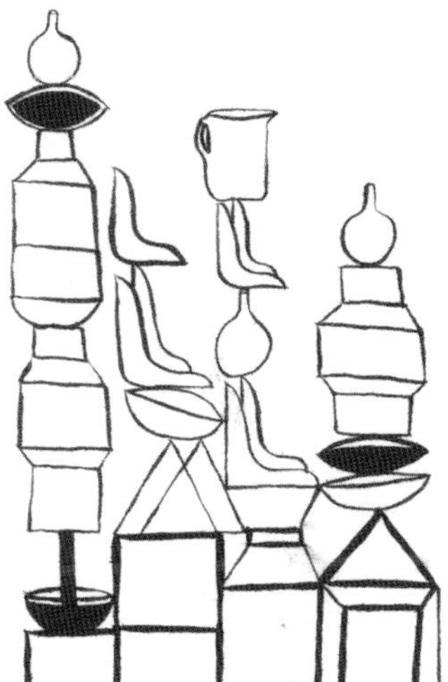

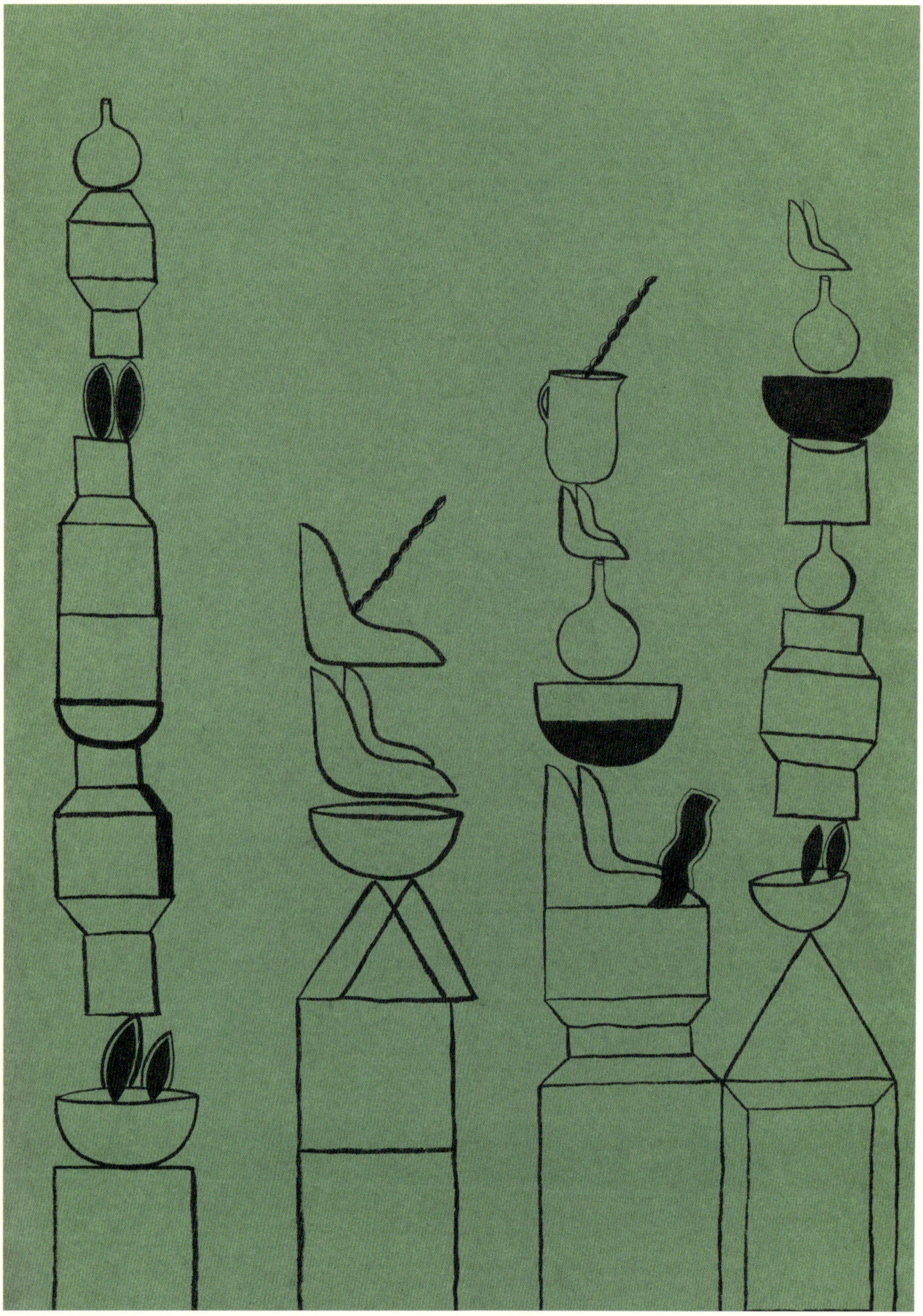

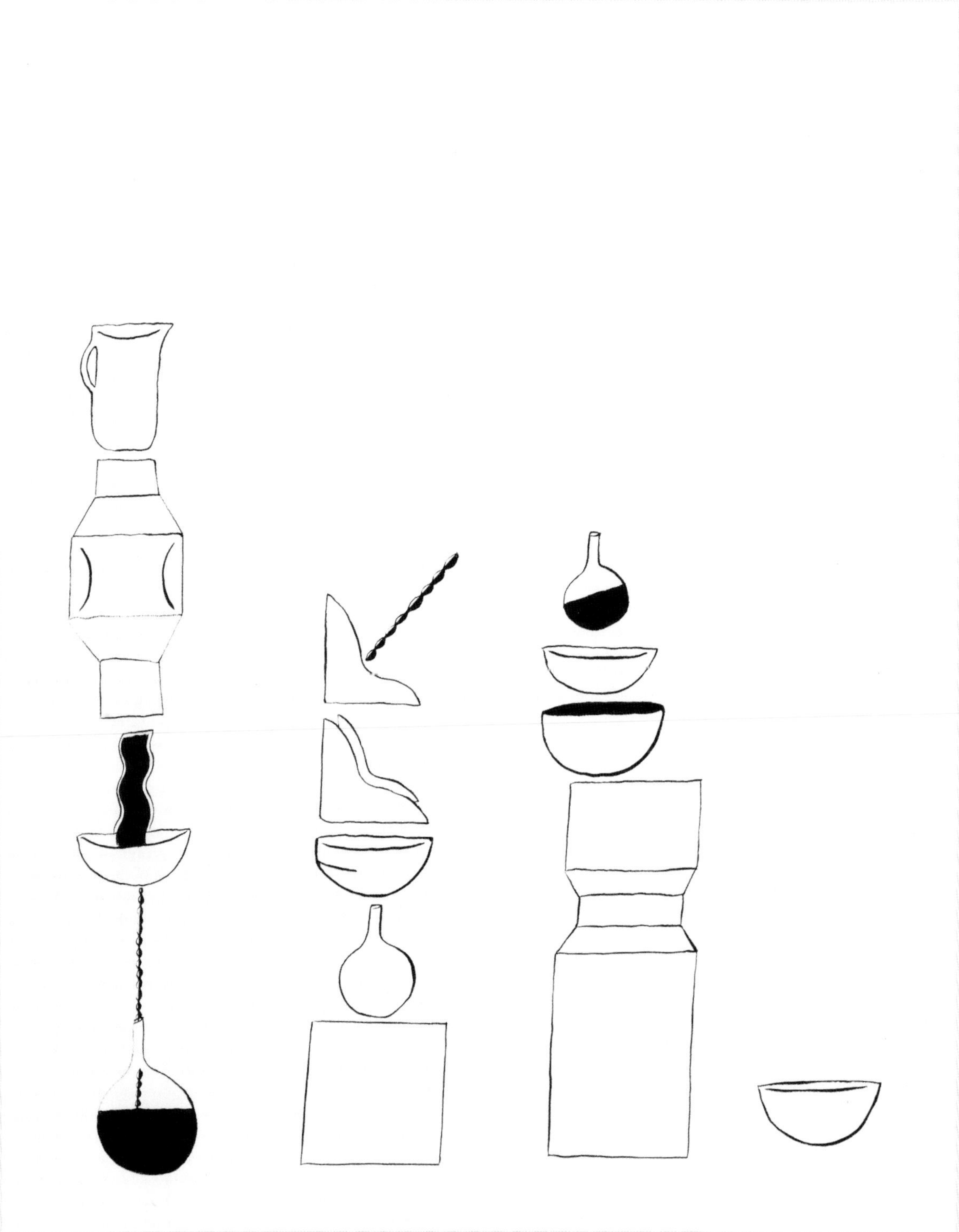

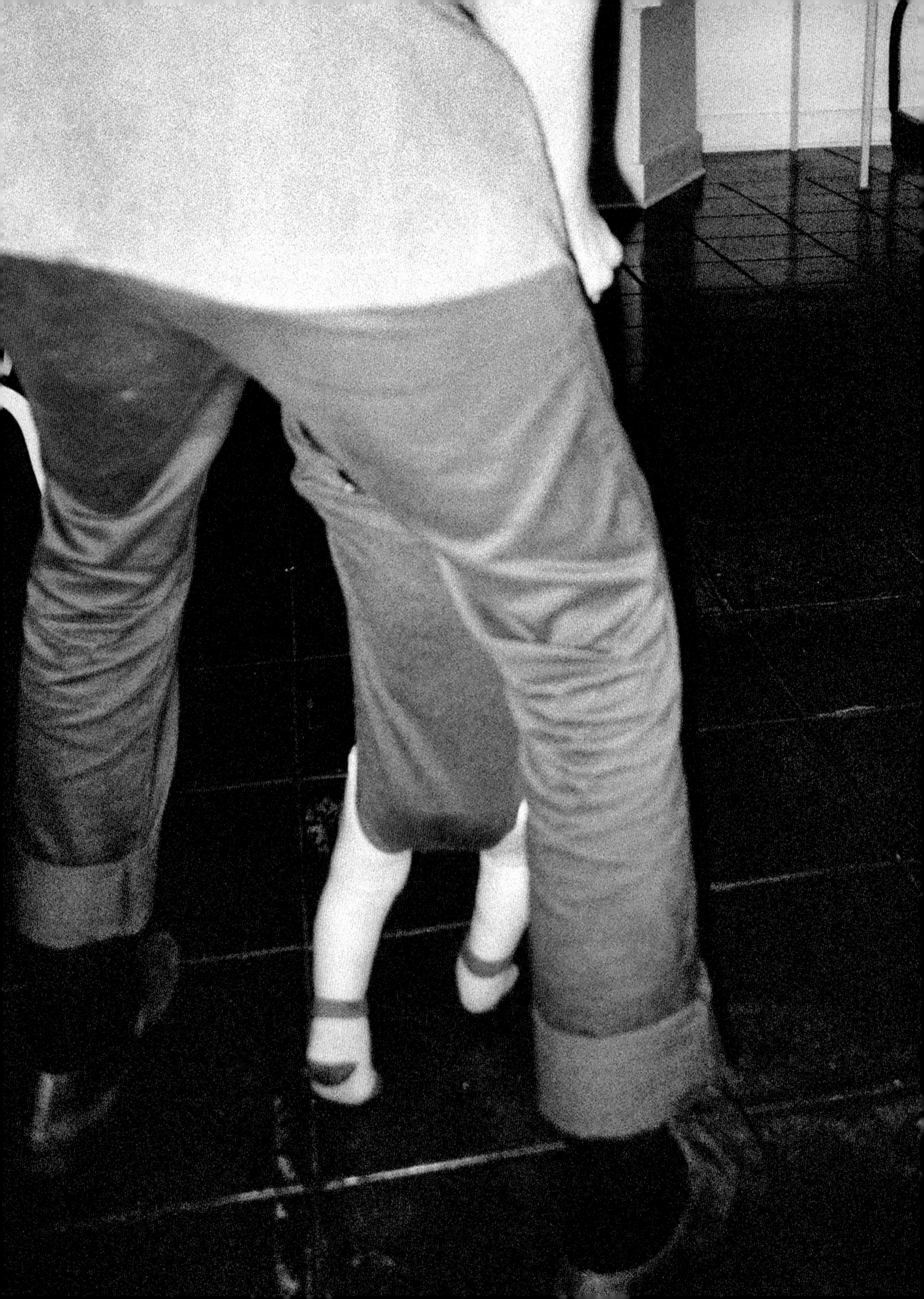

OH TO BE TREEMAN
SINGING SONGS GIVEN
BACK BY THE WINDS
WHAT JOY
OF NO MAN

- UNKNOWN JAPANESE
POET

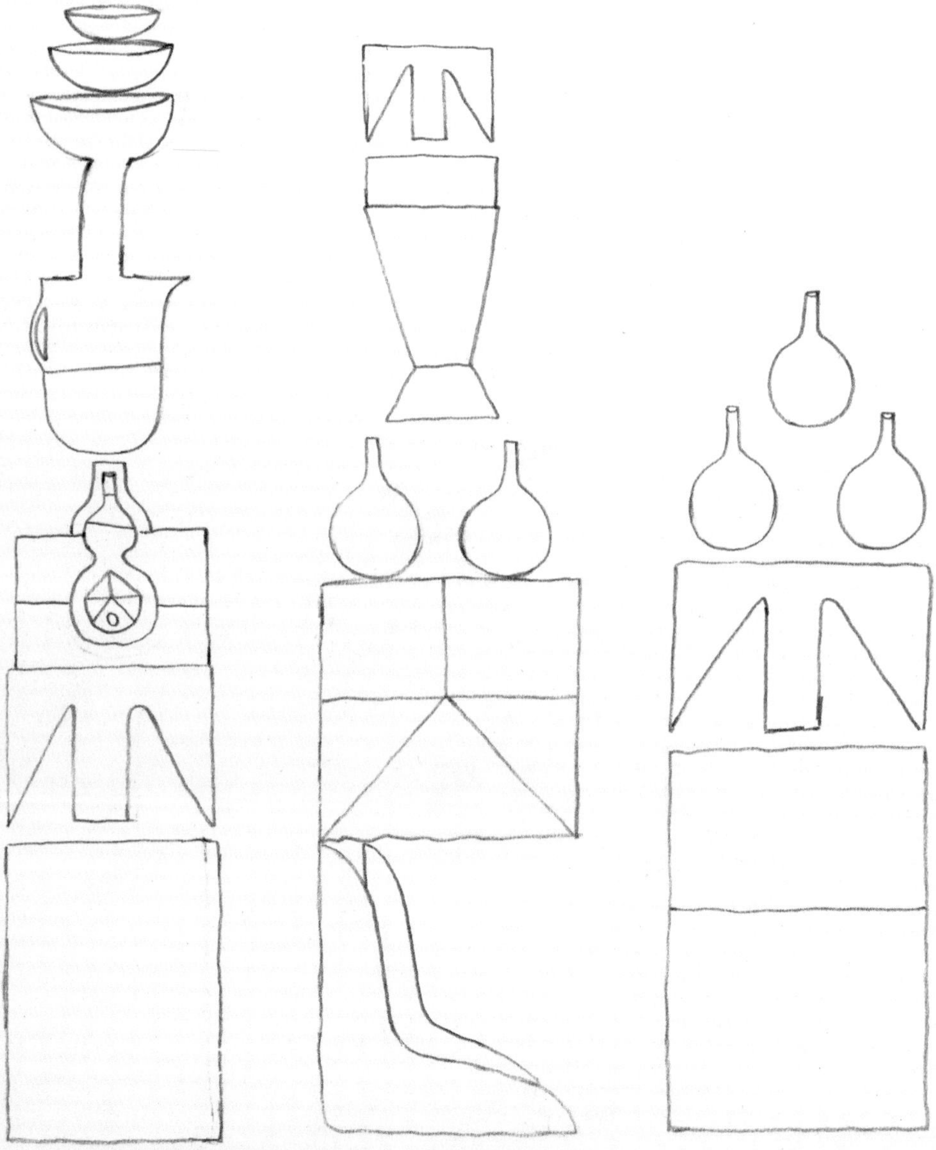

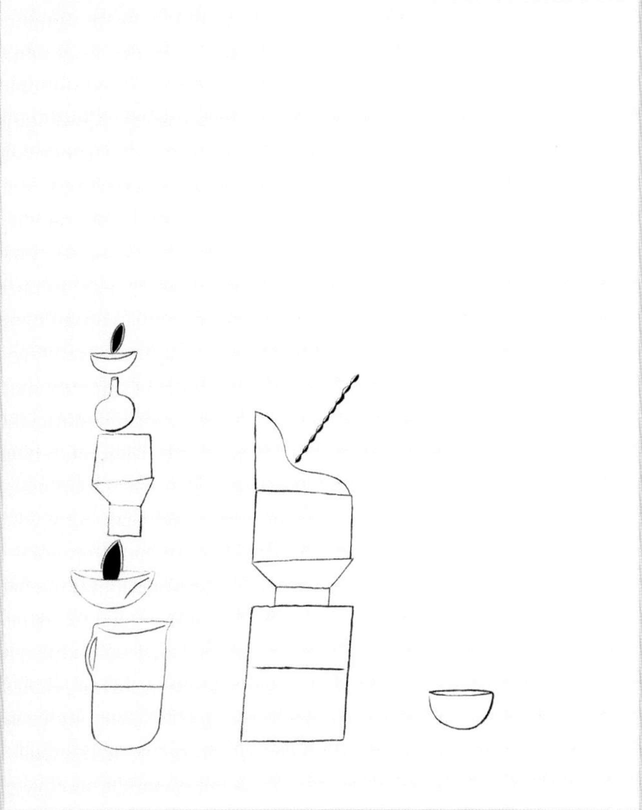

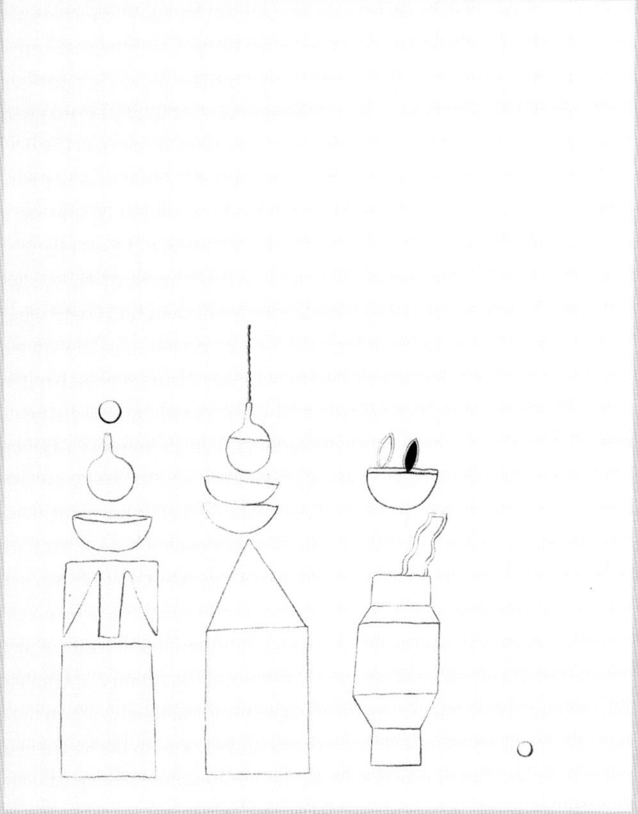

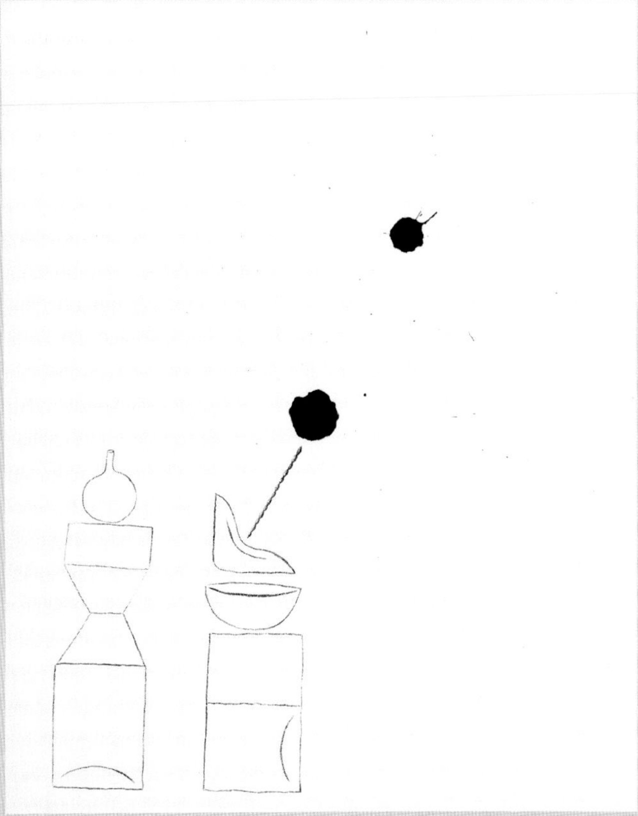

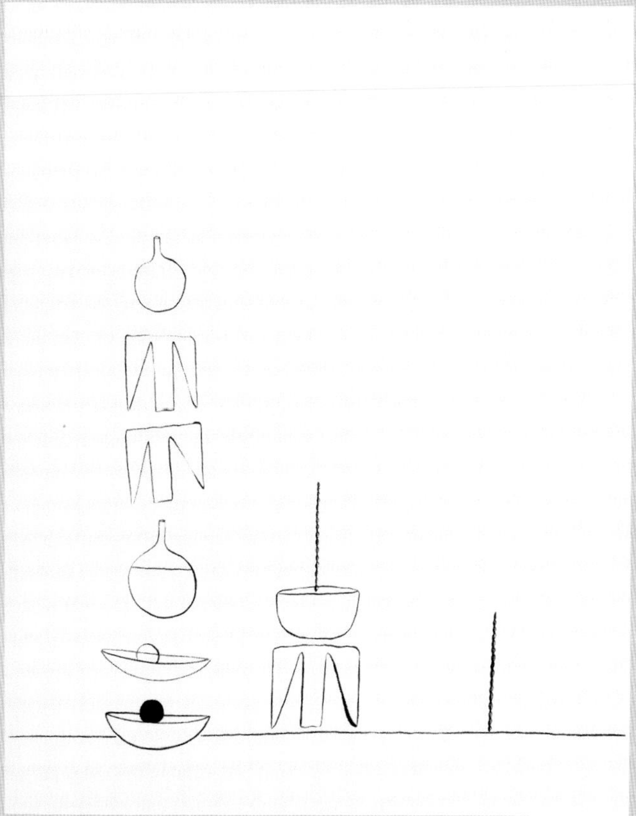

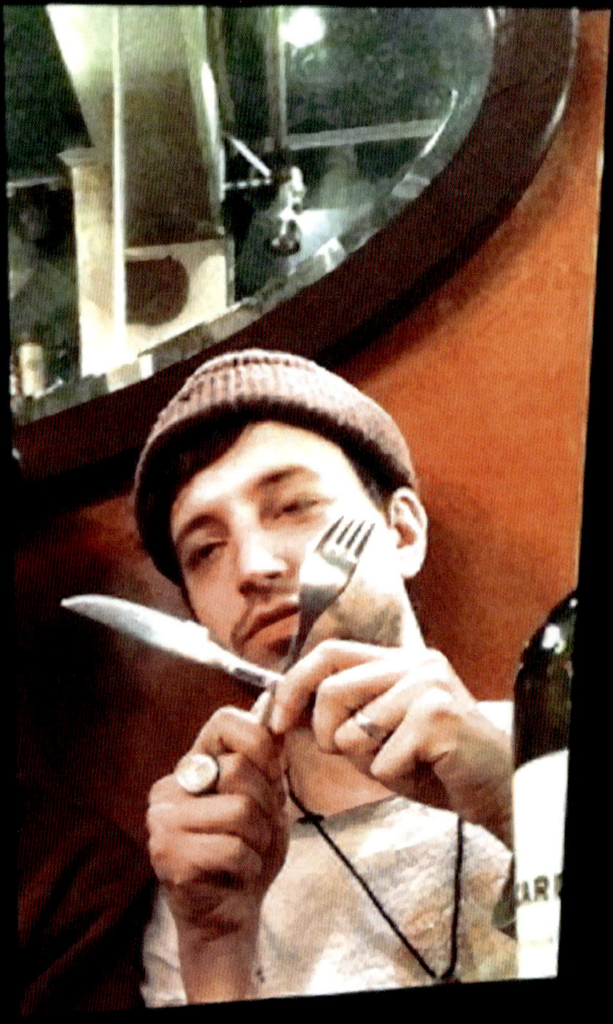

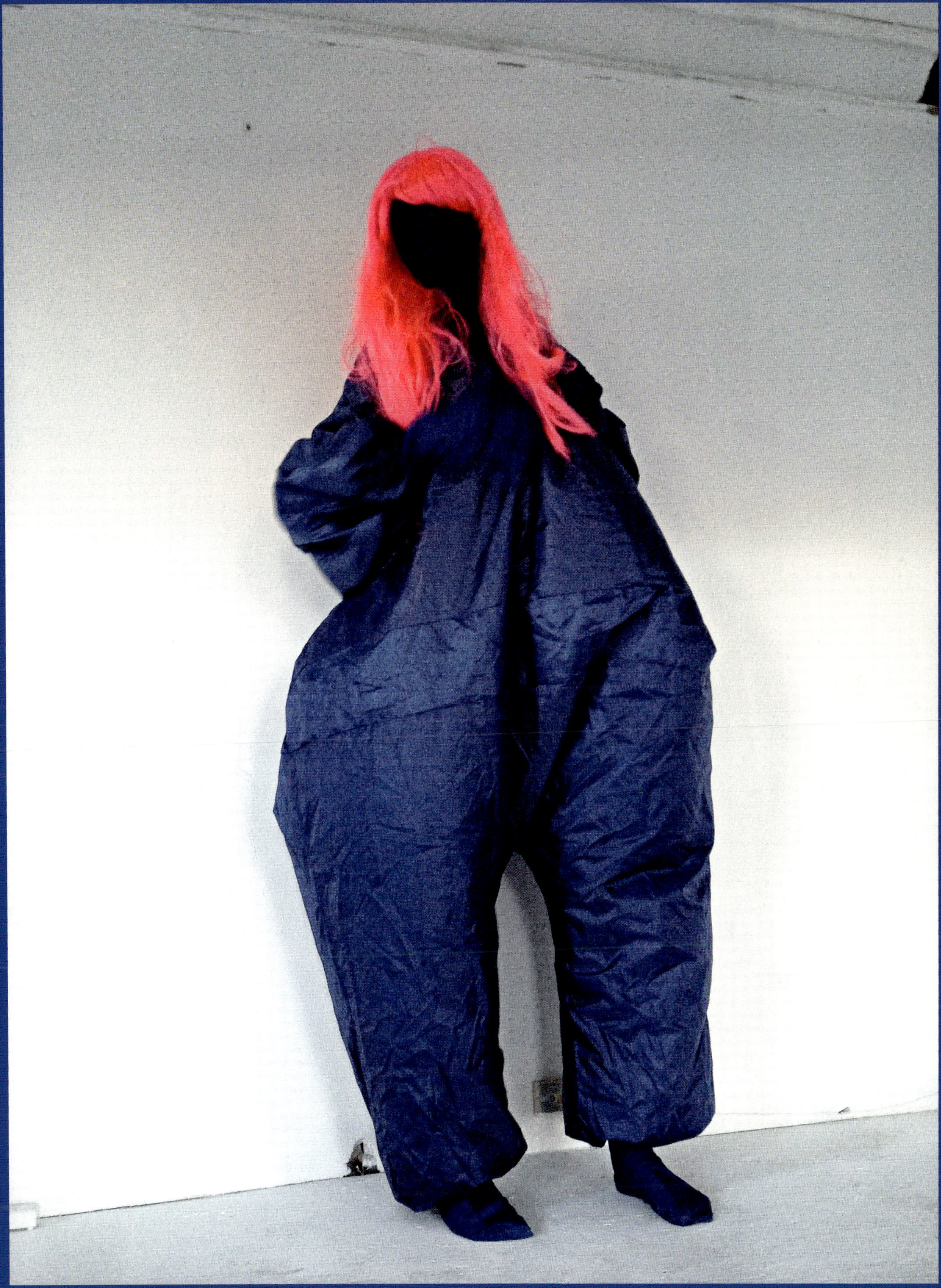

Portraits and
a self-portrait

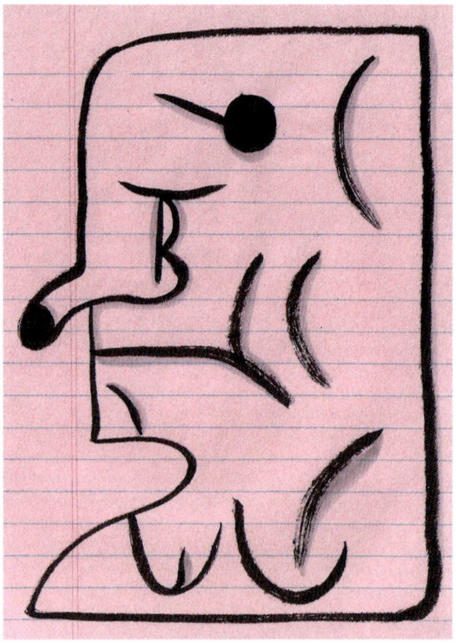

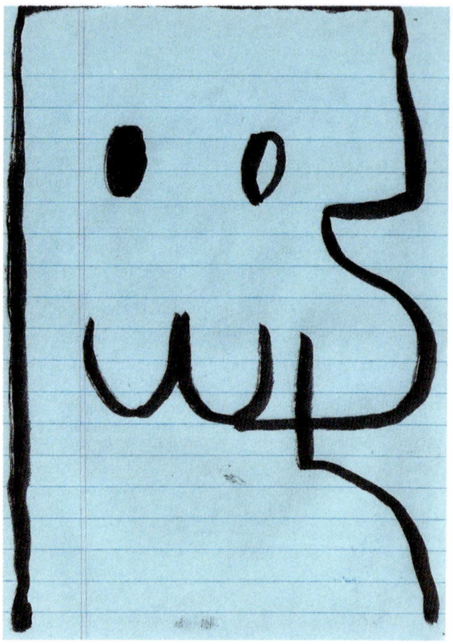

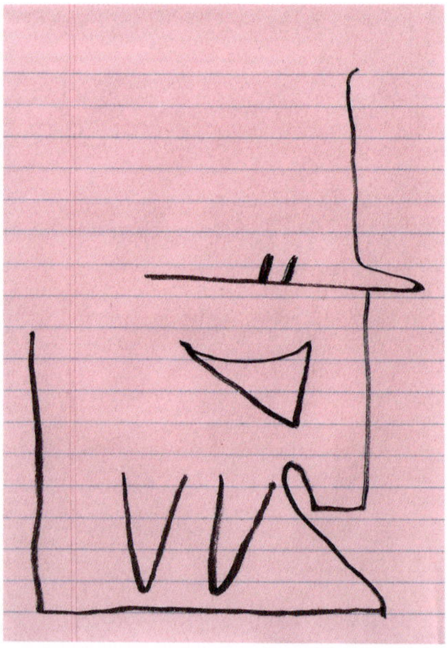

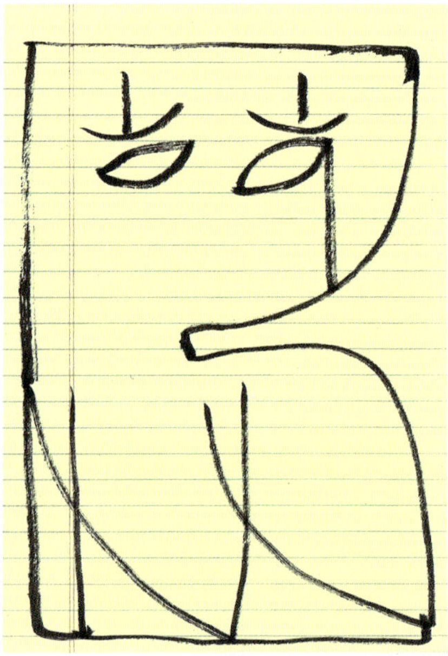

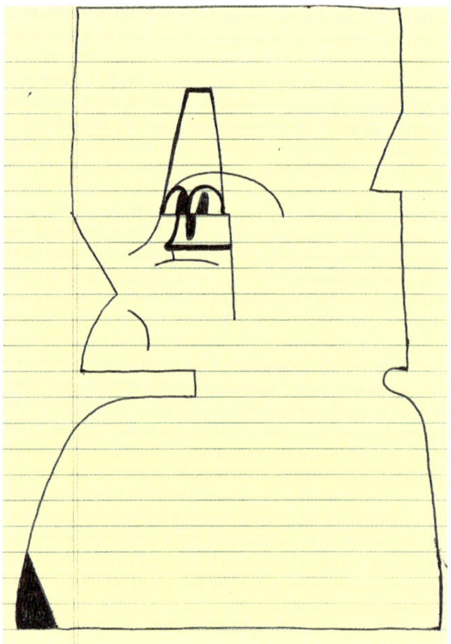

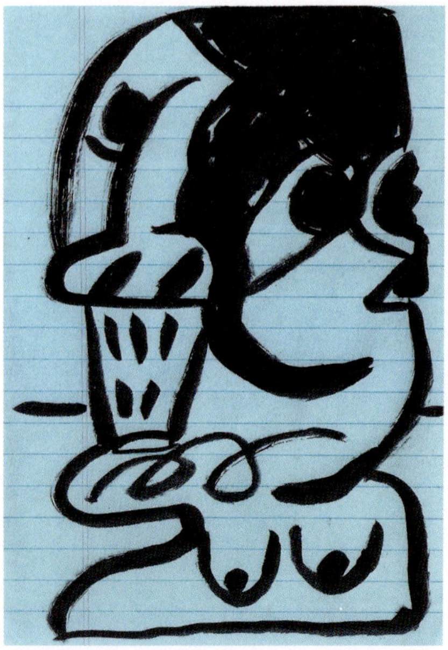

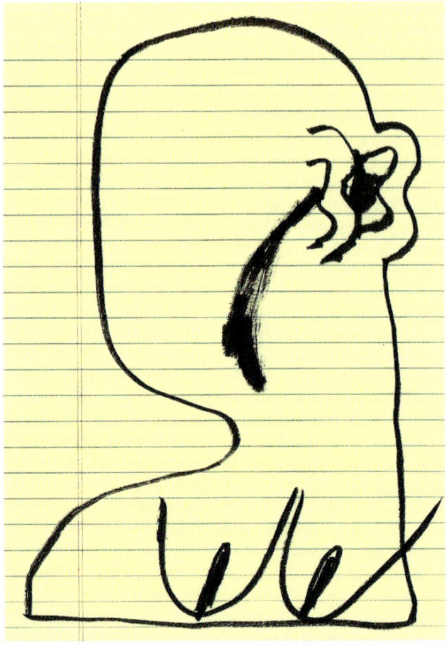

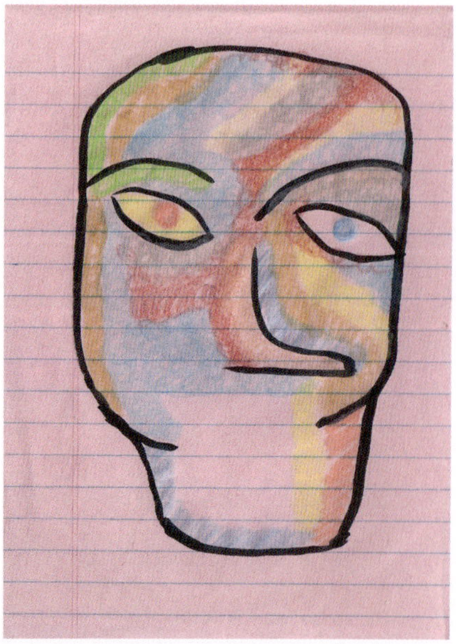

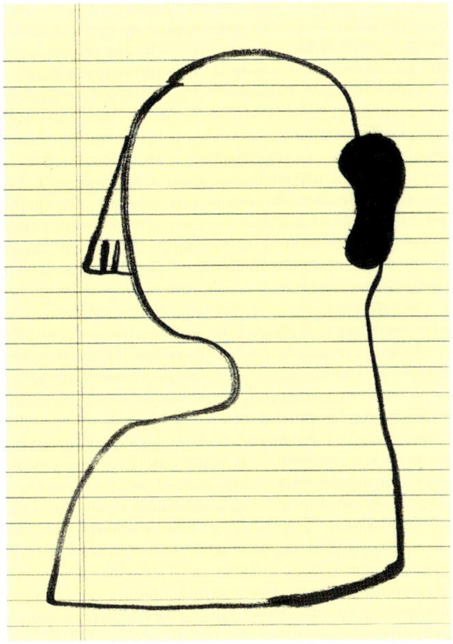
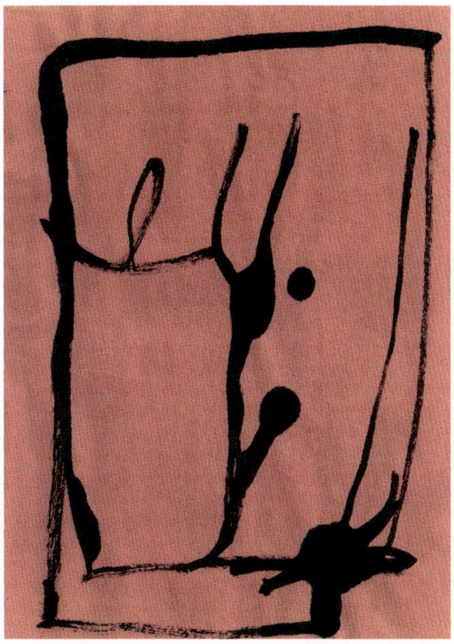
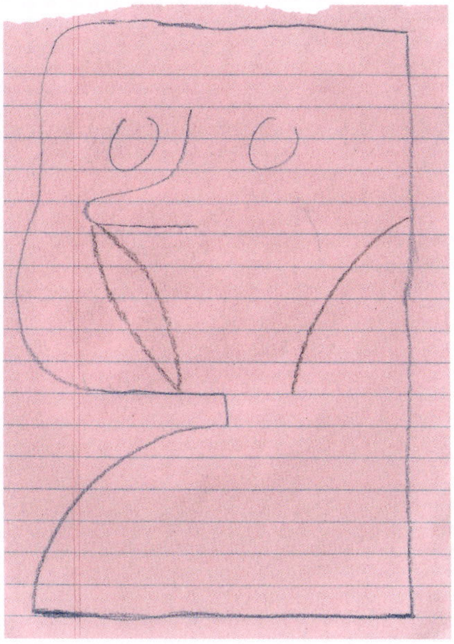
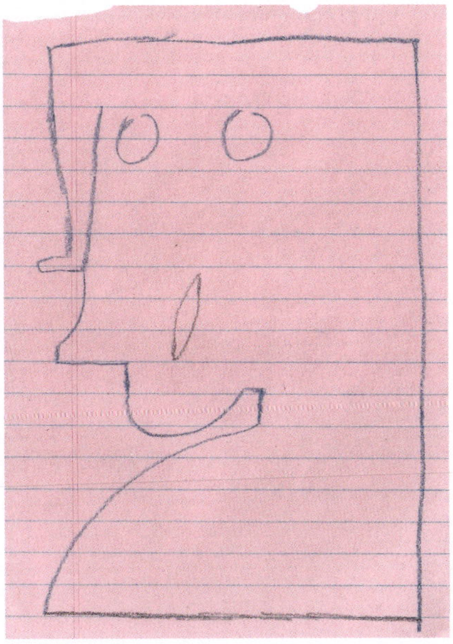
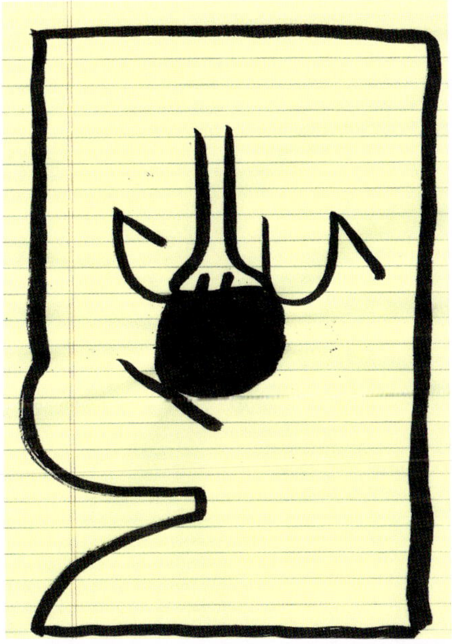
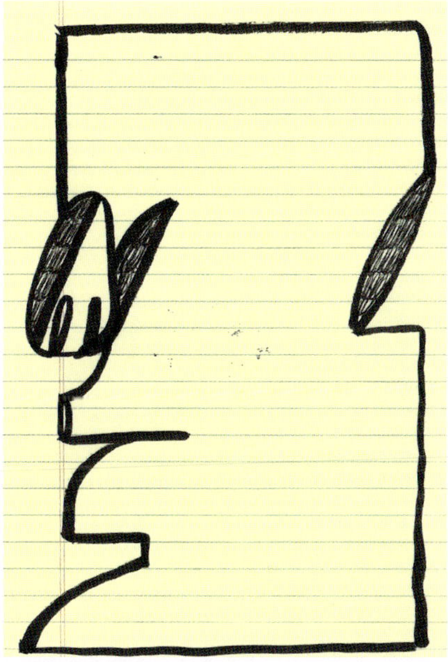
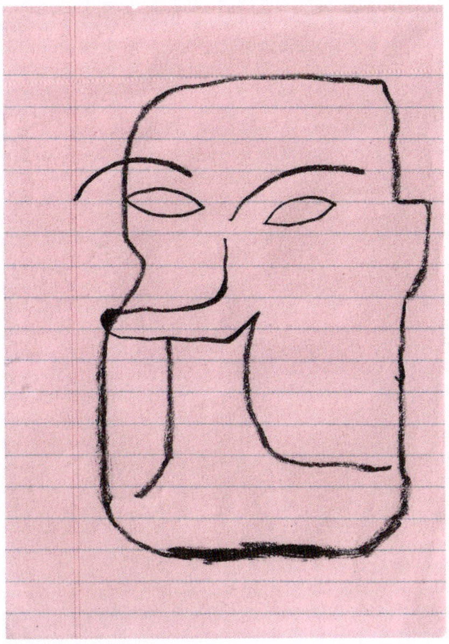
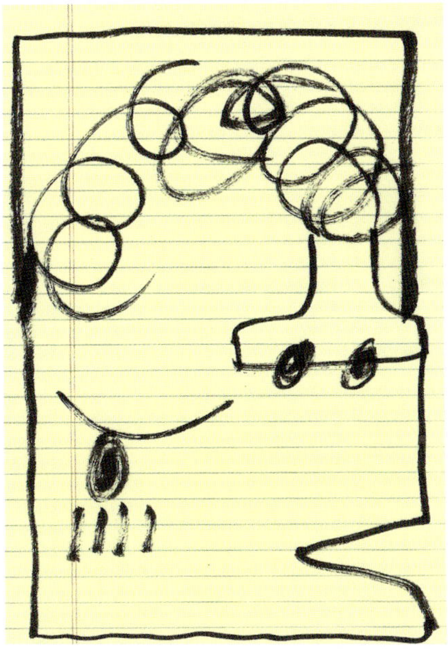
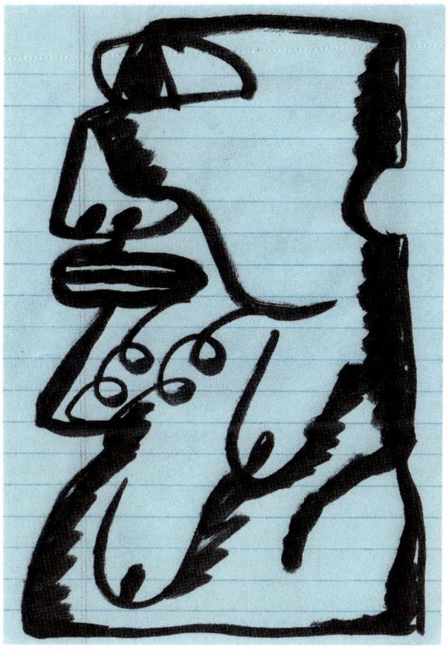

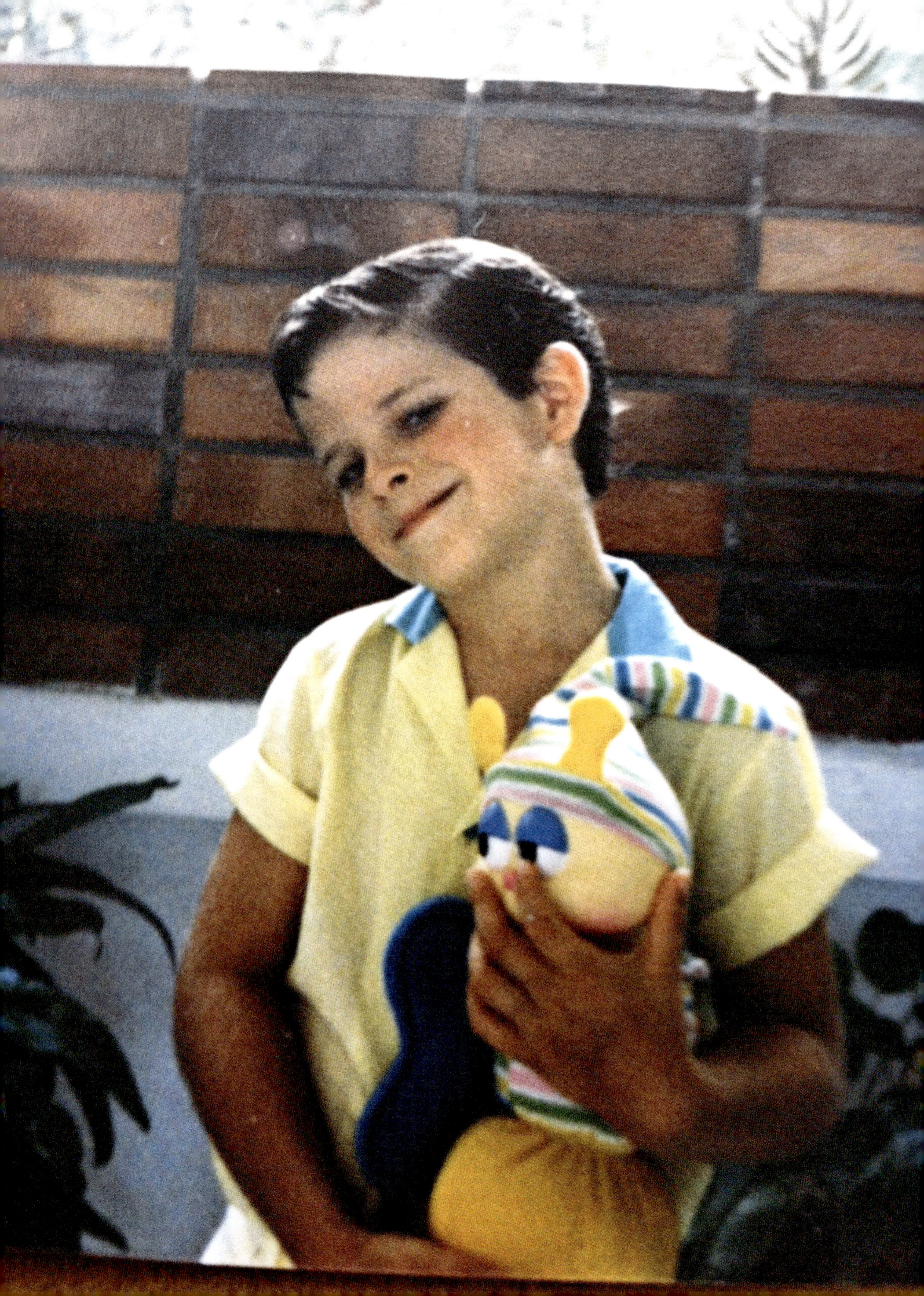

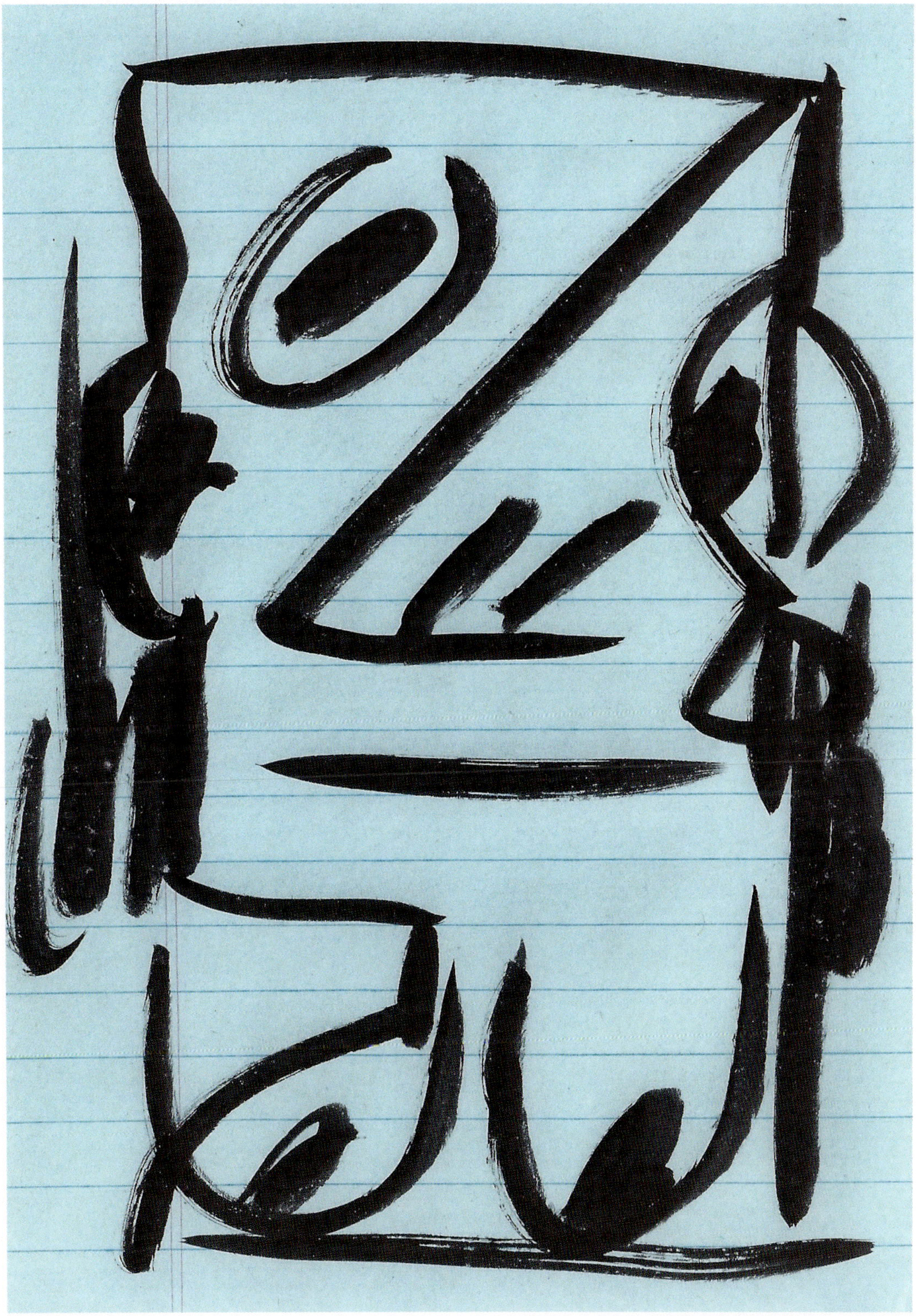

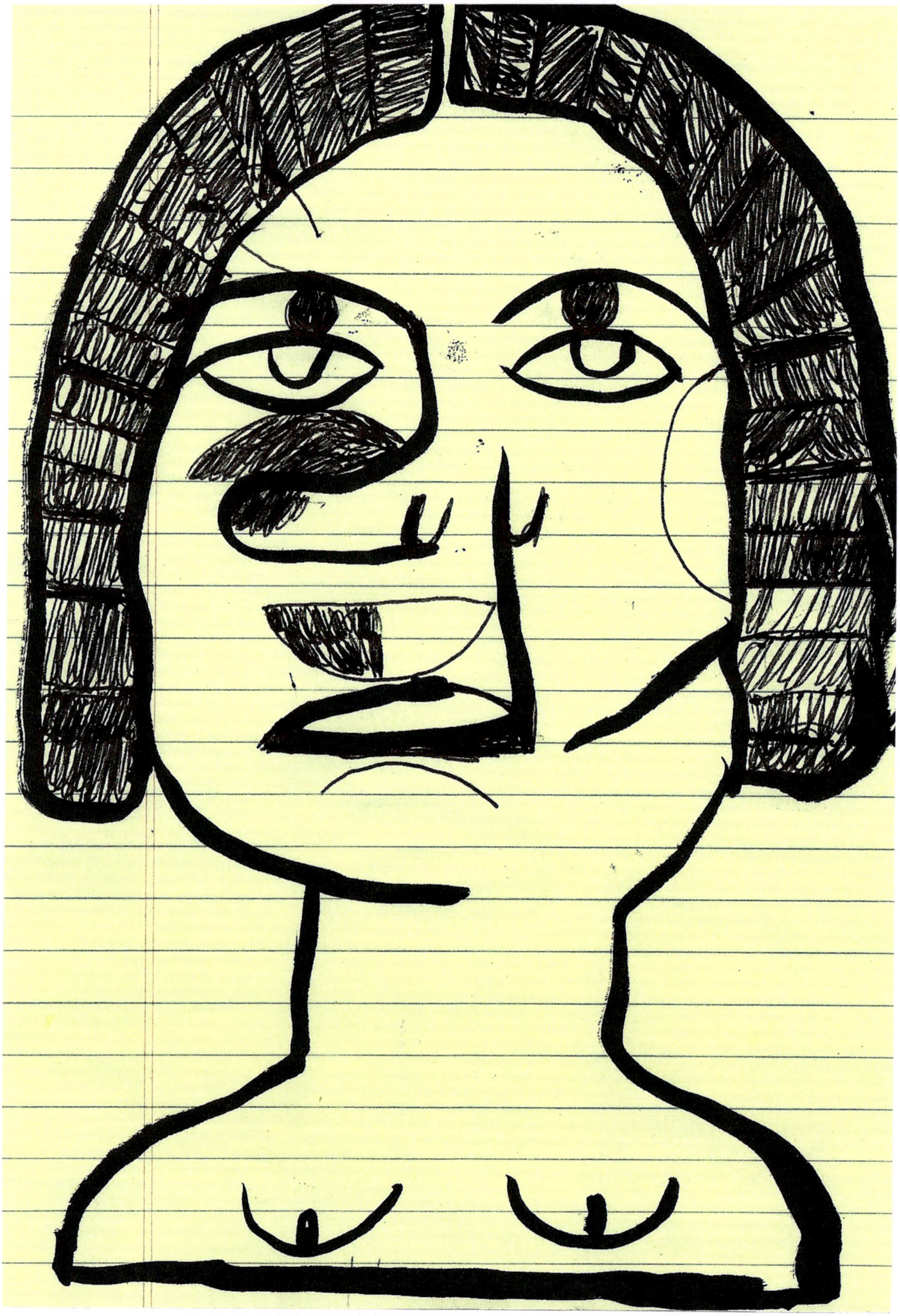

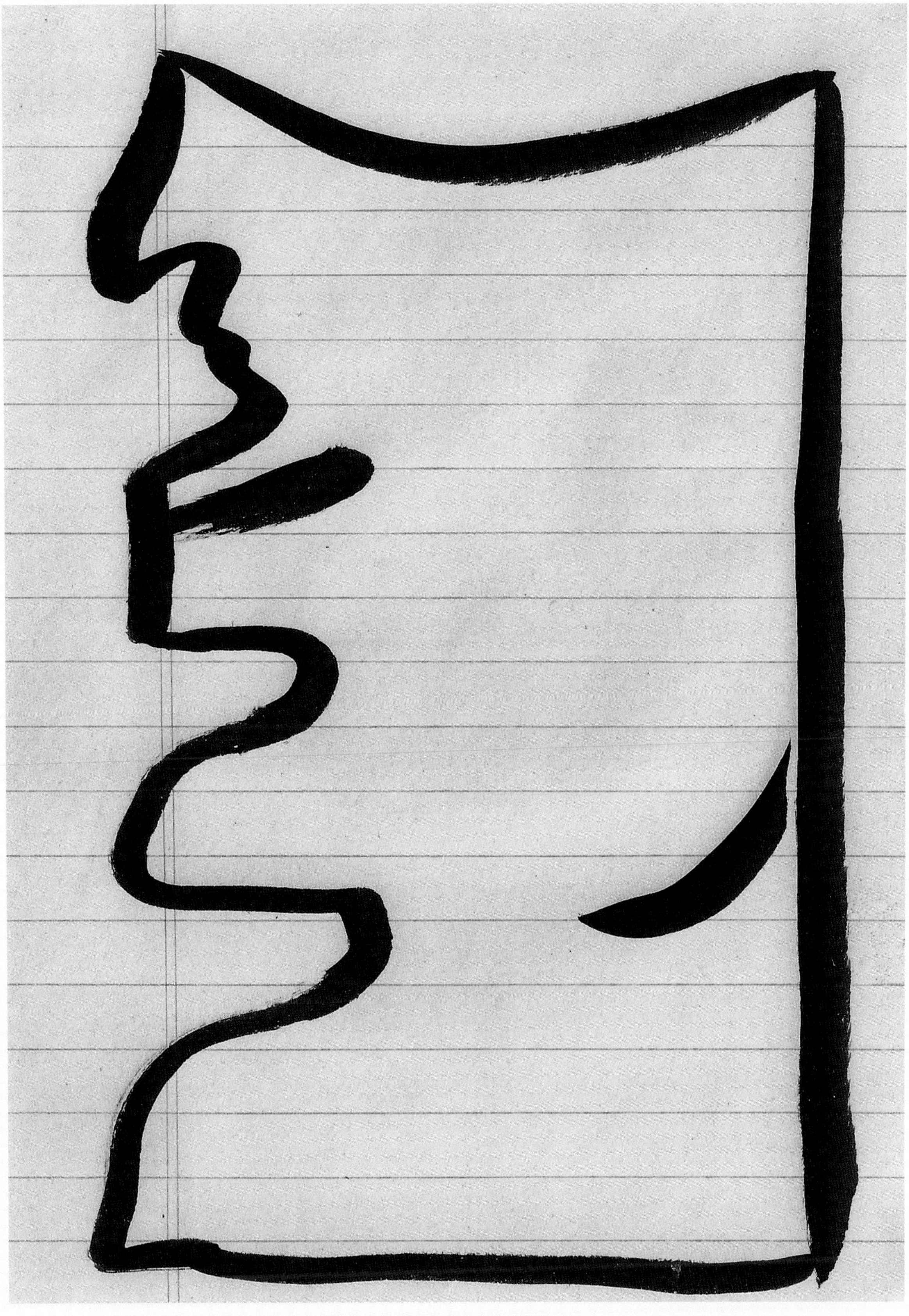

In the summer of 1998 The Specials played a free show in India Point Park, which is were I grew up going to for all the art fairs and world music gatherings, etc. Hippie stuff with the mother that I also always enjoyed. Although I wasn't really interested in them at that time (I was pretty squatty at this point… disgusting jeans all patched together and some crusty t-shirt) it was literally four blocks from my apartment and I felt nostalgic for being thirteen a few years earlier… which seemed like a lifetime ago. As I walked over the bridge* that crosses the 195 freeway to the park I passed two kids wearing Limp Bizkit shirts and thought, what the fuck is Limp Bizkit? They looked like shit. In a different way than I did.

Well, finally, after sixteen years, Limp Bizkit have reached their goal. Somebody has e-mailed me about Limp Bizkit. It sounds like those kids looked.

*I also just remembered the first time I did acid I watched the sun rising from this bridge but half the sky behind us was completely dark and the clouds were all goat skulls. We rode swings in the park after and were screaming from the euphoria… must have looked super cool to the people heading to work.

Josiah Steinbrick

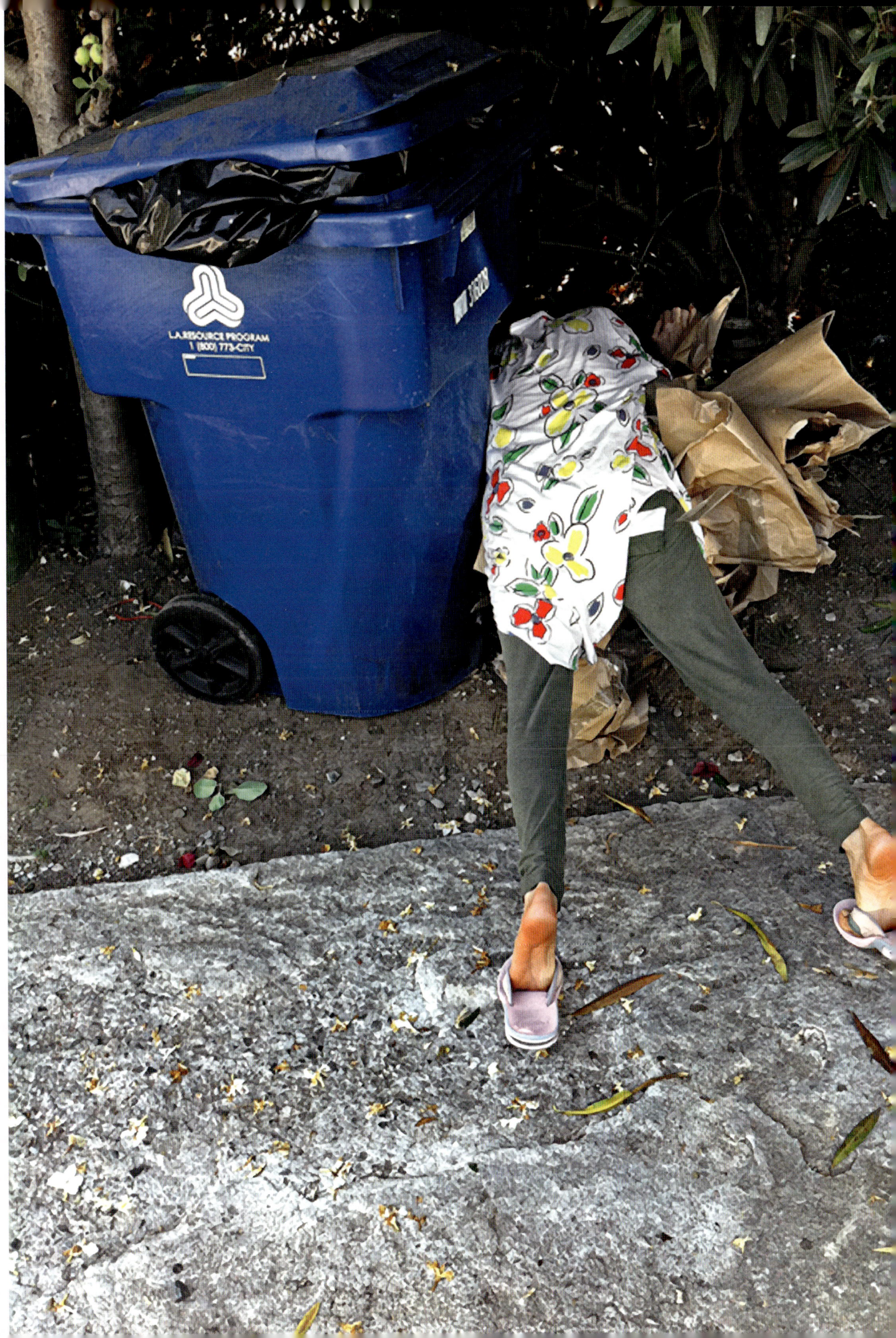
L.A.RESOURCE PROGRAM
1 (800) 773-CITY

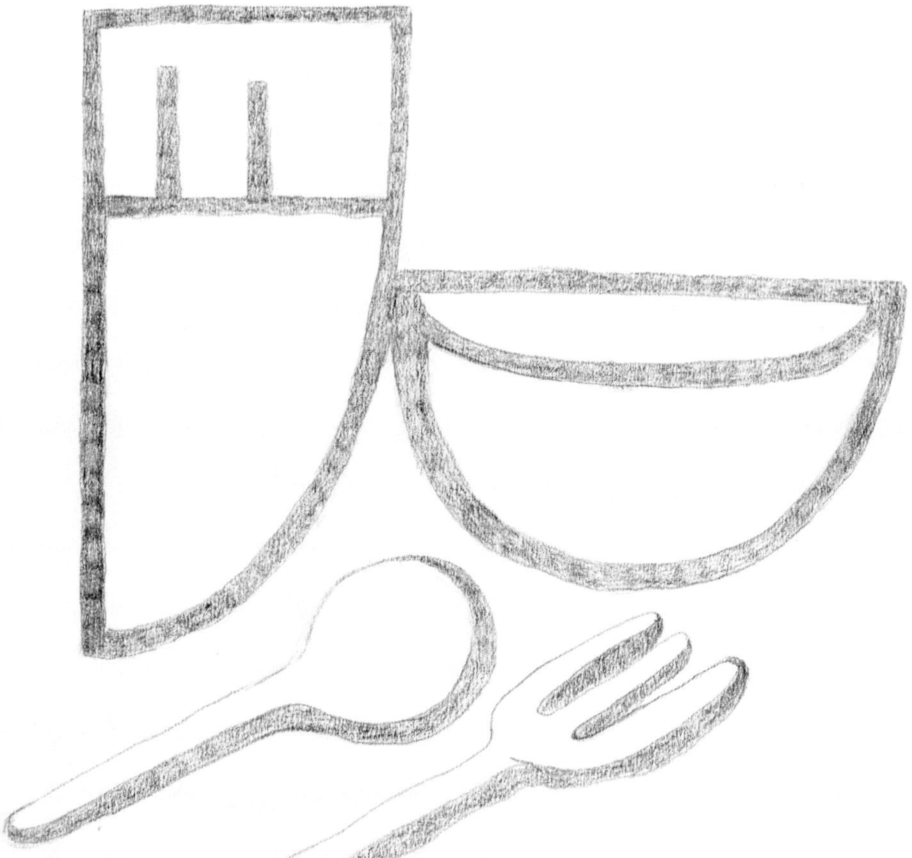

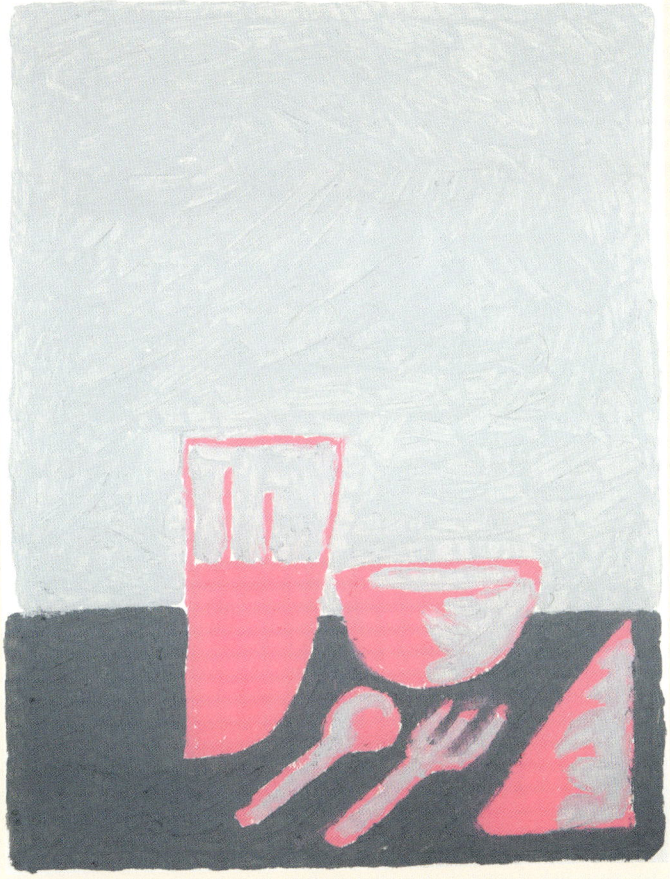

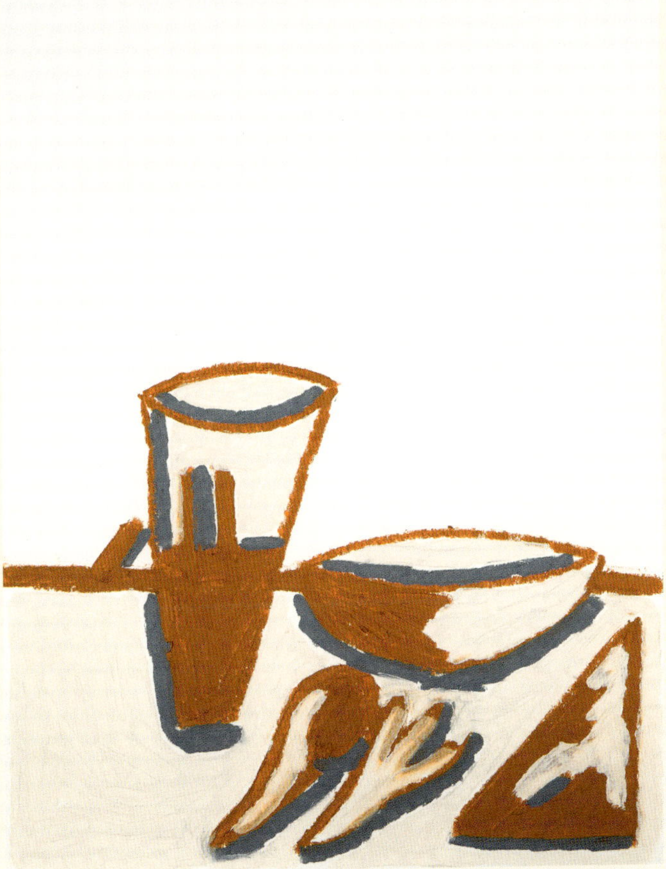

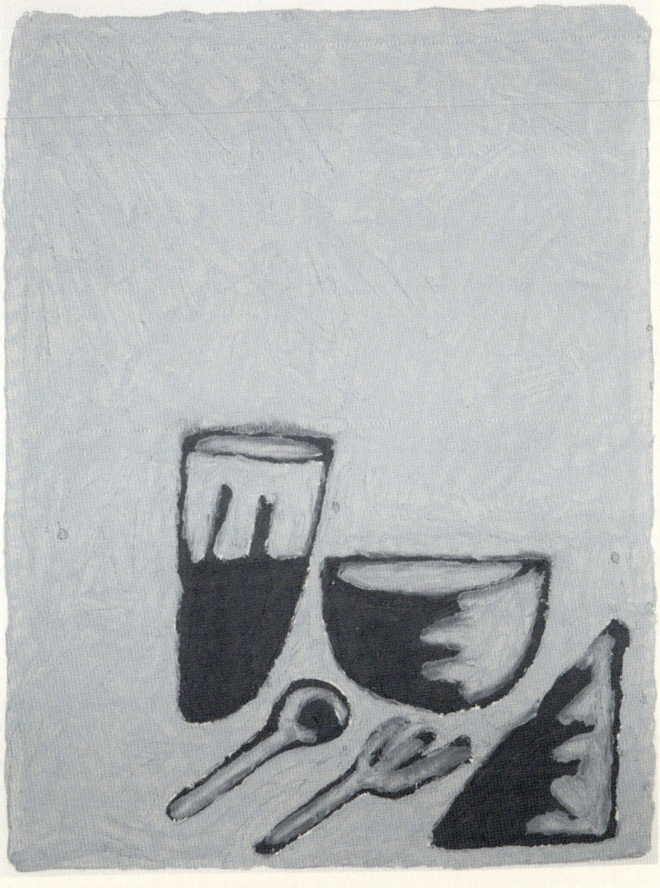

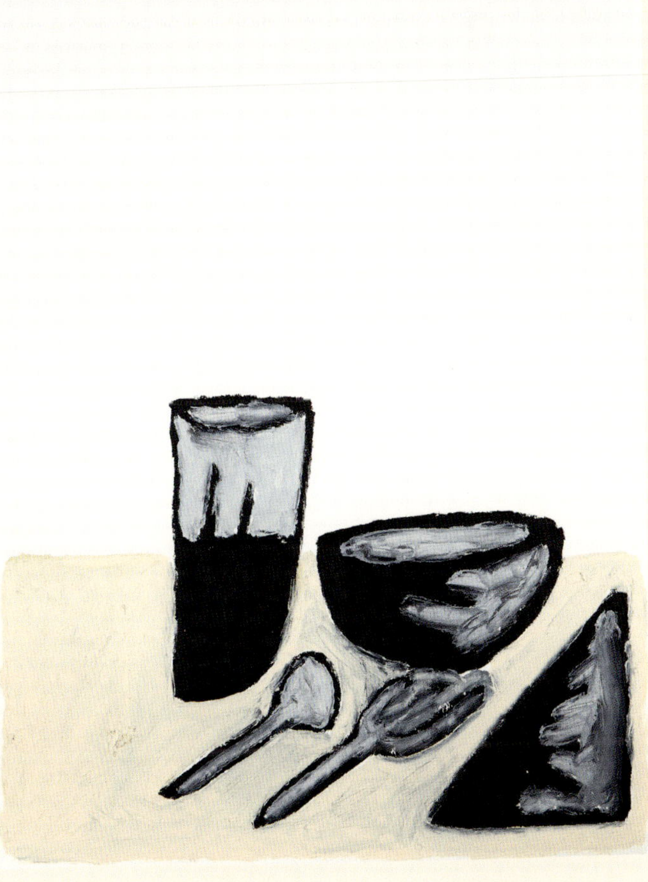

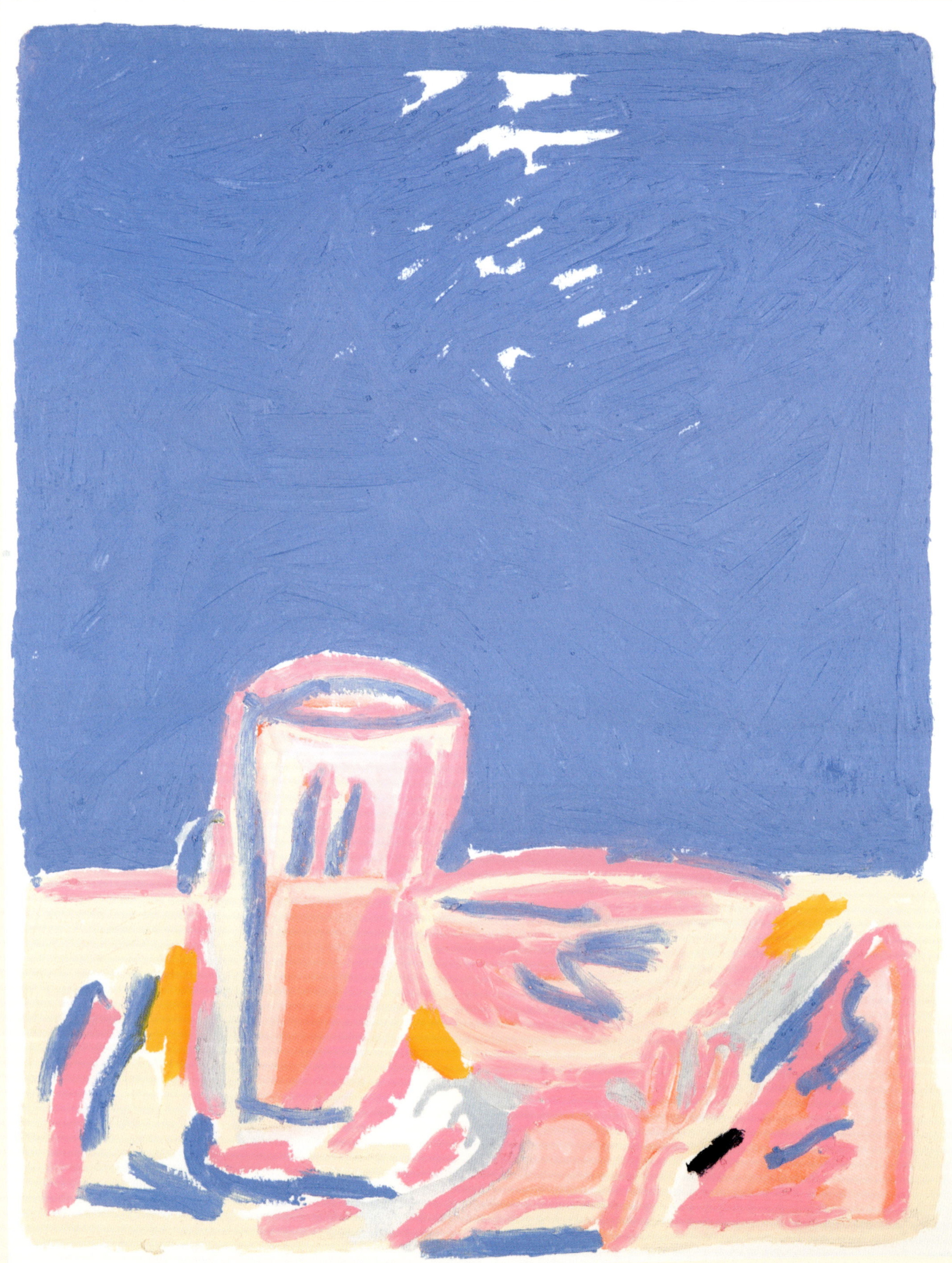

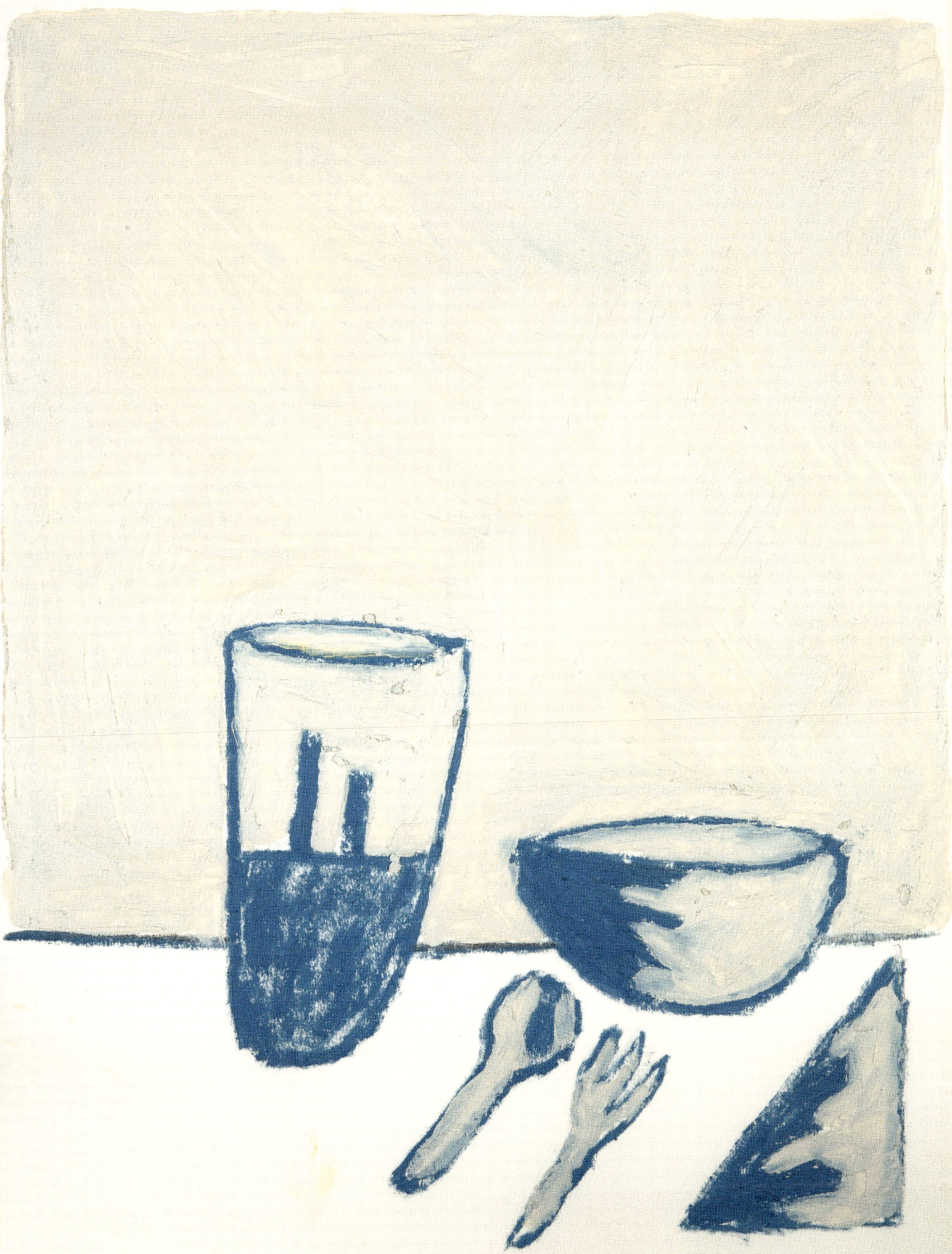

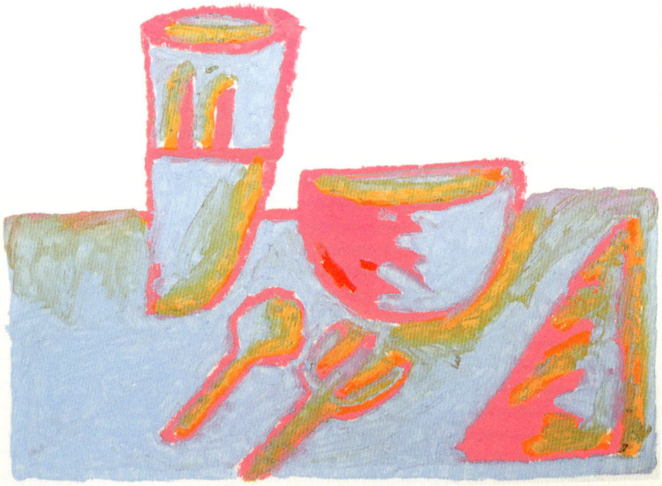
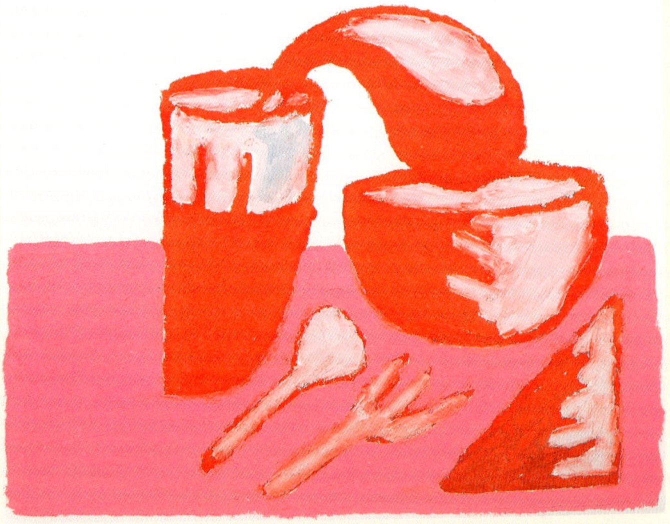
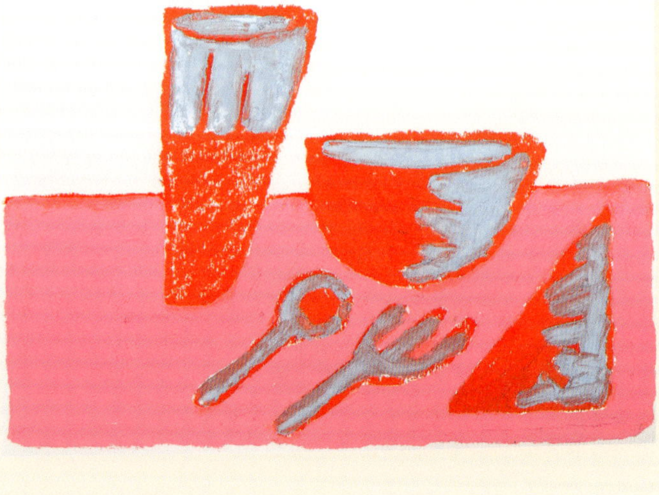
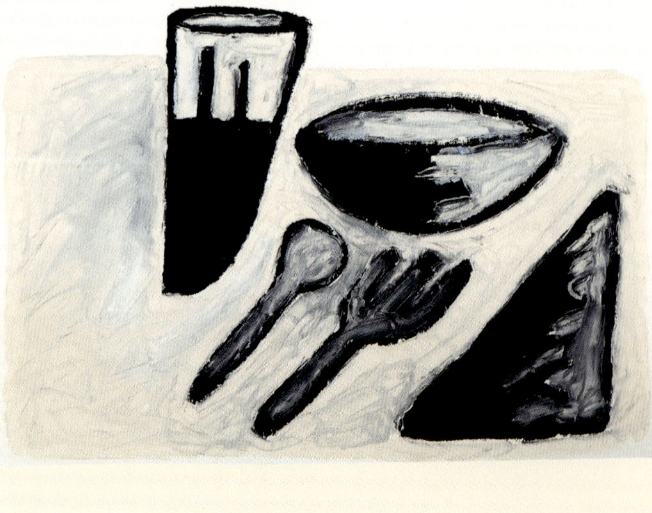

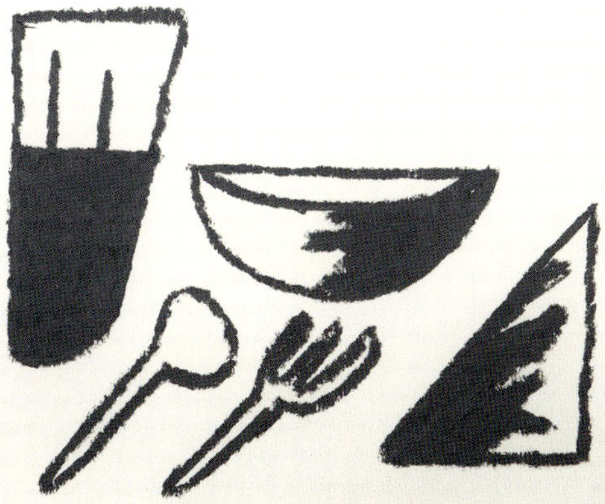

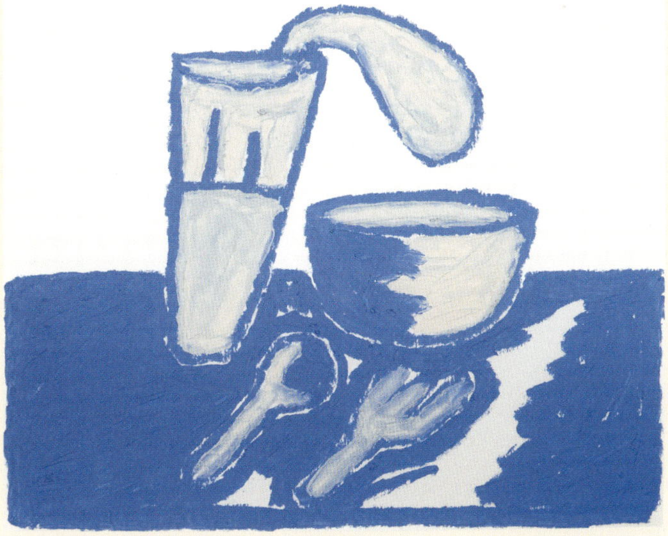

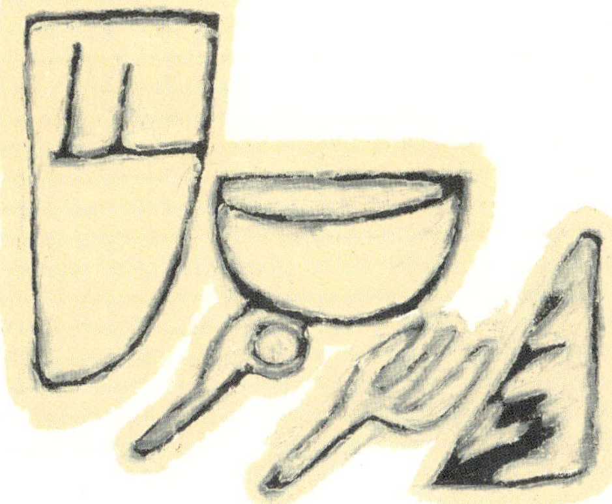

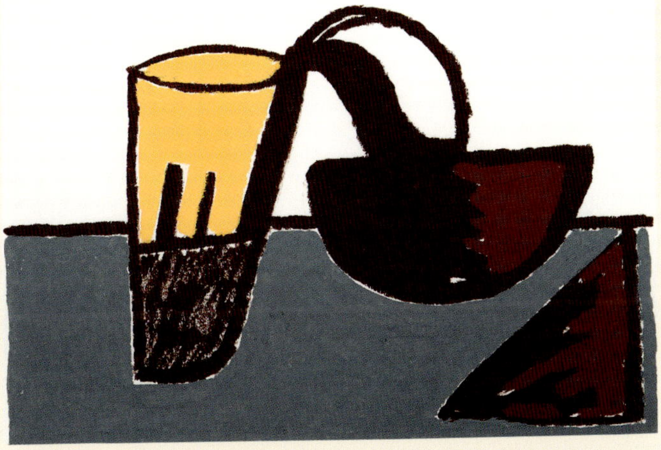

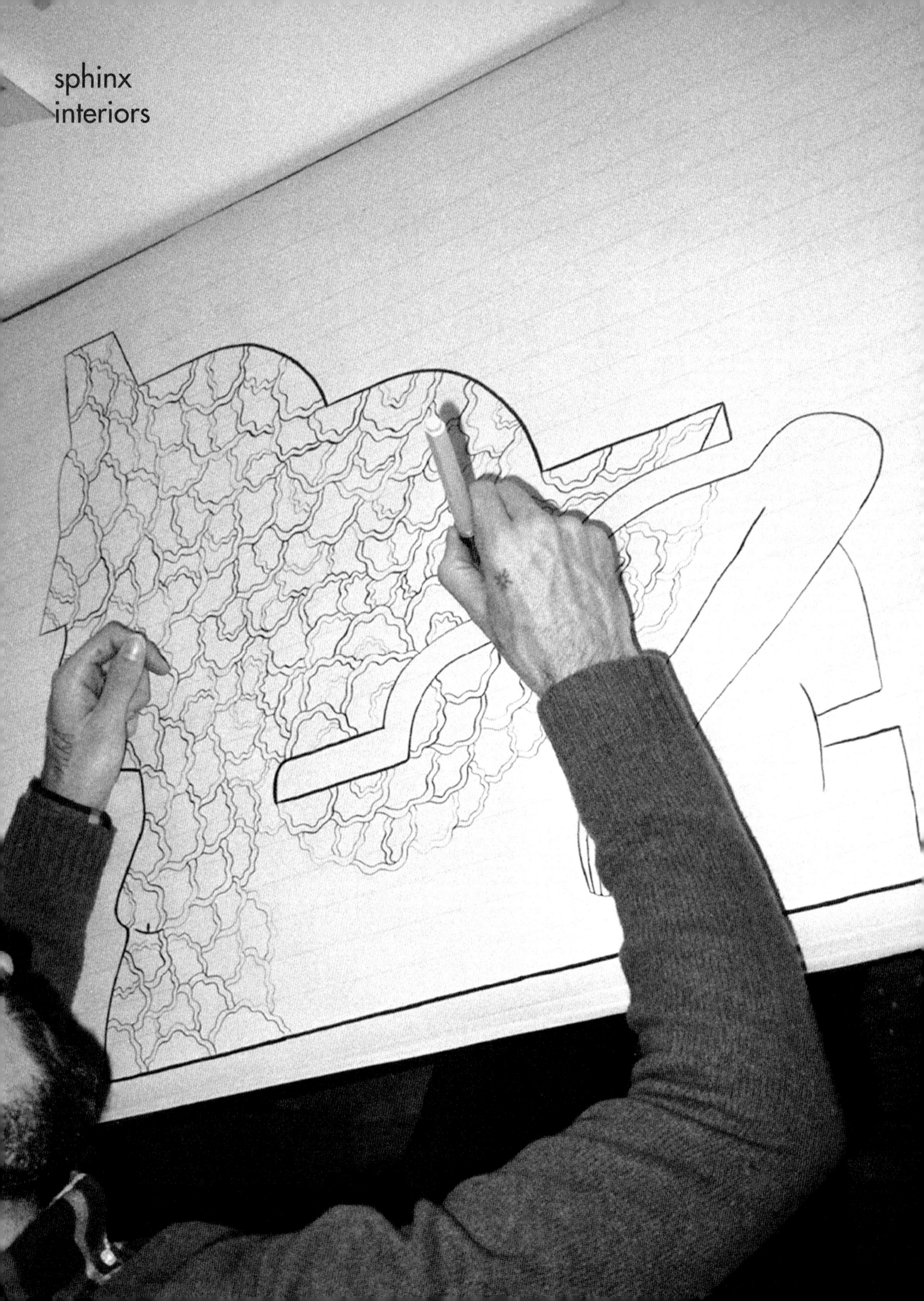
sphinx
interiors

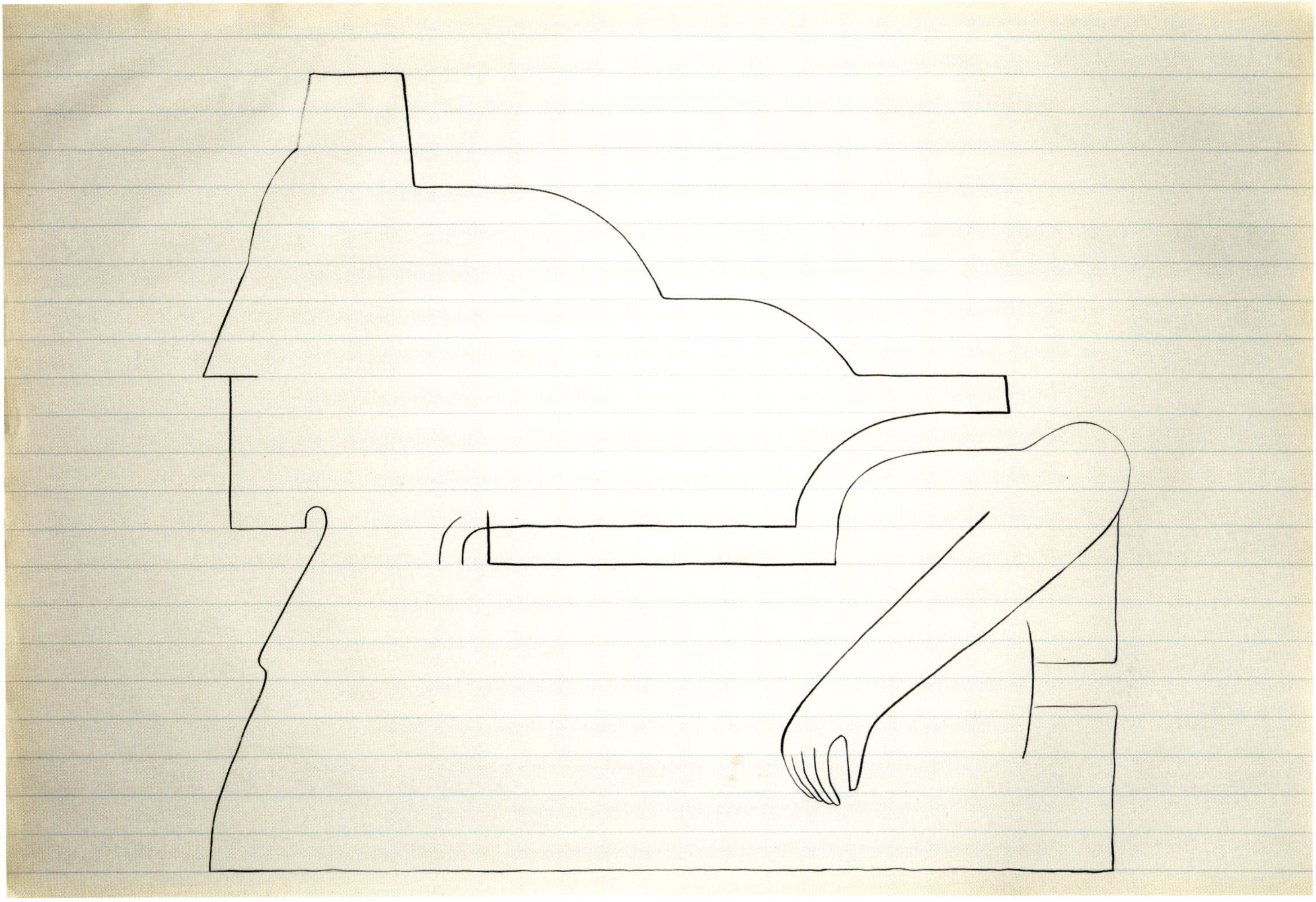

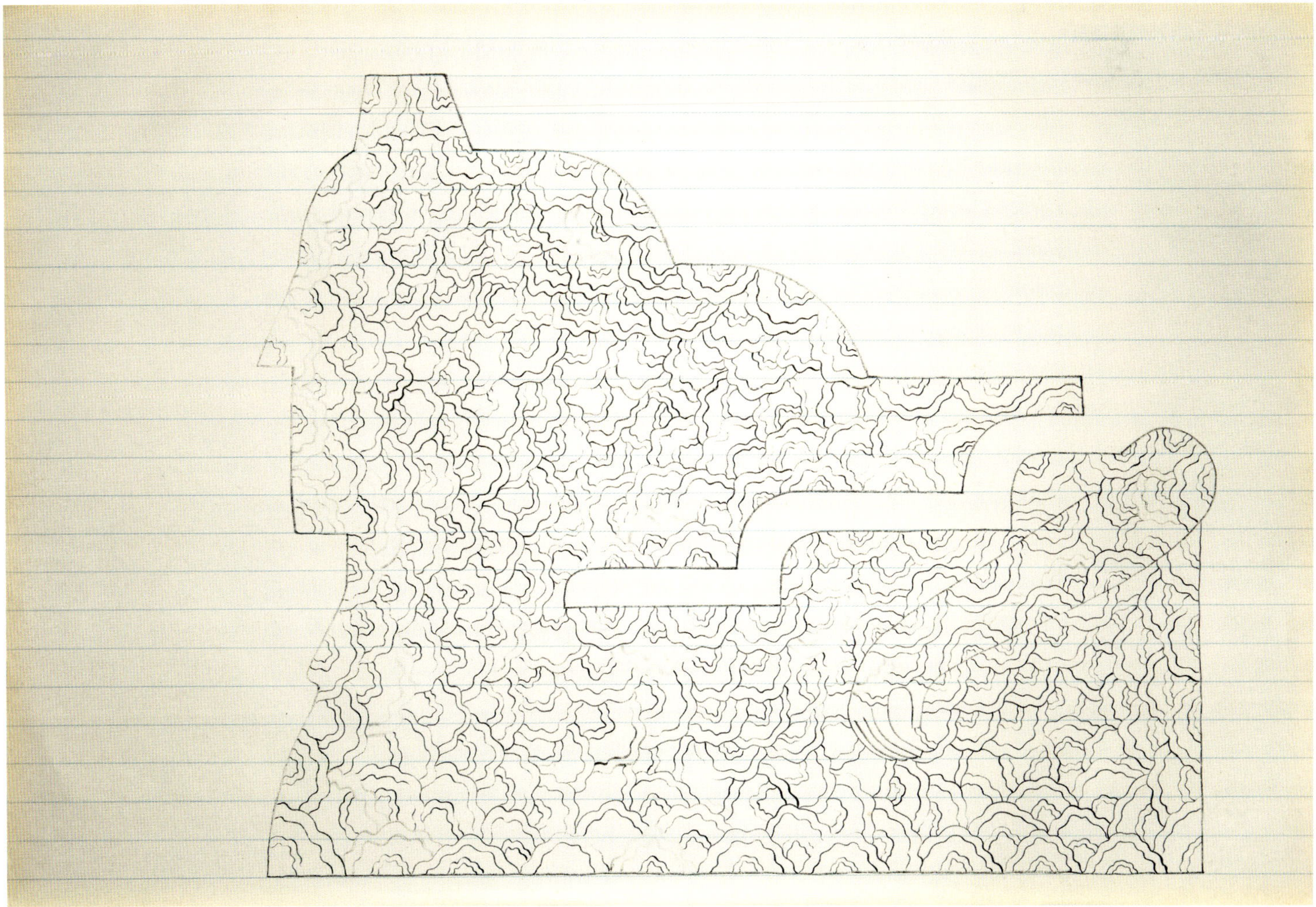

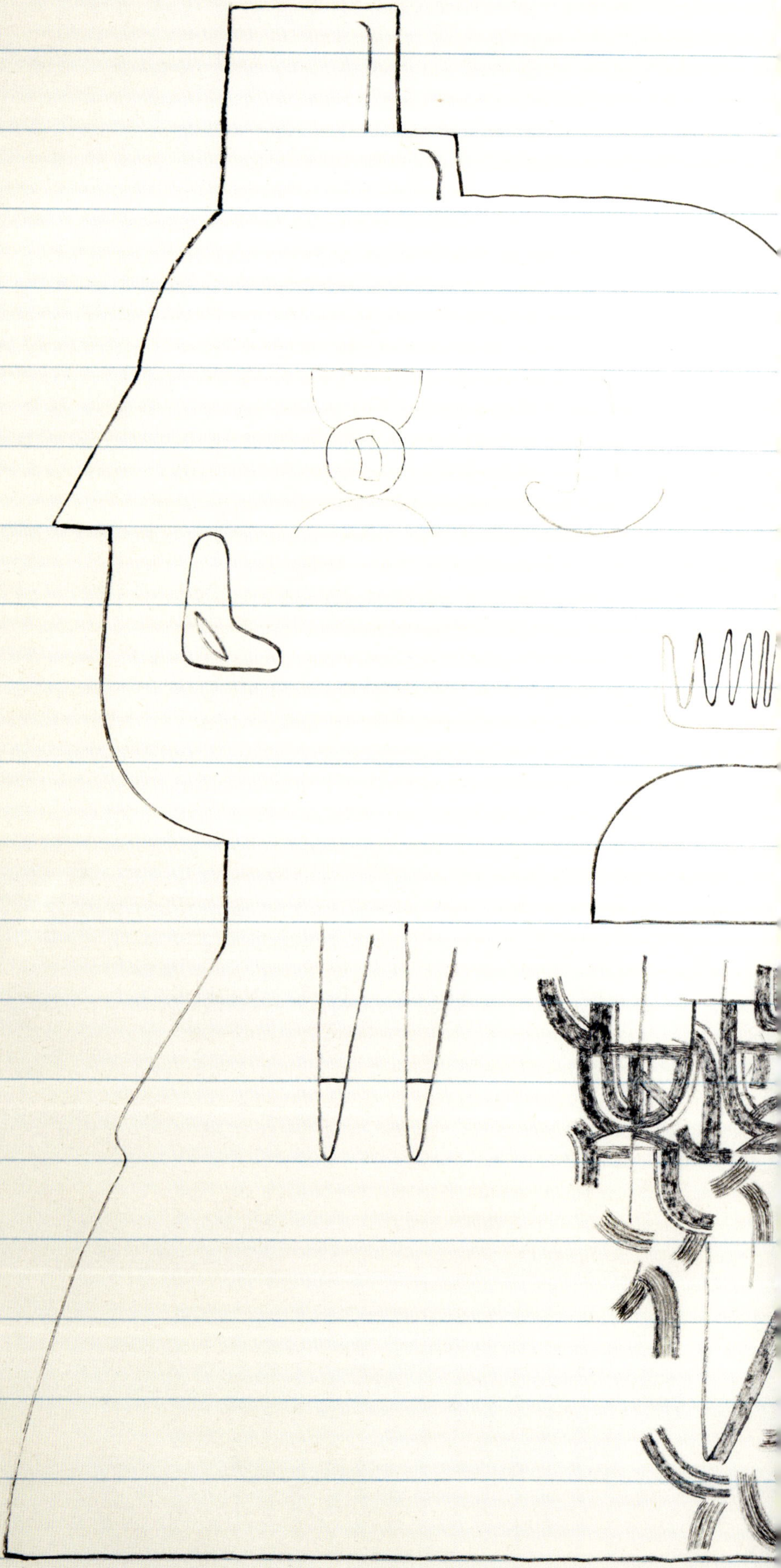

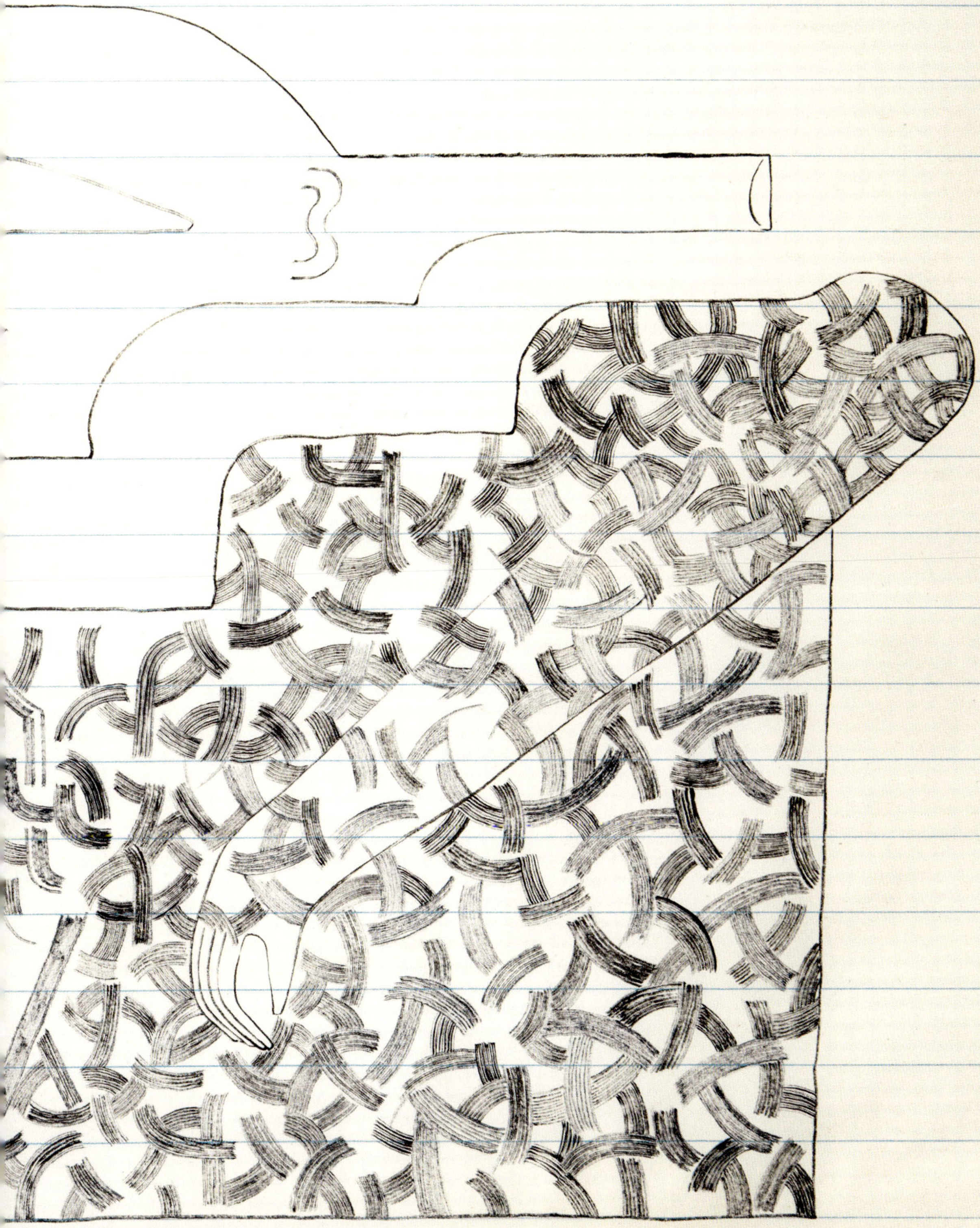

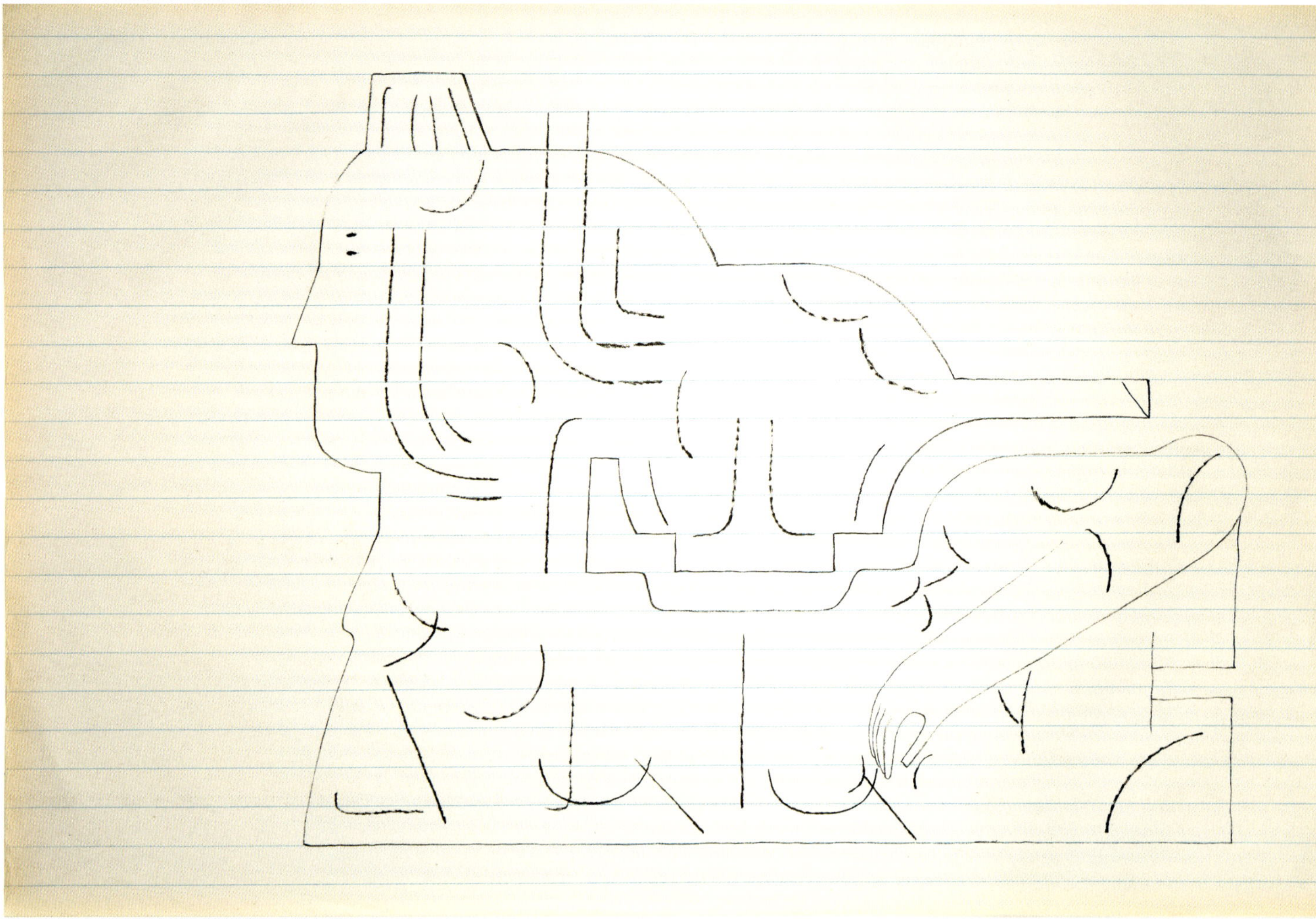

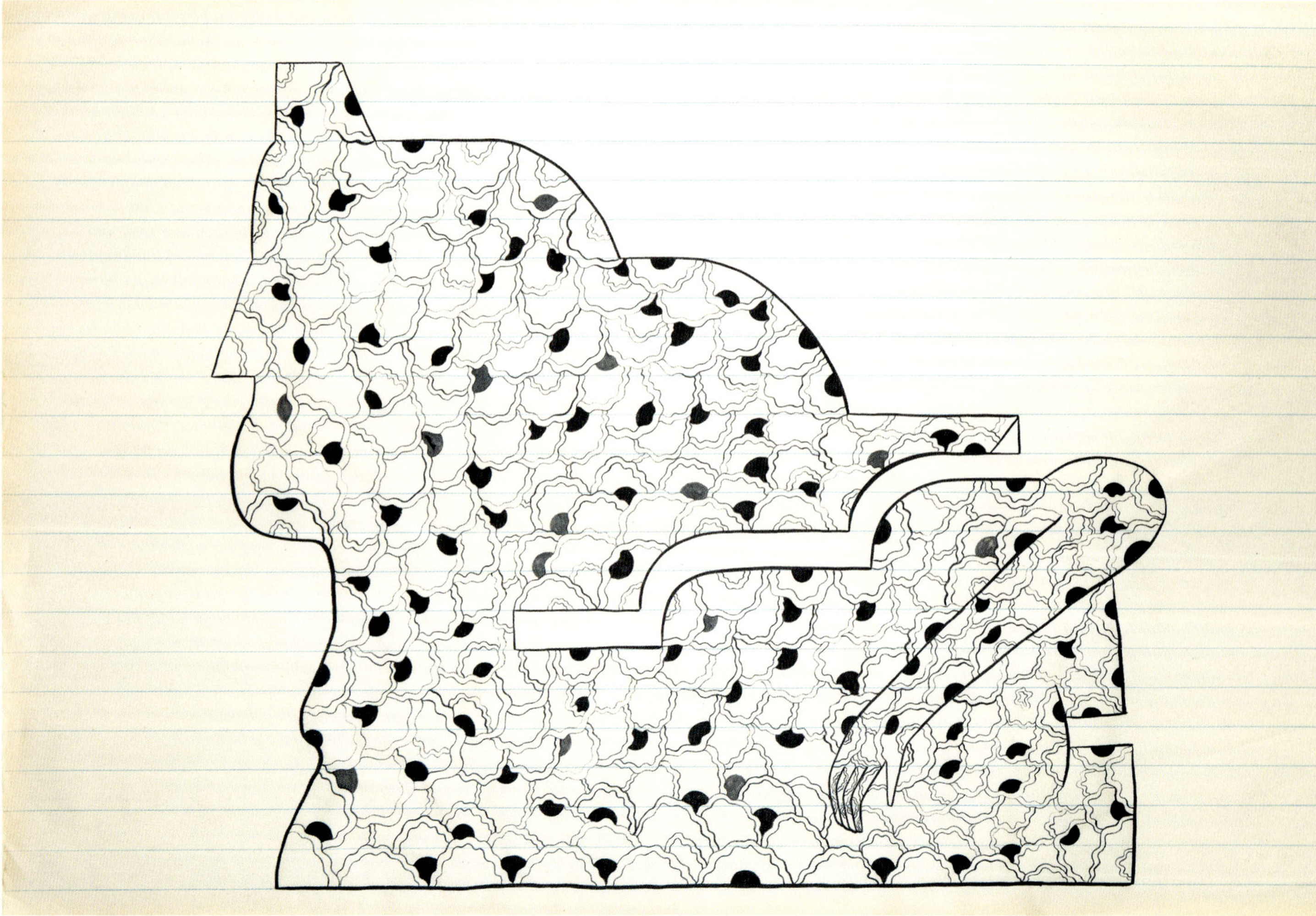

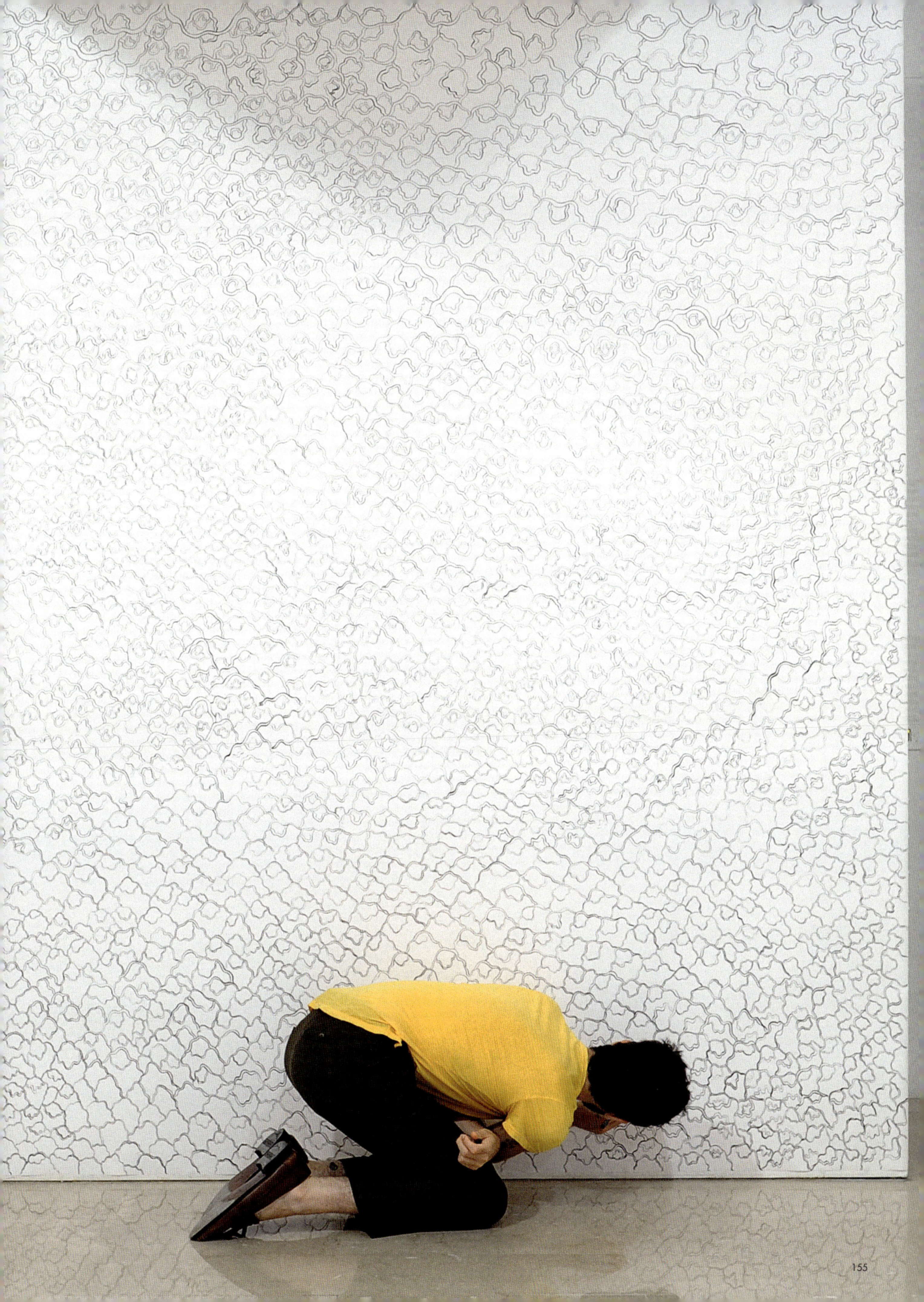

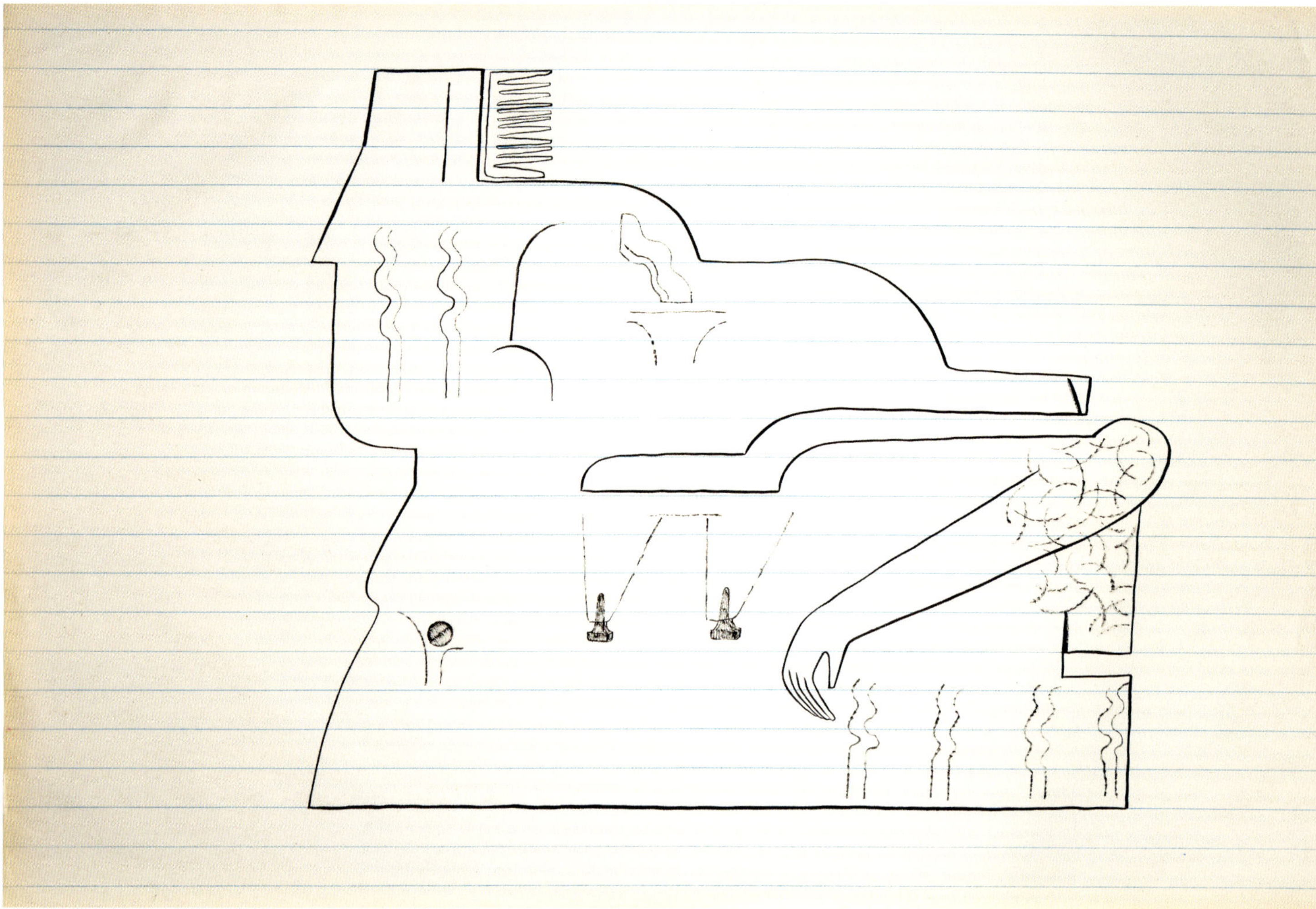

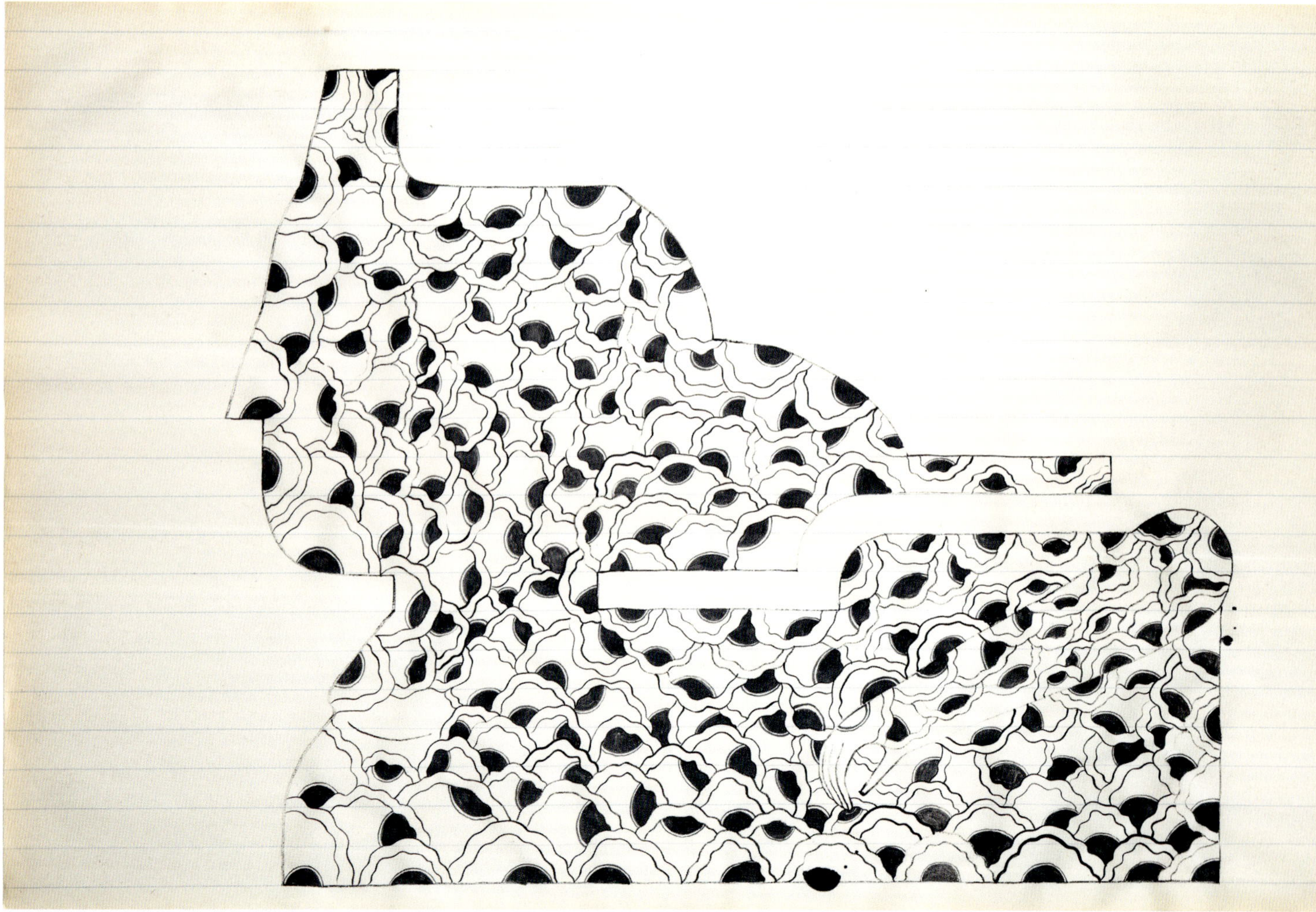

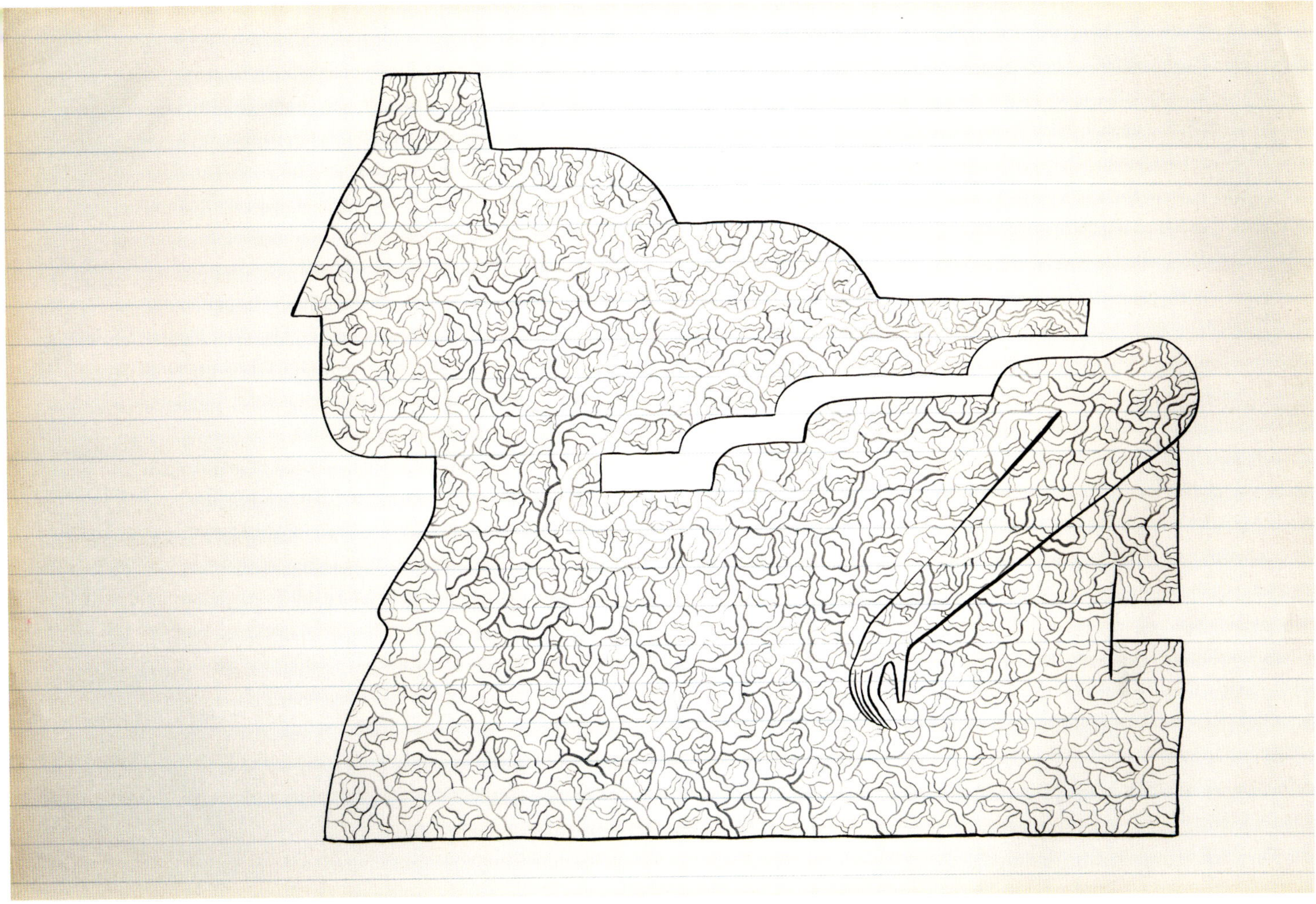

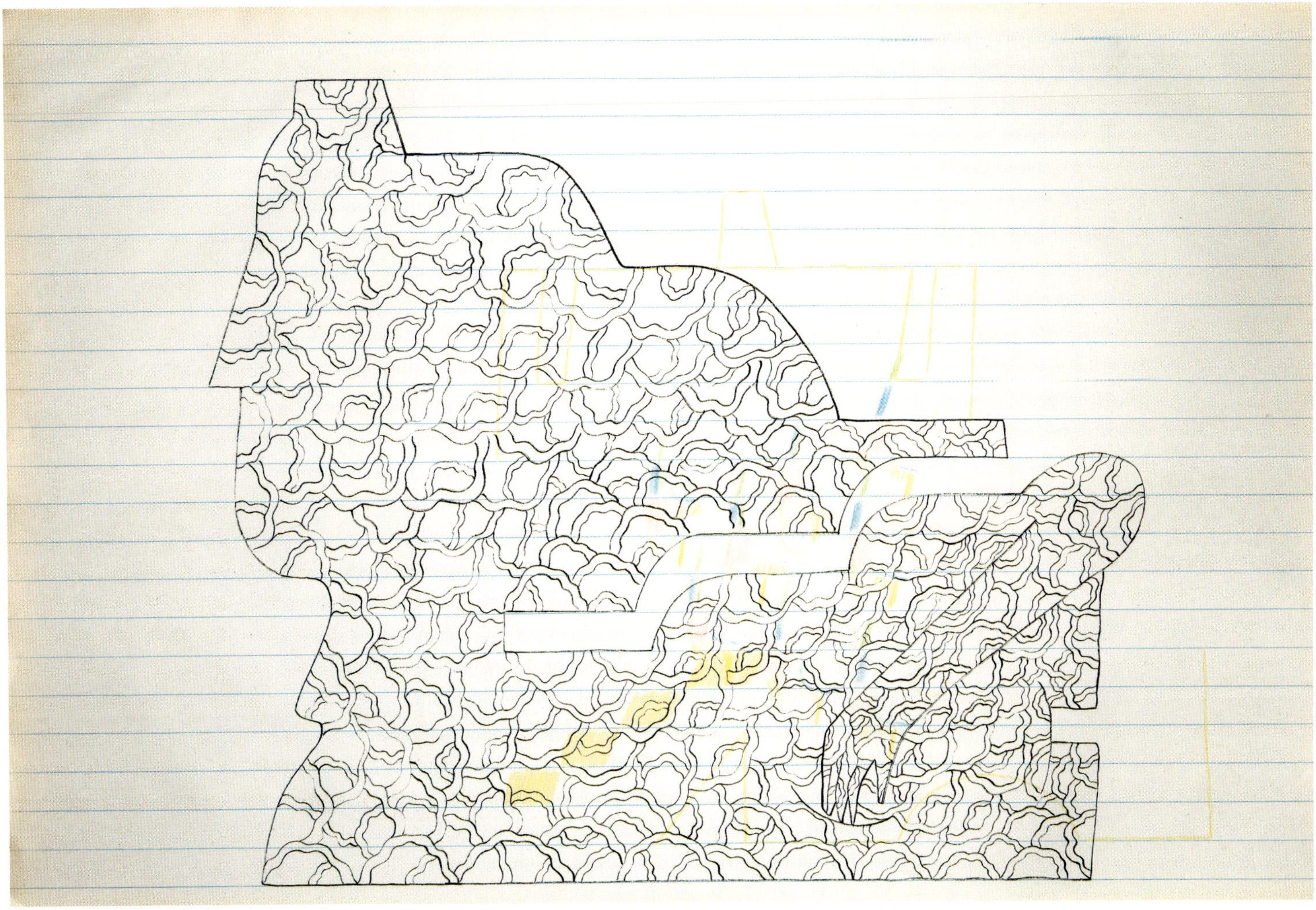

CATA TUMBO

OLO
GA

CONGO
MIRADOR

"DEBORA, IM OVER HERE"

SPEAK FREELY
TO YER BRO

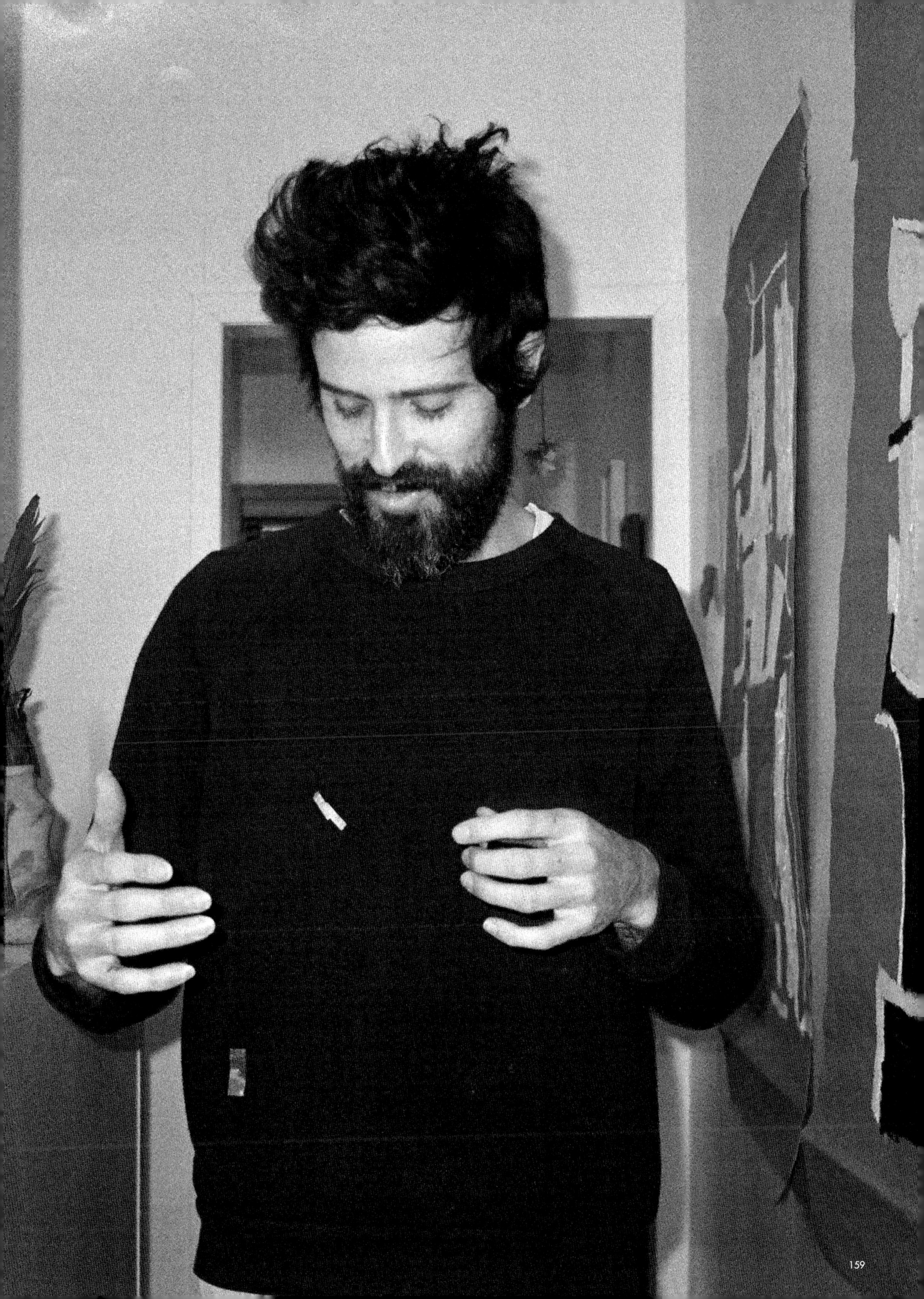

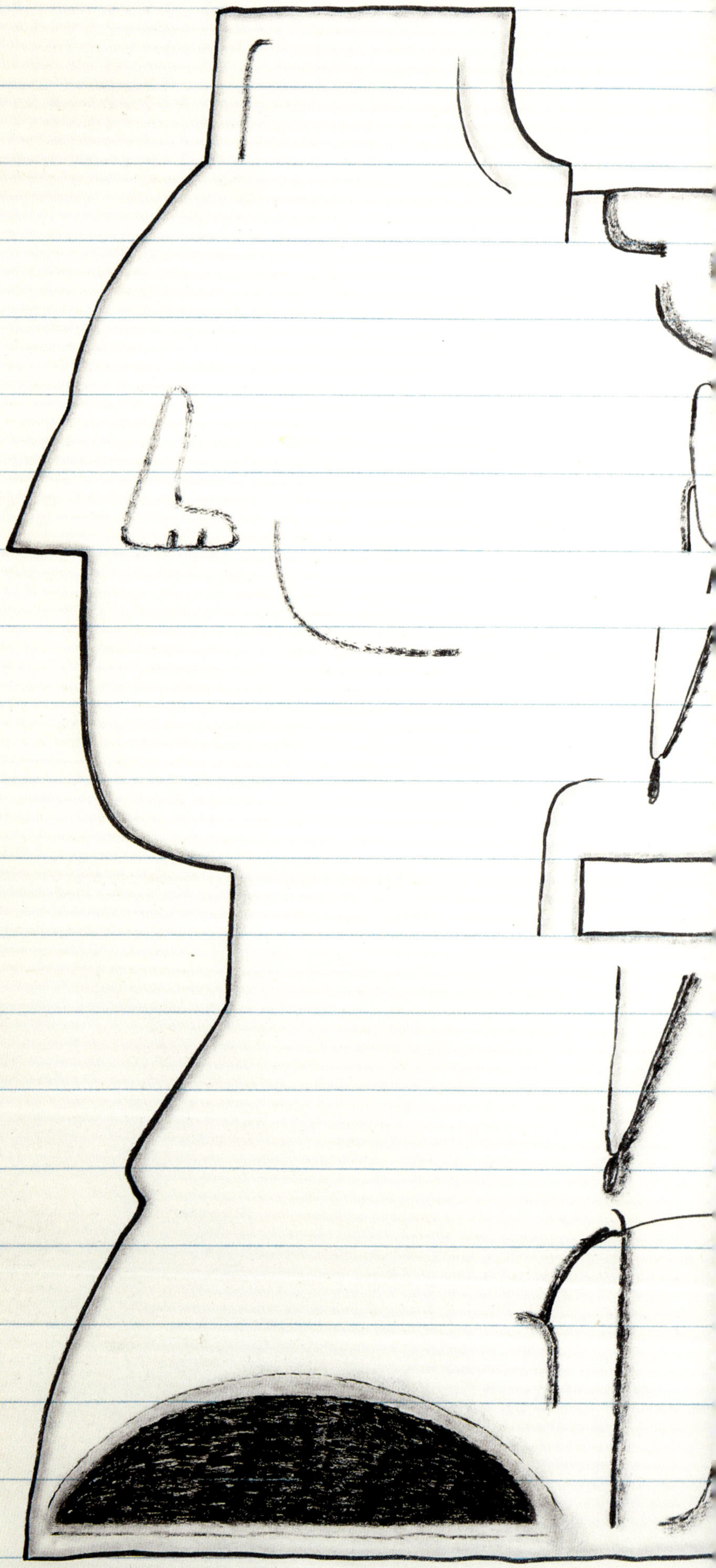

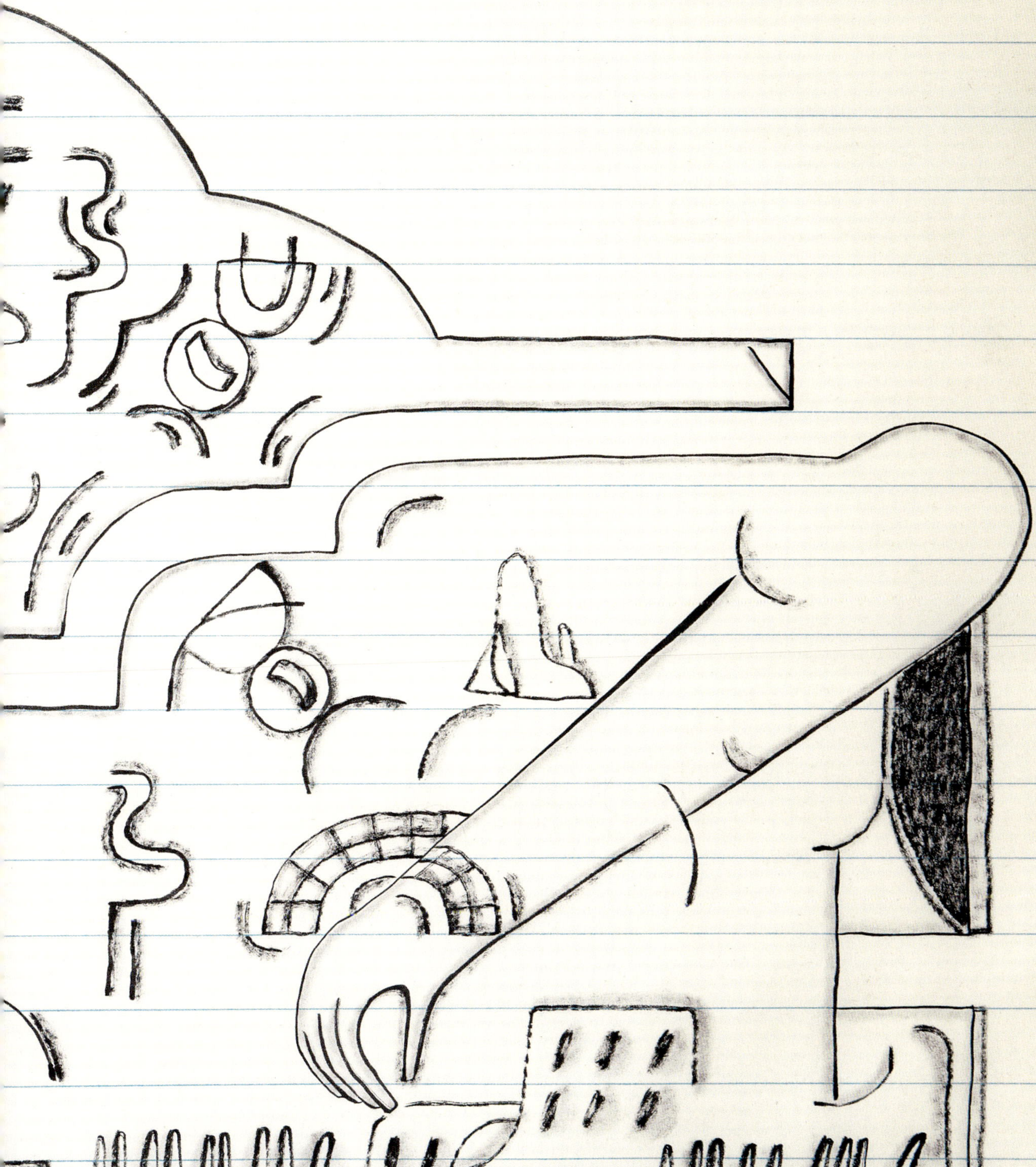

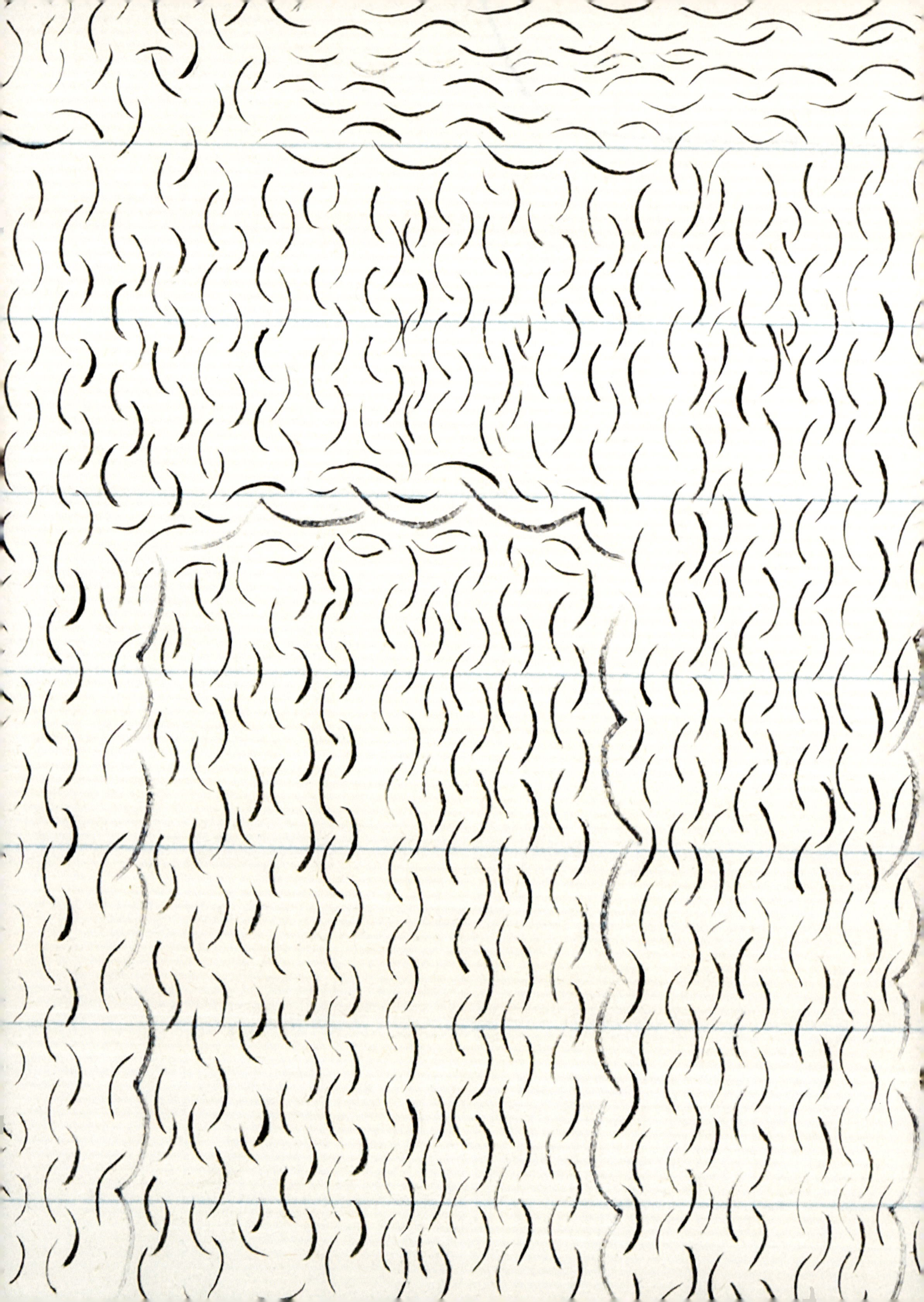

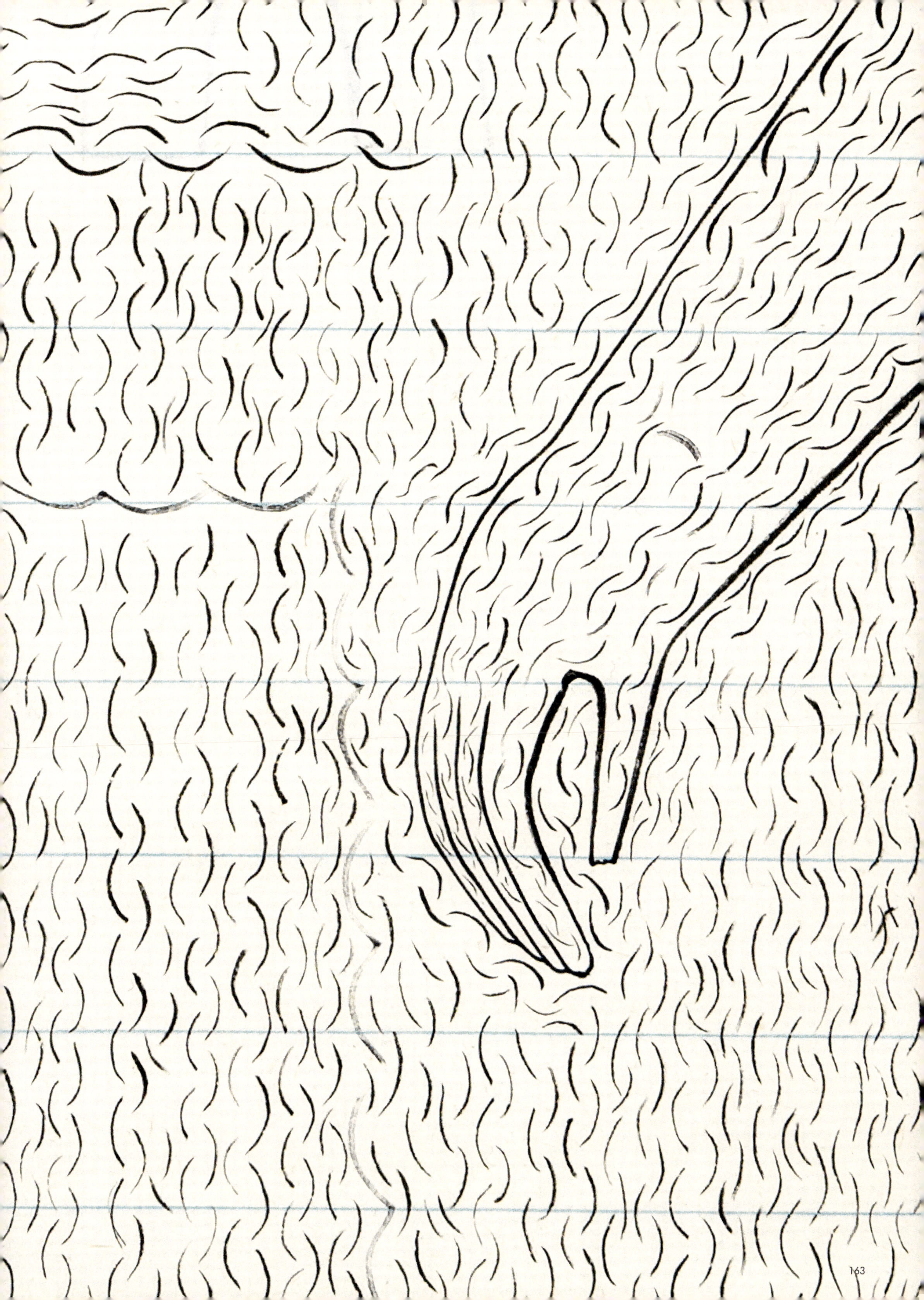

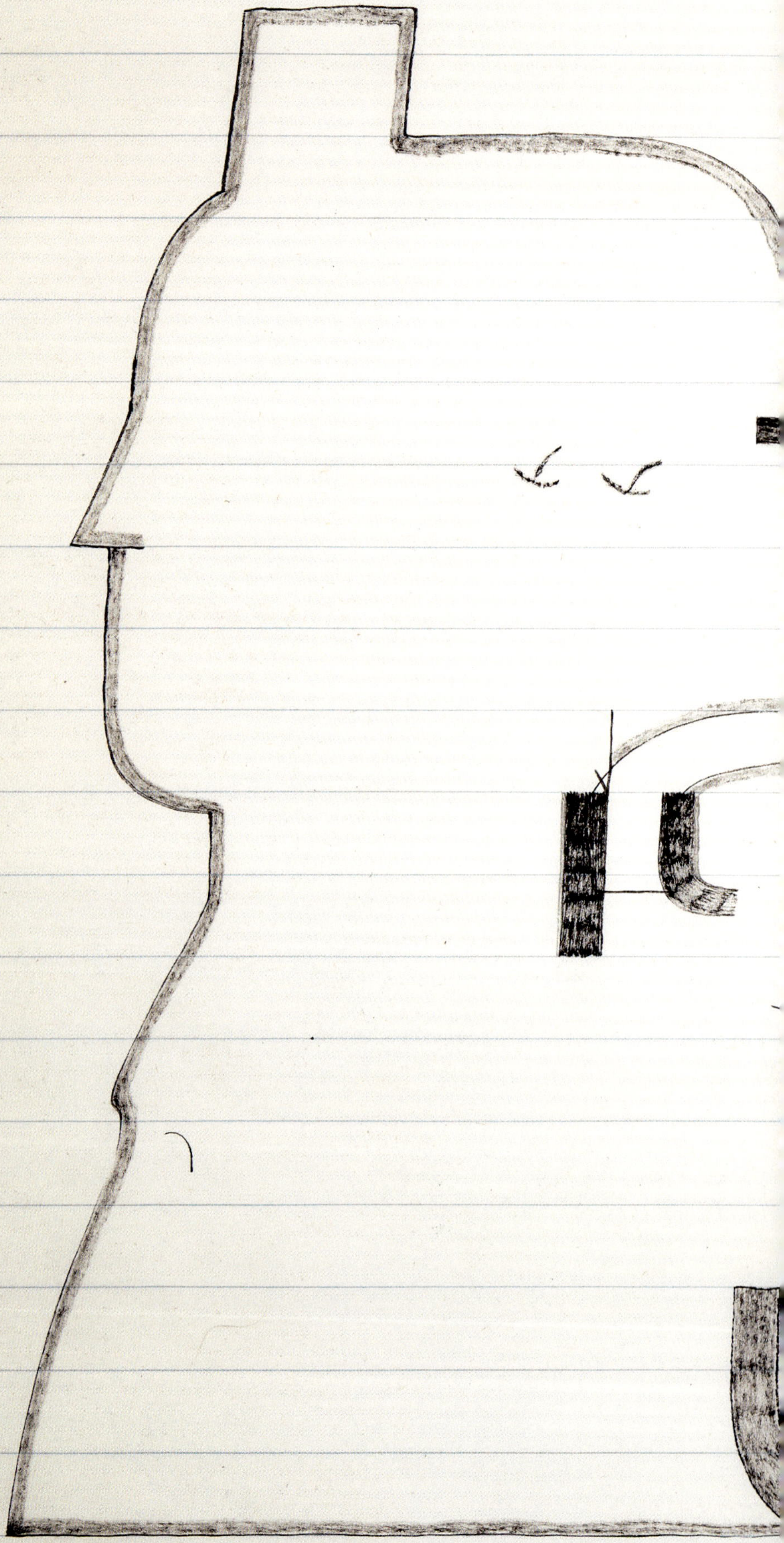

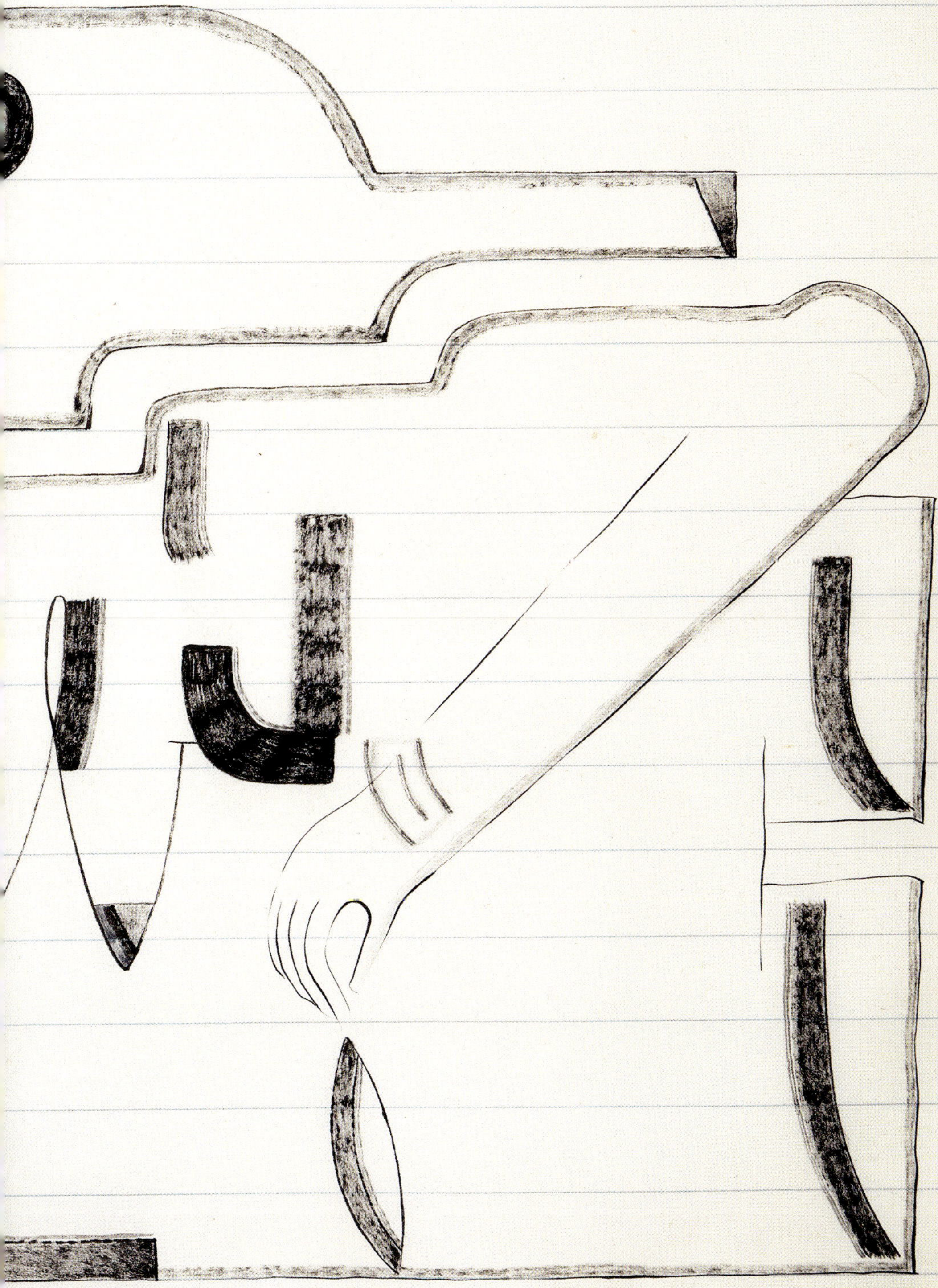

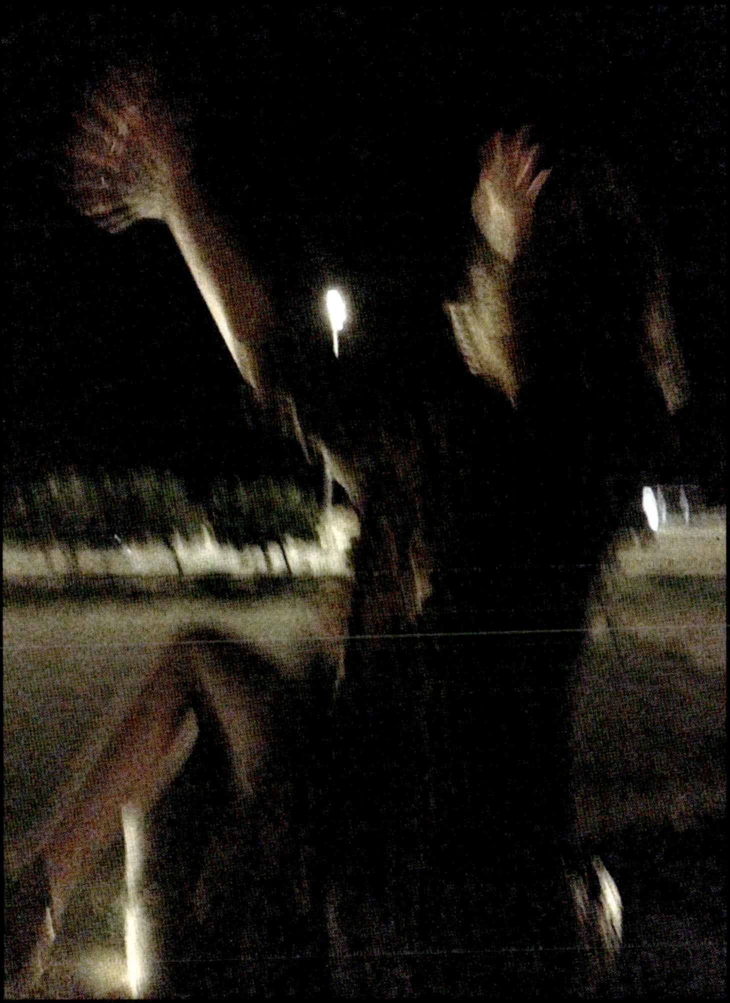

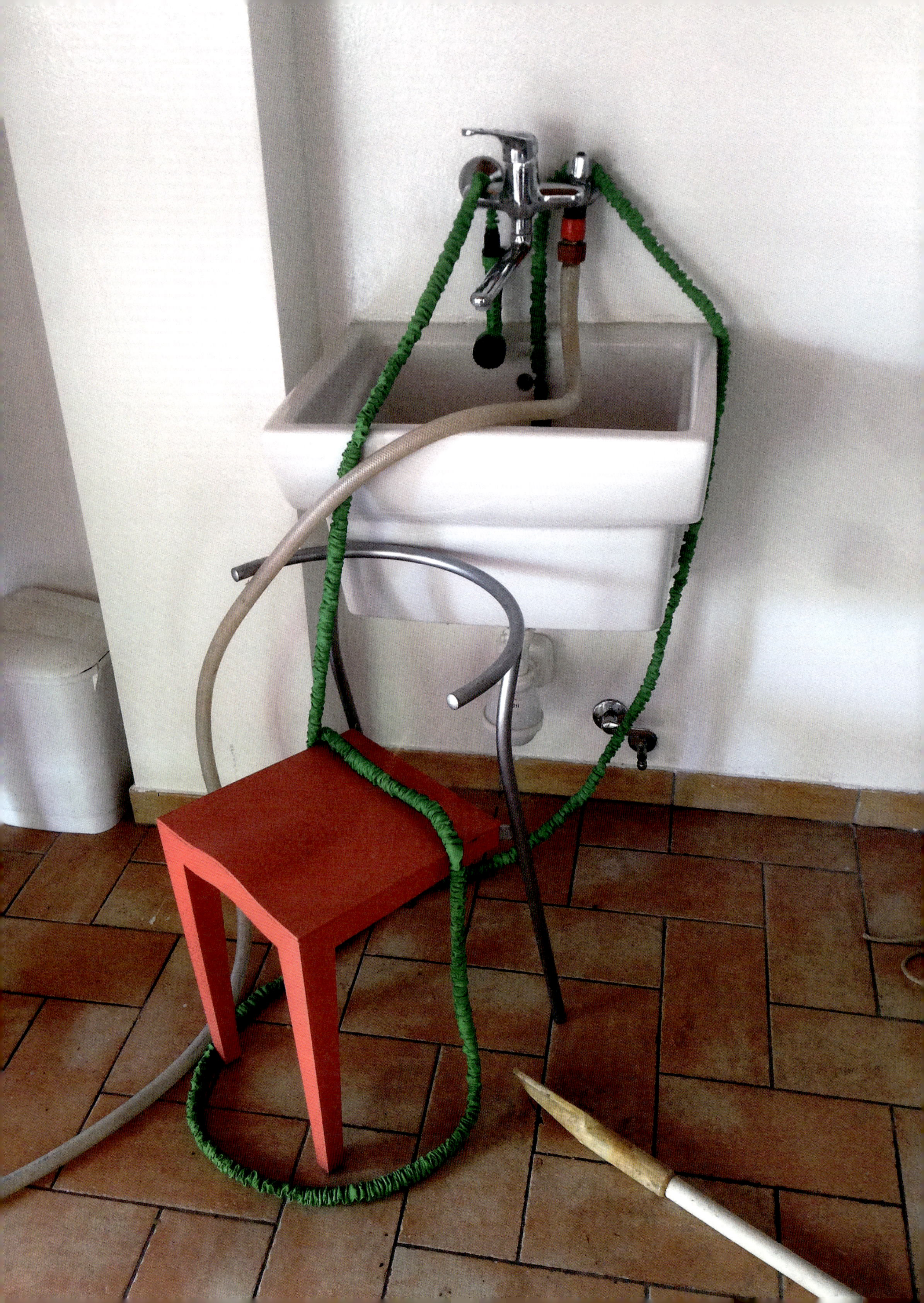

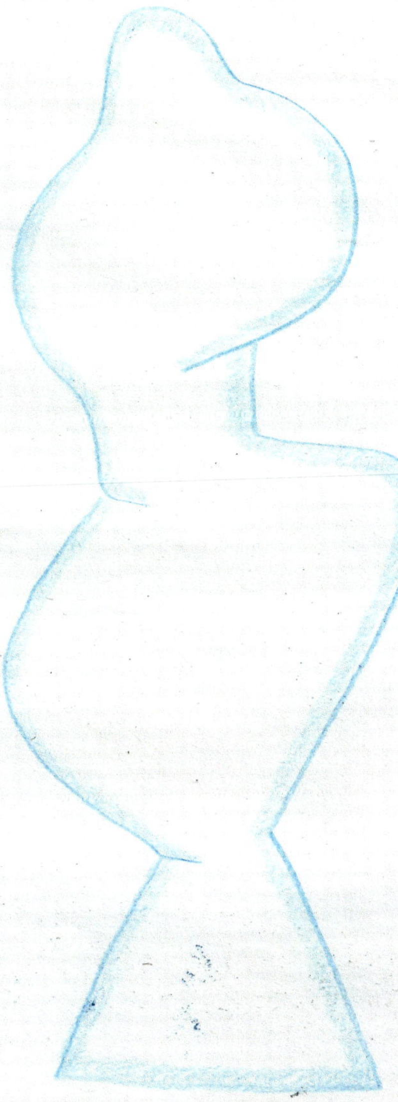

After "Haru Spring"
by Harold Budd

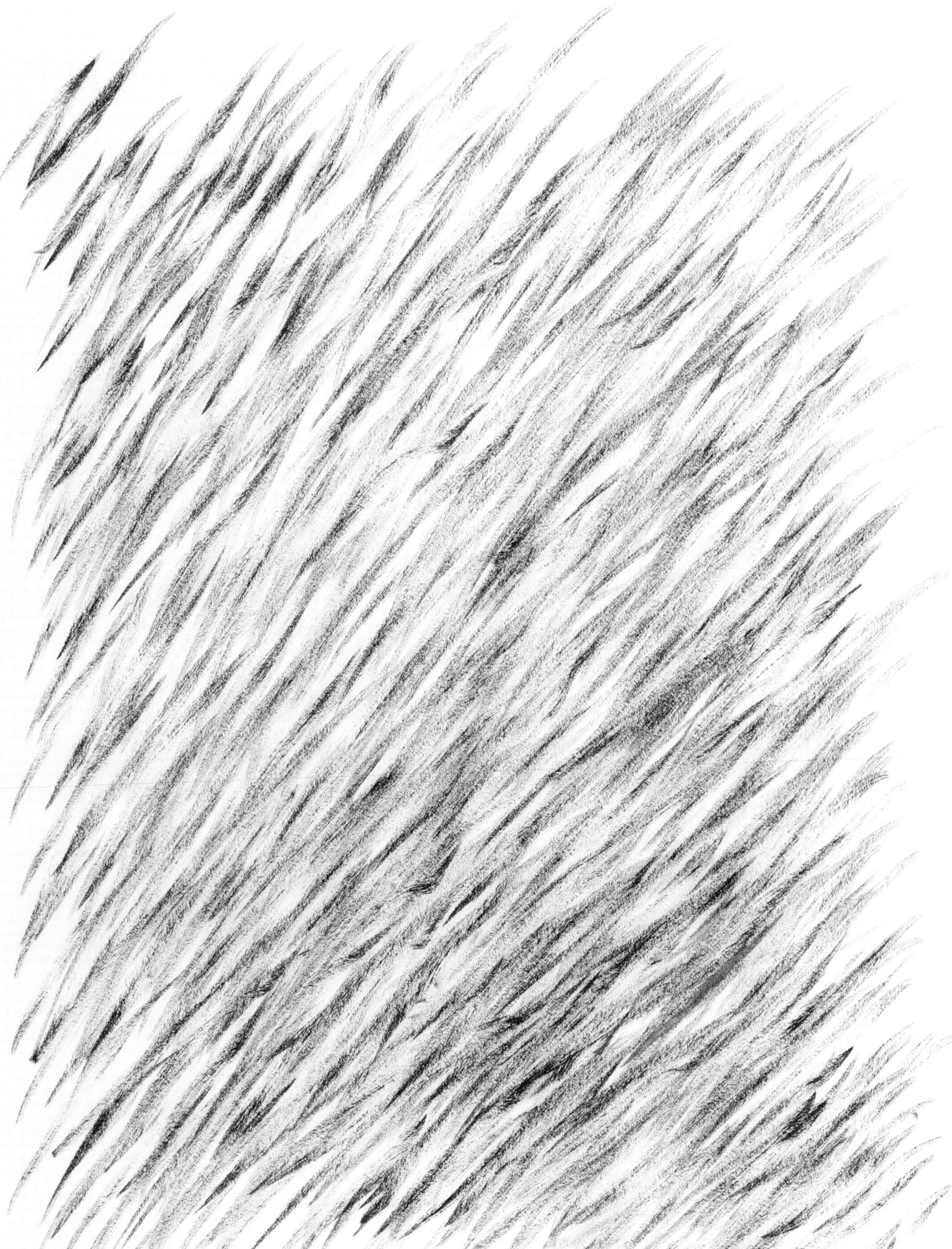

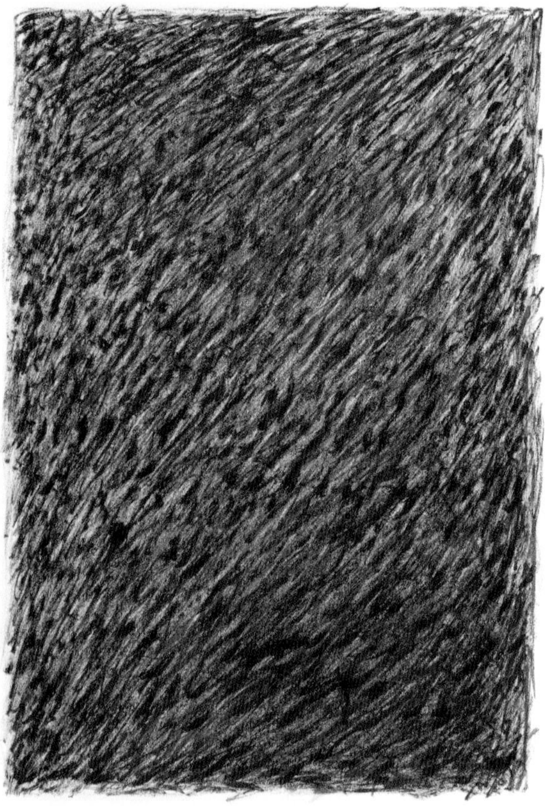

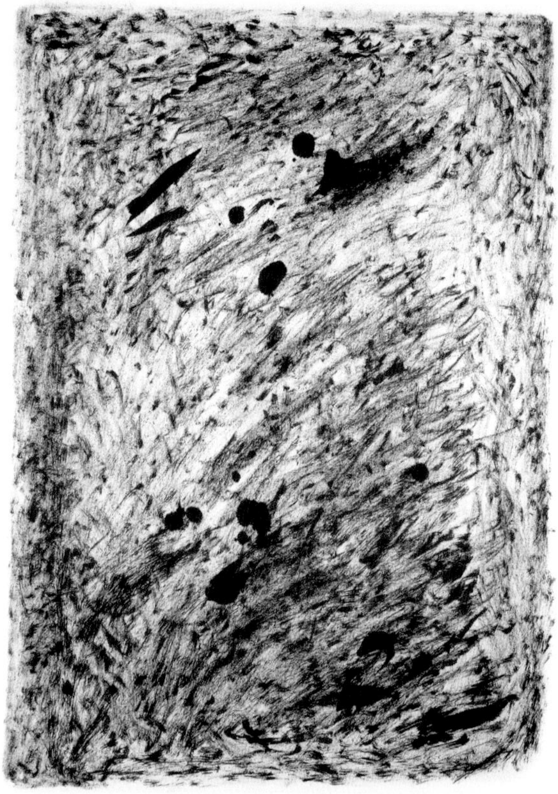

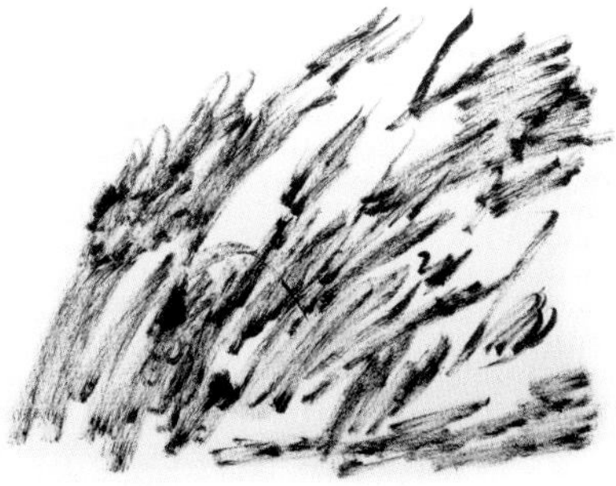
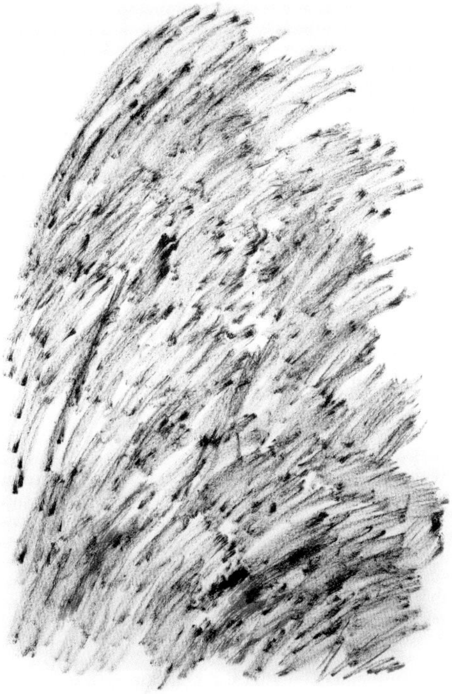
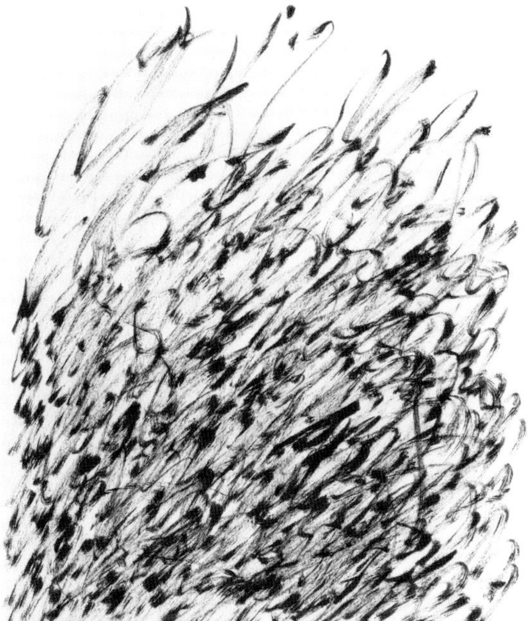
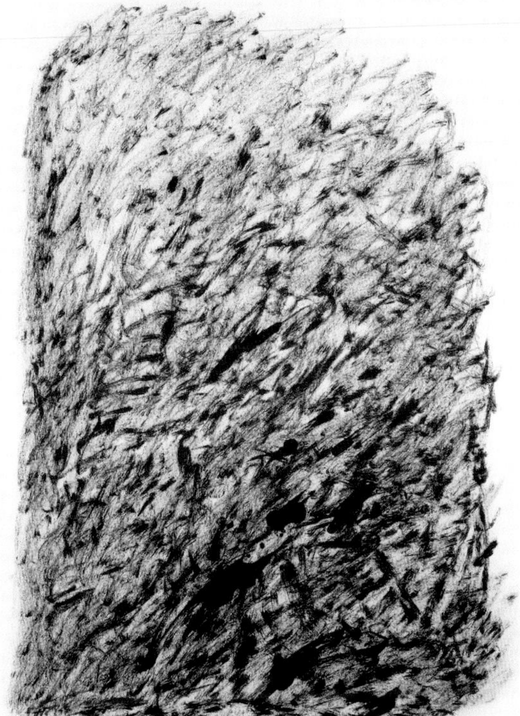

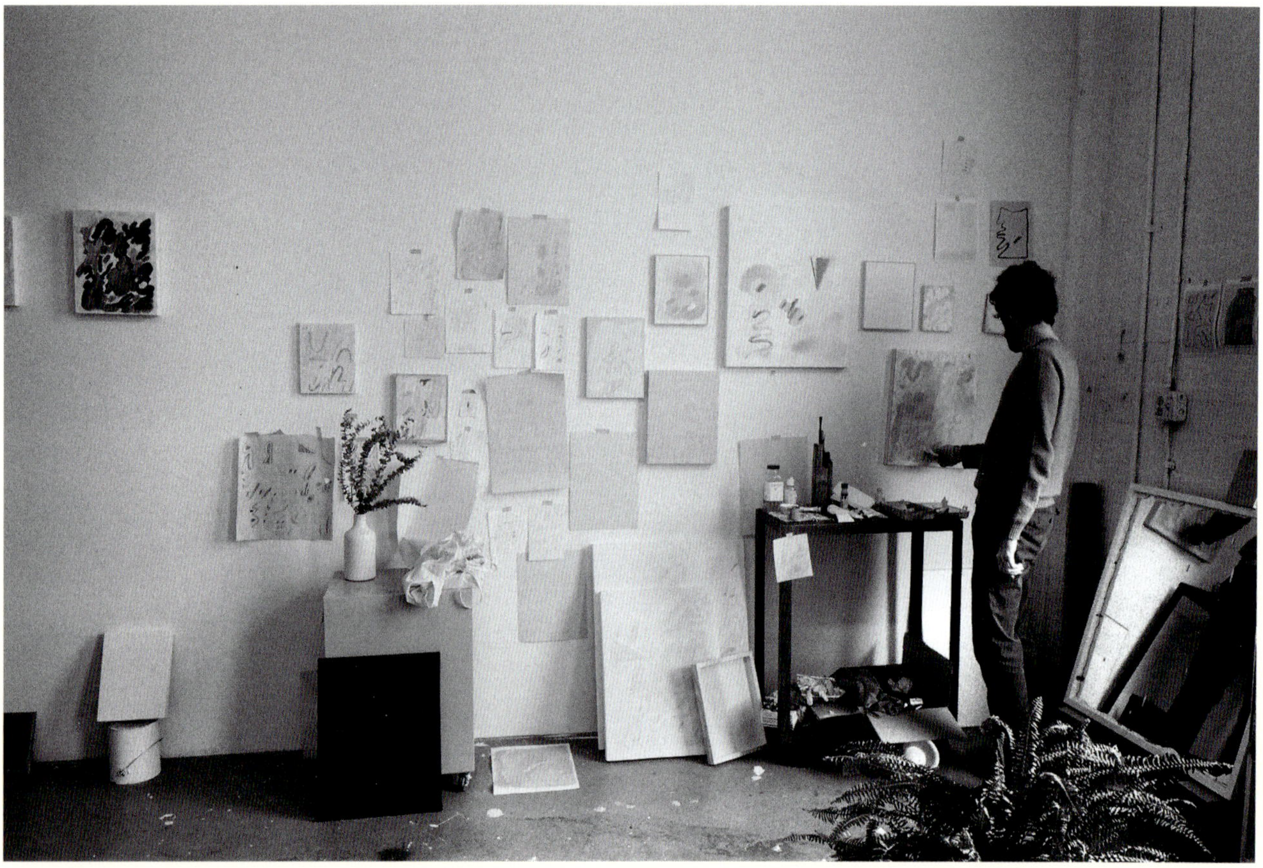

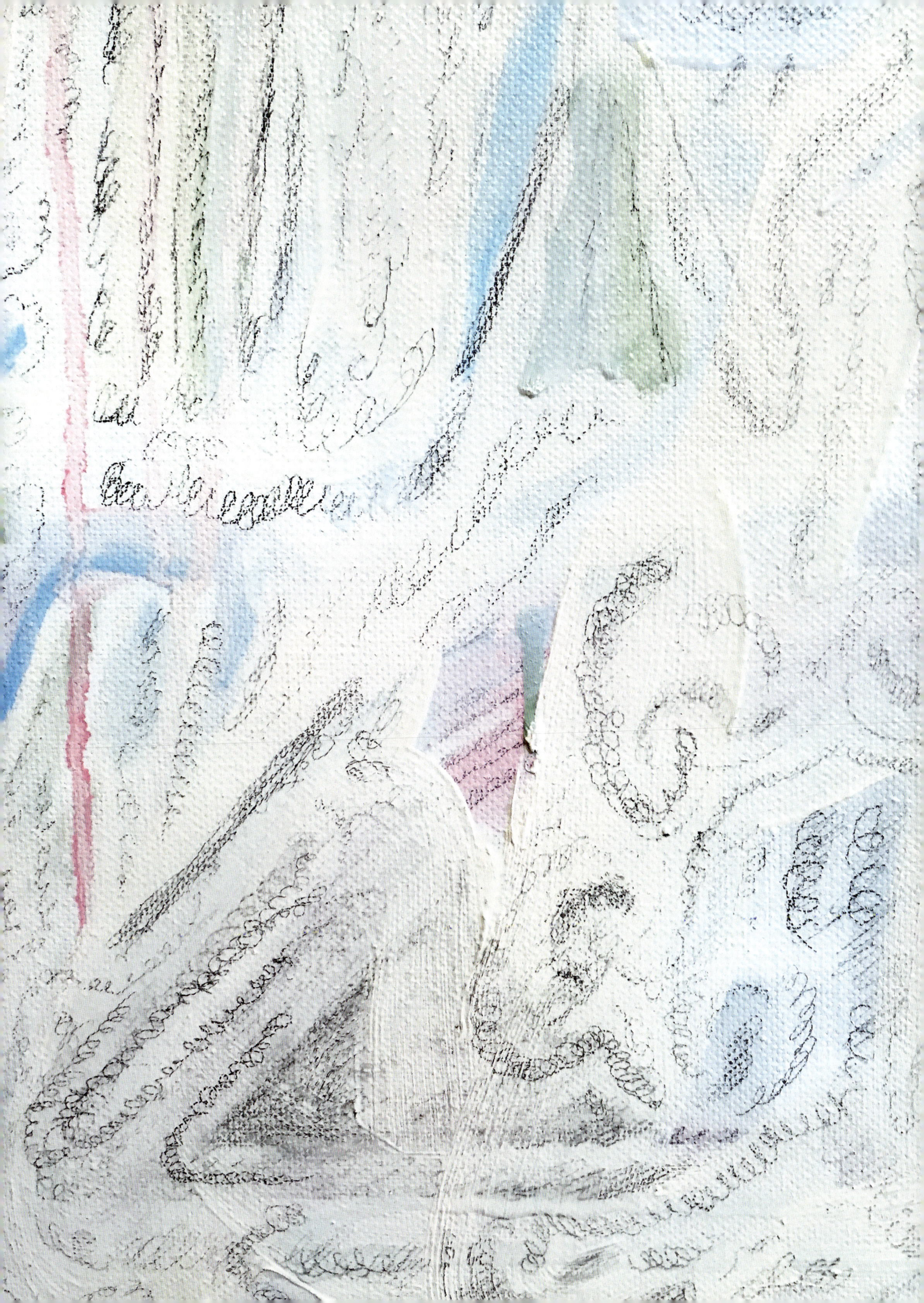

MOON PEOPLE

Two blue figures

synchronized to move

toward a blurred point

across the barest space imaginable—

will they make it?

—Bill Berkson

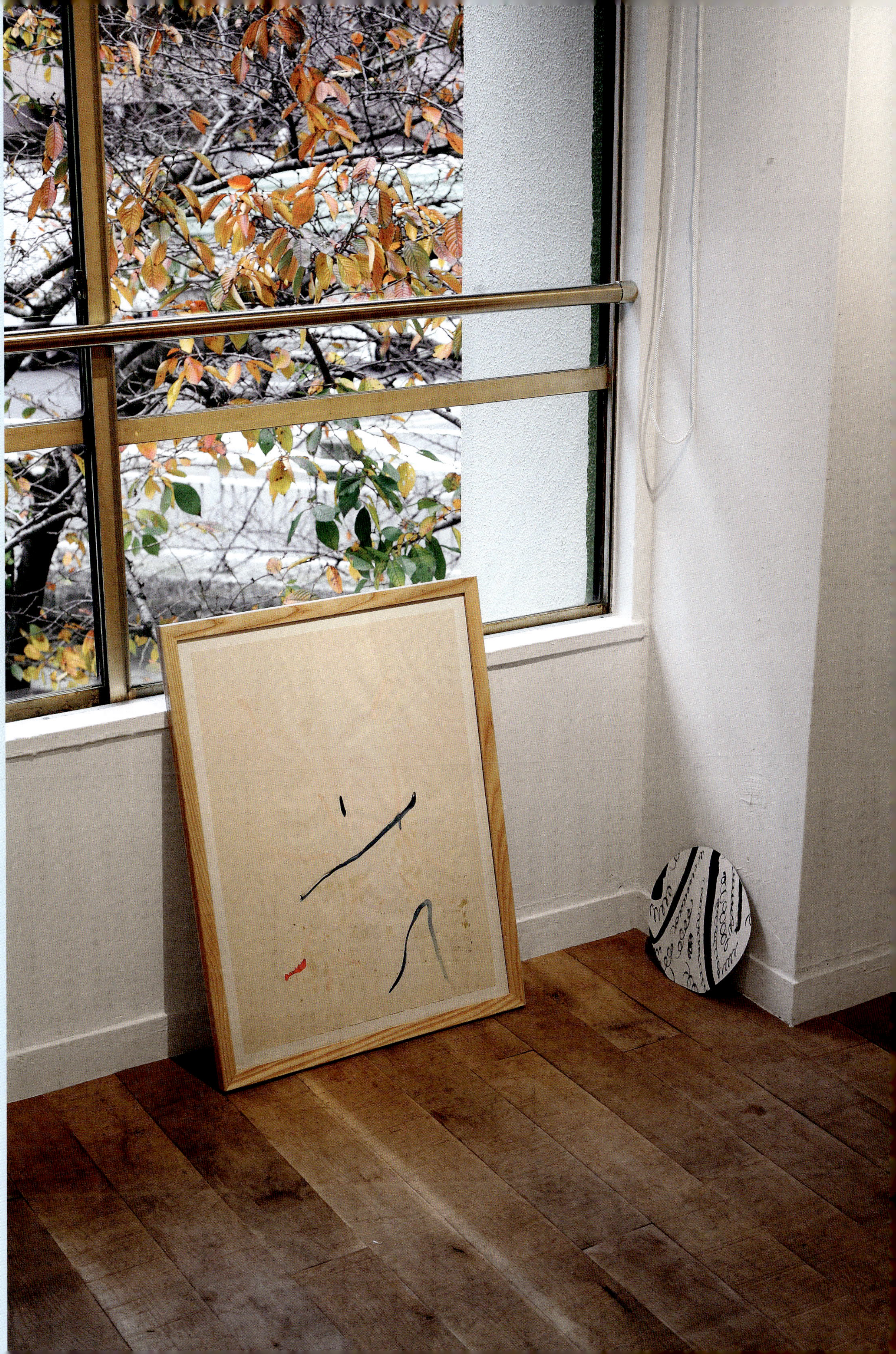

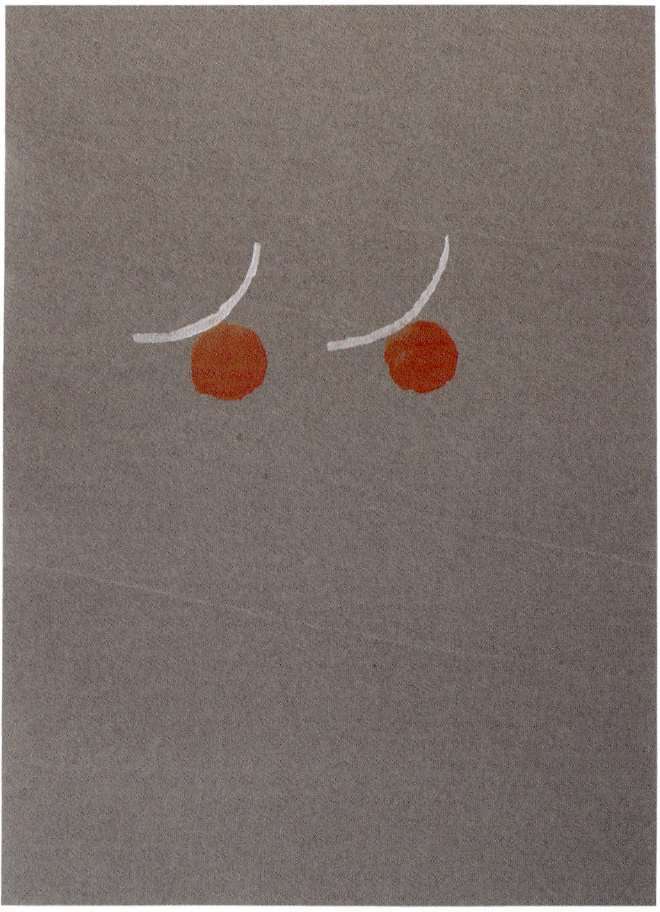

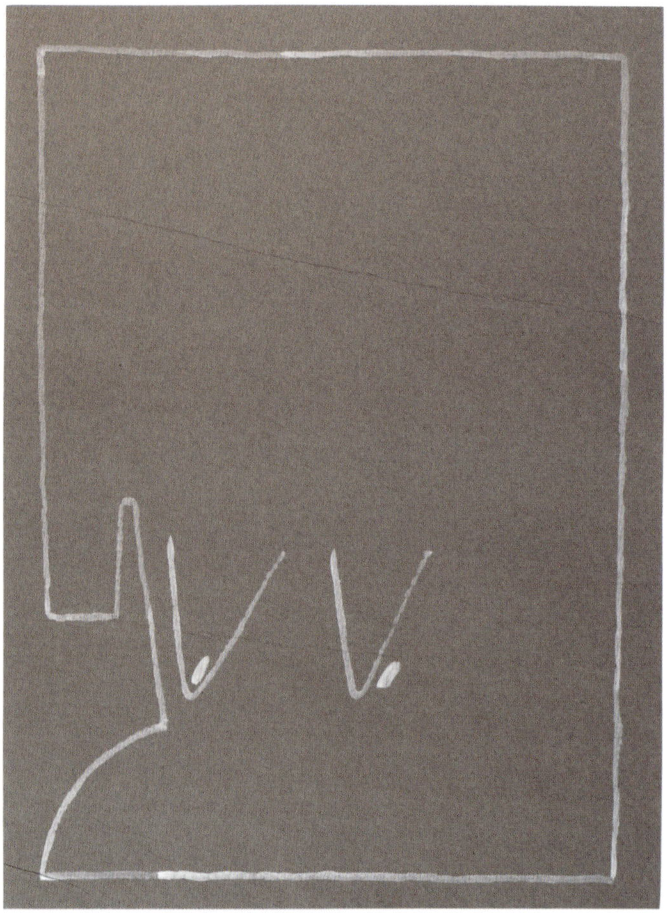

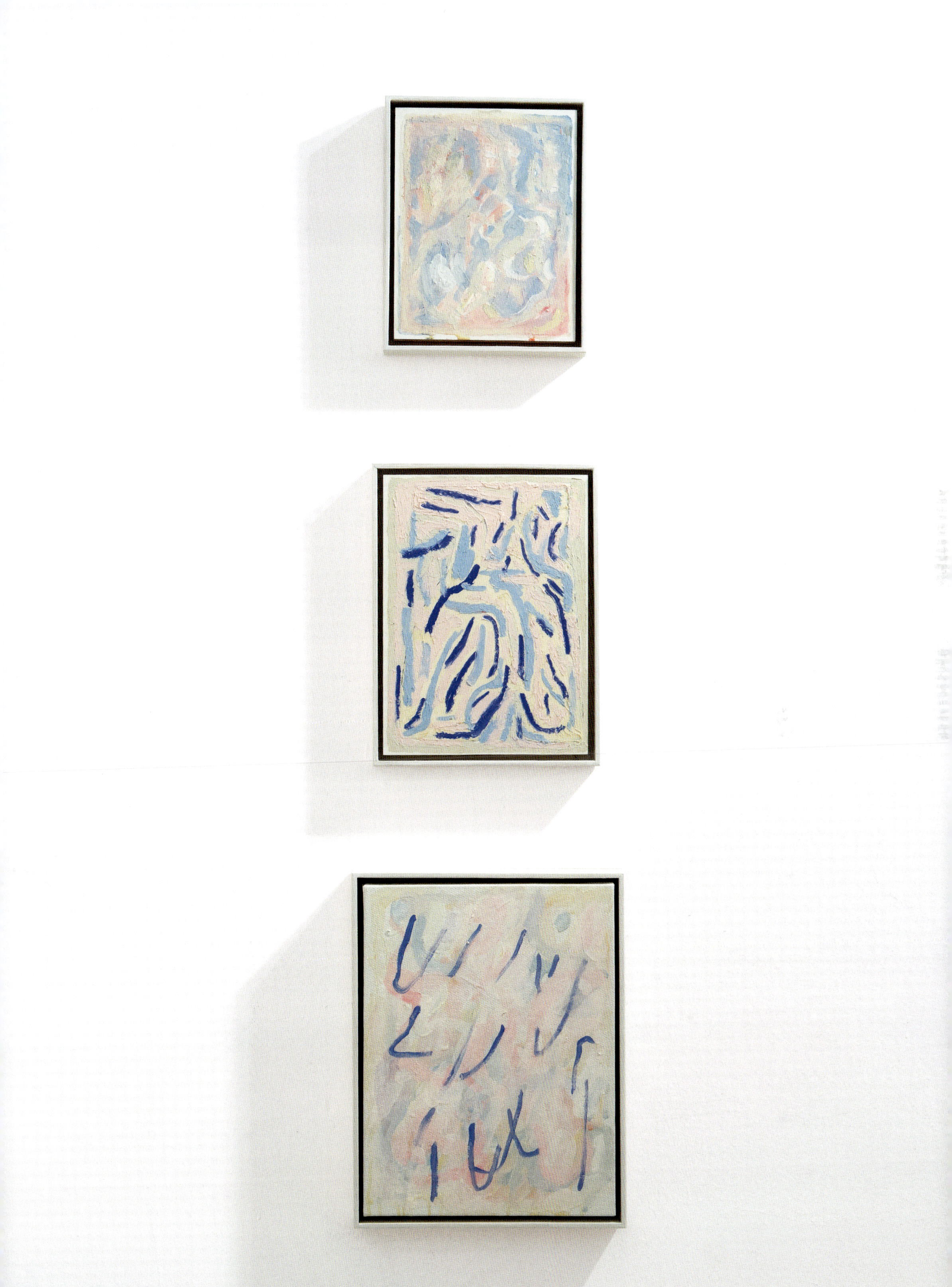

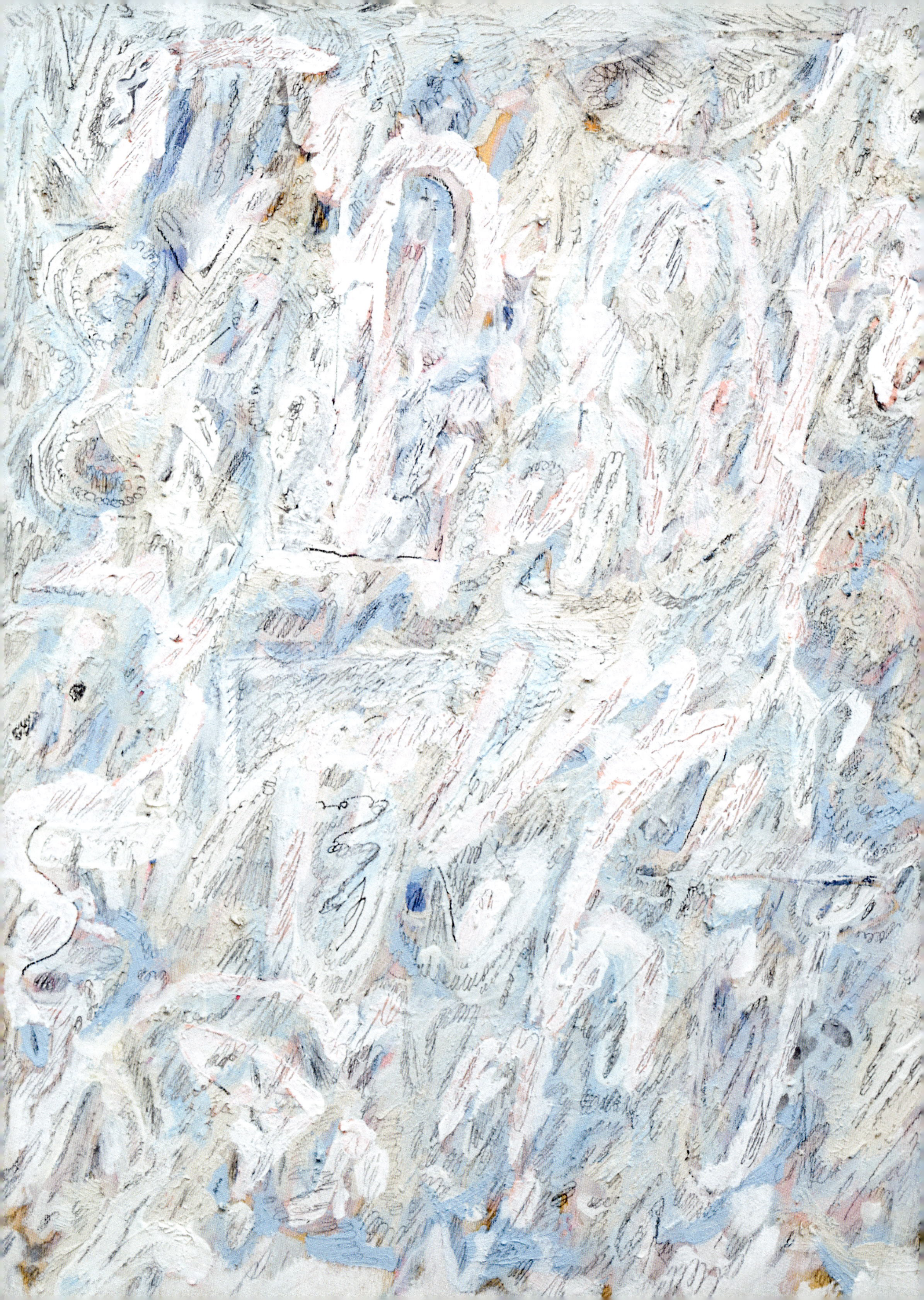

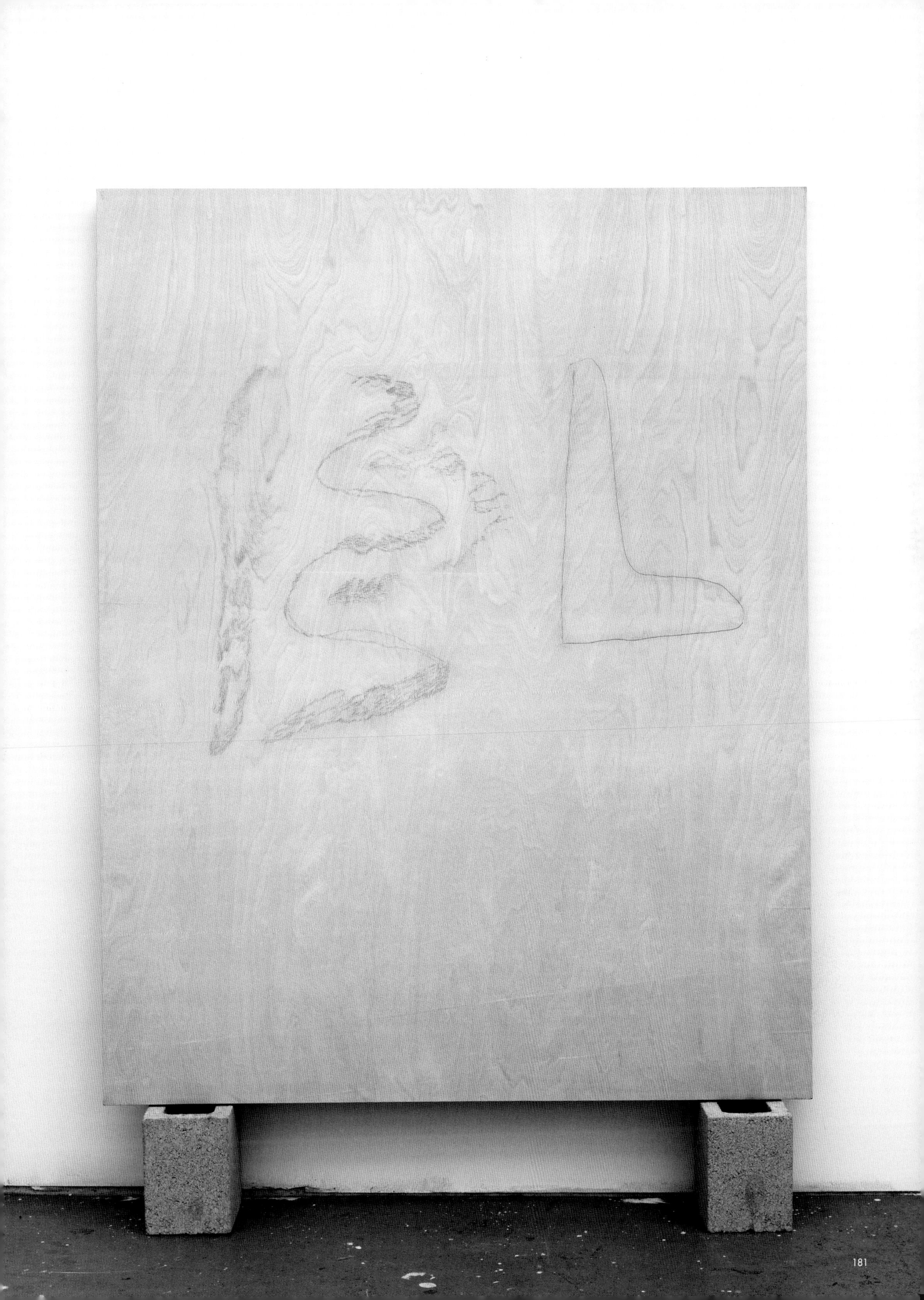

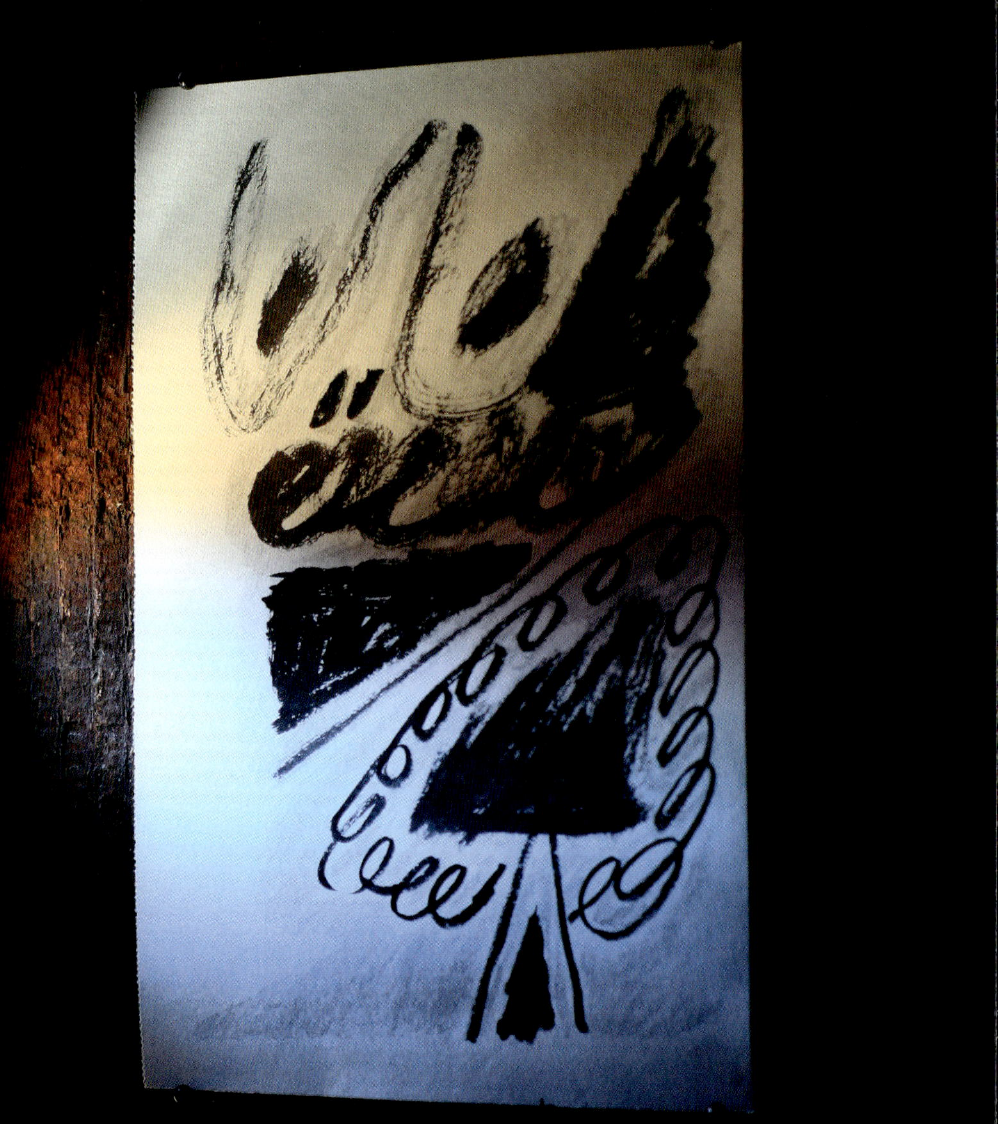

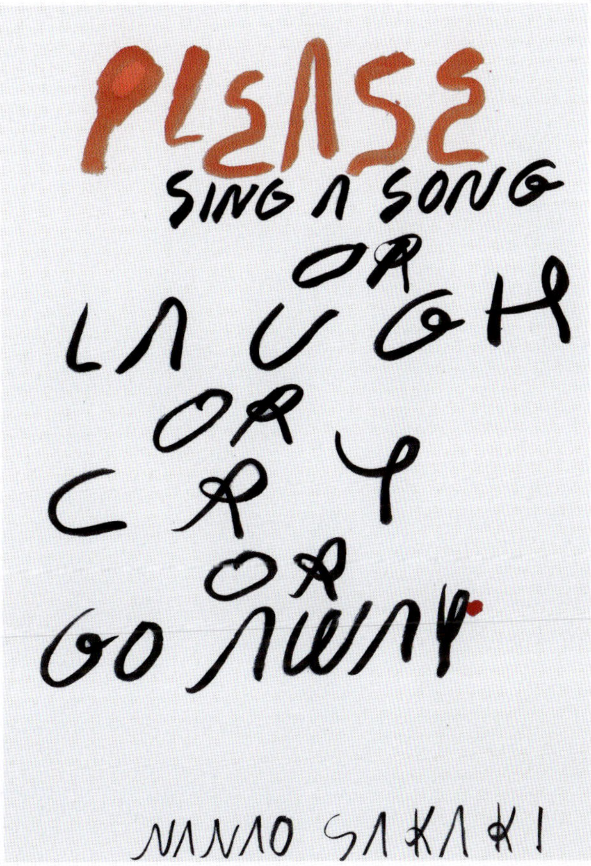
PLEASE
SING A SONG
OR
LAUGH
OR
CRY
OR
GO AWAY
NANAO SAKAKI

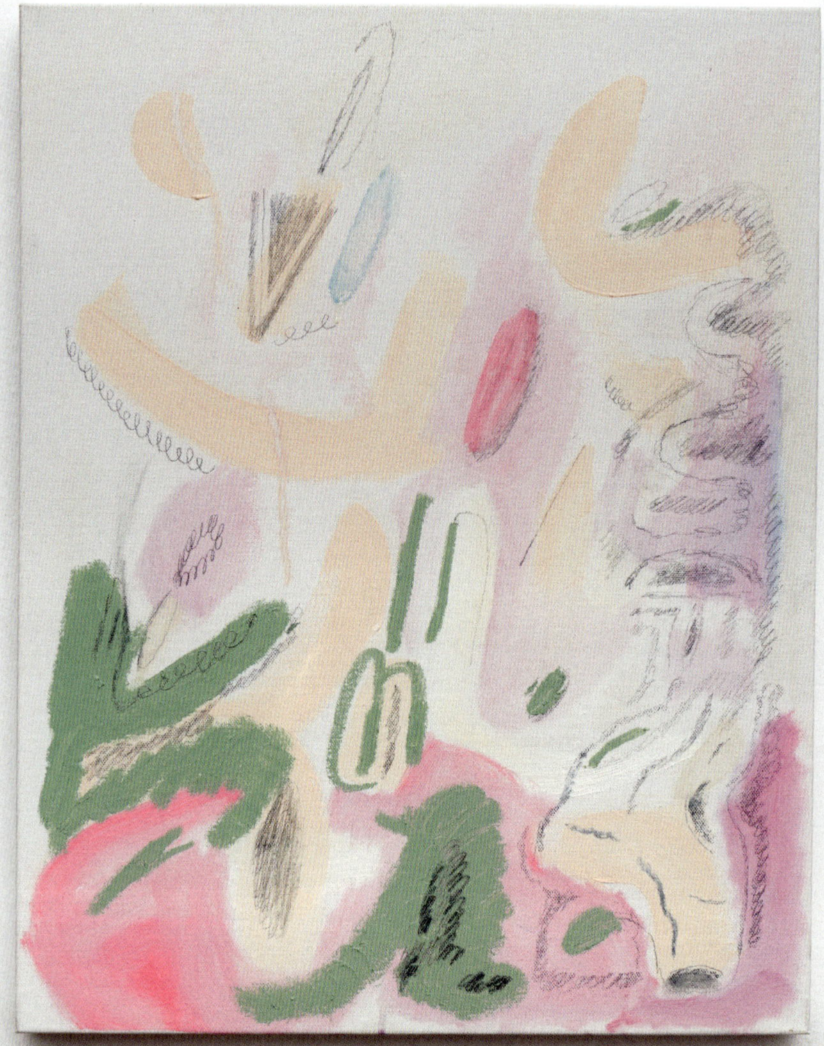

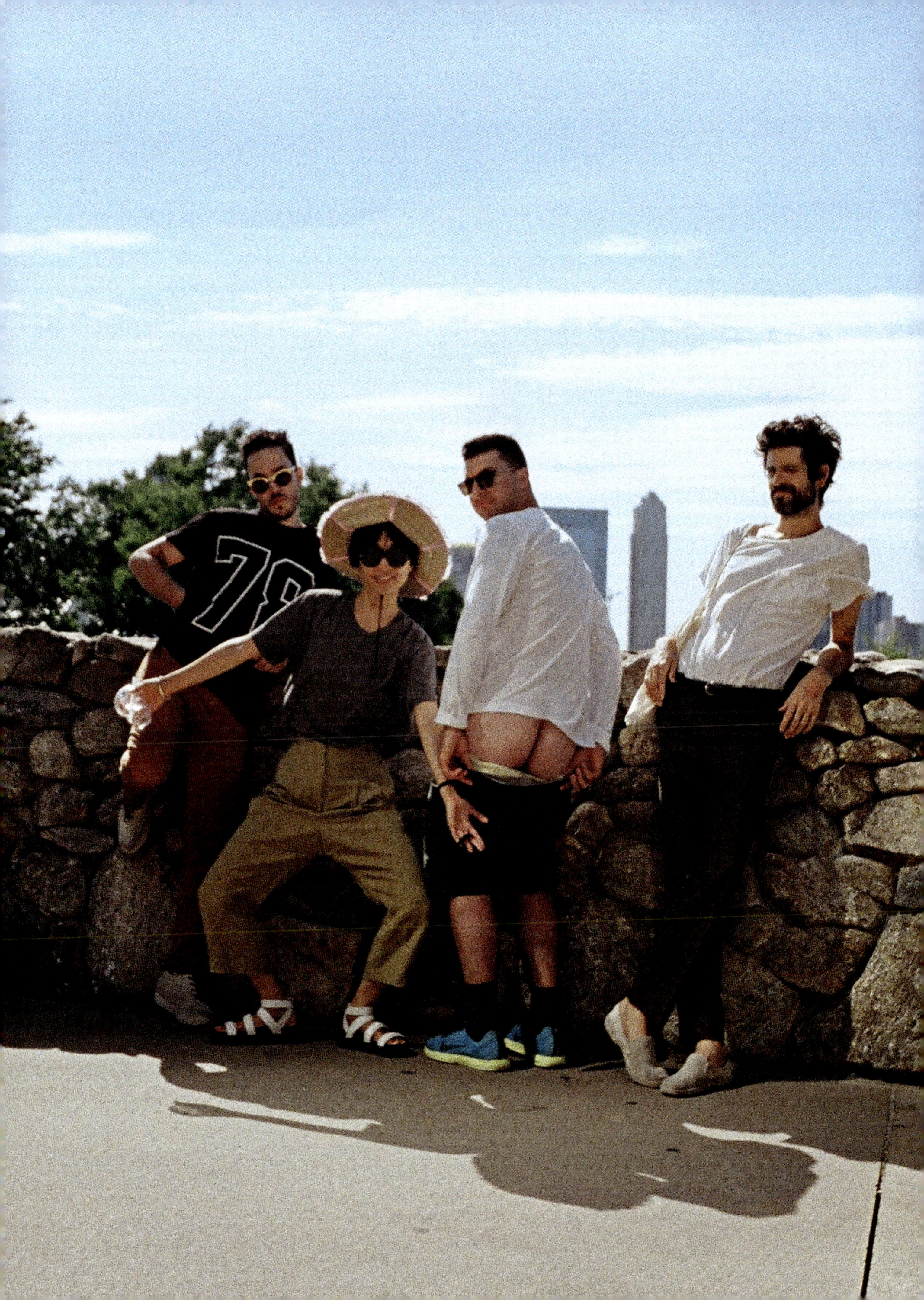
78

Index

PP. 1–2 Installation view of wall drawing in progress, Modena (upper arm: *lingam* by Kori Girard and *hermaphrodite temple* by Adam Tullie), 2014

P. 6 Hong Kong Charlie

Hong Kong Charlie told me her myth and it was a good myth…

P. 7 *it was Andy Cabic who, after reading this, fitfully remarked "So true"…*

P. 8 *Untitled*. Ink on paper, 2014

P. 11 *Untitled*. Ink on paper, 2014

P. 15 *how's pipi? what is this? some kind of ham-inspired bathroom keyboard? collective nostalgia for late 80s Berlin via mid-90s gardening magazines?*

cowboy boots, LA gears, or the humble flip-flop?

no, my amigos, this is meant to be the Zodiac in none of its glory

the mulling of mulch

cosmic spit

the guests have all gone home now. Ink on paper, 2014

P. 16 *Devendra called me up asking if I'd edit an interview that he and his long-time friend Adam Green, a fellow artist and musician, had conducted over the course of a day: "It's a billion hours of us drawing and talking. We got a little drunk, so please accept my apologies as you try to make sense of our conversation." The raw material I was given consisted of a computerized transcription of an audio recording with significant background noise that amounted to a seventy-page-long game of telephone. Would a human misinterpret Jodorowsky as Jody Rhapsody? Sure, but no. The challenge was immediately clear. I would become as much editor as translator for what can only be described as an ESL transcription service. This would prove a Sisyphean task since their repartee was abstract enough already. The resulting text reads like a two-person Samuel Beckett play, surreal but with a foothold in reality—besotted as it is.—Chris Fallon*

P. 17 *General with Gloves*. Oil, pencil, and crayon on paper, NYC, 2014

P. 18 *Cheeks Emperor*. Pencil on paper, NYC, 2014

P. 21 *Cat Sewage Heaven*. Oil, pencil, and crayon on paper, NYC, 2014

P. 23 *Receiver*. Oil and ink on paper, NYC, 2014

PP. 24–25 *Vagina Breather*. Oil, pencil, and crayon on paper, NYC, 2014

P. 26 *Gentleman*. Oil, pencil, and crayon on paper, NYC, 2014

P. 27 *Truck Truck*. Oil, pencil, and crayon on paper, NYC, 2014

P. 28 *Cave Computer Surprise*. Oil, pencil, and crayon on paper, NYC, 2014

P. 29 *Baseball Joseph*. Oil, pencil, and crayon on paper, NYC, 2014

P. 31 *Glove Untitled*. Oil and pencil on paper, NYC, 2014

P. 33 *Sheriff and Papaya*. Ink on paper, 2013

P. 36 San Francisco—2000

I think I said "high five Mom!" before taking this and you can see by her expression she's THINKING high five! hahaha! this was from the one slide I've kept since 2000, art institute days… why did I get a slide made? did I project this in class? I have no idea… but there it was, in my oldest trunk of ephemera… had it scanned and there was Mom giving me a high a five all over again, seemed like a fitting way to start the book… love ya Mum !

P. 37 *My New Art!*, San Francisco, 1998

P. 38 San Francisco—White-out and ink on polaroids, 2000

Out of necessity and convenience (they're already framed!) I would white-out over polaroids and draw on them. The top piece is the precursor to the monuments and the bottom are the beginnings of an ongoing exploration of anthropo-scaffolded-tit-entities and lettering…

P. 39 Bee vs. The Moth Costume—San Francisco, 2000

… Behemoth… I couldn't see anything and just ran around screaming until I ran into a tree… this was my final at the art institute, that's Matteah Baim filming (bottom left pic) and Sarah Cain adjusting my antenna (bottom middle pic).

P. 40 Black Forest, Germany, 2013

P. 41 *After the Single Petal of a Rose by Duke Ellington*. Watercolor on paper, 2000

P. 42 *Hands*. Ink on paper, 2002

what are the hands? are they some kind of UFO Childhood Farm Language? or are they the simplest illustration of acceptance that I can think of? a bit of both … none of the above? a bit of that too…

P. 43 Installing *Change Your Mind A Million Times*—solo show in Tokyo, 2014. Photo: Ryu Takahashi

P. 44 *The Three Secrets of Fatima*. Ink on paper, NYC, 2003

P. 45 *Puerta Abierta*. Ink on paper, NYC, 2003

P. 46 Ana and the light—Villa Lena, Italy, 2013

P. 47 Greg and Devendra—San Sebastián, Spain, 2007. Photo: Lauren Dukoff

P. 48 *Agora*. Ink on paper, 2002

P. 49 *Tathagata*. Ink on paper, 2002

PP. 50–51 *Red sun and snow with strange blue light*. Ink on paper, 2004

P. 52 On Lola's bike—Long Island, NY, 2013. Photo: Ana Kraš

P. 53 *Beginning of Nino Rojo/Hecate Void offering*. Ink on paper, 2000

PP. 54–55 *Untitled*. Ink on paper, NYC, 2003

P. 56 TOP: *For Antony's Turning*. Watercolor on paper, 2004

BOTTOM: *Untitled*. Watercolor on paper, 2004

P. 57 Mom—Caracas, Venezuela, 1985.

P. 58 *Untitled*. Ink on paper, 2003

P. 59 *Untitled*. Ink on paper, 2004

P. 60 Rodrigo Amarante—Fenway Park, Boston, 2014

P. 61 *And all your work, the space between*. Watercolor on paper, 2013

P. 62 *Goddess*. Ink on paper, 2005

P. 63 *Early study for "Rejoicing" cover*. Ink on paper, 2003

P. 64 *Two "Rejoicing" sketches*. Watercolor, pencil, and ink on paper, 2004

P. 65 *Rejoicing in the Hands*. Watercolor on paper, NYC, 2004.

P. 66 Bernardo's Poem—Caracas, 1989

translation:

April 15, 1989

Saturday
they cut
my nails

we shall see
when they
grow.

One weekend, mom dropped me off at my Aunt Margarita's house to play with my three cousins. Cristóbal and Andrés had already gone out to play, kick the can around, throw dog shit at each other, firecrackers, etc., but Bernardo was in his room. It's Saturday, what the hell's he doing in his room? I walk in and see him sitting at his little desk, hunched over this piece of paper, solemnly observing the page, then ceremoniously drawing the lines that conclude the piece… I thought, what the hell is this? is this homework? I've heard of diaries, is that what this is? he assured me it was neither… that this was just "una obra" (a piece)… suddenly I feel everything at once, super-fast slow motion, air knocked out, floors pulled from below, a weightless weight, watery-lead-like infrasonic bass note sending its time and space sound wave through my being… it was the first time I had seen words written for no reason, first time I had ever seen words outside of a scholastic context, this was the birth of division for me, between the Organ, the Organism, and the Organization… it was magic. Bernardo Rísquez, mi primo, mi pana, Granje, now, extraordinary artist living in Brussels, making tremendous, complex music with his partner Mike under the name Different Fountains, still making beautiful "obras"… I'm ever in awe of you, ever grateful, gracias Benny.

P. 67 *Nino Rojo*. Watercolor on paper, NYC, 2004

P. 68 *Untitled*. Ink on paper, 2006

you I cannot name,

too much power in naming,

too much risk in an imprecise naming,

can't be loosey-goosey with that!

in fact, there's a passage in Jerome Rothenberg's Smashing the Pumpkin (1972) that perfectly illustrates this:

"A person receives a name describing something odd & sexual about the namer. Here the namer is a woman or a transvestite, who makes the name public by shouting it after the man named when others are present. The man invariably accepts it & is regularly called by it, even by his wife & family. Such names include: Down-Dangling-Pussy-Hairs, Big Cunt, and Long Asshole."

P. 69 TOP: *Untitled*. Ink on paper, 2006

BOTTOM: *Untitled*. Ink on paper, 2006

PP. 70–71 *Untitled*. Watercolor on paper, 2006

P. 72 Encinal Canyon, 2004. Photo: Isabelle Albuquerque

PP. 73–77 *Light Aligns*. Watercolor and ink on paper, Saintes-Maries-de-la-Mer, France, 2004

P. 78 *Untitled*. Watercolor on paper, Encinal Canyon, California, 2000

P. 79 First Tour—with Entrance/Guy Blakeslee, somewhere in New Mexico, 2002. Photo: Tommy Awalt Rouse

P. 80 Apacheta—Incan, the word in Quechua meaning "the source where the flow begins"

an honoring and offering to Pachamama (Earth/Time Mother, Mother Nature, Universal Maternal Entity)

P. 81 *Monument*. Watercolor on paper, 2008

the monuments have always made the most sense to me,

a quantifiable, repetitive, and ritualistic act where

each line is proof of intention and devotion

Through the years I've always returned to these, as a meditative activity, as a palate cleanser between a new series, as a gift for a dear friend and as atonement for a wrongdoing. In the case of my first album, it was a monument to the dreams of a dog… and in the case of the first one I ever made, it was for INXS's Michael Hutchence.

P. 82 *Monument*. Watercolor on paper, 2007

P. 83 *Monument*. Pencil on wood, 2008

P. 84 *Oh Me Oh My*. Watercolor on paper, 2002

P. 85 Monument. Watercolor on paper, 2007

the monument is an even folksier version of the first health food store in Caracas (it was so funny, it was basically some flatbread and a few cookies made without milk or sugar)

P. 86 *Monument to Barbara Lewis*. Watercolor on paper, 2006

P. 87 Removal of unidentified cyst-like membrane—NYC, 2013

In a disparate culture, one ruled by a different set of customs, symbols, and myths, this would have been immediately diagnosed as a physical manifestation of a metaphysical, psycho-emotional trauma.

Especially (and ironically) since it literarily surfaced four months after I began a particular form of Western psychotherapy!

The Western view of what happened was that a little growth appeared near my ulna—in what is known as the twin muscles section of my right lower arm—in the period of one week the little pea grew to a marble and in a matter of days it ballooned into a golf ball... when I had it checked out, they didn't know what it was, just that "we better get it out, and fast!"...

the nurse was kind enough to take a pic while it was being removed...

PP. 88–89 *Monument*. Ink on paper, 2005

P. 90 Point Dume, 2013. Photo: Ana Kraš

P. 91 *Monument*. Watercolor on paper, 2008

P. 92 LEFT: *Monument*. Pencil on wood, 2008

RIGHT: *Monument*. Pencil on wood, 2008

P. 93 *Monument*. Watercolor on paper, 2008

P. 94 Ana holds candle/lights paper on fire—NYC, 2014.

P. 95 Studio—NYC, 2013. Photo: Ana Kraš

P. 96 *Untitled*. Pencil on paper, 2010, from *Strangers in the Night*—three-man show with Adam Tullie and Keegan McHargue at Galleria Patricia Armocida, Milan

P. 97 *What Will We Be Mask*. Watercolor on paper, 2009

PP. 98–99 *Folk Tale* (after *Mulata de Tal* by Miguel Ángel Asturias and Macunaíma by Mário de Andrade, respectively). Pencil on paper, 2010

PP. 100–101 Nezu Museum—Tokyo, 2014. Photo: Ryu Takahashi

P.102 CLOCKWISE FROM TOP RIGHT: Rodrigo Amarante on a ferry from Argentina to Uruguay; Ana Kraš in the morning, Villa Lena, Italy; Yusuke Nagai at Toku Tea in Shimokitazawa, Tokyo; Bernardo Rísquez in Echo Park, Los Angeles

P. 103 CLOCKWISE FROM TOP RIGHT: Izz and Jon at night, Los Angeles; Ana before Christmas, Belgrade; Aram Goldberg rehearsal space, Istanbul; Cy Gray, Upstate New York

PP. 104–105 LEFT TO RIGHT: Reykjavik, The Black Forest, Sioux Falls, 2014

P. 106 *Tapir*. Pencil on paper, Los Angeles, 2009

P. 107 Ana as Leigh Bowery, NYC, 2013 (background: Laptop #2—from Adam Green's 2010 show *Teen Tech*)

P. 108 *It's true, I did.*

P. 109 White plasteline on orange paper with blue cotton, Italy, 2013

P. 110 I am the Burger King, I can do anything—Love Hotel, 2013. Photo: Ana Kraš

P. 111 *What Will We Be Mask*. Watercolor on paper, Los Angeles, 2009

P. 112 Rio de Janeiro and Ana at M. Gira's wedding—Upstate New York, 2014

P. 113 *Untitled*. Pencil on wood, Los Angeles, 2011

P. 114 *Untitled*. Ink on paper, Los Angeles, 2009

P. 115 *Untitled*. Pencil on wood, Los Angeles, 2011

P. 116 *Untitled*. Pencil on paper, Los Angeles, 2011

P. 117 *What Will We Be Mask*. Watercolor on paper, 2010

P. 118 *Untitled*. Watercolor on paper, 2010

P. 119 LEFT: *Untitled*. Watercolor on paper, 2010

RIGHT: *Untitled*. Watercolor on paper, 2010

P. 120 *Arrow*. Watercolor on paper, Topanga, 2007

P. 121 Fab swings from a chandelier—Detroit, 2013

P. 122 Etretat—Normandy, France, 2013. Photo: Ana Kraš

Text is about just that, the Flamingo Hotel, a gateway to some sordid Shangri-la, degenerate El Dorado, and/or splendid Xibalba at the mouth of the Colombian Airport... neither malevolent nor benevolent, just a point of no return...

P. 123 *Arrows for Elliot and Aram*. Watercolor on paper, Topanga, 2007

PP. 124–125 LEFT: Web Master—Los Angeles, 2010. Photo: Adam Tullie

RIGHT: Objects, NYC, 2012

BACKGROUND: Josiah Steinbrick at massage parlor.

P.126 *Receptacles*. Ink on paper, 2013

P. 127 *Superb Honeymoon tour with Andy Cabic Receptacles*. Ink on paper, Japan, 2012

P. 128 *Receptacles*. Ink on paper, NYC, 2012

P. 129 *Receptacles*. Ink on paper, NYC, 2013

P. 130 Rowen and Jo—Kitchen Mouse, Los Angeles, 2014

P. 131 Unknown Japanese Poet

P. 132 *Receptacles*. Pencil on paper, 2013

P. 133 *Receptacles*. Pencil on paper, 2013

P. 134 Josiah Steinbrick—Buenos Aires, 2013

P. 135 Ana as Aranyani—NYC, 2012

PP. 136–137 *Portraits*. Ink and colored pencil on paper, South America, 2013

P. 138 Caracas, 1988. Photo: María Eugenia Rísquez

P. 139 *Self-Portrait*. Ink on paper, South America, 2013

P. 140 *Portrait*. Ink and ballpoint pen on paper, South America, 2013

P. 141 *Portrait*. Ink on paper, South America, 2013

P. 142 Josiah Steinbrick e-mail, 2014

P. 143 Mom—Echo Park, Los Angeles, 2011

P. 144 *Still*. Pencil on paper, Modena, 2014

PP. 145–149 *Still*. Oil on paper, Modena, 2014

P. 150 *Sphinx Interiors*

A series begun in NYC and completed in Modena for an exhibition of the same title. Ink on school paper given to me by Antony.

PP. 151–154 *Sphinx Interior*. Ink on paper, Modena, 2014

P. 155 Wall drawing. Ink on paper, Modena, 2014

PP. 156–157 *Sphinx Interior*. Ink on paper, Modena, 2014

P. 158 Catatumbo el gran relámpago!

Olga and Congo Mirador are its neighboring villages… very very special place(s)… many summers spent throwing rocks at a horse's dick there…

I'm Debora, and I also speak to her, but she never answers, I'm in the dark and want her to know I'm here… but I'm too frightened to make a sound… and then a voice says "speak freely"…

P. 159 NYC, 2014. Photo: Ana Kraš

PP. 160–161 *Sphinx Interior*. Ink on paper, 2014

PP. 162–163 *Sphinx Interior* (detail). Ink on paper, 2014

PP. 164–165 *Sphinx Interior*. Ink on paper, 2014

P. 166 *Smoke Doors Do Not Obstruct*, Italy 2013

P. 167 *Zingara*, Colombia, 2014

P. 168 Portions of Francesco's balsamic workshop, Modena, 2014

P. 169 *a protruding sweetness, an intruding tartness, both unburdened by meaning—For the love of a small Chinese woman, the specter of a sectarian war*. Colored pencil on paper, 2014

PP. 171–173 *After "Haru Spring" by Harold Budd*. Ink on paper, NYC, 2014

P. 174 Studio—Downtown Los Angeles, 2014

P. 175 *Untitled* (detail). Oil and pencil on canvas, Los Angeles, 2014

P. 176 *Bill was my teacher at SFAI, taught poetry, and other than the library was often the only reason I would refrain from skipping school. back then and to this day I love and admire him very much, am honored to be ever in his debt, and until those Gustons he has go missing, friends to this very day… hats off to you Bill… Love ya. p.s. hi Connie!*

P. 177 Change Your Mind A Million Times, Stall Baggage—Tokyo, 2014

P. 178 *Portrait of Avonte*. Watercolor on paper, NYC, 2013

I remember Avonte Oquendo

and it always makes me cry,

an autistic child

whose remains were found in queens…

after having gone missing for months

I remember reading what the loudspeakers blasted from the cars that circled the boroughs in hopes of getting his attention,

"Avonte
it's mom
come to the lights
come to the lights"

P. 179 TOP: *Bliss Void*. Oil on board, Modena, 2014

MIDDLE: *Homeless Mother*. Oil on board, Modena, 2014

BOTTOM: *Untitled*. Oil on board, Modena, 2014

P. 180 *Untitled* (detail). Oil and pencil on board, 2014. Devendra Banhart, solo show curated by Sylvia Chivaratanond at Reserve Ames, Los Angeles

P. 181 *Banish The One Object Of All Blame*. Pencil on wood, Reserve Ames, Los Angeles, 2014

P. 182 *Untitled*. Ink on paper, Reserve Ames, Los Angeles, 2014

P. 183 Poem—Nanao Sakaki

runner-up:

AMOR

Humor.

—Oswald de Andrade

and Carl just sent the third runner-up:

Even in Kyoto—
hearing the cuckoo's cry—
I long for Kyoto.
—Basho

P. 184 *Untitled*. Oil and pencil on canvas, Reserve Ames, Los Angeles, 2014

P. 185 Adam Tullie, Carol Nhan, Keegan McHargue—Battery Park, NYC, 2014

P. 190 Belgrade, 2013. Photo: Ana Kraš

All photos by Devendra Banhart unless otherwise noted.

RETRACTION: In Phaidon's *Vitamin D: New Perspectives in Drawing*, 2005, in respect to the ridiculous Rastaman Chant drawing they chose to include, they printed the BACK of my drawing. Finicky? Perhaps, but that's been bugging me for a decade!

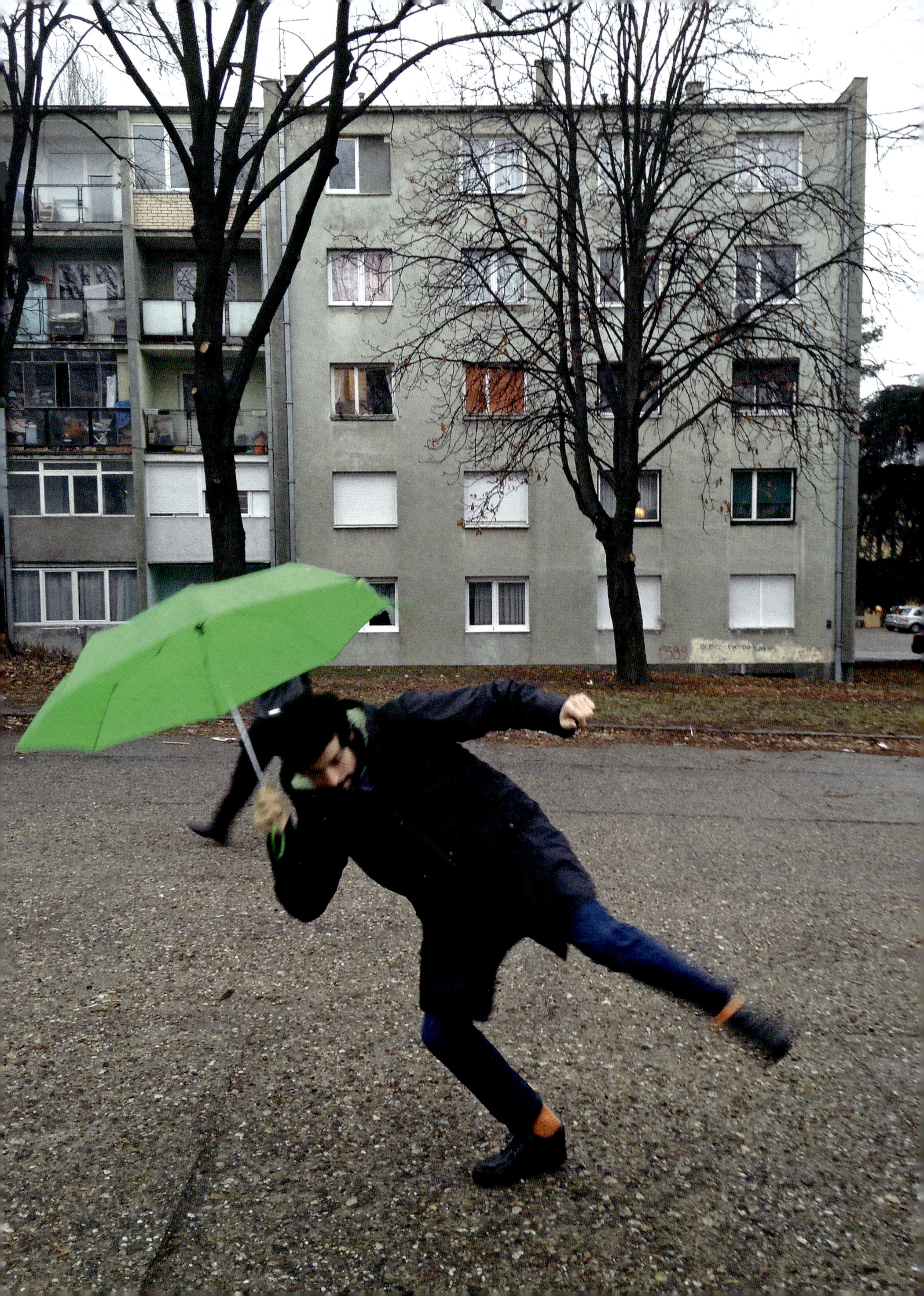

Thanks

Claudia Stäuble & Curt Holtz and everyone at Prestel
María Eugenia Rísquez
Loring Baker
Aram Goldberg
Lita Albuquerque
Jasmine Albuquerque
Isabelle Albuquerque
Jon Beasley
Ana Kraš
The Mazzolis
Adam Tullie
Antony
Diego Cortez
Beck, Marissa, Cosimo and Tuesday
Jeffrey Deitch
Andy Cabic and Alissa Anderson
Apsara DiQuinzio
Greg Rogove and Diana Garcia
Adam, Yasmin, and Zeba Green
Matteah Baim
Bill Berkson and Connie Lewallen
Vivian Elizabeth Ritchie Handler & Benjamin Lee Ritchie Handler
Sarah Cain
Alicia McCarthy
Lauren Dukoff
Rodrigo Amarante
M. Gira
Elliot Roberts
Colter Jacobsen
Patricia Armocida
Josiah Steinbrick, Erica Daking, and Rowen
Eric Owen
Fab Moretti
Ben Echeverria
Sylvia Chivaratanond
Amy Bouse
Keegan McHargue and Carol Nhan
Chris Fallon
Luckey Remington
Noah Georgeson and Erin Turnmire
Tahiti and Galen Pehrson
and finally,
Carl Williamson for his patience, cut-throat tenderness, impeccable eye,
and all around good human-ness.

In Loving memory of Gary Banhart.

EDITED AND
DESIGNED BY
CARL WILLIAMSON
AND DEVENDRA
BANHART.